D0344013

02

LIVERPOOL JMU LIBRARY

3 1111 00723 9831

THE THEATRE OF
YESTERDAY AND TOMORROW
Commedia Dell'Arte on the Modern Stage

James Fisher

The Edwin Mellen Press
Lewiston/Queenston/Lampeter

Library of Congress Cataloging-in-Publication Data

Fisher, James (A. James)
    The theatre of yesterday and tomorrow : commedia dell'arte on the
modern stage / by James Fisher.
      p.   cm.
    Includes bibliographical references and index.
    ISBN 0-7734-9529-0
    1. Commedia dell'arte. 2. Theater--Europe--History--20th century.
I. Title.
PQ4155.F57   1992
792.2'3'0904--dc20   94-14529
                                            CIP

Another volume in the continuing
"Studies in the Italian Theatre".
Dr. Christopher Cairns, General Editor.

A CIP catalog record for this book is available
from The British Library.

Copyright   ©1992 James Fisher.

All rights reserved. For more information contact

The Edwin Mellen Press   The Edwin Mellen Press
P.O. Box 450   Box 67
Lewiston, NY 14092   Queenston, Ontario
USA   CANADA L0S 1L0

The Edwin Mellen Press, Ltd.
Lampeter, Dyfed, Wales
UNITED KINGDOM SA48 7DY

Printed in the United States of America

For Dana

TABLE OF CONTENTS

List of Illustrations

ACKNOWLEDGEMENTS

This work could only have been realized with the support of many friends and colleagues who have nourished it from the beginning. Although it seems impossible to adequately express my gratitude, I particularly wish to note those without whose help it would never have seen the light of day.

The following institutions have assisted me in a variety of ways: the Bibliothèque Nationale, the Friends of Jacques Copeau (under the direction of Marie Hélène Copeau Dasté), the Humanities Research Center at the University of Texas at Austin, the Newberry Library, the Ellen Terry Memorial Museum, the Special Collections Department of the University Library at UCLA, the University of Florida at Gainesville Department of Classics Comparative Drama Conference (under the direction of Karelisa V. Hartigan), the Harvard University Library, the Indiana Humanities Council, *The New England Theatre Journal* (Charles Combs, editor), *Soviet and East European Performance* (Daniel Gerould and Alma Law, co-editors), the *Theatre Journal* (Enoch Brater, editor), the Theatre Museum of the Victoria and Albert Museum, the West European Center at Indiana University, the Max Reinhardt Archive at the State University of New York at Binghamton, and the Theatre Collection of the New York Public Library.

Many colleagues and friends, new and old, have offered invaluable help: David Allen, Christopher Cairns, Douglas Calisch, Helen Krich Chinoy, Laura Conners, Edward A. Craig, H. E. Robert Craig, Michael Bigelow Dixon and the Actors Theatre of Louisville, Diane Enenbach, Peter Frederick, Judith Greene, Thomas F. Heck, P. Donald Herring, Helen Hudson, Christopher Innes, Gerald Kahan, Dennis Kennedy, Kenneth Kloth, Ginger McNally, L.M. Newman, Herbert Richardson, Naomi Ritter, Arnold Rood, Julia Rosenberg, Warren Rosenberg, Mary Russo, Laurence Senelick, Richard Strawn, and Daniel Warner.

Special thanks are due to John C. Swan, Head Librarian of Bennington

College's Crossett Library and co-author of *The Triumph of Pierrot*, an excellent study of the influence of commedia's Pierrot on modern art, literature, film, theatre, and popular culture. John's keen understanding and knowledge of the subject, as well as his generous spirit and friendship, have proved indispensable at all stages of this project.

Herbert Stern, Milligan Professor of English at Wabash College, read an early draft of the text and generously contributed his broad and insightful knowledge of art and culture, as well as considerable moral support and friendship, for which I will always be grateful.

I must also thank Wabash College Deans Victor M. Powell and Paul C. McKinney and the Faculty Development Committee for approving support of various phases of this work over the course of several years. My receipt of the 1988 McLain-McTurnan-Arnold Research Award made it possible to spend a semester free of teaching duties to continue work on this book. I would like to thank the selection committee of P. Donald Herring (Chair), Edward B. McLean, and David Polley for that particular support. The staff of the Wabash College Library has devoted considerable time and effort to tracking down materials, but I am especially indebted to Debbie Polley. Marjorie Jackson, secretary of the Wabash College Theater and Speech Departments, assisted me greatly in the clerical aspects, and my Theater Department colleague, Dwight Watson, graciously tolerated my distracted ways while working on this project and read a draft of the manuscript to which he contributed many useful insights. Students at Wabash College, past and present, have helped me with this work in a variety of ways, but I particularly wish to single out Michael S. Abbott, Richard J. Haffner, Kaizaad Navroze Kotwal, Darin Prather, David V. Schulz, and Kenneth Siepman, as well as the members of two seminar classes on the influence of commedia on modern theatre.

Finally, I especially wish to acknowledge the help and support of my parents, my friend Erminie Leonardis, my son Daniel, my daughter Anna, and, most of all, my wife Dana Kay Warner, to whom this work is dedicated.

James Fisher
1992

INTRODUCTION

Children hear them, see them, know them;
See the things the fairies show them,
Harlequin in magic poses;
Columbine among the roses;
Pantaloon in slippered ease is
Laughing at Clown's ancient wheezes
In the Summer, in the Spring,
In the sunshine, in the rain,
Summon them and hear them cry --
"Here we are again."[1]

-- from *The Harlequinade. An Excursion* by Dion
Clayton Calthrop and Granville Barker

The Theatre of Yesterday: The Golden Age of Commedia dell'arte

The Italian Renaissance produced a myriad of dramatic entertainments and theatrical traditions. Architects in the larger cities constructed indoor theatres imitating the rediscovered ruins of outdoor classical theatres, adding proscenium arches and spectacular scenery constructed and painted in perspective. The art of acting, which had been largely reduced to wandering minstrels and mimes during the medieval era,[2] once more became a profession, although the social status of actors remained low. Relatively few important plays were written, however, and most seemed pedantically imitative of classical literature. Various courts and academies produced elaborate royal processions, street pageants, *intermezzi*, pastorals, operas, and formal neoclassical revivals, usually seen only by the privileged classes. In the midst of this sprawling era of artistic accomplishment appeared *commedia dell'arte*,[3] the most vital dramatic form of the era, and its most public and popular form of entertainment.

Actors in commedia, performing in tightly knit ensembles and playing broadly sketched stock characters after 1545,[4] worked from simple scenarios which were refined over a long period of time to permit maximum opportunity for absurd and imaginatively acted performances. The ability of commedia actors to perform *all'improvviso* became legendary. Commedia's stock characters, who evolved over many years into instantly recognizable stereotypes, made it possible for actors to master this complex skill. Typically, a commedia actor played one character throughout his career, although he could work extraordinary variations on the emblematic traits of his stock mask, depending on the requirements and opportunities presented by a particular scenario. The troupes also expanded their repertories to appeal to all tastes in their audiences, requiring even more flexibility and versatility from the actors.

The stock masks evident in surviving *scenarii* most frequently include the *innamorati*,[5] young lovers who professed their desires in lyrical poetry (often borrowed from published literary works) and who generally played their roles straight, setting a standard of normalcy against which the more grotesque and farcical characters were played. The lovers were typically dashing and elegant, if also slightly ridiculous, and their follies resulted from the heat of their passion. The comic roles were a collection of masters (*vecchi*) and servants (*servi*), most masked to exaggerate their appearances and to emphasize a few specific traits. Several of the masters that appear most consistently in extant *scenarii* include Pantalone, Dottore, and Capitano.

Pantalone, or *Il Magnifico*, was usually an elderly Venetian merchant who, despite his advanced age, was a pretender to youth and a ridiculous courtier of young women. He is often the father of one of the lovers. Pantalone's costume consisted of a soft cap, red breeches and stockings, soft shoes, and a long coat. He also wore a brown leather mask with a huge nose and a long, pointed gray beard.[6] He embodies the comic contradictions of old age: rich but cheap, impotent yet amorous. His typical ploy is to intrude on the young lovers in some fashion, absurdly attempting to take over the role of the ardent courtier. His vanity, lechery, and gullibility, however, lead to his exposure and defeat, usually as a result of the plotting of the servants.

Il Dottore was often Pantalone's friend or rival, and he was typically depicted as an academician or a doctor of medicine or law. An insufferable pedant who often spoke with a Bolognese dialect laced with half-learned Latin expressions and misunderstood sayings, he was, as scholar Joseph Spencer Kennard wrote, "a chattering, conceited ignoramus."[7] Like Pantalone, he is often a father of one of the lovers. Il Dottore typically wore the long black robe of the academician, and much of the humor in a commedia play resulted from his muddled pronouncements and absurd opinions. He has spent his life studying everything and understanding nothing.[8]

Il Capitano seems to descend directly from the *miles gloriosus* of ancient Roman comedy, and although he was initially seen as a relatively unexaggerated lover, he blossomed into an absurd braggart who crowed about his powers as a military man and his conquests as a lover. He was often depicted as Spanish and dressed in an outrageous cape and a feathered hat. His bold costume also included a sword which he tried his best never to draw. During the course of a typical commedia play, he usually took the role of an eager, but unwanted lover, and his exposure as a coward or rogue was typically a high point of hilarity in the action.[9]

Without question, the most universally recognized and beloved characters of commedia were the *zanni* (zany ones), who played the roles of servants. Among these, Arlecchino (Harlequin) emerged as an unprecedented theatrical icon whose mere appearance could be relied upon to create havoc on the stage and delight in the audience. In *The Italian Comedy*, author Pierre L. Duchartre quotes Jean-François Marmontel (1723-1799), who recorded his memorable impressions of Arlecchino in his *Mémoires*:

> His character is a mixture of ignorance, naivete, wit, stupidity, and grace. He is both a rake and an overgrown boy with occasional gleams of intelligence, and his mistakes and clumsiness often have a wayward charm. His acting is patterned on the lithe, agile grace of a young cat, and he has a superficial coarseness which makes his performance all the more amusing. He plays the role of a faithful valet, always patient, credulous, and greedy. He is eternally amorous, and is constantly in difficulties either on his own or on his master's account. He is hurt and comforted in turn as easily as a child, and his grief is almost as comic as his joy.[10]

Arlecchino is always hungry and represents, among other things, the wishes and desires of the common people. He embodies their rebelliousness against authority and power and their will to survive in the face of adversity. Numerous other servants appeared under different names, but most were variations on Arlecchino,[11] ranging from the venal Brighella[12] to the rascally Scapino[13] to the deformed and grotesque Neapolitan, Pulcinella.[14] Women *servants* included the memorable Columbina,[15] a clever and earthy compatriot and sometime lover of Arlecchino, who often served as a go-between for the lovers.

Numerous other stock characters appeared, depending on the needs of the plot and the unique skills of individual actors in various troupes.[16] As time passed, variant interpretations of the familiar masks appeared throughout Italy and in other cultures where commedic[17] theatre was seen.

Scholars have put forth various and conflicting theories to explain the origins of commedia, including the suggestion that it developed from the ancient Roman comedies of Plautus and Terence. The similarities between the Plautine and Terentian stock characters and the masks of commedia seem to support this theory, but there are equally compelling reasons to accept several other possibilities. Commedia may have sprung from ancient Atellan farces preserved by wandering mimes during the Middle Ages or it may have been brought to the West by Byzantine performers when Constantinople fell in 1453. Another theory suggests that it sprang from *commedia erudita*, scripted comedies based on classical models, which appeared during the fifteenth and early sixteenth centuries.[18]

Although it was not the first Italian paly of the era, Niccolo Machiavelli's (1469-1527) *commedia erudita* masterpiece, *The Mandrake* (c.1513-1520), depicts sinister, rather realistic Florentine characters, distinctly echoing the characters and plots of Roman comedy. Both comic and shocking, the play portrays Nicia, an old doctor of laws, who is tricked by a corrupt friar, Friar Timoteo, into approving of a sexual relationship between Nicia's young wife, Lucrezia, and their predatory young neighbor, Callimaco. As Machiavelli wrote in *The Prince*, "It may be said of men in general that they are ungrateful, voluble, dissemblers, anxious to avoid danger, and covetous of gain,"[19] and *The Mandrake* reflects a cynical view of human nature, which can also be found in the greed, cowardice, and vanity typical of commedia characters. Machiavelli's insightful grasp of the purposes of comedy, which also effectively describes commedia, are contained in the prologue to another of his surviving plays, *Clizia* (c.1520):

> Comedies serve two purposes: they are instructive, and they make people laugh. It is instructive, especially for the young, to witness the avarice of an old man, the madness of a lover, the wiles of a servant, the gluttony of a parasite, the misery of a pauper, the ambition of a rich man, the flattery of a whore, the faithlessness of men in general.[20]

If commedia did evolve from early Italian farces and *commedia erudita*, actor and playwright Angelo Beolco (1502-1542) might be the transitional figure. He first appeared as an actor around 1520, in the carnivals of Venice,

Ferrara, and Padua, his native city. His most significant works, *The Girl of Ancona* (1522), *The Flirt* (1528), *Ruzzante Returns from the Wars* (c.1528), and *Bilora, or the Second Rustic Play* (c.1528), give an extremely detailed observation of rural life. They generally center on the misadventures of Beolco's stock peasant character, *Ruzzante* ("playful" or "frisky"), a loquacious and shrewd rebel who evokes a simple and robust love of life. Significantly, his surviving plays are primitively constructed rough sketches written in the Paduan dialect, thus offering the actor ample latitude for improvisation within an extremely simple plot structure. The script for *Ruzzante Returns from the Wars*, for example, is barely more than a skit involving a beating Ruzzante receives from the protector of the wife he has deserted. Following the beating, which he mistakenly thinks has been at the hands of a gang, Ruzzante learns from his neighbor, Menato, that he was battered by only one man. With typical bravado and good humor, Ruzzante laughs off his pain in true commedic style:

> Oh, I'm used to it, good neighbor! I've grown myself a thick skin. I don't feel a thing now. But what does hurt me is knowing what you just told me--that there was only one of him. If I'd known that, well, I'd have thought up the best trick I ever cooked up in my life. I'd have tied him and her together and then, with the two of them stuck together like that, I'd have tossed them in the canal. Christ Almighty, wouldn't that have been funny? Hell, man, you should have told me! By God, what a laugh we'd have had. Mind you, I'm not saying I'd have gone so far as to give him a walloping. Out of love for her, I wouldn't do that. After all, I don't want to cause her any pain, because I still sort of love her, if you see what I mean. But it sure would have been damned funny! Ho! Ho! Ho! Ho![21]

Beolco's most significant rival was Andrea Calmo (1509-1571), a former gondolier who specialized in playing foolish old men not unlike commedia's Pantalone. Beolco and Calmo were truly folk playwrights and actors and the precursors to such actor/playwrights as Ettore Petrolini, Eduardo De Filippo, and Dario Fo.

Undoubtedly, *commedia dell'arte* emerged from an amalgam of sources and the spirit and social conditions of its time, but whatever influences led to its rise, it is clear that it had boisterously come into its own by the middle of the sixteenth century. During the golden age of *commedia dell'arte*, from approximately 1550 to 1650, the form reached a pinnacle of purity it rarely equalled again. The stock characters that were henceforth associated with commedia were clarified and fully formed; improvisation of dialogue and stage business from scenarios became the definitive rule. Over seven hundred scenarios survive from this era, the oldest and most representative of which were published in a collection by actor Flaminio Scala (1547-c.1620) in 1611. Little is known about Scala, except that he was a nobleman by birth. He is thought to have been an early manager of the celebrated Gelosi troupe and was later associated with the Confidenti troupe as an actor and author.

Much of the power of commedia came from these family-centered acting troupes. Children of the troupe endured rigorous apprenticeships that prepared them to replace their elders. These early professional actors were trained from childhood and most were accomplished and versatile in song, dance, acrobatics, and improvisation. They were often proficient in several languages, which, along with the highly entertaining and elaborate acrobatics of commedia, helps to explain the great success the troupes achieved when they toured outside of Italy. Although the repertory of commedia troupes often included tragedies and pastorals, the farcical comedies improvised from scenarios became the centerpiece of their performances. The puncturing of pretense and vanity, the love of mischief for its own sake, the contrast between earthy good-heartedness and venality and lechery and the struggle of the oppressed against the oppressor, supplied the conflict in most scenarios. Wildly inventive improvisations on the oft-repeated plots, surprises and practical jokes (*burle*), as well as the bits of comic business (*lazzi*) and stock speeches borrowed from commonplace books (*zibaldoni*), fueled by the fertile imaginations of the actors, typified a commedia performance. The form exploded in popularity with the appearance of the great troupes. These were best exemplified by the Gelosi ("zealous to please"), led after 1583, and at the height of their fame, by Francesco Andreini (1548-1624). Although the troupe of Alberto Naseli (d.1583?), known on stage as Zan Ganassa, was the first to achieve wide acclaim both within Italy and as one of the first troupes to travel widely outside of Italy, it was rapidly eclipsed by the Gelosi.

Andreini and his wife, Isabella Canali (1562-1604), an outstanding duo among commedia actors, elevated the quality of commedia performance and made it fashionable entertainment throughout Europe. They were invited by Henri IV to perform in France, where commedia subsequently became enormously popular and had an incalculable influence on the golden age of French drama in the seventeenth century. Andreini achieved fame playing *Capitano Spavento della Valle Inferna*, although he had initially played the young lover in the Gelosi company. In 1604, Isabella died in childbirth in France, and Andreini was so disheartened that he disbanded the Gelosi. Despite the fact that he had served as the titular head of the Gelosi, and was a popular actor, Isabella had become a theatrical legend through her beauty, grace, and comic skill. She had been a poet of considerable stature, and was elected Laureata of the *Accademia degli Intenti of Padua*, where her portrait hangs between those of Tasso and Petrarch. Three years after her death, Andreini published the first part of a memoir of his years as head of the Gelosi. *Bravure del Capitano Spavento*, whose second part appeared in 1618, is a rich source of material on the daily life, techniques of performance, and repertory of a commedia troupe. In the modern comic theatre, the husband and wife team of Dario Fo and Franca Rame are the most obvious heirs to the acting traditions exemplified by the Andreinis. When Andreini disbanded the Gelosi, many of the actors joined other troupes or started their own. Notable among these were the Confidenti (1574-1639), the Desiosi

(1581-1599), the Accesi (1590-1628), and the Fedeli (c.1579-1640's), whose principal actors were Giovanbattista Andreini (c.1579-1654), son of Francesco and Isabella, and his wife, Virginia Ramboni (1583-1630?). As the fame of the troupes spread during the sixteenth and early seventeenth centuries, audiences in England, France, Spain, Germany, and Eastern Europe, as well as in Italy, encountered and embraced this essential theatre of the streets.

The Theatre of Tomorrow: Commedia on the Modern Stage

Commedia dell'arte was the rarest of theatrical forms -- a non-literary theatre that emphasized the skill of the improvising actor. Commedia actors transformed human folly and vice into incisive satire as they literally created a play before the audience's eyes from a simple scenario. Its popularity grew over the centuries as the forms and characters it inspired evolved, supplying diverse and delightful entertainments throughout Europe's theatres. In many cultures, these commedic forms offered a style of ritualized carnival -- a popular street theatre that served not only as communal fun, but also as a political instrument through its ever present satire and mockery of the powerful. This seemingly casual and lowly form of theatre became a distinctly powerful *lingua franca* of the imagination, connecting cultures and artists throughout Europe. Like the best and rarest forms of theatre, commedia was both spiritual and intellectual. It proved to be universally malleable and national, adapting in each country where it appeared to the needs of that culture's artists and audiences. During the last decades of the sixteenth century, a central group of masked characters became widely recognized and beloved by audiences in market squares, fairgrounds, street corners, and eventually in palaces and castles all over Italy. This was impromptu street theatre that exaggerated reality, twisting it into fantasy, transforming the commonplace into the extraordinary, and, ultimately, transforming the art of the theatre itself. This was *commedia dell'arte.*

Although some nineteenth century dramatists, artists, composers, and writers had been drawn to commedia characters and images, at the beginning of the twentieth century, almost simultaneously, an astonishingly diverse group of playwrights, actors, directors, and designers rediscovered the art of commedia in ways that would permanently change the direction of the modern theatre. Luigi Pirandello, Edward Gordon Craig, Vsevolod Meyerhold, Max Reinhardt, and Jacques Copeau, among many others, sought liberation from the pervasiveness of Realism, as well as from the stale remnants of elaborate spectacles, overwrought melodramas, and artificial acting styles of the preceding century. Perhaps due to the lack of concrete literary and performance evidence, these artists had highly individual and, at times, distinctly contradictory notions about commedia. Their understanding of its spirit and traditions permitted their rich imaginations wide scope as they attempted to define commedia. Most of them viewed it as an amalgam of elements from traditional Italian improvised comedy, as well as its many commedic antecedents and derivatives: classical comedy, medieval jesters and farces, the comedies of Molière, the Venetian plays of Goldoni, the *fiabe* of Gozzi, Pierrot[22] in the tradition of Deburau, pantomimes, music hall, circus, carnival, street entertainments of all kinds, and the variety stage. Significantly, they rediscovered improvisation, masks, stereotypical characters, and movement through their understanding of commedia. They also noted the centrality of the commedic actor who, aided by masks, could rise above realistic illusion to create larger-than-life and universal human symbols. The spontaneity of the improvisatory commedic style with its buoyant energy and direct assault on the senses of its audience had virtually no parallel in modern theatre.

These twentieth century iconoclasts share the view that commedia is theatrical art at its pinnacle of expressiveness and creativity. Many of them were drawn toward a kind of archetypal Jungian vision which reduced and also transformed life into a handful of simple plots and stereotypical figures that confront us with spiritual and intellectual glimpses of our deepest beings. The characters of commedia thus became the expression of the universally human; to the modern mind the characters' magic was powerful because it was a kind of street psychology, revealing directly who we humans are. Particularly in the character of Arlecchino, the leading *zanni* of commedia, modern theatre found a model in which to embody an absurdly lyrical vision of contemporary humanity, leading to such creations as Chaplin's "Little Tramp" and Beckett's and Ionesco's existential clowns.

The rediscovery of commedia by these artists energized a new theatrical revolution, moving the theatre away from Realism toward a new theatricalism. More to the point, contemporary theatre appears to be in a state of perpetual revolution against various kinds of formal and controlled dialectical drama.

After 1900, many others joined Pirandello, Craig, Meyerhold, Reinhardt, and Copeau in looking toward commedia for inspiration. In Italy, where commedia originated, Pirandello's complex theatrical plays, which had been influenced by commedia, swept away the stagnant traditions of the Italian theatre, and set the stage for the later works featuring the actor as creator, such as those by actor/playwrights Eduardo De Filippo and Dario Fo. In Spain, Jacinto Benavente, Ramón Maria del Valle-Inclán, and Federico Garcia Lorca used commedic characters and situations in their plays. In England, George Bernard Shaw, Harley Granville Barker, and J.M. Barrie cautiously explored the use of commedic characters in a few of their plays. Meyerhold's contemporaries, Nikolai Evreinov, Alexander Tairov, and Eugene Vakhtangov, among others, found the naturalistic productions of Constantin Stanislavsky's Moscow Art Theatre too limiting. As they explored new production concepts, their imaginations led them to employ the themes and characters of commedia. Commedia decorated plays by Hugo von Hofmannsthal, Paul Ernst, Stefan Zweig, and even Bertolt Brecht, in German and Austrian theatres. Mostly as a result of Copeau's influence on a generation of actors that included Louis Jouvet, Charles Dullin, and Jean-Louis Barrault, commedic plays, productions, and performance techniques were commonplace in France, and supplied a multitude of images for the plays of the Absurdists. The techniques of modern mime pioneered by Etienne Decroux and popularized by Jacques Lecoq and Marcel Marceau owe much to commedia.

Elements of commedia can be found in many of the countries of Eastern Europe, and in the Americas, although modern commedia did not have much impact in the United States until the "Happenings" and guerilla theatre of the 1960's, when groups such as The San Francisco Mime Troupe began using commedic techniques to develop an ensemble acting style and improvisatory acting techniques suited to a radical theatre of the streets. During the last quarter of the twentieth century, commedia has clearly become a paradigm for theatre at the height of its expressive and technical powers; its echoes can be heard everywhere.

Martin Green and John Swan, authors of *The Triumph of Pierrot*, a chronicle of the influence of commedia, as exemplified by the figure of Pierrot, on modern art, literature, film, and theatre, rightly explain that for twentieth century artists commedia "is not an idea or a meaning, but a collection of images with many meanings."[23] For some, such as Meyerhold, Fo, and The San Francisco Mime Troupe, commedia offered a platform for potent political statements. For others, like Craig, Meyerhold, and Copeau, commedia provided techniques that helped them reconsider the art of acting and directing. Some, like Reinhardt, were commedia antiquarians, reviving a theatrical style to delight modern audiences as it had in its heyday. Playwrights including Pirandello, Evreinov, Brecht, and Beckett, found models for characters and situations that liberated them to examine their themes in meaningful ways. These artists, quite evidently, interpret commedia broadly and individually, and in this study I intend to do the same. The works of the playwrights, directors, actors, and scenic artists I examine here were unquestionably influenced by a wide variety of sources, but in most cases, the impact of commedia on their work has been overlooked. While Green and Swan's study impressively reports on the proliferation of commedia in modern culture, it is important to remember that commedia was, and is, a theatrical form, and no study currently exists which specifically focuses on how commedia influences modern theatre.

Past and present scholarship on commedia, including studies in Italian by Siro Ferrone, Luciano Mariti, Ferruccio Marotti, Cesare Molinari, Ferdinando Taviani, Roberto Tessari, and Ludovico Zorzi, and such English-language perennials as Allardyce Nicoll's *The World of Harlequin* and Pierre L. Duchartre's *The Italian Comedy*, along with several very recent works, such as Robert L. Erenstein's *De geschiedenis van de Commedia dell'Arte*, Virginia Scott's *Commedia dell'arte in Paris*, and Kenneth and Laura Richards' *The Commedia dell'arte. A Documentary History*, focus on commedia from its origins up through the attempts by Goldoni and Gozzi to revive it in the late eighteenth century. The references to nineteenth or twentieth century commedic plays or artists are slight. Studies of individual artists, particularly recent works on Meyerhold and Copeau, describe their interest in commedia, but do not examine the pervasive influence of commedia in twentieth century theatrical traditions at large.

This book will attempt to examine the impact of diverse notions of commedia on theatrical artists in the major cultures of Europe and North America since 1900. Each chapter begins with a brief introduction to the history of commedia's influence within the culture prior to 1900. Following that, most chapters will examine the work of the earliest and most influential post-1900 theatre artist to recognize the significance of commedia and to use its techniques, characters, or plots. Other artists also inspired by commedia will be examined down to the present day. Although this may seem, at times, to be a long list of names, it is my hope that the introduction of these individuals will prove a valuable resource to those interested in this subject. It also suggest something of the widespread influence of this extraordinary form of theatre. When possible, I have allowed the artists to speak for themselves in defining commedia and its impact on their work, as I trace commedia apparatus and perspectives found within their plays, productions, and theories of performance techniques. Although it is possible to a certain degree to define what *commedia dell'arte* was in earlier times, modern conceptions of it vary distinctly from artist to artist, and from culture to culture. The artists influenced by commedia in the modern era defined it through their own highly individual and eccentric visions of the form. What a Craig saw in his vision of commedia is vastly different from what a Reinhardt or a Meyerhold saw. My guiding notion in the selection of artists and texts was that these artists themselves identified commedia as an important influence on their conception of theatre. The reader may wish for one particular notion of what commedia was to modern artists: "Is it the influence on modern writers and drama of the techniques of the Italian professional improvised comedy of the sixteenth and seventeenth centuries?" "Is it the Franco-Italian comedy of the later sixteenth and seventeenth centuries?" "Is it the harlequinade?" "The pantomime?" "The pierrot show?" The answer to all of these questions must be, "Yes, it is all of these things and more, depending on the artist in question." My mission, to a large extent, is to expand knowledge about the wide-ranging and variant ways in which commedia and its influence on later allied forms nurtured the art of a staggering collection of modern artists. This study presumes, as I believe it must, that readers will be generally familiar with *commedia dell'arte* in its heyday, and the forms that it influenced during the seventeenth, eighteenth, and nineteenth centuries.

In 1912, Edward Gordon Craig wrote that "in the Commedia dell'Arte the Italians of the late 16th century gave to future generations a hint as to the possibilities of the Art of the Theatre."[24] Surveying the dazzlingly varied proliferation of commedia-inspired forms produced in this century, one can only suspect that Craig himself would have been astonished at how broadly this "hint" would be taken.

CHAPTER ONE

The Finger in the Eye: Commedia in Italy

Clowns are grotesque blasphemers against all our pieties. That's why we need them. They're our alter egos.[1]

-- Dario Fo

By the beginning of the eighteenth century, Italian troupes had exported their native *commedia dell'arte* to every corner of Europe. Ironically, at home, commedia had declined in quality, becoming repetitious, sentimental, and often obscene, in attempts to keep audiences from gravitating toward other entertainments. This situation reached alarming levels by the middle of the eighteenth century. In 1750, Carlo Goldoni (1707-1793) wrote *The Comic Theatre*, advocating improvements in commedia performances, especially a higher register of language and the total abandonment of masks. He also called for life-like situations to replace commedia plots which had become mindlessly absurd and fantastic. In these sweeping and controversial changes, Goldoni also shed improvisation, certain that leaving actors to their own devices led to the worst abuses evident in eighteenth century commedia. Goldoni reminded his readers that comedy

> was created to correct vice and ridicule bad customs; when the ancient poets wrote comedies in this manner, the common people could participate, because, seeing the copy of a character on stage, each found the original either in himself or in someone else. But when comedies became merely ridiculous, no one paid attention any more,

because with the excuse of making people laugh, they admitted the worst and most blatant errors.[2]

Although he wrote several tragedies and over eighty musical dramas, many formally scripted plays drawing inspiration from the commedia can be found among Goldoni's nearly one hundred and fifty play corpus. In *The Servant of Two Masters* (1743), *The Girl of Honor* (1749), *The Liar* (1750), *The Merchants* (1752), *The Loves of Harlequin and Camilla* (1763), *The Jealousy of Harlequin* (1763), and *The Portrait of Harlequin* (1764), among others, Goldoni made use of comparatively realistic situations (showing lives of both aristocrats and peasants) and stage effects, adding new and humanizing dimensions to the stock characters given to him by commedia tradition. His comedies fall into four distinct categories: satiric plays about the aristocracy, situation comedies about the bourgeoisie, Venetian dialect plays, and non-Italian comedies.

Several of Goldoni's plays, especially *The Servant of Two Masters*, were to figure prominently among these works most often staged by modern commedists. Indeed, few of his plays made better use of commedia's characters and situations. In the play, a noblewoman (Beatrice) arrives in Venice disguised as her brother (Silvio) to collect a debt from Pantalone and to find her lover (Florindo). Both lovers engage the mischievious and gluttonous Truffaldino as their servant, and much of the play's humor revolves around Truffaldino's attempts to keep both masters satisfied. After many confusions among the characters, Truffaldino mixes up some of the belongings of Beatrice and Florindo, and when they discover this, Truffaldino explains to each that the unfamiliar items belonged to his previous master, now deceased. Beatrice and Florindo, each believing that the other has died, appear with daggers poised over their hearts. But on seeing each other alive, their thoughts quickly change from suicide to love, and the play concludes with Beatrice collecting Silvio's debt from Pantalone, and marrying Florindo, as

Silvio marries Clarice, and Truffaldino is wed to Clarice's maid.

Goldoni's most significant rival, Carlo Gozzi (1720-1806), objected to Goldoni's reforms, and wrote for the *masked* commedia actor emphasizing improvisation and *fiabe* (fantasy). His *The Love for Three Oranges* (1760), *Turandot* (1762), *The King Stag* (1762), and *The Pretty Little Green Bird* (1765), were particularly popular in their day, and are among his most familiar works in the modern era.

Gozzi's tragicomic and fanciful Chinese fairy tale, *Turandot*, inspired many adaptations, most notably those by Friedrich Schiller, Giacomo Puccini, and several twentieth century commedists. Set in ancient Peking, *Turandot* begins with the beautiful Princess Turandot who poses three riddles to each of her suitors, all in hopes of marrying her and ruling all of China. Those who fail must forfeit their heads, which are then impaled on the gates of the city. Calaf, a deposed prince from Astrakhan, has seen a portrait of Turandot, and inspired by her great beauty, arrives in Peking determined to win her. Coming before Turandot, Calaf answers her riddles correctly, but she demands a retaliatory trial before accepting him. Turandot's father, the Emperor, demands that she comply with the original agreement, but Calaf galantly offers another proposition. He will submit to death if she is able to solve the riddle of his name and royal origin. Through an informant, Turandot learns Calaf's background and confronts him in triumph with the answer. Despondent over what he perceives as her intense hatred, Calaf contemplates suicide, but Turandot relents at the last moment, upon realizing her awakening love for him. Gozzi mixes such commedia characters as Pantalone, Tartaglia, Brighella, and Truffaldino into this exotic tale. They appear fundamentally to offer comic relief as ministers of the Emperor's court. As with most of Gozzi's *fiabe*, commedia's characters appear in a distinctive world of fantasy, clearly Gozzi's reaction against the social forces of the Enlightenment. While Goldoni satirized his world, Gozzi escaped into another one, and commedia's characters and traditions were but one mode of escape.

Although Goldoni and Gozzi[3] agreed on very little in the way of theatrical practice, they both admired and wrote plays for actor Antonio Sacchi (1708-1788), who was most often seen in the role of the *zanni*, Truffaldino. He had his own company, and was the first actor to perform the title role in Goldoni's *The Servant of Two Masters*. Unlike many of his contemporaries, he performed in both improvised and scripted plays, successfully skirting the tension that marked the demise of improvised comedy and the beginning of a relatively uninspired century of Italian theatre. By the end of Sacchi's life, commedia, and the Goldonian and Gozzian attempts to reform it, had essentially died as audiences turned to other entertainments. Commedia was to lie dormant in Italy until the early twentieth century when it rose again in the art of Italy's greatest modern playwright.

Luigi Pirandello

After Goldoni and Gozzi, the Italian theatre went through an era of decline, despite much activity. Aside from a few gifted actors, little of significance occurred until around World War I. Luigi Pirandello (1867-1936) emerged at this time as Italy's first internationally important dramatist since the eighteenth century. As a student, he distinguished himself in literary studies, and while still a student, he wrote his first dramatic work, *Barbaro*, which is no longer extant. After an unhappy time as an apprentice in his father's business, Pirandello enrolled at the University of Rome in 1887. Dissatisfied with the quality of education there, he went to the University of Bonn in 1888, where he taught until 1891. He was firmly committed to a life of letters, and returned to Rome in 1891 to pursue it. Pirandello married Antonietta Portulano[4] in 1894. A series of personal setbacks, including the failure of his father's business (which ended the possibility of family support for his writing), made it necessary for him to accept a position as a teacher of rhetoric in Rome, where he remained until 1923. In 1904, his father-in-law went bankrupt, causing his wife to suffer a nervous breakdown. Thus began a fifteen-year decline in her mental health, which finally forced Pirandello to commit her to an institution, where she remained for the rest of her life. His experiences during this time caused him to have what he later referred to as the trauma of his mind. Pirandello's speculation about the nature of sanity and madness arose at this time and later figured centrally in his most important plays.

Pirandello's earliest plays are written in dialect, and seem mostly inspired by Sicilian folk traditions; his final plays are highly symbolic, and untied to any particular traditions. His philosophical plays, written between 1917 and 1924, are his most acclaimed. These plays were seen and performed in Italy, and throughout Europe and America, beginning in the early 1920's. They are, among other things, his most commedic works. Although he uses Realism as a starting point, his plays stand within the broader theatrical traditions represented by commedia. In the philosophical plays, he examines the contradictory, paradoxical, and absurd aspects of life, through a mixture of comic and tragic elements, emphasizing conflicts between appearance and reality, and between the comic mask and the tragic face hidden by it. In every seemingly real situation or statement that he makes, Pirandello plays out its opposite as well. Illusion and reality, madness and sanity are perceived by his characters and audiences to exist within the same moment in time. In a sense, he was an Absurdist dramatist, viewing human beings as ridiculous creatures making their way in a world of shadowy and shifting realities and values. The action in his plays often escalates a normal state of affairs onto a plane of intensified farce where truth and reality are elusive and incomprehensible at best.

Placing extraordinary characters in absurd and densely complex situations with seemingly impossible resolutions delighted Pirandello. His plays, as commedia scenarios do, create surprising and fantastic situations that seem too complex to unravel. He manages a return to the ordinary through his magical ability to resolve the complicated contradictions and through flights into commedic farce. Pirandello's finest works are mature and polished *literary* achievements, not rough commedia scenarios, yet he depends heavily on the skill of the improvisatory actor in true commedic fashion. *Right You Are, If You Think You Are* (1917), *Six Characters in Search of An Author* (1921), *Henry IV* (1922), and *To-Night We Improvise* (1929), can fall as flat as any uninspired commedia scenario in the hands of uninventive actors.

Pirandello hoped to introduce new methods of theatrical production in Italy similar to those he had discovered in other European cultures. He was fascinated by puppets, having been familiar with traditional Sicilian puppets since boyhood. He also advocated the use of actual masks, but, more often, employed stylized make-up and lighting effects in his productions. The mask supplied him with a tangible symbol for the conflict between illusion and reality, the issue at the core of the four commedic plays. Masks were both protective and destructive to him, and they served as metaphors, as well as theatrical devices, in his plays. To Pirandello, the mask was a disguise, a way of hiding or obscuring truth, and creating a shifting sense of reality. Reality did not necessarily hide behind a single mask, for to Pirandello everything was masked: "Masks, they are all masks, a puff and they are gone, to make room for other masks."[5]

He admired "Reinhardt in Germany and Craig in England,"[6] but was less disposed toward the new scenic innovations of the day "which more or less overwhelms a work of art rather than defining it or realizing it completely."[7] He focused on a reform of acting that included experimentation with commedic performance techniques, especially improvisation. He saw the author, rather than the actor, as the true theatrical creator, despite his belief that "many bad plays have become excellent by what the actors have created and thus have triumphed on stage!"[8] As Russian dramatist Nikolai Evreinov had, Pirandello developed a philosophy of theatricality which suggested that "it was not the actors who had invented the improvisations of the *Commedia dell'arte*, but it was the playwrights who had become actors, who had lost all their artistic ambitions and had become attracted by *momentaneous* life."[9]

Pirandello strove to create a spirit of spontaneity and improvisation in the plays that he crafted with extreme care. He recognized, however, that "theater, before it is a traditional form of literature, is a natural expression of life,"[10] a grotesque carnival expressing both the madness and mystery of life. Looking to carnival traditions, he observed the "many sad things"[11] the songs of the carnival "say to those who know how to read into them!"[12] His plays presented, in his own view, "new problems to be resolved,"[13] and were "built entirely upon live impressions, which have flashed before my imagination as an artist."[14]

In addition to these "live impressions," it seems that Pirandello, like other Italian theatrical artists, found commedia a potent resource. In 1908, he published his lengthy essay "Humor," an early explication of his aesthetic principles, and of the diverse literary influences on his work. Noting that "Caricature, extravagant farce, and the grotesque are often mistaken for authentic humor,"[15] he examines the ironies, contradictions, and rhetoric of humor, along with a survey of Italian and international "humorists." Humor was not merely "a play of contrasts between the poet's ideal and reality,"[16] although

> a great deal depends on the poet's temperament and that his ideal, confronted by reality, may react with indignation, or laughter, or compromise; but an ideal that compromises does not really show that it is sure of itself and profoundly rooted. And is this limitation of the ideal all that humor consists of? Not at all. The limitation of the ideal, if anything, would be not the cause but rather the result of the

particular psychological process which is called humor.[17]

As the twentieth century's most philosophical commedist, Pirandello did not wish to confuse "comic spirit, irony, or satire with humor,"[18] but described humor as "an *eccentricity of style*."[19] In what may well be an allusion to the inherent humor of commedia, he explains that humor

> originates out of a special state of mind, which can, to some degree, spread. When an artistic expression succeeds in dominating the attention of the public, the latter immediately begins to think, speak, and write in accordance with the impressions it has received; thus, such an expression, originating from the particular intuition of a writer, soon penetrates into the public and is then variously transformed and regulated by it.[20]

He cites an example of an old woman, whose face is grotesquely made-up and whose clothes are absurdly out of fashion. The old woman, a commedic pretender to youth, is *comic* in her belief that she can create an impossible illusion, but Pirandello finds *humor* in a "*perception of the opposite*,"[21] that the old woman may indeed be distressed by her appearance, shifting the observer's reaction to one of pity. Basically, he is interested in the character's complex and contradictory inner emotions which exist, often in conflict, with the outer appearance. This suggests one reason why commedia, with its masked characters (a comic mask hiding a character inside who is also doubled in perception), was of great significance to him. Pirandello hardly mentions comic theatre or commedia itself in "Humor." Later, in his introduction to Silvio D'Amico's *The Italian Theatre*, commedia figures prominently in his essay, and he clearly identifies it as a significant force in his own drama, as well as that of his predecessors and contemporaries.

Commedia, he writes, was born out of authors, like Ruzzante, who "indulged their own personal tastes and ambitions,"[22] yet were acquainted with literary works. These authors were "so deeply involved in the Theater, in the life of the Theater, as to become, in fact, actors; they begin by writing the comedies they later perform, comedies at once more theatrical because not written in the isolated study of the man of letters,"[23] but in front of an actual audience. For Pirandello, it seemed absurd to imagine this as merely an accidental discovery of actors. The authors thus "lost all their serious artistic pretensions: the transitory, impassioned life of the Theater must have taken such full possession of them that the only interest left to them was that of the spectacle itself -- a complete absorption in the quality of the performance and communication with the audience."[24] No longer an author, or even an actor, the figure onstage became a type, with a vivid stage life of its own. In essence, what remained in these characters for Pirandello "was their sheer movement."[25] They required order in his view, and each was assigned specific tasks with distinguishing dress and dialect, leading toward "some sort of intrigue within a more or less logical pattern of development which the classical forms, long emptied of their content, easily provided."[26]

Pirandello saw commedia as an inheritance of Roman comedy, as part of a tradition, and not as a national naive form as so many more sentimental commentators have seen it. By the time commedia had reached its peak, it had developed as "a quicker and more prudent way, certainly a more decisive way, of profiting from all the material of classical comedy,"[27] from the ancients through Ruzzante and his contemporaries. Commedia provided internationally acclaimed entertainment because the Italian theatre had, above all others, "drained the recovered classical world of all that it had to offer."[28] Pirandello claimed that the triumph of theatre throughout Europe during the Renaissance was a direct result of the influence of Italian theatre, especially commedia. Craig had credited the Italians with supplying the theatre with its true spirit, and Pirandello concurred, emphasizing that the plays of Shakespeare, Molière, Lope de Vega, and others, were outgrowths of

the Italian matrix. Molière alone was frank enough to admit: "*je prends mon bien où je le trouve*," in answer to those who remarked that perhaps he had gone too far in appropriating not only situations and characters but entire scenes from our *commedia dell'arte*; and he was right in shrugging off such remarks, considering the narrow point of view reflected in them. The truth is that all these great authors, these originators of European Theater, had appropriated -- without being aware of it -- something quite different: the very spirit of our Theater.[29]

He felt that literary history generally overlooked the importance of Italian Renaissance theatre and drama, undoubtedly due to the lack of traditional literary evidence, and he regretted "that the Italian Theater, having reached at last the possibility of bringing forth a great author, should have given us, with Goldoni, simply a minor version of Molière."[30]

Yet, Pirandello did have considerable admiration for the plays of Goldoni, who he acknowledged was rightly recognized "for having relaxed the rigidity of the masks in their strained and artificial laughter and for having reanimated the now flexible muscles of the human face with the natural laughter of a life caught in the midst of the most vivacious and, at the same time, most exquisite and incomparably graceful activity."[31] Pirandello saw his own shattering of nineteenth century rigidities as similar to Goldoni's. Thus he shared English scene designer and theorist Edward Gordon Craig's view that although "Molière is purer *Commedia dell'arte*, more genuine theater of the grand and traditional manner, Goldoni is pure Italian comedy and of a little kind which has never been equalled: it is the best of its kind."[32]

Goldoni's most significant achievement, according to Pirandello, was more than just enlivening the fading characters of traditional commedia. Goldoni created new figures and transcended the old ones, "with an unapproachable facility, with an astounding lightness of touch,"[33] bringing to them "all the involubility, the fluidity, the contradiction, the spontaneity of life"[34] necessary to pave the way for the emergence of the contemporary theatre. He saw himself as a kindred spirit with Goldoni and commedia actors. Commedia had broken through the formality of Renaissance art forms, and Pirandello similarly attempted to break through the narrow bounds of the late nineteenth century stage. "Modernizing" theatrical traditions seemed appropriate to Pirandello, for whom theatre should never be archaeology but an ever renewing form in which "a work of art is no longer the work of the writer (which, after all, can always be preserved in some other way), but an act of life, realized on the stage from one moment to the next, with the cooperation of an audience that must find satisfaction in it."[35] Here Pirandello seems to empower the actor, the creator of the act, as in commedia tradition.

Pirandello believed that the contemporary Italian theatre succeeded where even the greatest of Europe's modern theatre had not, "in their greater realism and their greater fidelity to life"[36] and in the emergence "as in the Commedia dell'arte"[37] of "regional characters and forms of expression."[38] In a sense, the Italian theatre, through commedia, had rediscovered a "vast virgin world of the unexplored life of human personality,"[39] transforming the maschere of commedia into maschere nude, human characters minus the trappings of civilized behavior and social pretensions.

Pirandello's early plays most obviously demonstrate the influence of commedia and Italian folk traditions on his work. Most of these, including Liolà (1916), Think It Over, Giacomino! (1916), and Cap and Bells (1917), feature simple, stock comic situations with occasional elements of fantasy, and characters who are clearly inspired by commedia's masks (in Liolá, for example, Uncle Simone, the old man bragging of his potency, is an obvious variation of Pantalone). More importantly, they introduce themes developed later in his most sophisticated works: the relationship and duality of masks, sanity and madness, illusion versus reality, and the need for compassion in all human matters.

Cap and Bells is set in a realistic drawing room where Pirandello has combined aspects of Pantalone and Arlecchino in the character Ciampa, who is both a scheming servant (in this case, a bank employee) and a deceived elderly husband. Ciampa's wife is having an affair with his boss, Cavalier Fiorica, but Ciampa allows it to continue for the sake of keeping his job, as long as he and his wife can maintain an illusion of respectability. When the boss's wife, Beatrice, publicly reveals the affair, Ciampa has to stop the tidal wave of gossip her revelation starts in their small Sicilian town. He convinces his wife and her lover that since Beatrice's jealousy has caused a public embarrassment, the only way to rectify it is for Beatrice to be declared insane. The mask of madness works, and Ciampa, his wife, and Fiorica are able to resume their "normal" lives. This Machiavellian little play owes much to commedia in its stereotypical characters. Ciampa sees humans as merely puppets:

> I am a puppet, you are a puppet, we are all puppets. Is it enough, do you think, to be born a puppet by divine will? No, Signor! Each can make himself the puppet he wants, the puppet he can be or that he believes himself to be. And this is where the insanity begins, Signora! Because each puppet wishes to be respected, not only for what he has inside himself, but for the mask he wears to the world. Not one of the puppets is contented with his role, each would like to stand before his own puppet and spit in its face.[40]

Actor Angelo Musco (1872-1937), who had begun his career with a Sicilian marionette theatre and in the company of Giovanni Grasso, had significant impact on Pirandello's earliest plays. With his own company, Musco had popular successes with *Think It Over, Giacomino!*, *Liolá*, and and *The Jug* (1917), playing the *brillante* (another stock character, one that "sparkles" like a diamond). Critics applauded his infectious comic skill, and even Craig described him as one of the great actors of the day. Other critics, such as Silvio D'Amico, were offended by his flagrant improvisations and willingness to depart from the written text. Musco's obvious strength was his ability to act in response to the reactions of his audience. Like commedia actors, he moved freely within the loose confines of the scenario, nimble enough to seize a comic moment and play it for an engaged audience.

It is unclear why Pirandello tolerated Musco's flamboyant disregard for his dialogue, but he was undoubtedly as attracted to the actor's skill as he was repelled by the liberties Musco took with his plays. Once Pirandello was outraged at a dress rehearsal for *Liolá* when he realized that Musco's actors had not properly learned their parts. Refusing Musco permission to use his text, he grabbed his script and left in a fury, telling Musco in no uncertain terms that the performance was called off. Musco ran after him, insisting that he needed no script, his cast would improvise the play anyway. Actors like Musco, who continued to perform as commedia actors, were a rare breed. Most Italian actors of the day had abandoned the improvisatory and natural style in favor of a formal declamatory style, presumably to add seriousness and dignity to the literary dramas of the day. Pirandello, who found this type of theatre pretentious and its actors stiff, preferred a spontaneity typical of commedia, yet at the same time controlled by the structure and language of his polished scripts. Given the choice between Musco's liberties and the lifelessness of most Italian players of his time, Pirandello chose to endure, and even to admire, Musco's improvisations.

Pirandello's first important full-length play, *Right You Are, If You Think You Are* (1917), appears to be as loosely constructed as a commedia scenario: thus creating the illusion of improvisation. Eric Bentley, who has translated the play, describes the play's central character, Lamberto Laudisi, a *brillante*, a "Harlequin in modern dress, a Harlequin who has invaded the realm of philosophy, and who behaves there as he had behaved elsewhere."[41] Laudisi is the cynical observer who watches Councillor Agazzi and his family pry into the personal life of Signor Ponza, secretary to Agazzi. Mysteriously, Ponza's wife and her mother (Signora Frola) have never been seen together. Signora Frola claims to live alone to avoid interfering in her daughter's life, but Ponza insists that she has been isolated because she is insane. His first wife (Signora

Frola's daughter), he says, was killed some years before in an earthquake that conveniently destroyed any written evidence of the marriage. Signora Frola turns the tables by insisting that it is Ponza who is insane; she claims that his present wife is her daughter. Ponza responds by saying that he pretends insanity to humor Signora Frola, and he is distressed to become the "target of insufferable persecution."[42] Finally, Agazzi demands that Ponza's wife appear. She does, dressed in mourning with a thick veil, and announces that she is Signora Frola's daughter and the second wife of Ponza. She continues: "to myself I am no one. No one."[43] This is met with protestations from the others, but she concludes, "I am the one that each of you thinks I am."[44] Laudisi, laughing derisively at the "truth-seekers," proclaims that Signora Ponza has spoken with "the voice of truth!"[45] Pirandello's notion of *maschere nude* causes him to people *Right You Are* with stock characters recognizable as commedia types. Using the psychological language common in the early twentieth century, Stark Young suggests, "Mental Habits, Characteristic Human Emotions, Thematic Ideas"[46] are the stock characters of *Right You Are*. Undoubtedly, Pirandello would have preferred to think that he had put commedic characters on the stage rather than "Mental Habits." Along with his translation of *Right You Are*, Bentley includes some production notes suggesting that a director remember that:

> actors -- especially the actors of the *commedia dell'arte* whose skill Pirandello wished to revive -- once were, and can be again, the main part of the show. Tell your actors to let go. Have them shout, swagger, gesticulate -- at least in the earlier rehearsals. For you have to get them to act and talk instead of strolling and muttering like mannequins with a pin loose. And if they perform their roles from outside instead of pretending to *be* the people who are not people, Pirandello would be better served.[47]

Six Characters in Search of an Author (1921) gained international celebrity for Pirandello for its exposition of both the illusion and reality inherent to theatre and to life. In it, a Producer has assembled his acting company to prepare a production of a play by Pirandello (in an early extract, the Producer furiously derides Pirandello's plays: "And if you can understand them you must be very clever. He writes them on purpose so nobody enjoys them, neither actors nor critics nor audience."[48]) The rehearsal is interrupted by the appearance of a Father, a Mother, a Stepdaughter, a Young Boy, and a Baby Girl. The Family explains that they are characters from an unfinished play and they plead for permission to recreate a crucial moment in their lives, claiming that they would supply the director and his company with a scene from which they may construct a finished drama. The Producer and his actors are skeptical, but the Father proceeds to explain that his wife had fallen in love with another man and he has stepped aside, permitting her to live with the other man, by whom she has had three illegitimate children. He has also arranged for a legitimate child, a Son, to live in the country. The Mother contests the Father's account, claiming that he had tired of her and pushed her into the arms of another man, separating her from her Son. The Father continues to explain that some time later he failed to recognize the Stepdaughter in Madame Pace's bordello and only the appearance of the Mother at the crucial moment prevented him from dishonor. The Father convinces the Producer to improvise the scene with his actors. They resist, however, through an allusion to commedia:

LEADING ACTOR.	Is he serious? What's he going to do?
YOUNG ACTOR.	I think he's gone round the bend.
ANOTHER ACTOR.	Does he expect to make up a play in five minutes?
YOUNG ACTOR.	Yes, like the old actors in the commedia del'arte!
LEADING ACTRESS.	Well if he thinks I'm going to appear in that sort of nonsense. . .
YOUNG ACTOR.	Nor me.
FOURTH ACTOR.	I should like to know who they are.
THIRD ACTOR.	Who do you think? They're probably escaped lunatics or crooks.
YOUNG ACTOR.	Is he taking them seriously?

YOUNG ACTRESS.	It's vanity. The vanity of seeing himself as an author.
LEADING ACTOR.	I've never heard of such a thing! If the theatre, ladies and gentlemen, is reduced to this. . .
FIFTH ACTOR	I'm enjoying it!
THIRD ACTOR.	Really? We shall have to wait and see what happens next I suppose.[49]

The actors finally do attempt to play the roles of the Father and the Stepdaughter in this scene, but the characters, especially the Stepdaughter, protest the actors' vulgarized treatment of the scene. She insists that the scene be played truthfully, leading to a debate with the Producer which raises the idea that truth may be an impossibility in a theatre as well as in life. In this madcap philosophical scene, Pirandello grinds to dust the sentimentalizing excesses of the contemporary Italian theatre:

PRODUCER.	The truth! Do me a favour will you? This is the theatre you know! Truth's all very well up to a point but. . .
STEPDAUGHTER.	What do you want to do then?
PRODUCER.	You'll see! You'll see! Leave it all to me.
STEPDAUGHTER.	No. No I won't. I know what you want to do! Out of my feeling of revulsion, out of all the vile and sordid reasons why I am what I am, you want to make a sugary little sentimental romance. You want him to ask me why I'm in mourning and you want me to reply with the tears running down my face that it is only two months since my father died. No. No. I won't have it! He must say to me what he really did say. "Well then, let's take it off, we'll take it off at once, shall we, your little black dress." And I, with my heart still grieving for my father's death only two months before, I went behind there, do you see? Behind that screen and with my fingers trembling with shame and loathing I took off the dress, unfastened my bra. .

PRODUCER	(his head in his hands). For God's sake! What are you saying!
STEPDAUGHTER	(shouting excitedly). The truth! I'm telling you the truth!
PRODUCER.	All right then. Now listen to me. I'm not denying its the truth. Right. And believe me I understand your horror, but you must see that we can't really put a scene like that on the stage.[50]

The Father defensively explains that having found the Mother and her children destitute, he took them in with himself and the Son. The Stepdaughter continues despite this to blame the Father for her shame and the Son rejects them all. Requested to enact the scene in which he rejects the Mother, the Son refuses and exits to a garden, where he finds the Young Boy beside a fountain staring in horror at the drowned body of the Baby Girl. Before this news can be fully grasped, a shot is heard. The Young Boy has killed himself, sending the characters into shock, and causing the observing actors to protest hysterically that "It's all make-believe."[51] The Father, however, protests: "What do you mean, make-believe? It's real! It's real, ladies and gentlemen! It's reality!"[52] The Producer, perplexed by his inability to comprehend the clash between real life and theatrical illusion, finally dismisses them all: "Make-believe?! Reality?! Oh, go to hell the lot of you! Lights! Lights! Lights!"[53]

Depending on his experiences as a playwright and director, combined with his despairing but compassionate view of human nature and art, Pirandello makes use of his understanding of commedic improvisation to create and recreate the complex relationships of his emblematic characters. Caught up in the complex tangles of life, his "actors" and "characters" are ordinary people he uses as types, but like the characters of commedia they seem to have free expressions and movements that even their author did not give them. They also suggest commedia masks: the Stepdaughter is the innamorata, the Father is Pantalone, and the Actors and Actresses are the *zanni*. Pirandello succeeds at the unlikely task of combining Realism and nearly pure commedia in a single play. By using theatre as a metaphor he exposes his characters' tragedies, by breaking through the illusion of the theatre with the illusion of improvisation. In this remarkable achievement, Pirandello reveals the complex and ever-changing realities that always lurk beneath the mask of Realism. The result was

> what it had to be: a mixture of tragic and comic, fantastic and realistic, in a humorous situation that was quite new and infinitely complex, a drama which is conveyed by means of the characters, who carry it within them and suffer it, a drama, breathing, speaking, self-propelled, which seeks at all costs to find the means of its own presentation; and the comedy of the vain attempt at an improvised realization of the drama on stage.[54]

In less than a year after *Six Characters*, Pirandello completed another masterwork, *Henry IV* (1922). This play explores the tragedy of a middle-aged Italian nobleman who, after a fall from a horse at a carnival, lives with the delusion that he is Henry IV. Twenty years of tailoring his life to suit his madness leads five individuals, Matilde Spina (a former lover who had jilted him), Belcredi (her current lover), Frida (her daughter), Frida's fiancé (who is also the madman's nephew), and a doctor, to attempt to cure him. Henry is furious at their intrusions, since he has used his madness as a protective mask against reality. After he reveals to his attendants that he is actually sane, they inform Matilde, who refuses to believe them. Henry's emotions are stirred by seeing Frida, who reminds him of the youthful Matilde, and he admits that he regained his sanity some years before, but continues to find his particular masquerade as good as any other. In Act Three, he grabs hold of his costume and explains that

> This. . .for me this is an obvious, deliberate caricature of that other masquerade which goes on all the time, in which we're all involuntary clowns without knowing it. . . (Indicating Belcredi). . . when we dress up as who we think we are. You have to forgive them, because they

still don't see that clothes. . .habits. . .are the same as personality itself."[55]

In a climactic moment, Henry insists that his fall at the carnival was a result of Belcredi's dirty work. Henry stabs Belcredi, who is carried away dying, insisting of Henry, "You're not mad! He's not mad! Not mad at all!"[56] Henry realizes, however, that to escape the consequences of his act he and his lackeys must continue his masquerade: "Yes. . .no choice now. . .(He calls them round him, as if for protection.) Here together. . .here together. . .and for always!"[57]

In *Henry IV*, Pirandello's characters are again inspired by the masks of commedia. Frida and the nephew are the *innamorati*, Belcredi is the jealous lover, and the doctor is a semi-comic quack, resembling commedia's Il Dottore. Henry himself is a commedic clown, an Arlecchino, impersonating a madman. In a sense, he improvises his way through his masquerade and through his life, but finally, and tragically, he is permanently trapped behind his mask of madness.

Each in His Own Way (1924) also depends on commedic elements, and is similar in many ways to *Six Characters in Search of an Author*. Based on an actual newspaper account of a young artist's suicide over his lover's betrayal, Pirandello mixed the reactions of his audience with the drama itself. In the first part of the play, Doro Palegari defends the dead artist's lover (Delia) blaming her new lover (Michele) for the tragedy. Francesco Savio, however, takes the opposing view, and they quarrel. The next day they meet and both attempt to apologize, but they fall into a quarrel again, having now taken each other's former opinion. Delia appears herself and, after learning of the two versions of the story, she is confused over which is correct. During a supposed intermission, and with Delia and Michele angrily watching, the "theatre lobby" is shown and the "audience" visible in it argue about the play, which they generally consider a joke on them.

At the beginning of the second act, preparations are proceeding for a duel between Doro and Francesco, but Michele, wishing to defend his own honor, follows Delia to Francesco's house. A violent confrontation between Delia and Michele, born of a passion that has turned to hatred, makes it clear that neither Francesco's nor Doro's version of the tragedy is true. During the final intermission, the "real life" Delia and Michele appear to attack the director and the actors of the play, proclaiming that the version of their lives shown is ridiculous. They re-enact the scene, to the anger of the "actors," and the play concludes as the theatre management apologizes to the "audience." In *Each in His Own Way*, Pirandello merges the illusiveness of reality with his self-contradicting commedic characters. As he himself wrote, "life, as I said, is unstable. What I have attempted to do is capture the instability of life and fix it in dramatic form."[58]

In 1925, Pirandello established his own theatre company in Rome, the Teatro D'Arte, subsidized by grants from Mussolini's government. The troupe toured widely in Europe and the Americas, and Pirandello himself performed on many occasions, often taking roles in his own plays. During this time, his plays had become popular with international audiences and were often produced abroad. Oddly, some early international directors of Pirandello's plays, particularly commedist Max Reinhardt,[59] tended to overlook their commedic aspects, making them more elaborate and soberly realistic than Pirandello had intended. When he directed, Pirandello used simple settings and strove for lightness and spontaneity in the acting. He staged many of his own works as well as plays by Italian and European dramatists he admired. Among the productions during the troupe's first season at Teatro D'Arte was Evreinov's commedia one-act, *The Merry Death*. Pirandello made experiments with commedia techniques, and especially encouraged his company to improvise in rehearsals. He typically rehearsed for several days, and then had his actors improvise around a specific theme, aiming for the spontaneity he believed must be at the heart of theatre.

With his own play, *To-night We Improvise* (1929), which he produced in 1930, Pirandello presents, as he did in *Six Characters in Search of an Author* and *Each in His Own Way*, an examination of how theatre is created, emphasizing the idea that theatre comes alive when it is tied directly to the imagination of the actor. The stage directions for the play confirm his conviction that critics and audiences were unwilling to accept a play that emphasizes improvisation. In *To-night We Improvise*, a director, Hinkfuss (a broad caricature of Reinhardt), urges his actors toward commedic improvisation of their roles from a simple scenario. In his stage directions, Pirandello indicates that

> *Much curiosity has been aroused by the advertisement, in the newspapers and on the playbills, of an unusual sort of improvised show. The dramatic critics of the town are the only ones who have not thought it worth their while to come, feeling it will be easy enough the next morning to say what a hodge-podge the thing was. (Good Lord, you know, one of those hoary old commedia dell'arte things; but where will you find, in these days, actors who are capable of improvising like those funny devils of the real commedia dell'arte, who, so far as that goes, were helped out not a little by their traditional mask and other trappings, as well as by their repertory?) To tell the truth, they are a little put out by the fact that the name of the writer who has provided stage manager and actors of the evening with their scenario does not appear on the playbills or anywhere else; accordingly, deprived of any hint that might conveniently enable them to fall back upon a ready-made opinion, they are in dread of contradicting themselves.*[60]

After a noisy fracas backstage that alarms members of the "audience," Hinkfuss comes forward to try to prepare them for the "unusual performance,"[61] and to confess that the author of the "scenario" to be performed is, in fact, Pirandello. This is greeted with some distress from planted actors in the audience, and Hinkfuss acknowledges that

> He's played the same trick twice, on a couple of colleagues of mine, sending one of them Six lost Characters in Search of an Author, which created a riot on the stage and upset everybody very much, while on

the other one he palmed off a trick comedy that caused the audience to rise up and stop the show; but it's different this time; there's no chance of his doing that to me.[62]

Following some further explanation of how the play-within-the play will be performed, Hinkfuss sets the scene in Sicily where four beautiful young women, Mommina, Totina, Dorina, and Nené, encouraged by their liberal mother, entertain several aviators. One conservative young man in the group, Verri, is attracted to Mommina, but resents her free-wheeling manner with the other men. He fights the other men off and proposes marriage to Mommina. When Hinkfuss attempts to interrupt the flow of the "improvised" story, he fails, and the play proceeds on its own without him. Mommina's father has been killed in a café brawl, and feeling she has no choice, she marries Verri.

In the last act of the "improvised" play, Mommina has had two daughters by Verri, but her life with him has been a living hell, due to his intense jealousy and brutality. Suffering from a weak heart and Verri's roughness, Mommina drifts away from sanity into memories of her parents and sisters, and her love of music. Images from her past float by her as she tells her daughters of the happiness she might have had if she had not married Verri. Singing her favorite aria, she dies, leaving Hinkfuss protesting the artificiality of the play and its author. The actors counter by proclaiming the artificiality of the director and the significance of the author. Despite the conflicts, Pirandello proves the necessity of theatre -- and its unique ability to capture the conflicting and shifting emotions of life as they seem to actually occur.

To-Night We Improvise, like *Six Characters in Search of an Author* and *Each in His Own Way*, resembles commedia in its character transformations, the sudden changes of direction in the action, the conflict between the play and the play-within-the-play, and what Pirandello described as the "*aggressive vitality* of the *commedia*."[63] He also makes it clear in his plays, as in commedia, that the emphasis is on the illusion of the actors' creativity, not on any realistic happening. A feeling of urgency and spontaneity is created by the playwright, as in commedia, despite the fact that the actors work from a complete and carefully constructed script with finished dialogue. It was necessary for an actor in a Pirandello play, as A. Richard Sogliuzzo writes, to "function skillfully within these various levels of reality while appearing to be confused as to the distinctions between fact and fiction, art and life, and his identity as character or actor."[64]

Between the founding of Teatro d'Arte and his death in 1936, Pirandello worked steadily as a playwright and director, and also wrote novels and contributed screenplays for some of his works. Although he supported Mussolini and the Fascist regime at first, he ultimately kept his distance, creating considerable controversy. His ambiguity can perhaps be understood in his statement that "I am unpolitical -- *apolitico*; I feel myself merely a man upon the earth."[65] He won the Nobel Prize for Literature in 1934, and his international fame peaked at that time. His plays were produced and published throughout Europe and America, where they continue to be produced and to influence theatre practice. In introducing a published collection of three of his most performed plays, *Six Characters in Search of an Author, Each in His Own Way*, and *To-night We Improvise*, he wrote that each

> presents characters, events, and passions peculiar to it and having nothing to do with those of the other two; but the three together, however different, form something of a trilogy of the theatre in the theatre, not only because there is action both on the stage and in the auditorium, in a box and in the corridors and in the foyer of a theatre, but also because the whole complex of theatrical elements, characters and actors, author and actor-manager or director, dramatic critics and spectators (external or involved) present every possible conflict.[66]

Imbued with a love of theatre, a theatre that supplied characters as symbols for ever-changing and contradictory human emotions, and with his despairing, ironic, and finally compassionate view of the human condition, Pirandello concluded that "All that remains to me is a great pity for humanity, forced to live out its allotted span upon this cruel earth."[67] Using the characters, techniques, and spirit of commedia, he brilliantly illuminated humanity's struggle on this "cruel earth."

Commedia in Italy After Pirandello

With the exception of Pirandello and a few extraordinary acting talents such as Eleonora Duse, Tommoso Salvini, Adelaide Ristori, and Ernesto Rossi, the state of theatre in Italy, despite considerable activity, was at a low ebb during the late nineteenth and early twentieth centuries. Old forms and old plays were tiresomely revived, production and acting standards were low, and there were few interesting playwrights. Some sprinkled commedia characters or plots into their plays. Giuseppe Adami's (b.1880) *Pierrot in Love* (1914), *Arlecchino* (1935), and his libretto for an operatic version of Gozzi's *Turandot*, as well as Enrico Cavacchioli's (1885-1954) *Pierrot, Lottery Clerk* (1925), borrowed commedic characters and situations to explore contemporary problems, but none of these achieved anything approaching the transcendent theatricalism of Pirandello.

Before Pirandello's emergence, the Futurist movement had supplied the first significant energy for a rejuvenation of the Italian stage. Few of the Futurists were specifically interested in commedia. That the movement's fantastic theatricalism was commedic can be seen in Filippo Tommaso Marinetti's (1876-1944) *King Glutton* (1905), which created controversy by using the human digestive system as a symbol for corruption. In the staging of his plays, Marinetti was said to hark "back to the platform stage of the French mystery plays, where Heaven occupied one end of the stage, Hell the other, and between them appeared half a dozen other places."[68] His incorporation of improvisational and spontaneous acting has reminded critics like Kenneth Macgowan of commedia.

Among those influenced by Futurism, director and critic Anton Giulio Bragaglia (1890-1960) wrote and directed commedic plays at his Teatro degli Indipendenti, including *Commedia dell'arte* (1943) and *Pulcinella* (1953), and edited a five-volume edition of Renaissance comedies. Although he has been largely neglected in English translation, he was, within Italy, one of the signal theatrical figures of the generation following Pirandello. He contributed to a growing understanding of the value of commedia traditions on the modern Italian stage as both a director and an essayist. Bragaglia advocated greater creativity in theatre production, assigning more significance to the individual responsibilities of the director, designer, and actor. The actor, in Bragaglia's theatre, would have to work as part of an ensemble, and learn to improvise (at least in rehearsals) as commedia actors had. This, he believed, would ultimately banish the "star" system which permitted one actor to dominate at all times. Changes were slow, however.

Of Pirandello's contemporaries, Luigi Chiarelli (1884-1947) was the most significant experimenter with commedia. Chiarelli was a major figure in the *teatro grottesco* movement, which featured exaggerated and grotesque perspectives in its imagery and humor. It was closely related to the capricious fantasy of commedia, although few playwrights of the movement consciously subscribed to commedic techniques. *Teatro grottesco* was truly a creation of critics, especially Silvio D'Amico, who interpreted it as "a theatre in which the characters were, in reality, marionettes and puppets animated by means of a complicated system of strings. They were not human beings capable of acting independently."[69]

As defined by D'Amico, *teatro grottesco* was best exemplified by Chiarelli's play *The Mask and the Face* (1916), a study of a man in contemporary society who, confronted with rampant hypocrisy, hides all true feeling under an expressionless mask. Late in his career, Chiarelli brought the tenets of *teatro grottesco* together with obvious commedic overtones in his 1939 play, *Pulcinella*. His other plays included melodramas, *The Lover's Death* (1921), and whimsical comedy, *The Magic Circle* (1937), but he is most effective at the ironic parody and fantasy of *The Mask and the Face*, and one later similar play, *Fireworks!* (1923). *The Silken Ladder* (1917), with its near allegorical presentation of character types, also establishes a link with commedic tradition in its tale of an unprincipled rascal's climb to success. Chiarelli's own acting company, *Ars Italica*, staged revivals of Goldoni along with his own plays. Although his achievements were ultimately overwhelmed by Pirandello's, Chiarelli's recognition of the significance of masks in modern theatre allies him with Russia's commedic playwrights, especially Evreinov.[70] No literary playwrights capable of challenging Pirandello's predominance appeared after World War I. Some theatre companies, especially since World War II, and a few individual actors, have brought sweeping changes and a renewed interest in recreated commedia in Italy during the last fifty years.[71]

The Piccolo Teatro di Milano, founded in May, 1947 as a *teatro stabile* (permanent theatre company), has been the troupe most responsible for reviving commedia. One of its founders is critic and director Paolo Grassi (b. 1919), who has written that the Piccolo Teatro was established to free the Italian theatre "from the commercial criteria which held it fatally in bond to the old *boulevard* type of repertoire, and should seek in the concept of *public service* -- in its highest meaning -- a new gauge of appreciation. This function of cultural, civil and moral education, which always has been that of dramatic art in its most splendid moments, would then give the theatre a new and far nobler *raison d'être*."[72] The Piccolo Teatro's first director would put Grassi's notions onto the stage with a particularly commedic spin.

The dominant creative force of the six-hundred seat Piccolo Teatro from its beginning was director Giorgio Strehler (b. 1921).[73] He has staged a wide range of dramas, the best of which demonstrate a keen intelligence and a brilliant sense of theatrical artifice and spectacle. He introduced and widely promoted the plays of Brecht in Italy, but the seminal production of the Piccolo Teatro was Strehler's revival of Goldoni's *The Servant of Two Masters*, first seen in 1947 and repeated many times thereafter. The role of Truffaldino (often called Arlecchino) was acted memorably by Marcello Moretti (1910-1961)[74] and masks made by Donato Sartori. Grassi recalled that this production, the most internationally acclaimed commedia revival of the post-war Italian stage, peeled away the traditional interpretation of the play as a "drawing-room comedy" and

> threw light on the social aspect of this work -- a satire of 18th century behaviour. A largely unknown Goldoni was revealed, even to the experts, rich in interesting complexes and far removed from the reputation for easy-going good nature and optimism which the traditional interpretation of the 19th and 20th centuries had pinned on him.[75]

This was accomplished, Grassi believed, because the Piccolo Teatro aimed to offer its audiences productions featuring the varied artistic and intellectual currents "which meet in our present culture. These different plays are presented as contemporary -- in the sense that history is always contemporary -- i.e., by showing their direct relation to our own problems."[76] Strehler and Grassi viewed commedia as "a phenomenon of theatrical decadence, a unique and marvelous phenomenon: a moment when the actor, having no good texts, had to take the entire responsibility of the theatre upon himself."[77] Despite their feeling that most efforts to revive commedia as a dramatic form tended to be artificial, they believed the commedia tradition was accountable for "certain good things about Italian actors -- their power of invention, their embroidery upon a dramatic theme."[78]

Strehler's rambunctious production of Goldoni's play embodied the spirit of anarchic commedia; it was received rapturously throughout Europe and America and applauded for its commedic vitality. Jan Kott remembered "the strong, almost physical joy I experienced watching that performance. It was a rare revelation of pure theatre, one that inspired the imagination."[79] Strehler significantly rethought the production in three different treatments. The first played down the action in favor of stylization, while the second, the one most widely seen and written about, was an historically accurate recreation of traditional commedia. The final version, which was seen on tour in Europe, offered a modern interpretation of *The Servant of Two Masters*, and of eighteenth century Italian acting traditions. Here, the modern director and cast "transmitted to a modern audience simultaneously the old dramatic text and the modern attitude to that text -- a combination of knowledge, affection, and admiration."[80] Critics noted with delight that the production had a vitality that most reconstructions of classic forms lacked. Kott claimed that this version too was faithful to commedia traditions, that it was as "refreshing as a cold shower. Theatre at last, true theatre at last, theatre we had dreamed of. . . .Harlequin's return is a triumph."[81] Strehler's basic understanding of theatre is in keeping with Kott's response. In his notes for a 1967 production of Pirandello's unfinished last play, *The Giants of the Mountain*, he writes of

> . . .the mystery of the theatre. A place where things do themselves, where everything is possible. The receptacle of all "instruments" of the theatre: actors, mimes, puppets, Dancing Jacks, dolls, make-up, illusions, sets, costumes, screens, machines, objects, battens, artifices, manners of acting, sound and visual solutions, which animate, give life, in its diverse possible "forms" (genera), to the performance, to the representation: prose theatre, interlude or variety show, cinema, mimes, musical hall.[82]

Significantly, Strehler does not limit his sense of theatre only to productions of overtly commedic works. When he directed *The Good Woman of Setzuan* at his Piccolo Teatro di Milano, he recognized the commedic possibilities of Brecht's epic actor, and he emphasized the fairytale qualities of the play "drawing heavily on the tradition of *commedia dell'arte*, insisting that his actors move as expressively as dancers, while at the same time augmenting the caricaturing tendency of popular farce (the policeman as *miles gloriosus*) with techniques drawn from slapstick and expressionist cinema."[83] While preparing *The Giants of the Mountain*, he wrote that the "Theatre-carnival" he attempted to create offered the "demystifying function of the *mascarade*"[84] in the invention of "a poetic projection of one's own self."[85] The carnival environment he created offered another escape from Realism in its freedom to show characters as larger-than-life fantastic creatures that were deeply human, but also much more.

During the 1977-78 Piccolo Teatro season, Strehler directed Shakespeare's *The Tempest*, which he had first staged in Florence in 1948. The later production was a spectacular theatrical fantasy similar to the style of Max Reinhardt's treatment of *A Midsummer Night's Dream*, employing commedia masks and lush music by Alessandro and Domenico Scarlatti.

Strehler's vision of *The Tempest* also brought Shakespeare's play "back to its Italian lineage: Prospero was to return to Milan for the second time."[86] This delicate production featured Guilia Lazzarini as an Ariel who was "half fallen angel, half *commedia dell'arte* Pierrot"[87] and Strehler also discovered commedic parallels in Trinculo (Pulcinella) and Stephano (the Capitano).[88] One of the production's most effective sequences was the encounter between Caliban and Trinculo. Once again, there were echoes of commedia "as the two *strange bed-fellows* huddle together, sheltering one another from the storm."[89] All of the characters in the play indulged in cruel commedic pranks aimed at Caliban, and this harsh rambunctiousness was set in counterpoint to the delicacy of the lovers and Ariel. As he had with *The Servant of Two Masters*, Strehler modified the production twice, altering the final version so that at the end the whole structure collapsed into a "spectacular nothingness and from this nothingness once again emerged the stage."[90]

In the year following *The Tempest*, Strehler directed *The Taming of the Shrew* at the Piccolo Teatro, in an elaborate Reinhardtian production emphasizing the Italianate qualities of the play, and the broad comedy and vulgarity typical of both Elizabethan and commedia comic actors. Through use of commedic acting techniques, he transformed *The Taming of the Shrew* from a vehicle for two stars into a riotous ensemble comedy. During the 1984 season, Strehler staged Lessing's *Minna von Barnhelm*. Even with this play, seemingly so far from commedia, he managed to create a theatrical environment more commedic than Saxon or Prussian. Thanks to Strehler's vision,

> Lessing's didactic comedy has grown wings of love and light humor, wings feathered by Goldoni, one of Strehler's most consistent sources of inspiration (*Arlecchino, The Servant of Two Masters, Il Campiello*). Even the caricatural French of the ridiculous gambler and fop, Riccault de la Marliniere, whose appearance on the stage provides one of the bravura pieces in the play, seems to have issued from the kind of fun-making levied by the *Comediens Italiens* at their French hosts when the latter invited them to settle in Paris.[91]

Under his direction, Andrea Jonasson as Minna, was "endowed with the fluttering grace of Marivaux maidens, these Parisian extensions of the Colombines of *commedia dell'arte*."[92] The success of Strehler's commedic techniques with the Piccolo Teatro have led to other experiments, and many imitators.[93]

In 1961, Strehler and Grassi set up The State School of Milan, a training studio for the Piccolo Teatro, under Grassi's direction.[94] Since its inception, the main focus of the training has been on the development of the actor in classes involving mime, dance, stage combat, and scene work. Despite changes over the years, the school has kept faith with an emphasis on the actor, and the development of such commedic techniques as mime and improvisation.

Other theatre schools, like the Bologna Theatre School founded in

1977 by Alessandra Galante Garrone, also place a strong emphasis on commedic performance techniques. Garrone, who trained with Lecoq, stresses that the school's mission is to look at the basics and traditions of the Italian theatre, including "(commedia dell'arte, farce, experimental theatre, dramatic theatre, cabaret, circus, dialect theatre in the grand tradition of Naples and Venice). This legacy of ours has to be reclaimed, examined in detail, and handed on, and we need to find the meeting point between our great roots and the theatre in our own time."[95] In her school, Garrone avoids traditional approaches to actor training and features a program which emphasizes particularly Italian theatrical traditions, especially commedia, in the development of the modern actor. In a statement strikingly similar to some of Edward Gordon Craig's pronouncements of a half century earlier, Garrone says:

> Our school in fact is a school based on improvisation, and tends therefore to be not so much a school for actors, but more of a school for creative performers. Improvisation is a discipline in which rules are assimilated through meticulous preparatory work. Good improvisation is the result of a delicate balance between the chosen "subject" and the performer's capacity for inventiveness, between study and spontaneity.[96]

The energy supplied by the *teatro stabili* and training schools revitalized Italian theatre during the 1970's and 1980's, while reminding audiences and actors alike how significant commedia performance techniques and traditions were to knowing theatre in Italy.[97]

Even more recently, director Carlo Boso and his Tag Teatro company, founded in 1975, have taken up the study and performance of commedia because "people want to go to the theatre to dream. So we have to invent magical characters. Nowadays, we need to use the same methods and techniques as in the original commedia dell'arte, but to change the subjects, to find situations that are more interesting for modern audiences."[98] To do this, Boso has resurrected the characters of commedia who "are not at all spiritual. They're earthy."[99] Boso uses them in their traditional guises set "in stories from today which you keep as up to date as possible,"[100] instead of creating new characters from today's society that have the same characteristics as commedia characters. For example, Boso notes, Jarry's *Ubu Roi* is "simply the story of a commedia Captain, just another Scaramouche. Or Brecht -- all his characters are social stereotypes."[101]

At a November, 1988 conference on commedia held at the Italian Institute of Culture in London, Boso stated that, in his opinion, his troupe has captured the spirit of commedia, but not its elusive technique. He stressed that it will probably take several generations to comprehend and master commedia technique, although the way to begin is "to go back to the tradition that exists in the theatre, which is the criticism of the society on a level of fairy tales, but with great seriousness, though at the same time joyfully."[102] Boso and his troupe have successfully produced a number of commedia plays based on traditional scenarios and early Italian plays, including *The Servant of Two Masters* (1979), *The False Magnifico* (1983), and *Scaramuccia* (1986). Their production of *The Madness of Isabella* (1988), based on a Scala scenario, followed the principles of traditional commedia performance. Boso limited his nine actors to the use of a few props and a small stage platform, and, as a result, "the vitality and physical discipline of the piece intensified."[103] One critic claimed that the "achievement of Carlo Boso is to prove that the legendary commedia dell'arte can work today."[104]

During the mid 1980's there was an explosion of interest among new Italian theatre companies in commedia. In Venice, in 1985, Claes Oldenburg, Coosje van Bruggen, and Frank O. Gehry staged a Venetian extravaganza, *Il Corso del Coltello* (*The Curse of the Knife*), which was inspired by many eighteenth century commedic elements. Many other groups have similarly borrowed commedia characters, plots, and performance traditions, as well as modern conceptions of commedia, since the 1980's.

Most Italian theatre artists have recognized that commedia is essentially an actor's art. Some individual actors have continued the tradition of improvisation during the nineteenth and early twentieth centuries, but only a few have succeeded in bringing the ancient craft alive. In actor and playwright Eduardo Ferravilla (1846-1916), "the old spirit of the commedia dell'arte seemed reborn,"[105] in his creation of Milanese character types in his own modest plays, within which he would improvise during performances. But the Italian actor who epitomized commedic acting in the first half of the twentieth century was Ettore Petrolini (1886-1935). He had begun his career in Roman cafés as a light comedian. After World War I, his style matured: he became more satiric and bitter, while retaining the rambunctious fun and improvisatory quality inherent in commedia. Petrolini became extremely popular when he appeared in his own sketches (*machietta*), and he later formed his own company. With his troupe, he performed his own works as well as plays of the contemporary and classical Italian stage, including the one-act plays of Pirandello. Regardless of the text at hand, he approached it as a scenario which he would embellish with his improvisations; in his own sketches he developed a character for himself based on commedia's Pulcinella. He was particularly adept at altering the relationship between the actor and his audience through the *slittamento*, a breaking of character to address the audience spontaneously.

In 1921, Petrolini began performing in his own adaptation of a commedia scenario entitled *The Farce of Pulcinella*, and the following year he adapted Molière's *The Doctor in Spite of Himself.* Although he took extreme liberties with Molière's text, his version was a great success, even when he performed it at the Comédie-Française, the bastion of Molière productions. When Edward Gordon Craig saw Petrolini perform during the Volta Theatre Congress in Rome in 1934, he felt that he was seeing "the most vital actor, the artist of richest vein, that Italy, if not all Europe, has today."[106]   Silvio

D'Amico, who described commedia as "the oldest, the most authentic; the eternal theatre of the actor, which is sufficient unto itself because the performance is the actor's,"[107] admired Petrolini because he discovered "beneath the grimaces of this comedian something profoundly different from the tactics of the ordinary funny-man. Rather a comic force which belongs, not to any one manner or tradition, but to all humanity."[108]

Petrolini, in the mode of the true commedia clown, seemed disinterested in critical analysis of his style or the influences on it, claiming that "I do not descend at all from the old *maschere* to which you compare me; I merely descend, each morning, from the front steps of my house."[109] He was an instinctive comic actor who also possessed the skills of a playwright, and the emotional depth of a tragedian. He was especially attuned to the importance of interplay with the audience: "I am both actor and spectator,"[110] he declared. Petrolini was in no sense a commedia antiquarian. He brought from the commedic form those elements which worked most usefully for a modern audience. He is clearly a forerunner of Eduardo De Filippo and Dario Fo, both of whom would further the study of the relationship between the individual arts of the playwright and the actor in the creation of a modern equivalent of commedia.

Eduardo De Filippo (1900-1984), an illegitimate son of actor Eduardo Scarpetta, worked for a time with his father's company, and in musical comedy before he joined the Molinari Company in 1929, with his brother Peppino and sister Titina.[111] He worked with the Molinari troupe for two years, appearing in many productions as well as writing variety sketches and short plays. With his brother and sister, he formed a company, *I De Filippo*, in Naples, that performed plays which he wrote in collaboration with his brother. The troupe toured Italy with great success and also made several films during the mid-1930's. *I De Filippo* performed together throughout World War II, but separated after the war.

De Filippo's more than fifty plays are mostly written in the Neapolitan dialect. They carry the infectious spirit of Pulcinella and a core of matter-of-fact earthiness, compounded of love and mockery, that characterizes the Neapolitan temperament, and which may have given rise to commedia originally. As he himself wrote, "The main influences on my work as an actor have been life, humanity, nature, the *commedia dell'arte* tradition."[112] His commedic plays, beginning with *Pulcinella, Dream Prince* (1932), a light-hearted revue, and continuing through his full-length plays, *The Son of Pulcinella* (1959) and *Saturday, Sunday, and Monday* (1959), are, as most of his works, overtly realistic. He rarely made use of symbols or obvious political or social issues, and, like Petrolini, rarely involved himself in the never-ending debate over theatrical theory. He wrote that although he admired "the major theorists of the modern theatre, I have always preferred to seek my inspiration from the natural source of art, life."[113] De Filippo was influenced, however, as most of his generation was, by the works of Pirandello, with whom he worked when he staged *Liolá* in 1935 and *Caps and Bells* in 1936. Pirandello and De Filippo also collaborated on *The New Suit* (1936), a comic scenario performed by De Filippo, with his brother and sister, as a traditional Neapolitan comedy.

Despite his work in dialect and his heavy use of stock characters, De Filippo was not interested in an antiquarian revival of commedia, but instead worked toward a living theatrical form which would illuminate contemporary Neapolitan life. Using commedia masks, he enlivened them by creating, as Eric Bentley wrote, "a fine blend of comedy and drama, the naive pathos, the almost noble seriousness of what might easily be ludicrous."[114] De Filippo was intensely proud of his commedic heritage; his poetry, collected in a volume called *Naples, the Country of Pulcinella* (1951), is imbued with its spirit. He was in tune with the deeply-rooted dramatic impulses of the Neapolitans and instinctively identified commedia as the obvious form for presenting them.

Describing the typical Neapolitan actor, De Filippo stressed that he "has a naturalness, spontaneity, rhythm, creativity; he knows how to improvise (an extremely difficult thing for an Italian actor); he has a traditional sack of scenic conventions, subterfuges, tricks, that add up to a useful inheritance if they are accompanied by sensitivity and education."[115] Marina Confalone, who acted with De Filippo during his later years, however, indicates that he rarely permitted improvisation and that he achieved his effects by "almost mathematically precise rules."[116] As his career moved into its final phase during the late 1950's, Italian actor and playwright Dario Fo was to take De Filippo's ideas much further.

In 1957, Fo (b. 1926) and his wife Franca Rame (b. 1929) founded the Compagnia Dario Fo-Franca Rame and produced a string of Fo's satirical comedies. Fame from cabaret performances and television sketches led to the formation of a spin-off troupe, *Nuova Scena* (1967), which had links to the Italian Communist party, and which gave birth to Fo's distinctive brand of political commedia. Fo has acted in films and television, directed in theatres throughout Europe and America, was nominated for the Nobel Prize, has been jailed as a subversive, has toured international theatres, and faced censorship, derision, and acclaim in a remarkable career as playwright, actor, and activist.

Fo and Rame are both adept improvisers. Rame had come from a theatrical family, *Teatro Famiglia Rame*, a touring troupe, and had a successful film career during the 1950's. From the mid-1960's, Fo and Rame became increasingly more committed to political theatre forged from the tradition of the strolling, improvising actor. In support of this goal, Fo's plays are written hurriedly and often depend on improvisation and revision in performance to keep the material topical. For Fo, the connection between politics and improvisation is total: "The choice of an improvisational form of theatre is already a political one -- because improvisational theatre is never finished, never a closed case, always open-ended."[117] His most representative works satirize governmental and industrial corruption and the resultant problems of survival for the middle and lower classes. Fo, Rame, and their fellow actors improvised in the tradition of commedia actors, drawing their ideas for characters and situations from the headlines and popular culture. The content of Fo's plays, and his interest in Marxism, have created considerable international controversy; his life has been threatened by those opposing his political views, Rame suffered a brutal kidnapping, and because of his links with the Communists, he has been an unwelcome visitor in several nations, including, until the mid-1980's, the United States.

Fo depends on satire to make his social and political statements, believing that "Nothing gets down as deeply into the mind and intelligence as satire. . .The end of satire is the first alarm bell signalling the end of real democracy."[118] Many of his plays are allegorical political satires calling for a non-violent revolution, and he has recently explained that his style proposes two possible directions:

> First, theatre as a retrieval of medieval peasant culture, linked to the important moments of our history, and tied up with class struggle, religious conflicts and so on. Second, theatre as counter-information about the events which occur in our social reality: exposing the violence of the system, police repression, and using the grotesque and satire in such a way that the comedian's distorting lens enables the public to experience a synthesizing, didactic vision, which means giving them alternatives or moments of critical reflection, etc.[119]

Typically taking the anarchic Clown role himself (Fo often refers to this character as "the maniac"), he has performed in most of his own plays, which include *Archangels Don't Play Pinball* (1959); *He Had Two Pistols With White and Black Eyes* (1960); *Seventh: Steal a Bit Less* (1964); *The Lady's Not for Discarding* (1967); *Grand Pantomime* (1968); *Mistero Buffo* (1969), a collection of original monologues taken from popular religious works of the

Middle Ages; *Accidental Death of an Anarchist* (1970); *Can't Pay? Won't Pay!* (1974); *Trumpets and Rasberries* (1981); *Elizabeth* (1984); *Hellequin, Arlekin, Arlecchino* (1985); and, *The Pope and Witch* (1991), among others. "Pirandello and I deal with the same themes [illusion and reality] but I'm an optimist,"[120] states Fo, despite the intensity of the satire and the cynical view of human nature apparent in his plays.

Among the many influences on his work, Fo acknowledges the plays of De Filippo, Strehler's commedic productions, and several Italian clowns, particularly Totò (1898-1967), the beloved Neapolitan clown. Fo admired his improvisatory skill and his recreation of past comic traditions, especially commedia. In the late 1950's, Fo and his actors performed his play (co-written with Franco Parenti and Giustino Durano) *The Finger in the Eye* (1953) at Strehler's Piccolo Teatro di Milano. The play "was based upon a story whose origins go back to the goliard tradition,"[121] and mixed elements of commedia, cabaret, and the influence of what Fo called Strehler's "truly revolutionary"[122] productions.

Fo's production, however, differed greatly from cabaret traditions, which, he felt, required "a very private and intimate form of speaking."[123] *The Finger in the Eye* "was something better than *cabaret*,"[124] because "everything was flung out: the action, the amount of physical expression inherent in our way of acting -- a pantomime learned not from the tradition of the white mime (Pierrot) but from commedia dell'arte."[125] The production was staged in a permanent setting that was similar to that of the Elizabethan theatre. The actors wore black leotards and only used the simplest of props and theatrical effects. Emphasis was placed on the ability of the actors to use themselves to create whatever visual situation was required. The production provided "a real shock"[126] to audiences "because of the amount of pantomime and the great precision of the improvisations. The performance was always changing, adjusting, modifying itself according to the reactions of the public."[127]   Fo, like Petrolini, emphasizes the significance of the audience, his involvement with it as an actor, and the audiences' engagement in the subject of the play:

> The comic fishes for laughs by virtually throwing out a comic line, or a hook, into the audience. He indicates where the audience's reaction has to be gathered in and also virtually where the hook is cast, because otherwise the tension built up between stage and audience would die down. Winding in the hook doesn't mean snuffing out the audience reaction, but correcting its flow with a flick of the rod. The comic's ability lies in knowing that if he carries on for a while on the same tack he'll snap the audience's capacity to keep up with his theme. So he breaks into the stage action, using something extraneous (a spectator's funny way of laughing, for example, or imitating the way La Malfa [Ugo La Malfa, former leader of the Italian Republican Party] speaks). . .All popular theatre requires the audience to be 'inside', and take part in the rhythm of laughter.[128]

As an actor, Fo is a sophisticated pantomimist, but completely disassociated from the white-faced mime.   Grotesque and vulgar, his performances have a directness and clarity that traditional mime avoided.   In 1988, at the Italian Institute of Culture in London where Carlo Boso spoke, Fo recreated one of his most emblematic pantomimes, based on a traditional commedia *lazzi*, from his play *Hellekin, Arlequin, Arlecchino.* His clown drinks a love potion that causes his penis to grow almost as large as the rest of him. He then goes through an hilarious array of subterfuges to hide the offending organ, including disguising it as a baby. When a group of village women come by and see him with the "baby," they coo over it and pet it, triggering a kaleidoscopic variety of reactions suggesting variations on both the clown's erotic joy and his fear of discovery. Here, as in most improvisatory situations, the actor is a playwright, or at least, an active commentator, on the situation being portrayed.

Fo's characters, like Bertolt Brecht's, are not acted, "but represented, and, since they are familiar, the actor can't talk about himself, but to others about particular situations which the character indicates."[129]   To accomplish this, the actor must act in the third person, as in Brecht's epic style, serving as "a *call boy* who represents the character to the audience, props it up or humiliates it, reports it or condemns it, hates it or loves it, as the case requires."[130]

Having mastered the skills of actor and mime, Fo set out to learn the necessary skills of playwriting. From the ancient comedies of Plautus, he discovered "how to dismantle and re-assemble the mechanisms of comedy, and to write directly for the stage without any literary intermediary. I also realised how many antiquated, useless things there were in many plays which belong to the theatre of words."[131] Through his study of pre-Renaissance Italian theatrical traditions, he rediscovered and was impressed by the history and techniques of medieval street entertainers (*giullare*) and their French (*jongleur*) and Spanish (*juglare*) equivalents. Fo has also drawn much from his interests in circus, puppetry, carnivals, music halls, *teatro grottesco*, Punch and Judy, and, most obviously, commedia. He does not accept commedia as a generic, unified form, but as a form in which there are distinctly variant styles. He acknowledges that there is "a *part* of the Commedia dell'Arte, which I have taken and used,"[132] but stresses that many original commedia troupes, such as the Gelosi, and others like them, were "generally conservative, and often downright reactionary in content,"[133] because of the patronage they accepted from the Italian nobility. He suggests that the great commedia troupes were "a bit like those football teams nowadays that are owned by big industrialists."[134] Fo's plays, again, like sporting events, are not static or permanently fixed; even his best known, most produced works have undergone continual revisions to keep them as fresh as today's headlines.

Fo is certain that the freelance commedia performer who had a significant and immediate influence on the life of the general populace in the Renaissance was worthy of emulation. They were "also professionals, who didn't frequent the courts and nobility, but worked in taverns, worked in town squares, worked in far lowlier circumstances."[135] To recreate commedia, he insists that "you have to decide which political line, which cultural direction you are going to take as the basis for your work."[136] His clearly articulated mission is to "advance certain democratic appeals, to form public opinion, to stimulate, to create moments of dialectical conflict."[137] The approach is that of an "epic" actor, who sees art as political empowerment, and his work can only be understood as it represents a creative reaction to the most topical social, political, and moral issues.

Accidental Death of an Anarchist, Fo's best known farce, examines the events surrounding the actual 1969 bombing of the Agricultural Bank in Milan. Following the incident, an anarchist named Giovanni Pinelli is arrested. Shortly thereafter, when Pinelli dies in a fall from a window in police headquarters, the police and local officials claim that the anarchist committed suicide. It is at this point that Fo begins his play. He exposes the lies and cover-ups perpetrated by the police who, as it turns out, pushed the anarchist from the window. As he describes it, the plot involves a "maniac who gets inside a police station and puts the police on trial, reversing the usual process."[138] In Accidental Death of an Anarchist, as in many of his plays, Fo uses commedia elements and farce in order to tell tragic events, and although the audience is aware that it is watching a farce, they never forget the fact that "what we are describing is true, is a reality. The element of farce heightens the tragic element of what they are portraying. In fact, the key to the tragedy is that which enables the comic to take on a satyrical dimension."[139]

Another of his internationally known plays, Can't Pay? Won't Pay! (1975), borrows the tradition in old Neapolitan and Venetian farces that "the starting point, the fundamental impetus, is hunger."[140] The play is set in a middle-class apartment where a housewife, Antonia, suffering from a variety of economic problems, has returned after her involvement in a looting incident at a neighborhood market. Eventually it becomes clear to Antonia, and to the audience, that her attempt to solve her problem has turned into "a need to work collectively, to get organised and fight together -- not just for survival, but to live in a world where there are less brightly-lit shop windows, less motorways, and no government corruption, no thieves -- the real thieves, the big fish, that is -- and where there is justice, justice for all."[141]

Among Fo's most recent plays, *Hellekin, Arlekin, Arlecchino* (1985), brings him full circle and back to his commedia origins. Combining aspects of the *giullare*, Brechtian alienation techniques, and the traditions of commedia, he includes an introductory prologue outlining the significance of commedia, and underscoring its basis in social satire and political activism. As with his earlier works, *Hellequin, Arlekin, Arlecchino* provides him with a platform for his savage satire of prominent figures and issues in contemporary politics.

Since the early 1970's, Fo's plays have been performed throughout Europe and America, and he continues to write and perform in Italy. His use of commedia techniques and traditions to create an immediate and startling form of political theatre has stirred controversy because he demands that it be forcefully political. As Fo clearly understands, "There is a community dimension in performing theatre, and the characters are a pretext to make the people *speak*,"[142] adding that "It goes without saying that all theatre, and all art, is political."[143]

Commedia belonged first and foremost to the Italians, and its spirit is alive today in its land of origin. Numerous theatre companies and individual artists[144] are exploring its characters, *scenarii*, and performance techniques as they apply to the difficult social and political times in Italy. Commedia also remains Italy's most potent calling card on the international stage. In the hands of Pirandello, commedia became a medium for exploring contemporary life through ancient forms. More recently, in the work of gifted theatre artists such as Strehler, Boso, and Fo, commedia has been a significant element in the reconstruction of performance techniques. Commedia was a natural and necessary means of expression for the Italians, as Fo has articulated:

> We Italians "enjoyed" the industrial revolution after a long time-lag. So we are not yet a sufficiently modern nation to have forgotten the ancient feeling for satire. That is why we can still laugh, with a degree of cynicism, at the macabre dance which power and the civilisation that goes with it performs daily, without waiting for carnival.[145]

CHAPTER TWO

The Bonds of Interest: Commedia in Spain

The theatre is one of the most expressive and useful vehicles for the edification of a country's people, and a barometer that marks the country's greatness or decline. . . .The theatre is a school of tears and laughter and an open tribunal where people can place outmoded or erroneous mores on trial and explain through living examples the eternal standards of the human heart and feelings.[1]

-- Federico Garcia Lorca

Zan Ganassa's troupe visited Spain in 1574,[2] and commedia proved to be an essential force in the development of native theatre and the popular *capa y espada* (cape and sword) comedies of the sixteenth century. Ganassa's visit also inspired the formation of several Italo-Spanish troupes beginning in the 1570's. Although Spanish dramatists and actors did not create many counterparts of the traditional commedia characters, the visits of the Italians gave direction to and set a standard for the emerging Spanish theatre. One Italian commedia actor, Bottarga, was so popular that his name gave the Spanish language its word for clown (botarga). It was, however, Lope de Rueda (1510?-1565), the first important actor-manager and playwright of the Spanish theatre, who had arranged Ganassa's visit. Rueda himself played comic fools in the manner of commedia, and his plays, some of which were commedia-inspired, later influenced other Spanish dramatists of the era as well as William Shakespeare.

Novelist, poet, and sometime playwright Miquel de Cervantes (1547-1616) admired Rueda[3], and although he himself struggled for success in the theatre, Cervantes' plays never achieved the popularity of his other writings. In his plays, the lovers, comic servants, and cuckolds are clearly inspired by commedia types. Commedic elements also have a prominent place in his novel, *Don Quixote* (1605), particularly in the characters of Quixote and his comic foil, Sancho Panza. Cervantes was undoubtedly influenced by Ganassa, whose name in Spanish is *quijada*, one of the several names given to Quixote in the novel. A commedia character, Zan Panza, also appeared in Spain during Cervantes' time, and was probably the model for Quixote's comic squire. At approximately the same time, Spanish ecclesiastic Tirso de Molina (Fray Gabriel Tellez; 1571?-1648) introduced the Don Juan legend in his play *The Deceiver of Seville and The Stone Guest* (c.1630), although this legend may have appeared earlier in an undated commedia scenario, *The Stone Guest*. Don Juan became a powerful image for commedic playwrights and directors, including Molière. The ambiguous personality of Don Juan, who is usually seen as a mixture of appealing and repellent characteristics, is evident in most interpretations. Don Juan's often courageous resistance and indifference to both earthly and heavenly values appealed to commedic playwrights and directors in most eras.

Of the nearly two hundred plays and *auto sacramentales* written by Calderón (Pedro Calderón de la Barca; 1600-1681), *The Great Theatre of the World* (c.1633) owes the most to commedia. In this play, God is depicted as an *Autor*, who assigns life's roles to humans and rewards or punishes them according to their success in those roles. As the characters of the play "improvise" their way through life, the significance of commedic traditions on this play's theme becomes clear.

In the eighteenth century, poet and playwright Leandro Fernández de Moratín (1760-1828) combined traditional Spanish characters and situations with the commedic plays of Goldoni, and techniques he had learned from the French stage. He greatly admired Molière's comedies, and freely translated *The School for Husbands* and *The Imaginary Invalid*, suggesting performances which emphasized commedic moments. Commedic elements were ingrained in Spanish culture by the late eighteenth century, but the nineteenth century was a period of theatrical decline in Spain.

The more than sixty plays of José Echegaray (1832-1916), winner of the 1904 Nobel Prize for Literature, are commedic in his recurrent use of a play-within-a-play formula, as well as in the illusion he creates of some characters' independence from their author. His are among the few Spanish plays that continued commedic traditions on the late nineteenth century stage. At the beginning of the twentieth century, one of the most significant artists among commedia modernists, Pablo Picasso, was Spanish, and commedic elements appeared in puppet plays, folk entertainments, and musical genres. Composer Manuel de Falla (1876-1946) made a profound commedic connection with Don Quixote in his marionette-opera *Master Peter's Puppet Show* (1916), an elaboration on an incident from Cervantes' novel.

Despite a considerable volume of theatrical activity, few interesting dramas or theatrical innovations appeared to regenerate the Spanish stage, until some young writers at the turn of the century, who became known as the "generation of '98," brought Spanish drama into the modern era. Members of this group were bound together by their belief that the human mind is fundamentally unable to make sense of existence, but, despite this fact, it was necessary for individuals to strive for a spiritual and intellectual re-birth, if the world itself was to have hope of one. This, along with a heritage of commedic influences from the Golden Age of Spanish theatre, led many of the "generation of '98" to create their own versions of modern commedia.[4] Commedic writers in Spain were also influenced by French commedists and the Symbolist movement.

The most active and successful Spanish dramatist of the first two decades of the twentieth century, and the one most inspired by commedia, was Jacinto Benavente (1866-1954). As the predominant playwright to emerge from the "generation of '98," he wrote over one hundred and seventy-five plays and adaptations, and served as director of the Teatro Español beginning in 1920. Winner of the Nobel Prize for Literature in 1922, Benavente wrote plays that demonstrate a startling range. Fantasy, fairy tales, and the theatrical life are some of the sources for his works, which feature stories centering around love, family, and marriage. Some plays are tragedies, some are comedies, some are social drama, and some are social satires. He even wrote a good many plays for children. In his youth, Benavente had been interested in circus and puppets (he owned his own puppet stage), and it is thought that he worked in a circus for a time. His plays *Brute Force* (1908) and *The Cubs* (1918), as well as the unfinished *¡Clown!* (1945), all equate circus with life. He especially loved the clowns of the circus, whom he did not view as frivolous creatures. He was aware, as many modern commedists were, of their inherent sadness and ironic perspective.

Benavente's works on society's conventions and mores often were presented in a highly theatrical manner. *The Téllez Woman's Husband* (1897), *Rags of the Royal Purple* (1930), *The Demon of the Theatre* (1942), *Don Magin the Magician* (1944), and *Life in Verse* (1951), are Pirandellian in their use of the theatre itself as a source for characters, themes, and situations. As many modern commedic plays, his works examine the role of theatre in a world moving toward the apocalyptic changes brought on by World War I. Benavente also translated and adapted plays by Molière, such as *Don Juan* (1897), and Shakespeare, including *Love Story* (taken from *Twelfth Night*; 1899) and *The Favorites* (taken from *Much Ado About Nothing*; 1903). His last play, *The Buffoon of Hamlet*, unproduced until after his death, combined his interests in Shakespeare and circus.

Throughout his long career, Benavente filled his plays with commedic characters and situations. *Spring Story* (1892), published in his earliest collection, *Fantasy Plays*, includes a prologue that offers insight into his interest in commedia. He writes that although he is not part of the "glorious stock" that produced Lope de Rueda, Shakespeare, and Molière, his play "is a puppet farce, with an absurd plot, and is completely unrealistic."[5] Here commedic fantasy is a childlike dream, a revelation of his wish to move the theatre beyond intellectual and didactic purposes. He attempted to release the audience's imagination so that it could completely enter the world of the play. His early commedic plays are extremely sentimental and emphasize theatricality over reality; for example, his character Arlequín in *Spring Story* informs the audience that he will make fun of everything. Benavente attempts to dilute the extreme sentimentality of the plays with irony, as Russian commedists did, but he is seldom as effective in achieving a balance between emotional excess and sharp-edged undercutting.

Spring Story places characters from commedia into a court setting, anticipating many modern German and Russian commedic plays. A later, expanded edition of *Fantasy Plays* included four other commedic works: *The Whiteness of Pierrot* (written prior to 1892), *Italian Comedy* (written prior to 1892), *The Magic of an Hour* (1892), and *The Path of Love* (written prior to 1892). Benavente's finest play, *The Bonds of Interest* (1907), is also his most commedic. Its great vitality is created in part by the vivid characters based on commedia masks. Elements of early Spanish theatre also give *The Bonds of Interest* a commedic atmosphere.

The Bonds of Interest illustrates how love is often united with material interests. It was thereby a modest forerunner of the Italian *teatro grottesco* movement in its combination of "satire and humour with a higher idealistic philosophy."[6] The play's theme, which is perhaps the most representative of all of Benavente's works, suggests that the bonds of mutual interest between human beings govern their actions more than any of society's laws or sacred tenets. The skeptical and lightly satiric viewpoint is apparent from the outset. *The Bonds of Interest* includes a prologue indicating that the characters are the grotesque masks of commedia, but less frivolous than their original counterparts; the characters, after all, have had several centuries to think. They remain, however, "puppets and marionettes of cardboard and cloth, with strings which are visible even in little light and to the most near-sighted."[7]

The play begins with the arrival of the handsome charmer Leander and his clever servant Crispín in an Italian city. Crispín overcomes Leander's resistance to a scheme to convince the entire community that Leander is a wealthy aristocrat in disguise. They successfully convince the gullible local citizenry and obtain a virtually unlimited amount of credit. Leander encounters and falls in love with the beautiful Sylvia, daughter of a wealthy merchant, Polichinelle. Leander confesses the truth of his poverty to Sylvia, but Crispín has already convinced Polichinelle to oppose a marriage between Leander and Sylvia. Regretting his actions, and desiring to help the lovers, Crispín spreads the rumor that Polichinelle has plotted to have Leander murdered. As creditors become suspicious, Crispín convinces them that their only hope of payment is to assist him in convincing Polichinelle to permit a marriage between Leander and Sylvia. When Polichinelle and the law confront Crispín with his deceptions, he easily persuades the assembled crowd that the lovers truly belong together. Sylvia, addressing the audience, expresses the meaning of the play's title and its theme:

> In our play, as in life's comedy, you have seen puppets like human beings moved by thick strings that are their interests, their passions, their deceits, and all the miseries of their condition; some are pulled by their feet and driven to sad wandering; others pulled by their hands, work by the sweat of their brow, fight fiercely, hoard skilfully, commit dread murders. But amongst all of them, at times there descends from heaven a fine thread, woven as it were of sun and moonlight, the thread of love which makes yon puppets that are human in appearance seem divine; and it lights up our brow with the splendour of dawn;

adds wings to our heart, and tells us that not all is make believe, for there is in our life something divine, an eternal truth, which cannot end when the play ends.[8]

The Bonds of Interest has remained popular and it has often been produced outside of Spain. Its popularity inspired a 1916 sequel, *The Joyous and Confident City*, which premiered on May 18, 1916, at the Teatro de Lara Madrid. This play presents a somewhat bleaker perspective than *The Bonds of Interest*, using the same characters (Leander has become a philanderer) suffering defeat and death, but ultimately achieving spiritual regeneration. Benavente attempts to express "the aspirations of the Spanish people during the World War,"[9] but his heavy-handed politicizing makes the characters seem unnecessarily wooden, and, therefore the play lacks the deft satiric quality of *The Bonds of Interest* and the commedic impulses are less evident. Reacting to Spain's involvement in World War I, Benavente's city (Spain) is being sold out by its leaders, without the knowledge or consent of the common people. Clearly, Benavente's outlook changed during World War I; he felt humanity was disillusioned and confused, and his commedic characters lost their tone of fantasy and became symbols of society's decay. Although *The Joyous and Confident City* was not well-received critically, it was very popular with audiences.

Among Benavente's many imitators, Gregorio Martínez Sierra (1881-1948), who worked in collaboration with his wife, María de la O Lejárraga, wrote a play called *Love's Magic* (1908), which is overtly commedic. Azorín (José Martínez Ruiz; 1873-1967), another leading writer of the "generation of '98" movement, was also interested in commedia. In *Racine and Molière* (1924), *Old Spain* (1926), in which his character Mr. Brown is a typical commedia clown, and *Comedia del arte* (1927), a play about actors, Azorín incorporated commedic elements. As early as 1923, he had written an essay entitled "Comedia del arte" in which he states that "the *comedia atelana* of ancient Rome is the precursor of the *commedia dell'arte*. His own theoretical examples take the *commedia dell'arte* a step further than Pirandello did by actually mixing fantasy with life completely removed from the theater to make the differentiation between the play and life psychologically impossible."[10] None of his plays were particularly successful, and his impact on the development of Spanish drama was minimal. Other modern Spanish playwrights of this period influenced by commedia include Darío Lugones and Manuel Machado (1874-1947).

Ramón María del Valle-Inclán (1866-1936), another "generation of '98" writer, demonstrated a more sophisticated understanding of commedia than Benavente. Anticipating Fo, Valle-Inclán believed that commedia thrived among the lower classes who used it as a mouthpiece for their

> socio-religio-economic jeers and aspirations. The simplicity and spontaneity of format, the universality of characters, the variety and vigor of the *lazzi* (tricks), the presence of women on the stage, the lewdness of word and action, the contemporaneity of comments, and the underpinnings of ancient paganism were some of the reasons for its success.[11]

Valle-Inclán's best plays offer commedic elements combined with characters inspired, in part, by Cervantes. Many of his plays were farces and grotesque tragi-comedies (*comedias bárbaras*) that he eventually labelled *esperpento* (the technique of systematic distortion or defamation of traditional values), a literary style looking ironically at the world from a superior angle, and taking the view that the characters of the plot are inferior to the author.[12] He intended *esperpento* to be the dramatic equivalent of the effect created by a concave fun-house mirror, transforming reality into a distorted, absurd image. This, he believed, enhanced the play's underlying tragedy. In similar fashion, he also attempted to satirize contemporary society. Commedia seems to interest him as a result of his love of theatricality, especially in the creation of his characters. His Arlequín, for example, is a mixture of traits taken from traditional commedia, nineteenth century French Pierrot plays, and Spanish Golden Age drama. At the same time, he satirizes aspects of early Spanish drama, particularly the traditional values of honor and virtue. He manages through the use of irony, the grotesque, and ambiguity to debunk the romantic and sentimental qualities that typically diminish the effectiveness of Benavente's plays. Valle Inclán's emphasis on theatricality, as represented by commedia, makes it impossible for the audience to view his works as realistic. Whereas Benavente projects his views through his commedia characters in his highly theatrical works, Valle-Inclán maintains a detachment, at times cynical or bemused, that, despite the non-realistic elements, keeps his audiences from too much empathy towards his characters, or the plays from falling too far toward Benaventian sentimentality.

Valle-Inclán had briefly been an actor (appearing in Benavente's 1899 play, *The Wild Beast's Banquet*), but he lost an arm as a result of a barroom brawl. This infirmity, combined with the moderate success of his first play, led him to concentrate on his writing. His play, *The Dragon's Head* (1909), was a light-hearted satire with commedic touches lampooning the Symbolist movement as epitomized by the plays of Maeterlinck, Yeats, and others. Partly influenced by the poems of Rubén Darío and Benavente's plays, especially the strikingly similar *Spring Story*, Valle-Inclán's *The Marchioness Rosalinda*, produced March 5, 1912, at the Teatro de la Princisa by the Guerrero-Mendoza company, owes much to commedia. It is a farce in which Arlequín brings a troupe of actors to court to seek the patronage of the Marquis d'Olbray. Anticipating Pirandello's play-within-a-play structure, *The Marchioness Rosalinda* "ranges from refined lyricism to broad slapstick."[13]

The Marchioness Rosalinda begins with the arrival of Arlequín and his troupe at the court of Aranjuez. They hope that the Marquis d'Olbray will become their patron. That evening, as part of their performance, the troupe draws those at court into the commedia play being performed. Arlequín then completes the triangle in two love affairs, one between the marquis and his wife, Rosalinda, and the other between Pierrot and Columbine. The marquis, angered by Rosalinda's relationship with Arlequín, sends her to a convent. He then has Arlequín threatened by thugs; at the same time, Pierrot attempts to entice Arlequín into a duel. Arlequín is also caught up in the machinations of Columbine, who exposes him to the marquis's henchmen, but later Columbine has a change of heart and helps Arlequín escape imprisonment by the marquis. Despite Rosalinda's declaration of love for him, a disillusioned Arlequín slips away with his troupe to continue wandering the world.

This play is filled with visual and verbal contrasts, and requires actors who are equally adept verbally and physically. Although he uses several commedia characters, Valle-Inclán significantly transforms many of them. Pierrot, for example, has few of his traditional traits; he "is neither melancholic, nor vicious, nor a fool," [but] "has become cunning."[14] Pierrot, Arlequín, and Columbine are identified by their familiar names and costumes, but other commedia types appear in different guises: the marquis is Pantalone, and Dottore can be found in the person of El Abate. Valle-Inclán seeks to mix commedia masks with modern character types to "give continuity to his characters both artistically and historically."[15]

Other Spanish dramatists similarly transformed commedia traditions. Federico García Lorca (1898-1936), probably the most internationally produced Spanish playwright of the twentieth century, is best remembered for his folk tragedies, including *Yerma* (1934), *Blood Wedding* (1933), and *The House of Bernarda Alba* (1936). Earlier in his career, however, he wrote brief comic scenes (including *Buster Keaton's Promenade*), many of which were published in a collection in 1928. As a child, Lorca had been interested in puppets and had performed puppet plays for his family and friends. Later, he wrote two puppet plays, *The Tragicomedy of Don Cristóbal and Doña Rosita*

(1928) and *The Puppet Play of Don Cristóbal* (1931). His most frequently produced and best comedy, influenced by the traditions of Spanish farce (from Cervantes to Juan del Encina) and by *Cristobitas* (Spanish Punch and Judy shows) and other Spanish manifestations of commedia, was *The Shoemaker's Prodigious Wife* (1926). It was first produced in 1930, and later revised and produced again in 1933. He wrote it in reaction to European avant-garde artistic movements, intending its simplicity and directness as an antidote for abstract art. In it, he attempts to "weave an invisible thread of poetry, but where the comic gesture and the humour would stand out clear and undisguised at the surface."[16]

The Shoemaker's Prodigious Wife assimilates many folk and theatrical traditions in telling the commedic story of an unhappy young wife married to an old man. It begins with the appearance of The Author himself, a convention typical of many modern commedic plays. In the play, Lorca incorporates many surprises and startling tricks (water spewing from a hat, etc.) to emphasize that theatre is an illusion. Describing the character of the wife, he wrote that she is "at once a type and an archetype,"[17] a Columbine, who is both real and a creature of the stage. Other characters in the play are similarly patterned, creating an interesting duality between reality and the magic world of the stage.

In production, Lorca applied many of the theories of modern theatrical practice, particularly drawing from the theories of Edward Gordon Craig and from the plays of Maurice Maeterlinck, when he stressed that all of "the arts should combine in the art of drama."[18] He maintained an allegiance to the puppet theatre and commedia even in his mature, poetic dramas. *Blood Wedding*, for example, includes such stereotypical commedic devices as a love triangle, runaway lovers, and angry parents. He combined these elements with what Pamela Robertson calls "a most powerful and tragic theme interspersed here and there with light but significant touches in the form of the Servant Woman's broad humour and the peasant girls' singing and dancing, the introduction of which is very much in the tradition."[19] Lorca[20] and several other significant artists lost their lives in the cataclysm of the Spanish Civil War (1936-1939).

After the Civil War, Victor Ruiz Iriarte's (b. 1912) sad comedies were influenced by the plays of Pirandello and Benavente. Iriarte's *The Grand Minuet* (1950), a "farce-ballet," clearly inspired by Benavente's *The Bonds of Interest*, begins with a prologue in which the character Diana invites the audience to join in a game in which actors in makeup, music, and words will harmonize. The theatricality of the play serves as an obvious metaphor, especially when the character Crispín declares that "life is a party where music serves to cover up words and words to hide our thoughts."[21]

During the late 1960's, despite the repressions of Franco's regime, several independent groups formed in attempts to break away from the formal, and heavily censored, written drama. Tábano and El Búho, Los Goliardos, Els Joglars, and Els Comedians presented controversial satiric and anti-establishment performances expressed through such commedic elements as the grotesque, pantomime, masks, and music. Since the death of Franco in 1975, many restrictions on Spanish theatre have been relaxed, and along with 1960's avant-garde theatre groups, commedia has played a part in the explosion of cabaret entertainments on Spanish stages during the 1970's and 1980's.

CHAPTER THREE

"Here We Are Again!": Commedia in England

Arlecchino is immortal and Columbina can never die. Their spangled jackets and waving skirts are a mere mortal livery, for they are ideas, not material beings; they are mirrors which reflect the life around them and the sunlight above them and the laughter and movement and folly and wisdom and love and gaiety and tears of life as well in the twentieth century as the sixteenth, but which render no dull photographic reproduction of actuality, but a vision of life all silvered over with laughter and coloured with romance.[1]

-- Edward Gordon Craig

Commedia troupes appeared in England frequently from the middle of the sixteenth century, and were regularly seen by the 1570's. Zanni, Pantalone, and Arlecchino became models for British variations called Zany, Pantaloon, and Harlakeen; the Capitano inspired the bravos and Dottore was the forerunner of the pedants popular in English drama of the period.

Although the true impact of commedia on its contemporary William Shakespeare (1564-1616) is difficult to ascertain and verify, it is not surprising that many connections with commedia can be found in his plays. The plot of *The Tempest* (1611) is similar to several earlier commedia scenarios, but is most like Scala's *The Enchanted Wood*, which describes the comic misfortunes of several shipwrecked characters in a magician's forest. Viola's masquerade and the occasional buffoonery in *Twelfth Night* (1599-1600), the pastoral

setting of *As You Like It* (1599-1600), the combined fantasy and clowning in
A Midsummer Night's Dream (1600), the trickery of Autolycus in *The Winter's
Tale* (1610-1611), and the vulgar slapstick of *The Merry Wives of Windsor*
(1599-1600) and *The Comedy of Errors* (1591-1592), are but a few examples
of commedic elements in Shakespeare's plays.[2] Shakespeare made use of
many typical elements found in commedia scenarios, with mistaken identities
and brother-sister twins appearing in several of his comedies; however, it must
be noted that such conventions undoubtedly were known to him through his
familiarity with ancient comedies and early English farces as well. There is
no mistaking the awareness of commedia in his plays, however, and those of
his contemporaries, revealed through occasional references to commedia
characters.[3]

Among other Elizabethan and Jacobean dramatists, commedic images
or characters appear in most of the plays of Ben Jonson (1572-1637),
including *Volpone* (1606) and *The Alchemist* (1610). In the twentieth century,
Jonson's *Volpone* was directed or adapted by modern artists in several cultures
in commedic style. Jonson's comedies feature broadly stereotypical
characters, and although they depend on verbal wit more than slapstick, they
are strongly reminiscent of commedia. *An Humorous Day's Mirth* (1597) by
George Chapman (c.1560-1634), *The Widow* (c.1616) by Thomas Middleton
(c.1580-1627), and *What You Will* (1601) by John Marston (1576-1634), also
contain references to commedia, but the sole English play of the Renaissance
which is unmistakably based on a commedia scenario is Sir Ashton Cockain's
Trappolin, Creduto Principe.

After the Restoration, Italian commedia troupes continued to appear
and Molière's plays achieved some popularity on the English stage,[4] bringing
the French brand of commedia to the British. More significantly, "Punch"
made his first documented appearance in Samuel Pepys' diary on May 6, 1662,
and he quickly became an all-purpose buffoon in virtually every puppet play

of that time. With his hump-back and hooked nose, Punch bore great similarity to commedia's grotesque clown, Pulcinella. During the eighteenth century he adopted his now familiar high-pitched voice and became a popular staple of English country fairs. Punch's wife, Judy (originally called Joan), was added shortly thereafter, and Punch and Judy have remained familiar figures since that time.[5]

Combining aspects of commedia with contemporary satire and classical mythology, pantomime became one of the most popular forms of entertainment in England by the 1720's. Although John Rich (1692-1761) is most often credited with creating the pattern for English pantomime with *Harlequin Executed* (1716) and *Amadis, or the Loves of Harlequin and Columbine* (1718), Aphra Behn (1640-1689) had anticipated him with her 1687 play, *The Emperor of the Moon*, a farce based on a commedia scenario (in 1677, she had included Harlequin and Scaramouche in *The Rover*).[6] Behn was the first English dramatist to assimilate commedia fully into her drama, but it was Rich who popularized pantomime, and shaped it into its traditional form by combining serious episodes of classical mythology with music and commedia characters in mute comic scenes.[7]

The harlequinade, which evolved from the fusion of Parisian fairground dumbshows and the convention that Harlequin could be transformed into someone else by a magic wand, was also an important element in the development of English pantomime. When Joseph Grimaldi (1778-1837) made his purely English "Joey the Clown" the dominant character of the harlequinade, Harlequin and Columbine became peripheral figures who died out completely by the twentieth century. Until then, however, most pantomimes and harlequinades centrally featured Pantaloon, Columbine, and Harlequin.[8]

Another significant step in the creation of modern commedia was the appearance and popularity of music halls. The survival in England of broad humor in the theatre and the relationship between a single performer, playing a stereotypical character, and the audience, was mostly due to music halls. Comedians such as Albert Chevalier (1861-1923), Dan Leno (1860-1904), and "Little Tich" (Harry Relph; 1868-1928), created contemporary equivalents of commedia masks in their vivid characterizations of stock types found in the society of their day. Chevalier's Cockney costermonger ("The Coster's Serenade") and Leno's officious Shop-walker and bewildered Beefeater became instantly and delightfully recognizable stereotypes to their audiences. Most music hall performers also appeared often in pantomime and harlequinades, especially during the Christmas season. Although harlequinades had diminished in popularity after Grimaldi's day, pantomimes rarely failed to include a "transformation" scene in which the raising of a series of gauzy curtains brought forth the magical appearance of Clown, Pantaloon, Columbine, and Harlequin, with the Clown shouting the traditional greeting, "Here we are again!" The broad stereotyping in these forms permitted male comedians to play outrageous female characters in the pantomimes. Grimaldi had appeared as the Baroness in *Harlequin and Cinderella; or, The Little Glass Slipper* (1820), and Leno was still playing that role and similar ones at the beginning of the twentieth century. When Leno died at age forty-three, *The Times* wrote that to "find anything like a close parallel to his style we should probably have to go back to the Italian *commedia dell'arte.*"[9]

By the end of the nineteenth century in England then, commedia traditions and characters survived solely on variety stages, and were generally regarded as relatively unimportant forms of entertainment. The variety stages, however, as commedia, served to offer the common people an outrageously immediate and entertaining theatre, while the formal legitimate stage exemplified a dignity and restraint typical of "official" culture.

Edward Gordon Craig

The first English theatrical artist to view commedia as a revitalizing force for the modern stage was Edward Gordon Craig (1872-1966). As the illegitimate son of architect and theatrical designer Edward William Godwin, and the legendary English actress Ellen Terry, Craig began acting as a child under the direction of Terry's co-star, Henry Irving, manager of London's Lyceum Theatre. In his mid-twenties, however, Craig gave up acting, anxious to develop a new art of the theatre. As a director, scene designer, and theorist, he began to advance his ambitious ideas in a series of periodicals and books.[10] He introduced a notion central to his aesthetic -- that of a master artist capable of conceiving and realizing all aspects of a theatrical production. In his desire to move the theatre away from its dependence on Realism, and the superficial nineteenth century melodramas he had participated in at Irving's Lyceum, Craig created a Nietzschian vision of the "über-marionette," a larger-than-life puppet, as as a means by which to describe the actor's role. Curiously, he seemed to be rejecting the wooden acting of melodrama and replacing it with a wooden actor. Craig later insisted that he did not mean to supplant the live actor, but only wanted actors to achieve greater control over their bodies, voices, and egos.

Craig's published theories, especially his essay on the über-marionette, as well as his flamboyant manner and temperament, generated considerable controversy in the established theatre world, and he found himself in a self-imposed exile from England that led him to Florence. Aside from attempts to realize his ideas in a few iconoclastic productions, particularly between 1900 and 1912, he remained in Italy, where he spent productive years as an author and designer of spectacular imaginary productions.

Italy was the inspiration as well as the scene of Craig's interest in commedia. In an unpublished manuscript for a planned history of the European theatre between 1500 and 1900, Craig expressed his admiration for the artistry of the Italians. "I might well have called the book 'The History of the Italian Theatre'," he wrote, "for I am strongly inclined to think that the Theatre of Europe *is* the Italian Theatre."[11] In the October, 1924 issue of *Theatre Arts Monthly* he proclaimed, as he had many times before, that Italian artists had given world theatre the fundamental principles of scenic design and the finest traditions in acting. He added that playwrights owed a similar debt to it, noting that although Molière was a great playwright, it was important to remember that much of Molière's significance had to do with the fact that Italian commedia "is passed to us by his hands."[12] Ettore Petrolini and the De Filippo family were among the select group of contemporary Italian theatrical artists for whom Craig had much admiration. Actor and playwright Eduardo De Filippo, especially, was, for Craig:

> a man born of the C dell A -- a genius & any word he might utter of more value than the talk of anyone else in Europe. He is I can well suppose descended from the Andreinis -- distinction is his: strength & wit. . . .I have seen that man act. Not a Tommaso Salvini -- he is at once *less* & much more.[13]

This susceptibility to commedia had predated Craig's time in Italy. In his autobiography, he recalled his earliest experiences with commedia in the guise of French pantomime. He had attended the Prince of Wales' Theatre with Irving and Terry in July, 1891 to see *The Prodigal Son*, "a Mimo Drama, from Paris. Jane May as Pierrot. H.I. [Irving] and E.T.[Terry] not wildly enthusiastic. I was."[14] On a seaside holiday in England in 1897, Craig and his friend, composer and conductor Martin Fallas Shaw, encountered a troupe of Pierrots performing in the open air.[15] They made a profound impression on Craig, as on many other artists and writers of his generation. He did not see these seaside Pierrots as simple carnival clowns, but as larger than life visions of humanity in his own theatrical dream world. Pierrot so fascinated him and Shaw that, as Shaw remembered, "I arranged and partly composed some music to a little scene he [Craig] had devised around one of the 'What the Moon Saw' stories of Hans Christian Andersen. . . .Craig had secured a trial runthrough at the Palace in Cambridge Circus, . . .The orchestra was quite good and Craig looked a handsome Pierrot."[16]

Craig's scene was based on the "Fifteenth Evening" of Andersen's *What the Moon Saw*, which places Pulcinella (who Craig changed to Pierrot), Harlequin, and Columbine in a tragi-comic tale of love and death. In Andersen's story, Columbine prepares to choose between her two suitors, Pulcinella and Harlequin. She selects Harlequin, thus breaking the heart of Pulcinella, who must continue to play the boisterous clown of commedia for his audience. When Columbine dies, Harlequin is given the day off from performing, but Pulcinella must appear on the boards. Despite the despair in his heart, he performs ably and the audience showers him with applause and cheers. After the performance, Pulcinella goes to the deserted churchyard and places a wreath on his beloved's grave, where he is left in the moonlight frozen with grief like a grotesque monument. Andersen concludes that if the audience could see their favorite clown at this particular moment, they would cry "Bravo!"

What the Moon Saw was never publicly performed, but Craig's selection of this particular piece suggests his awareness of the potent mixture of absurd commedia characters with darker strains, leading to a mixture of lightness with Hoffmannesque grotesque. French Romantic writers had discovered this several decades before, and similar connections would be made by a number of Craig's contemporaries, especially in Russia.

A few years later, commedic touches could be seen more clearly in Craig's Purcell Opera Society production of *The Masque of Love*, which he adapted in 1901 with Shaw.[17] Here he used a basic setting of light gray curtains and a chorus of Pierrots as marionettes manipulated by another chorus of Harlequins in a fantasized meditation on a mythical love story. Max Beerbohm, a major supporter of Craig's theories and productions, wrote of

The Masque of Love that "those solemn and slow-moving harlequins, with surcoats of dark gauze over their gay lozenges, setting the huge candles in the candelabra of the Prison of Love -- they and the rest are ineffaceable pictures in my memory. Mr. Craig must give us many more such pretty pictures."[18]

In the program for a revival of *The Masque of Love* (on a double bill with Craig's production of *Acis and Galatea*) at the Queen Street Theatre on March 10, 1902, writer Christopher St. John synopsized the plot of the masque, presumably to assist the audience in following a performance that included mostly pantomime and dance. Set in the palace of the God of Love, *The Masque of Love* delicately balanced the pathos of star-crossed lovers with commedic imagery.

The symbolic nature of the production was emphasized by imaginative lighting that changed both the color of the setting and the fabric of the costumes. Stylized choreographic movement set to music accentuated the emotional content of the piece. The result was that Craig successfully tested many of his evolving theories while exploring the visual possibilities suggested by the universality inherent in commedia's characters. William Butler Yeats saw *The Masque of Love*, and wrote that it

> gave me more perfect pleasure than I have met with in any theatre this ten years. I saw the only admirable stage scenery of our time, for Mr. Gordon Craig has discovered how to decorate a play with severe, beautiful, simple, effects of colour, that leave the imagination free to follow all the suggestions of the play. Realistic scenery takes the imagination captive and is at best but bad landscape painting, but Mr. Gordon Craig's scenery is a new and distinct art. It is something that can only exist in the theatre. It cannot even be separated from the figures that move before it.[19]

Yeats added that the production would be "remembered among the important events of our time."[20] Craig was inclined to agree. In later years, he was often critical of his few realized productions, but he wrote in his 1957 autobiography that *The Masque of Love* was "the best thing I ever did on a stage."[21]

For *Acis and Galatea*,[22] in 1902, Craig designed provocative half masks similar to those of commedia, and in his design for the Fool in Yeats' *The Hour Glass* in 1911, elements of a modified Harlequin mask and the familiar patched costume are found.[23] Craig never again demonstrated obvious commedia techniques in his productions, but he soon turned his attention to writing about commedia in his journal of the art of the theatre, *The Mask.*

From the beginning of his publishing career, Craig paid attention to commedia. As early as 1899, *The Page* (Vol. 11, No. 2) included an S.M. Fox story called "The Last of the Pierrots." It was in *The Mask*, however, especially between 1910 and 1913, that he suggested that contemporary theatrical performance could find a model in commedia. He published excerpts from diverse works on commedia history and performance techniques by several writers and artists,[24] including pieces on noted actors, troupes, and several old scenarios translated into English. In 1910, Craig "filled a little book with a mass of fact relating to the Commedia dell'Arte which I hope shortly to publish"[25] for "the sincere student of the stage of the future."[26] Although he never completed the text, an unpublished manuscript on commedia entitled *Notebook 24: The Commedia dell'Arte* (1910-1911) survives[27]. It is laden with research on the activities of major commedia troupes, actors, and other historical material, much of which eventually turned up in some form in *The Mask*. In all cases, he called for a renaissance of commedia, not for its antiquarian value, but as a source of inspiration for theatrical artists of the future, for whom commedia would be "an affectionate whisper from the dead: nothing dry about it, nothing boisterous; something beautiful, exciting and full of promises."[28]

But what were these promises? In commedia Craig sensed a vital form that confirmed his ambitious vision of a theatre composed equally of acting, words, color, movement, and rhythm. Perhaps he also saw a validation of his "über-marionette" theory in the symbolism inherent in the masked, improvising commedia actor. Bold theatricality, improvisation, masks, and pantomime were all primary characteristics of commedia, and Craig's writings repeatedly promote the idea that a revitalized theatre can be founded on these very qualities. His intense and long-time study of commedia history, particularly his painstaking lists of actors, characters, and dates of important events in commedia history, testify to his scholarly interest in Italian commedia of the sixteenth century, but this historical cataloguing was a means to an end. Craig wanted to immerse himself in these dates and facts to see what of the original Italian works still lived, and could guide the formation of a new theatre.

Craig's confidence in commedia's importance to the modern theatre was based not only on his study of Italian commedia at its height, but also from later derivatives, including such eclectic sources as the plays of Goldoni and Gozzi, Pierrot and the French pantomime, music hall, variety entertainments and harlequinades, and early English farces and puppet plays (which he scrupulously collected during his later years). He looked for commedic elements in classical drama and Oriental and Indian theatre as well.[29] These forms, as commedia did, emphasized movement, masks, and stock characters.

Commedia was at heart a vibrant *comic* theatre and distinctly farcical. Craig believed that farce was the essential theatre. As he noted, "Farce refined becomes high comedy: farce brutalized becomes tragedy. But at the roots of all drama farce is to be found."[30] Like his near contemporary Chekhov, Craig also believed that even in the acting of tragedy, a playfulness, similar to that of farcical acting, should be evident. Conversely, no farce could be truly effective without a hint of tragedy. Although Craig does not explore farce as a concept in his writings, he was always full of praise for the skillful comedian and popular variety entertainments. He found a clear parallel between music hall performances and commedia. When Sarah

Bernhardt was widely criticized for leaving the legitimate theatre to perform in a London music hall, Craig applauded her appearance there. His retort to critics was direct: the "variety stage is the sole remaining link connecting us with that stupendous achievement of the sixteenth century known as the Commedia dell'arte."[31]

In a more scholarly vein, Craig studied commedia scenarios and found them illuminating. They made the plays of literary dramatists such as Shakespeare and George Bernard Shaw seem restrictive to him, because they needed nothing added, and "did not inspire me to create. But the bare framework of *The Four Madmen* [a traditional commedia scenario published in *The Mask*] inspires me -- It calls for me to exert myself. I am all on the alert -- already at the first glance I have seen where the flesh is to cling to its skeleton. The promise of colour and form and the rhythms excites me -- It is what I have been waiting for so long."[32]

Craig always considered himself an actor, although he never again acted after leaving Irving in 1897. He wrote that in commedia scenarios "all parts are ready for the comedian who cares to undergo the training which gives the power to improvise."[33] Responding to the widely held criticism that improvisation led to coarse and vulgar performances, he cleverly defended commedia by comparing it to contemporary realistic theatre:

> And what if the old Commedia dell'Arte were what the critics consider so over-frank in its rendering of life? It is true enough that three hundred years ago the players had all kinds of amazing adventures upon the stage with birth and death, doctors and marriages and bridal nights and surgical operations and feeding bottles and other intimate factors of life. But today the very theatre which regards that as a barbarous age gives us seductions and confinements, bath-room scenes and bedroom scenes and hospital scenes, only gives them all with a smug solemnity which has none of the frank merry healthy spirit of an earlier day.[34]

In *The Theatre Advancing*, he theorized on the improvisatory skill of commedia actors as a potent influence on the greatest English playwrights, including Shakespeare. For example, he convinced himself that the leading actors in the first production of *Much Ado About Nothing*, and particularly the secondary comedians, improvised choice lines from minimal stage directions and a scenario supplied by the playwright. Shakespeare, Craig believed, later "took the whole play and polished it; and if he removed some of its spontaneity and grossness, he left in the richest, cleverest part of the decoration which those actors of genius had contributed to the structure."[35] In his view, great theatre was a true collaboration of playwright and actor, and commedic actors were responsible for "helping Shakespeare, suckling Molière and creating Goldoni."[36]

Craig believed that the fundamentally realistic dramas of Ibsen, Shaw, and others, were weakened by an adherence to formally constructed literary manuscripts, which stifled creative contributions by the skillful actor. Liberation of the actor, he insisted, was required, and he went so far as to question the value of language in the theatre. Action was the key, and Craig concluded that tragedy was "petrified action. Comedy is action out of all bounds tumbling over itself -- breathless -- speechless."[37] His study of commedia history, however, offered few clues about how players moved on stage. He could sense the carnival-spirit and roughness in an old scenario, but he became increasingly aware that the true nature of commedia in performance was inaccessible to him: the central action, commedia's heart, was perishable and elusive.

He nonetheless pressed his attack on the literary and realistic theatre, insisting that a sophisticated form of improvisation could return the vigor of commedia to the theatre. Primarily, Craig decided that "effort should be made to *simplify*."[38] This would allow theatre artists to escape the failures and pitfalls of literary theatre, and the theatre of Realism it spawned. He suggested that "the very *material* of the theatre"[39] be simplified and returned to "a *noble tradition*"[40] rebuilding on old truths -- which in art never grow to look old. In this respect art and life differ -- in this art is superior to life -- for art is the expression of the spirtual life and artists are but the instruments of the Gods.[41]

Craig's material for accomplishing his ends would include the playing place itself: "I must have only open air theatres,"[42] he wrote, as were found in Greece and Rome, and "where Arlecchino lived in Italy. . .at the corner of some street, against some palace; he leaned there in the sun, and delivered his monologues. Does that reality offend you? That is the real reality."[43] He drew many parallels between classical drama and commedia, describing the ancient tragedies as sacred and commedia performances as profane and grotesque. To rise to the playwright's intention, the actor must be "both Priest and Zany, the two extremes of mankind."[44]

Craig believed that the theatre could only call itself a "creative" art when the actors were "creative" artists like commedia's Andreinis, superior performers skilled in improvisation, highly intelligent, and physically versatile. Following the Italian model, he went so far as to suggest that actors ought to be born and bred within a theatrical community. He suggested that modern actors use the Italians as models. Pointing out that surviving commedia scenarios, speeches, and *lazzi* were rich in allusion, "myth and legend, ancient history and contemporary fact,"[45] he stressed "how keen must have been the intelligence, how fertile the imagination, how ready the wit of the men who could seize on all and give so richly and inexhaustibly, who could so swiftly and splendidly weave their web of fantasy upon the stage before the people's eyes."[46] Although Craig's vision of commedia was clearly a romantic one, his depiction of the facility of commedia actors was intended to be accurate as well as inspirational. Craig also suggested that actors should again wear masks, "that paramount means of dramatic expression, without which acting was bound to degenerate."[47] He wrote many articles promoting the return of the mask to theatrical performance, particularly in *The Mask* and *The*

Theatre Advancing. *The Mask* also ran essays on masks by other authors, most notably excerpts from Friedrich Nietzsche's *Beyond Good and Evil*. "Everything that is profound loves the mask,"[48] wrote Nietzsche, to which Craig added:

> Masks carry conviction when he who creates them is an artist, for the artist limits the statements which he places upon these masks. The face of the actor carries so much conviction; it is over-full of fleeting expressions -- frail, restless, disturbed, disturbing. It once would have seemed doubtful to me whether the actor would ever have the courage to cover his face with a mask again, having once put it aside, for it is doubtful whether he would see that it would again serve as any gain.[49]

His persuasive if idealistic argument on the value of masks was not drawn from an antiquarian's pedantry any more than his interest in commedia was, although he studied masks, and designed and constructed them with skill. Instead, he was conscious of their worth as a performance element in the theatre of the present and the future. He believed that the true actor "hates the natural. That is why he plays the Role of the Stage. He loves the disguise -- the mask."[50] He recognized that the control offered by masks could create a symbolic vision of "facial" expression that would be highly selective and deeply moving, more so than the unplanned and unconscious expressions appearing on an actor's face. In his theatrical designs, Craig always attempted to eliminate unnecessary detail and useless information which might obscure the effectiveness of specifically chosen visual images. His scene designs were ambiguous environments, achieving a powerfully mystical mood, typically planned to the last detail of lighting, movement, and gesture. The mask would make a similar control possible for the actor himself and, as such, the director could achieve a greater artistic consistency by relating scene and actor.

Craig indicated that a return of symbolic acting, through use of the mask, was essential for a revitalized theatre. Although it could be said that his controversial 1908 essay, "The Actor and the Über-marionette," was an intentionally provocative attempt to shake off the grip of dead traditions in the theatrical world, it is more likely that his life-long interest in puppets and marionettes inspired his über-marionette theory and enlivened his interest in commedia. It is also true that his memory of the strange, trance-like acting of Irving encouraged his notion of a dominating, supremely talented, larger-than-life actor. He recalled that Irving rehearsed his actors unceasingly, attempting, in a sense, to make good marionettes of them. According to Craig, Irving too had been a great believer in puppets, and lamented that his actors were made of flesh and blood. It is clear that Irving pared down scripts for his productions, allowing free range to a technique that hinted at a return to commedic tradition.

In "The Actor and the Über-marionette," Craig seems to anticipate Brecht's epic theatre. Craig suggests that modern actors can escape the bondage of realistic acting when they "create for themselves a new form of acting, consisting for the main part of symbolic gesture. Today they *impersonate* and interpret; to-morrow they must *represent* and interpret; and the third day they must create."[51] He wished for "improvised dramas that were elegant and even exquisite. Perhaps here we would drop speech and pass to the dance. . .but dance based upon the movement of perishable things in nature."[52]

Craig was impressed by the dancing of Isadora Duncan, whom he met in 1904, and who subsequently became his lover. She expanded his understanding of the symbolic possibilities of movement, and he spent years attempting to capture the feeling of movement in his scene designs. Duncan created a new language of movement that Craig found uniquely expressive and uplifting. In her dancing, she combined the joyous liberation he sensed in the physicality of commedia actors and the symbolic expressiveness of the puppet. His interest in movement also included a fascination with Emile Jacques-Dalcroze's eurythmics, as well as with silent screen comedians, especially Charlie Chaplin. He felt that pantomime, which mixed dance, movement, and gesture, was "a universal means of expression. An Act. . . .a thing done. . . .is always Dramatic. . . .it must be so by reason of its nature. A thing said is only sometimes Dramatic. A gesture says more than a speech and says it better."[53] Ultimately, he could only lament that "Dancing, Pantomime, Marionnettes, Masks; these things so vital to the ancients, all essential parts of their respected Art of the Theatre at one time or another, have now been turned into a jest."[54]

Craig's critique was as personal as it was harsh. Although his native English theatre largely ignored his theories, commedia itself proved to be a powerful influence on many of his European contemporaries. It must have been difficult for Craig, whose work was rarely produced, to see his theories so magnificently embodied in such diverse productions as those staged by Meyerhold, Reinhardt, and Copeau. Many of his fellow artists credited his contributions, however, and the quality of his commedia research has been acknowledged by numerous scholars. Sheldon Cheney, for example, writing in 1914, listed the standard commedia histories as sources for his book, *The Theatre. Three Thousand Years of Drama, Acting and Stagecraft*, but also noted that "I am most indebted to the spirited if scrappy treatment in the noted issues of *The Mask*."[55]

Although it is true that most of his theories, including those on commedia, depend as much on his unique and eccentric intuitive vision of theatre as on historical facts, it is also true that Craig's ideas have been successfully carried forth in the work of countless twentieth century directors and actors. He envisioned a new theatre, clearly based on many of the theatrical characteristics that had reigned for over two centuries in commedia, and he never wavered in his hope that it would eventually come to pass. Responding to a letter from art historian and commedia iconographer David Allen in 1955, Craig, at the age of eighty-three, still in self-imposed exile from the theatres of Europe, wrote wistfully of his theatrical struggles and his love for commedia:

> the C dell A always has & always will be to me a thing I love -- & alas know little of. . . .The Theatre of today has a few links still with the Commedia -- its actors *are* still of it though ignorant of the fact or of its great traditional laws. No matter -- they are still of it. . . .C dell A was & is a live thing for me.[56]

Commedia in England After Craig

Craig had exiled himself from England at the beginning of his most important work, so he had little immediate effect on theatrical developments there. The modern revival of commedia was, like Craig himself, relatively unappreciated in England, and with a few significant exceptions, it was slow to filter into the work of English theatre artists, despite its widespread popularity in ballet and its influence on the disreputable music halls and variety stages. Shakespeare's plays were continually produced, melodramatic nineteenth century entertainments continued, but little of either the realistic drama exemplified by Ibsen's plays, or the modern anti-realist theories typified by Craig, were seen in England at the time. George Bernard Shaw (1856-1950) pressed the case for Ibsenesque Realism, transforming himself into a dramatist in the process, and once his struggles with censorship were over, and after an initial lukewarm response by the audience, Shaw's plays dominated the English stage during the first quarter of the twentieth century.

Although he initially embraced much of Ibsen's style of drama, many of Shaw's plays made considerable use of theatricalism, humor, and fantasy, central commedic traits. In the Preface to his *Three Plays for Puritans*, he compared his plays to earlier theatrical traditions, including commedia:

> my stories are the old stories: my characters are the familiar harlequin and columbine, clown and pantaloon (note the harlequin's leap in the third act of *Caesar and Cleopatra*); my stage tricks and suspenses and thrills and jests are the ones in vogue when I was a boy, by which time my grandfather was tired of them. To the young people who make

their acquaintance for the first time in my plays, they may be as novel as Cyrano's nose to those who have never seen Punch; whilst to older playgoers the unexpectedness of my attempt to substitute natural history for conventional ethics and romantic logic may so transfigure the eternal stage puppets and their inevitable dilemmas as to make their identification impossible for the moment. If so, so much the better for me: I shall perhaps enjoy a few years of immortality.[57]

Although Shaw was unmistakably a literary playwright, and hardly inclined to employ such commedic techniques as improvisation or pantomime in his plays, he often captured commedia's spirit without resorting to imitation of the form. As a drama critic, he typically did not care for the farcical plays of his day, but he astutely noted that only in the "fantastic atmosphere of moral irresponsibility"[58] of such plays could the hero realize himself totally.

Many of Shaw's characters emerge as modern parallels of commedia masks, or his own inventions along similar lines. One particular commedic type is the ruthless businessman, such as Sir George Crofts, seen in Shaw's early play, *Mrs. Warren's Profession* (1893), and in late works such as *Heartbreak House* (1913-1916), in the person of Boss Mangan. Crofts is a one-dimensional character, but Mangan turns out to be wearing a mask -- he is not what he initially seems to be; in contrast to his image as a successful hard-nosed industrialist, he is actually comparatively sensitive and emotional, and in financial ruin. Shaw's use of the idea of the mask clearly displays commedic origins, despite the fact that his characters do not necessarily do so.

Androcles and the Lion (1912), which combines discussions of religion with Aesop's fable of a henpecked tailor who befriends a wounded lion, features commedic touches. The gentle, slightly befuddled Androcles is a Shavian variation on Pierrot in the Deburau tradition, while Androcles' harridan wife, seen only in the prologue, is a stock shrew. It may be stretching a point, but the Lion gives the play a touch of Gozzian *fiabe*. Among Shaw's other works, the one-act burlesque, *Passion, Poison, and Petrification; or The Fatal Gazogene* (1905), has commedic aspects, as does

You Never Can Tell (1899), in which the twins Philip and Dolly, whose words and actions seem to merge them into a single identity, appear at the play's climax dressed as Harlequin and Columbine. In an essay entitled "Less Scenery Would Mean Better Drama," Shaw calls for a return to simpler stages, like those of the popular entertainments of the Renaissance. Although he flirted with some of its elements, Shaw could hardly be considered a true commedist.

One of Shaw's contemporaries, J. M. Barrie (1860-1937), author of popular light dramas and comedies, found inspiration in commedia via the traditions of English pantomime and harlequinades. His perennial *Peter Pan* (1904) is a memorable fairy tale which, in several forms, remains a stage vehicle for actresses specializing in "breeches" roles. Along with its debt to English pantomime, Barrie adds a dash of cynical Gozzian fantasy through the use of animals with human qualities, fairies, and buffoons. Aside from his longer dramatic works and novels, Barrie wrote one-act plays, many of which are delicate experiments with themes he pursued at length in his major works. Most notable is *Pantaloon* (1905), a sensitively written and gently cynical harlequinade, based on Chapter Twenty-Two ("Joey") of Barrie's novel *The Little White Bird*. It was written eleven years before his other (and longer) work, *A Kiss for Cinderella*, in which pantomime figures prominently.

In two short episodes, *Pantaloon*, which was produced in England with Gerald du Maurier in the lead, combines both the theatrical fantasy and harsh irony of commedia. At one point,when Clown brutally thrashes Pantaloon, the old man can only respond with great reverence: "What an artist!"[59]

Barrie points out that he has not portrayed the characters in their typical milieu: "Pantaloon is presented not on the stage but in private life, yet he is garbed and powdered as we know him in the harlequinade."[60] Barrie eschews any similarity between his characters and modern actors: "Pantaloon was never an actor in their sense; he would have scorned to speak words written for him by any whippersnapper; what he said and did before the footlights were the result of mature conviction and represented his philosophy of life."

Harley Granville Barker (1877-1946), Craig's contemporary, also worked to liberate the English theatre from its slavish dependence on the practices of the nineteenth century stage. Barker, too, was an actor in his early career (Barker and Craig had, in fact, once acted together in a provincial production of *She Stoops to Conquer*). Though he shared many of Craig's concerns, Barker more successfully combined a playwright's skill with an awareness of the needs of the actor. Deeply interested in the classics, especially the plays of Shakespeare and Molière, Barker stopped short of suggesting, as Craig had, that Shakespeare was aided by commedic improvisation in the creation of his comic plays. He did, however, acknowledge the centrality of the actor's contributions, pointing to commedia as a model:

> Shakespeare's own plays might pull through without extempore funniments, but where would some of the others have been? For the Commedia dell'Arte action was outlined and dialogue largely left to the actor. And one could find in melodramas being played in booths to-day what are called "carpenter's" scenes, in which, before a cloth showing a street or country lane or what not, the villain or the comic man is expected to improvise talk for the five minutes' extra, it may be, which the carpenters need to turn the scenery behind from the baronial hall of the wicked uncle into the humble heroine's cottage.[61]

Barker's use of commedia in his directing work seems modest, but as a playwright, he anticipated Shaw and Barrie, as well as Meyerhold, whose 1906 production of Alexander Blok's *The Fairground Booth* has long been held up as the quintessential modern commedia.

Barker's best known plays[62] are recognized today as solidly constructed social problem dramas in the Ibsenesque mold, second only to those of Shaw as scathing assaults on bourgeois hypocrisy and middle-class morality in turn of the century England. Although these works remain his finest achievements as a dramatist, Barker's most popular plays during his lifetime include two overtly theatrical works inspired by commedia: *Prunella, or Love in a Dutch Garden* (1904) and *The Harlequinade* (1913).

Barker collaborated with Laurence Housman (1865-1959) on *Prunella*, and he directed and played the role of Pierrot himself. *Prunella* is not in the rambunctious and physical commedic mode in any respect, and despite its touches of cynicism, it is essentially a slight and sentimental poetic love story, owing much to Deburau's vision of Pierrot. It is significantly more verbose, but is similar to both Blok's *The Fairground Booth*, and to Craig's production of *The Masque of Love*, which anticipated *Prunella* by nearly three years.

Prunella is a gentle, repressed young woman who lives in a secluded garden which represents no particular time or place, but where it is always afternoon. Worldly love arrives in the person of Pierrot, leading a band of strolling players. He immediately sets out to charm Prunella:

> Oh, I'm nothing: I'm nothing in the world but a poor Pierrot. I'm an orphan, I haven't got a home, I haven't got a leg to stand on, I haven't got a bed to sleep in, I haven't had a bit to eat, and I haven't had a drop to drink for three whole hours. [*Changing his manner, seeing that he has made an impression on her.*] There, now you know all about me,-- as much as I know myself, almost. Oh, I'm so giddy, I can't stand. If you don't look sweet at me, I shall be dead in a minute.[63]

In the climactic scene of Act Two (a third act was added in 1930), the personification of Love appears to the repressed Prunella. A chorus of mummers enter and encircle her and her would-be lover. She is caught up in the whirl of life, leaving her dream-like garden and her existence as Prunella, proclaiming "I am -- Pierrette!"[64] In the added third act, a disillusioned and abandoned Prunella returns to her garden, only to learn, in the arms of the remorseful Pierrot, who has returned transformed by her pure love, that "a little weeping does not blind the eyes of love."[65]

Housman remembered that Barker worked feverishly on the

production, paying particular attention to "how much music was wanted to accompany words and action at certain points of the play, and how much music could be allowed for atmosphere, with action, at other points."[66] The first performance of *Prunella* was given on December 23, 1904, and the critics were respectful, but somewhat puzzled by the play's fantasy. Since it was clearly not a typical harlequinade for children, they were at a loss to categorize the piece. The production was almost immediately in jeopardy, and it gave its final performance in the middle of January. As Housman recalled in his memoirs, the play failed with most critics and audiences:

> "Quaint, but feeble," I heard a lady say, as I came away from the first performance. The press damned it with faint praise; the general line taken by the critics was that the authors were ambitiously trying to produce a new *genre* which was scarcely worthwhile; Granville Barker and I were put severely in our places -- in our anxiety to be original, we had merely been fantastic;. . .[67]

The failure of the original production of *Prunella*, however, proved to be only an initial and somewhat inexplicable one. By 1955, Barker's biographer, C.B. Purdom, could write that it had been "the most often played of all the dramatic works bearing Barker's name, and when published ran through fourteen impressions in the next twenty years."[68] Less than two years after the original production, it was revived at the Court Theatre under the Barker/John Vedrenne management for eleven matinees and this time it caught on and remained in the Court repertory until 1910. On October 28, 1913, it opened in New York at the Little Theatre, produced by Winthrop Ames, with Marguerite Clark as Prunella and Ernest Glendinning as Pierrot. It ran for one hundred performances, and was enthusiastically received by critics, who referred to it as "an exceptionally lovely thing done in an exceptionally competent way."[69]

Prunella, however, has disappeared from the stage in more recent years, undoubtedly because its overt sentimentality undermines the potential impact of the play's themes. What has often been overlooked is Barker's original interpretation of the play, particularly in his own performance as Pierrot, which Housman recalled as being played along "cold macabre - lines."[70] In a letter to William Poel in January, 1905, Barker explained that he strove to capture the traditional appearance of Pierrot: "My white face! Yes -- I tried it less and more but in getting expression you somehow lost the definite Pierrot quality which was half the character. I feel that someone with cleverer gesture than I could have made you forget the expressionless white face."[71]

Housman felt that Barker's interpretation of the role "was the best, but it was the least popular; it had too much *bite* in it -- the audience preferred a Pierrot whom they could like -- and forgive -- more easily."[72] Clearly Barker intended the performance of the play to undercut at least some of the sentimentality of the script. Other actors who played the role, as Housman points out, gave in to the sentimental and winsome qualities typical of the Pierrot of the harlequinade, completely avoiding the cynical and amoral quality seen in the style of such late nineteenth century French Pierrot plays as Paul Margueritte's *Pierrot Assassin of His Wife* (1882), which Barker seems to have instinctively discovered.

By contrast, there was no mistaking the childlike fantasy of Barker's collaboration with Dion Clayton Calthrop (1879-1937) on *The Harlequinade*. It opened on September 1, 1913, at the St. James' Theatre, on a double bill with Shaw's *Androcles and the Lion*, under the management of Barker and Lillah McCarthy. The play was a fanciful theatrical history told by a little girl named Alice and her Uncle Edward, using elements of mythology and commedia to tell the story of man as symbolized by the theatre. *The Harlequinade* is clearly not up to the standards of *Prunella*. It is disappointing in its avoidance of any bitter edge that might have made the play's more saccharine moments bearable. It is, however, more revealing than the earlier play of Barker's understanding of commedia. The published version includes an introduction by Calthrop and Barker, referring to the play as an "excursion":

> Now in any excursion you get into all sorts of odd company, and fall into talk with persons out of your ordinary rule, and you borrow a match and get lent a magazine, and, as like as not, you may hear the whole tragedy and comedy of a ham and beef carver's life. So you will get a view of the world as oddly coloured as Harlequin's clothes, with puffs of sentiment dear to the soul of Columbine, and Clownish fun with Pantaloonish wisdom and chuckles. . . .[73]

The play opens with Alice and Uncle Edward sitting onstage waiting for the audience to fill their seats. The orchestra tunes up, and Uncle Edward informs Alice that it is time to begin. Calthrop and Barker have attempted in this prelude to break the theatrical fourth wall, even allowing Alice to address the audience directly. The authors attempt to employ commedia characters as symbols, as when Alice describes Harlequin as the spirit of man wanting to come to life. The symbolic use of mythology and commedia can best be seen in Alice's elaborate description of Columbine:

> Psyche, who is the Soul, comes down. . .whenever a baby's born, of course, a little scrap of Psyche is sent down! . . .But this is how the story goes. . .That she comes down from Mount Olympus where the gods live to adventure on the earth. And in the Harlequinade she's Columbine, but that only means a dove, and a dove is the symbol of the soul.

The attempt to mix the stereotypical characters of commedia with elements of Greek mythology in a recreation of a harlequinade emphasizing human comedy, requires almost endless exposition by Alice in setting up each small play-within- the-play. The prelude to the second scene, for example, finds Alice explaining that "the next part is going to be all in dumb-show, because it's in the fifteenth century, and that's how they used to play things in the fifteenth century, when they played heaps of Harlequinades."[74] Explaining that the gods almost ceased to exist because people stopped believing, Alice emphasizes the eternal quality of the theatre:

> Mercury knew that if people won't believe a thing when you say it's real, they'll just as good as believe it and understand it a great deal better when it only seems make-believe. And that's Art. And as the easiest art in the world is the art of acting. . .I hope they didn't hear. . .the gods became actors.

Alice introduces the time-worn commedia plot, which Calthrop and Barker have attempted to enliven by setting it within the context of her explanatory remarks:

> Columbine has run away again. The story's always got to be that. Either Columbine runs away from somebody, or somebody runs away with her. That's because the soul is always struggling to be free. This time Cousin Clown and Uncle Pantaloon helped her. She could twist them around her little finger. And she made a great mistake in running away with this very sham-serious young man.[75]

Columbine marries her suitor, but he turns out to be dull and inattentive, and she seeks excitement with The Man of the World. Fortunately, however, Alice tells us that

> just in time comes Harlequin-Mercury. He has no wings left to his feet, because you wear off wings rather soon if you wander about the world. And his wand hasn't any snakes left. It's just painted white wood. And it's a good thing we've come to the jokes about the sausages, because, now Harlequin's only a strolling player, he's sometimes awfully hungry.

The "dumb-show" takes place in the third scene, and Alice and Uncle Edward offer commentary and prompt the backstage crew to remember the appropriate romantic lighting and a moon effect. Columbine and her husband (Gelsomino) are brought together in a commedic charade, and, as Uncle Edward proclaims, "that's how they [the actors] get back among the gods."[76]

Two additional scenes move the characters through an eighteenth century comedy of manners and, in the final scene, Alice introduces the mechanized and inhuman modern era, which

> is to knock the spirit out of a man. Which is his magic. Clown and

Pantaloon and Harlequin and Columbine are very simple folk, you
know. They let themselves be just what it's most natural to be, and
only try to give their friends in front. . .kind friends in front, they call
them. . .just what will make them happiest quickest. So this is what
they've come to be by this time, Clown and Columbine, Harlequin and
Pantaloon. No names but those, no meaning, no real part at all in the
rattle and clatter of machinery which is now called Life. They're out
of it.

And, in an attack on the realistic stage worthy of Craig, Alice reports
that Clown, Pantaloon, Harlequin, and Columbine "clung to the skirts of the
theatre for a bit. But the theatre, aching to be *in it*, flung them off. The
intellectual drama had no use for them, no use at all."[77]

Alice continues to explain that businessmen took over the theatre,
conducting it on a sound commercial basis while draining the spirit from it.
The four characters beg for a job, but are informed that the theatre has
become completely automated. Plays are now "turned out by our Number
Two Factory of Automatic Dramaturgy; Plunkville, Tennessee."[78] They are
shown Act Three of "Love: a Disease" which is "Number seventy-six of the
High Brow Ibsen series."[79] Calthrop and Barker manage an effectively nasty
satire of modern realistic dramas, including a box set with wallpaper
"stencilled in the worst Munich style"[80] and characters represented by two
gramophones which speak to each other. The outraged clowns react by
creating bedlam in hope of destroying the theatre to save it, as Alice, from the
sidelines, calls for the traditional transformation scene of harlequinade. The
characters return to the heavens as gods, waiting, as Alice concludes, for us
to "Summon them and hear them cry -- *Here we are again.*"[81]

The Harlequinade had a moderately successful run, helped by sharing
the bill with Shaw's comedy, but the critics were fairly ruthless, with *The
Times* noting that "A theatre audience is in no mood for these subtleties."[82]
The Harlequinade was produced in New York in May, 1921, and had a five-
week run at the Neighborhood Playhouse (tranferring for a few more weeks

to the Punch and Judy Theatre) and a somewhat more agreeable critical response, with the *New York Times* critic calling it a "gay little diversion."[83] *The Harlequinade*, however, like *Prunella*, is seldom produced today.

Barker's final brush with commedic theatre came in 1920, when he translated and directed *Deburau*, a verse drama by French boulevardier Sacha Guitry, which opened in New York on December 27, 1920, starring Lionel Atwill as Deburau. Less than a year later, the play was produced in London on November 2, 1921, again translated and directed by Barker.

Guitry's play begins with a prologue set outside the legendary Théâtre des Funambules with a barker attracting a crowd to a performance featuring Deburau as Pierrot. The prologue dissolves quickly into a play-within-a-play performance which, in the published script of *Deburau*, is suggested by Theophile Gautier's synopsis of "The Old Clo' Man."

Deburau attempts to capture the bittersweet longing for elusive love that legend suggests inspired Deburau's sad-eyed Pierrot. The play's theme is summed up aptly in the final scene when Deburau, at the end of his career, tries to impress upon his son and theatrical heir, Charles, which things in life are important:

> I look back over my life,
> Its failures and successes,
> Its impotence and strife;
> Now, at the end of it, this is
> The lesson I've learnt by heart.
> There are two unfading things,
> Love and Art.[84]

Deburau ends with Charles taking over the role of Pierrot from his ill and heartbroken father.

Commedia characters and performance techniques crept into many English plays and productions between 1910 and 1930.[85] Clifford Bax (1886-1962), a dramatist heavily influenced by the poetic dramas of Yeats, experimented with commedia in *Midsummer Marriage* (1923), in which his modern characters, a middle-aged merchant, a young scholar, a widow, and a maid, become confused with the commedia characters they dress as for a midsummer carnival.

Many revues and musicals, as well as a wealth of ballets, included songs featuring commedia characters or imagery, especially romanticized treatments of Pierrot and Pierrette. Noel Coward's (1899-1973) "Parisian Pierrot," written for the revue *London Calling!* (1923), is among the most memorable of these. Pierrot plays continue to appeal to English audiences. The Pierrotters, a 1980's group of white-faced clowns, are only one example of performers recreating this entertainment for contemporary audiences. Making use of considerable social commentary in their zany performances, The Pierrotters contributed to the rise of many alternative avant-garde entertainments that began to replace traditional cabaret and music hall performances in England during the 1960's.

Since the 1930's, commedia has influenced a few significant English directors. Joan Littlewood's (b. 1914) distinctive style, shaped by the socially-conscious left-wing dramas of the 1930's, and a taste for collaborative working methods, was inspired, in part, by commedia. Littlewood joined a group in Manchester called the Theatre of Action (previously known as the Red Megaphones) in 1934. She participated in their controversial political performances and studied the art of the German Expressionists and Russian theatre artists of the first three decades of the twentieth century. She later moved to London and formed the Theatre Union, producing a varied repertory of classics: Shakespeare, Molière, and Schiller, as well as avant-garde contemporary works.

The Theatre Union disbanded before World War II, but Littlewood prevailed upon several key members to join her in starting the landmark Theatre Workshop in 1945. Its manifesto stressed a special relationship with its audiences in developing a theatre of the people:

The great theatres of all times have been popular theatres which reflected the dreams and struggles of the people. The theatre of Aeschyus and Sophocles, of Shakespeare and Ben Jonson, of the Commedia dell'Arte and Molière derived their inspiration, their language, their art from the people.[86]

Commedia was not only an inspiration to Littlewood and the Theatre Workshop, it was the foundation of their performance technique. For their production of Molière's *The Flying Doctor*, the acting style was drawn from commedia, thanks to the group's study of popular farce dating to the earliest known theatres. Influenced by her knowledge of commedic acting, Littlewood wanted her actors to be as versatile as possible. While they did not actually use masks, she encouraged her actors to work as if they were encumbered by them. The result was that the actors developed a broad array of expressive physical gestures and a unique ensemble style, and depended less on facial expression and language. In her production of *Volpone*, Littlewood set the one-dimensional characters of Jonson's play in a contemporary Italian setting, connecting with every possible stereotype, commedic and otherwise, to create a corrosive satire on post-World War II British society. Although she left the Theatre Workshop in 1961, she returned to stage *Oh, What a Lovely War!* in 1963. This critically acclaimed production, later made into a film, owed something to commedia and music hall traditions in its broad theatricality. Pierrot costumes were also used, drawn from traditional English Pierrot shows.

In more recent years, commedia has had little visible effect on English theatrical developments. The dramatists of the Absurdist movement after World War II made use of commedic characters and techniques, especially the image of the solitary clown in the style of Harlequin or Pierrot (or Chaplin) as an existential Everyman. Playwrights such as Tom Stoppard (b. 1937) and Joe Orton (1933-1967) could be considered commedic in their use of farcical elements, irony, satire, and emblematic characters, but perhaps the most commercially successful commedic production of the last two decades was the Young Vic's *Scapino!* (1970), freely adapted from Molière's *The Tricks of Scapin*, by director Frank Dunlop (b. 1927) and actor Jim Dale (b. 1935), who played the lead. *Scapino!* is loosely constructed to create the illusion of spontaneity, and is filled with anachronistic contemporary references mingled with Molière's basic plot and characters. The play is set on a cluttered stage mixing elements of several locations into a circus environment. Comic Italian songs were worked in and particular emphasis was placed on acrobatics and sight gags. The production's considerable success in England and America (1974) was due in large measure to Dale's energetic and inventively commedic performance as Scapino.

During the same decade, Peter Brook (b. 1925) staged his landmark production of *A Midsummer Night's Dream* for the Royal Shakespeare Company. Brook, a truly international director, has often expressed his admiration for Craig, Meyerhold, and many of their contemporaries. He believes the theatre must fulfill a socially worthwhile purpose, and he has been powerfully influenced by classical drama, Oriental theatre, and other ritualized forms. He has seen the work of some of the finest theatrical companies in the world, including a faithful revival of Vakhtangov's 1922 commedic production of Gozzi's *Princess Turandot*.

His affinity for Craig, whom he met in the 1950's, is not surprising. Although fascinated by the theatre's historical accomplishments, Brook was not interested in resuscitating a dead form or genre for its own sake, but, like Craig, he sought to understand the techniques that gave that form its vitality. Brook wrote in his 1968 book, *The Empty Space*, about his understanding of the theatre's purpose. He doesn't mention commedia by name, but he is clearly thinking of it when he asks: "What is this theatre's intent? First of all it is there unashamedly to make joy and laughter, what Tyrone Guthrie calls *theatre of delight*, and any theatre that can truly give delight has earned its place. Along with serious, committed and probing work, there must be irresponsibility."[87]

Much of Brook's finest work has been in overtly serious productions of the classics, Chekhov, and adaptations of literary masterpieces, but he also has tackled a variety of comic works.[88] His 1977 adaptation of Alfred Jarry's *Ubu* plays, which he called *Ubu aux Bouffes*, marked his Centre International de Recherche Théâtrale group's rediscovery of a "sense of fun, so apparent in their improvisations around the world, and both healthy and liberating after the bleakness"[89] of many of their earlier productions. Brook's most notable comic production to date was his internationally acclaimed *A Midsummer Night's Dream* (1970). No antiquarian commedia embellishments were present, nor did he impose commedia masks and costumes on Shakespeare's characters. Instead, he created a spontaneous, wildly inventive comic environment before a set made up of little more than white walls. The actors were clothed in nondescript baggy and colorful costumes belonging to no discernable period. Brook's version was a joyful celebration of theatricality, the play as "play." It was a production stripped of the familiar conventions of the stage, and featured a return to a bare stage peopled with commedic clowns. This stripping away liberated the actors, and in this way, Brook was able to realize a production filled with electrifying movement and pantomime.

The play-within-the-play performed by Shakespeare's "hempen homespuns," as staged by Brook, was "a patchwork pierrot show, or a human Punch-and-Judy in close-up,. . ."[90] He did not, however, restrict this spirit to Shakespeare's low comedy characters. Puck became the pivotal character in the treatment, looking, as one critic wrote, "like a more than usually perky Picasso clown,"[91] and the play's fantastic characters became comic grotesques. Critics made much of the circus connections, but few identified the obvious parallels with commedia.

Brook has not obviously returned to the commedic vein in his more recent productions, and he eventually left England for Paris, where, under the influence of Polish theatre artist Jerzy Grotowski, he has staged his more recent works, including *The Conference of the Birds* (1976), *The Mahabarata* (1985), and *The Tempest* (1990). In the latter, he experimented with masks, as he had in several earlier plays, undoubtedly inspired by his understanding of traditional masked forms, including Oriental drama and commedia, in an attempt to rediscover their value for the contemporary stage.

It is certainly the case that commedia had considerably less impact on the British stage, than it has had on the Russian, German, French, or Italian. Those most interested in commedia, like Barker and Craig, were discouraged from producing plays in that vein by unwelcoming critics and audiences. They had shared a belief in the inspirational value of commedia, and in the fundamental similarities between the genres of drama which ranged, as Barker wrote, "from the austerity of Greek tragedy to the freedom of the *Commedia dell'arte*."[92] It is quite clear that Barker recognized, as all commedists must, that "The antics of Harlequin are not essentially different from the art that shows us Oedipus."[93]

CHAPTER FOUR

Dr. Dapertutto and Company: Commedia in Russia

The public comes to the theatre to see the art of man, but what art is there in walking about the stage as oneself? The public expects invention, play acting and skill. But what it gets is either life or a slavish imitation of life. Surely the art of man on the stage consists in shedding all traces of environment, carefully choosing a mask, donning a decorative costume, and showing off one's brilliant tricks to the public -- now as a dancer, now as the intrigant at some masquerade, now as the fool of old Italian comedy, now as a juggler.[1]

-- Vsevolod Meyerhold

In the early eighteenth century, the Russian stage was essentially dominated by the German theatre. During this same time commedia companies began to appear,[2] followed by the influence of the French Baroque theatre and the plays of Goldoni, deeply effecting the stage and most aspects of Russian aristocratic life. The evolution of a strong native Russian theatre reflected diverse commedic influences.

The first important native dramatist, Denis Fonvizin (1745-1792), authored several comic fables satirizing aspects of the reign of Catherine the Great. Fonvizin's style was reminiscent of Molière's, and his first play, *The Brigadier* (1769), lampooned the Russian Francophilia of this era. A fierce moralist, Fonvizin also attacked the institution of serfdom, through his creation of stock characters in a commedic mode, including servants and foolish old women.

Less than seventy years later, Nikolai Gogol (1809-1852), the supreme Russian satirist, wrote plays which offer a brilliant amalgam of realistic, romantic, psychological, and grotesque insights into the fate of the little man pummeled by society. Thus began a golden age of Russian theatre that flourished until Stalin's repressions in the late 1930's. Gogol's masterpiece, *The Inspector General* (1836), was revived often during this century, and was especially popular during the years immediately following the Russian Revolution, when it was given several commedic productions. Gogol paralleled the modern Russian commedists in his insistence on the moral function of drama, and comedy's value in purging society of its ills. In this, he was clearly a forerunner of the great era in Russian theatre to come.

Anton Chekhov's (1860-1904) light-hearted short stories and early one-act plays, *The Bear* (1888), *The Proposal* (1889), and *The Wedding* (1890), seem connected to the farcical spirit of commedia. His major plays, *The Seagull* (1896), *Uncle Vanya* (1899), *Three Sisters* (1901), and *The Cherry Orchard* (1904), focus on the struggles of daily life and the waste of talent, energy, and human spirit, and were produced by the Moscow Art Theatre, where they would serve as a vehicle for an emphasis on realistic staging and acting techniques that would ultimately be resisted by Russia's anti-realist, commedic theatre artists.

Vsevelod Meyerhold

In March, 1935, when Stalin's policies were beginning to cripple the modern Russian theatre, an aging Edward Gordon Craig visited Moscow as an honored guest of the Russian theatres. When he arrived in Moscow's train station he was surprised to be greeted by a brass band and the theatrical elite of Russia. Craig, still in exile from the English stage, must certainly have been touched by the affection of his Russian colleagues, many of whom considered Craig's theories on the art of modern theatre as seminal.

For his part, Craig was impressed with much of what he saw in the Russian theatre, even then. He had made periodic visits between 1908 and 1912, while collaborating with Constantin Stanislavsky on a production of *Hamlet* at the Moscow Art Theatre. Craig's anti-realistic theories and backward glance at earlier theatrical traditions, especially commedia, had puzzled Stanislavsky, who found Craig's notion of a return to open air theatres particularly "sentimental."[3] Stanislavsky worked with his Moscow Art Theatre company to achieve an exquisite level of reality in performances of contemporary dramas. Although he occasionally attempted to move his actors toward verse plays or classics, he and his actors rarely felt comfortable or equipped to deal with the stylized aspects of such plays. *Hamlet* satisfied neither Craig nor Stanislavsky, both of whom believed that despite the production's memorable qualities, they had failed to achieve unity between the realistic acting style and Craig's highly symbolic visual concepts. In his memoirs, written more than twenty years after the production, Stanislavsky stated that he felt that his company had failed Craig.

Craig would undoubtedly have found a more suitable collaborator in Vsevolod Meyerhold (1874-1940), who stood among those greeting Craig on the railroad platform in 1935. Both were unabashed theatricalists and both valued the contribution of the actor more highly than that of the playwright. Despite their similarities, there was one great and obvious difference between them. Meyerhold's art was deeply and completely political in a fundamental way (although he disdained official politics and bureaucracy), while Craig unceasingly avoided overt political statements in both his art and his life. He was interred briefly in a prison camp during the Nazi occupation of France, where he was then living, but Craig's only concern with politics was the fear that his work would be disrupted by changes in the political climate. In a surprising departure from his political indifference, Craig wrote to *The Times* in 1938 to state his outrage at attempts by Soviet officials to stifle Meyerhold's art. Craig's sympathetic outcry does not reflect an understanding of the political forces that would eventually suppress the Golden Age of Russian theatre and bring about the arrest and subsequent murder of Vsevolod Meyerhold.

Meyerhold, for his part, admired Craig and his theories. When he visited Berlin in 1907, he learned of Craig's early English productions, and in 1909, in the *Journal of the Literary Artistic Society* (No. 9), Meyerhold translated two of the essays from Craig's *The Art of the Theatre* (although a pirated Russian translation had already appeared by 1906), adding a biographical sketch praising Craig's productions and theories.

The influence Craig's ideas had on his development was unmatched, but Meyerhold had the advantage of experimenting with these concepts in production while Craig could only theorize about them in writing. Meyerhold, like Craig, turned to the traditional devices of masks and puppets, to the ancient Greek and Roman theatres, to the ritualized performances of primitive and Oriental theatres, and, preeminently, to commedia, in his search for style and technique.

Also, like Craig, Meyerhold's art was built on the foundation of rebellion against the theatrical conditions prevalent as he began his career. He was born in Penza to a middle-class family, and after one year's study, he quit the Law School of Moscow University, and enrolled in the acting classes of Vladimir Nemirovich-Danchenko[4] at the Moscow Philharmonia. After graduating in 1898, he joined the company of the Moscow Art Theatre, originating roles in two of Chekhov's plays: Treplyov in *The Seagull* and Tusenbach in *Three Sisters*. The emphasis on Realism there, particularly as promoted by Stanislavsky, chaffed Meyerhold. He left the company to run his own provincial theatres for two years in Kherson and Tiflis, before returning to Moscow.

Meyerhold's ideas about the purpose of acting had formed early in his time at the Moscow Art Theatre, where he was unable to act on them. In a frustrated letter to Nemirovich-Danchenko he wondered if actors were "to do nothing but *act*? We want to be able to *think* while we act! We want to know *why* we are doing what we are doing, *what* it is we are acting, and *whom* we are instructing or criticizing."[5]

Despite Meyerhold's objections, the Moscow Art Theatre was the most prestigious theatre in Russia, and when Stanislavsky invited him back in 1904 to direct the newly established Theater-Studio, he returned, understanding that the studio setting would offer him some much desired opportunities for experimentation. His first productions there did not please Stanislavsky, who did not permit them to open. In anger, Meyerhold went back to his work in provincial companies until 1906, when actress Vera Komissarzhevskaya[6] offered him the opportunity to direct a new company she had established in St. Petersburg. Although Meyerhold parted company with her after a relatively short time, several of his first significant productions were staged there, including a definitive version of Alexander Blok's commedic play, *The Fairground Booth*.

During his short tenure with Komissarzhevskaya, many of the theories which had been formulated during his years in the provinces began to take firm shape in Meyerhold's productions. In 1908, he became director of the Imperial Theatres in St. Petersburg, beginning a ten year period during which he staged his major pre-Revolutionary productions. Demonstrating an extraordinary range of skills, he acted, directed plays and operas,[7] and published many theoretical essays. Of equal significance, with regard to his interest in commedia, was the work he did in St. Petersburg's many experimental theatres under the pseudonym Doctor Dapertutto.[8] The beginning of the Soviet era saw little interruption in his prolific work, especially during the 1920's, and his achievements continued unabated until his theatre was closed by Stalin in 1938.

Although commedia was only one of many influences on Meyerhold, his particular and unique understanding of it was one of the most powerful forces in his work. The highly stylized productions typical of him were laced with scathing political satire and grotesqueness, inspired by both commedia and the works of the German Romantic writer, E.T.A. Hoffmann.[9] At the same time, he intended to strip theatre down to its essentials, inspiring many subsequent theatre artists, including Jerzy Grotowski, whose "Poor Theatre" carried this concept forth several decades later.

Meyerhold had great sympathy for the Symbolist movement, and his principles of "biomechanics," suggested in part by the Constructivist movement, called for a recreation of the actor as an acrobat who transcended his own ego in order to become a symbolic human image in fantastic motion. At the same time, Meyerhold also wished to cut away the Symbolists' often overwrought attempts at profundity by intentionally blurring the division between audience and actor. It was often his intent to implicate the audience into the action of the play, and even his simplest attempts, such as leaving the houselights up in the auditorium during the performance, were designed to put the audience inside the world of the play.

To unify the contradictory and diverse elements of his productions, Meyerhold used music. It established a rhythm, which he had observed in opera, and made it impossible for actors only to enact events or psychological motivations; accompanied by music, the actor had to act the score itself. The result was a unity in movement and gesture that Meyerhold had seen in the performances of opera singer Fyodor Chaliapin in which "thanks to pantomime and movements of the actor, ruled by the musical design, the illusory becomes real, the expression which hovered in time is materialized in space."[10]

In studying commedia, Meyerhold found striking contrasts between the three-dimensional realistic portraits of character typical of the Moscow Art Theatre, and the few defining details of the stock commedia characters. From 1910 onward, commedia "became the central inspiration in his quest for new formulas to combat realism."[11] This was apparent in his productions of both old and new plays, and especially in the acting techniques he developed. He wrote that the improvisations of commedia had a "firm basis of faultless technique,"[12] and he hoped to recreate the actor in the style of the medieval strolling troubador, the *cabotin*, as he explained in his seminal essay, "The Fairground Booth." He wrote that the "cabotin is a strolling player; the cabotin is a kinsman to the mime, the histrion, and the juggler; the cabotin can work miracles with his technical mastery; the cabotin keeps alive the traditions of the true art of acting."[13]

Explaining that the Russian theatre needed to be saved from its desire to become the servant of literature, Meyerhold argued that we must spare nothing to restore to the stage "the cult of cabotinage in its broadest sense."[14] The purpose of the techniques of the *cabotin* and "the commedia and the mime is to transport the spectator to a world of make-believe, entertaining him on the way there with the brilliance of his technical skill."[15] To educate the modern Russian actor in this direction, he opened The Meyerhold Studio in 1913. Its curriculum included a course called "Methods of Staging Commedia dell'Arte Performances," and although he didn't teach it himself, Meyerhold required his actors to take it. He insisted on the highest level of technical skill so that the actors could serve the needs of both the play and the director's concept.

At the studio and in his productions, Meyerhold, like Craig, emphasized the close kinship of the comic and the tragic revealed through masks, improvisation, symbols, puppets, and movement. In 1912, a year after Craig devoted two complete numbers of *The Mask* to commedia, Meyerhold wrote: "The new *theatre of masks* will. . .build its repertoire according to the laws of the fairground booth, where entertainment always proceeds instruction and where movement is prized more highly than words."[16] Later, in his journal *The Love for Three Oranges* (1914-1916), written under his pseudonym Doctor Dapertutto, he continued to promote the significance of the "theatre of the mask" which:

> has always been a fairground show, and the idea of acting based on the apotheosis of the mask, gesture and movement is indivisible from the idea of the travelling show. Those concerned in reforming the contemporary theatre dream of introducing principles of the fairground booth into the theatre. However, the sceptics believe that the revival of the principles of the fairground booth is being obstructed by the cinematograph.[17]

Meyerhold acknowledged that the "theatre of the mask" had been banished from the modern stage, but its principles could be found in "temporary refuge in the French cabarets, the German Überbrettl, the English music halls and the ubiquitous varietes."[18] Less outspokenly opposed to literary drama than Craig, Meyerhold placed more value on movement and visual elements than on the verbal aspects. As he said, audiences of commedia "came not so much to listen to dialogue as to watch the wealth of movement, club blows, dizzy leaps, and all the whole range of tricks native to the theatre."

The road to a return of the theatre as art, for Meyerhold, passed through an understanding of commedia and its emphasis on the centrality of the actor, who combined the skills of the mime, the athlete, and the improvisor. "I will never renounce the right to stimulate an actor to improvise,"[19] he wrote, and added that the "actor of the new theater must establish an entire canon of technical devices such as he will discover by studying principles of acting in truly theatrical eras of the past."[20] It was not Meyerhold's aim, however, to separate the actor from the other production elements; he hoped to unify them by supplying "*every means to assist the actor to blend his soul with that of the playwright and reveal it through the soul of the director.*"[21]

One of the most important means of liberating the actor, he reasoned, was to return to the mask. Like Craig, he had studied commedia history in some depth, and, also like Craig, Meyerhold was not truly an antiquarian. He seemed never to have used an exact recreation of a commedia mask, but was instead interested in the ambiguity and complexity that the wearing of a mask supplied the actor in the construction of a character. While obscuring facial expressions, the mask permitted a chameleonic diversity in the personality barely hidden under the mask. Drawing his examples from commedia, Meyerhold explained that

> The mask enables the spectator to see not only the actual Arlecchino before him but all the Arlecchinos who live in his memory. Through the mask the spectator sees every person who bears the merest resemblance to the character. But is it the mask alone which serves as the mainspring for all the enchanting plots of the theatre?
>
> No, it takes the actor with his art of gesture and movement to transport the spectator to the fairy-tale kingdom where the bluebird flies, where the wild beasts talk, where Arlecchino, the loafer and knave sprung from subterranean forces, is reborn as a clown who performs the most astonishing tricks. Arlecchino is an equilibrist, almost a tight-rope walker. He can leap with amazing agility. His improvised pranks astonish the spectator with hyperbolical improbability beyond even our satirists' dreams. The actor is a dancer who can dance a graceful monferrina as well as a hearty English jig. The actor can turn tears to laughter in a few seconds. He bears the fat Doctor on his shoulders, yet prances about the stage with no apparent effort. Now he is soft and malleable, now he is awkward and inflexible. The actor can command a thousand different intonations, yet he never employs them to impersonate definite characters, preferring to use them merely to embellish his range of gestures and movements. The actor can speak quickly when playing a rogue, slowly and sing-song when playing a pedant. With his body he can describe geometrical figures on the stage, then sometimes he leaps, happy and free as a bird in the sky. The actor's face may be a death mask, yet he is able to distort it and bend his body to such a pose that the death mask comes to life.

For Meyerhold's actor, the mask supplied a necessary level of detachment from emotion that would permit his actor to "act" as well as to "be." Quite obviously, the mask required the development of a sophisticated level of physical dexterity from the actor and permitted the body to express and react in contrast with the fixed expression. His emphasis on movement, coupled with the skillful manipulation of the mask, meant that the actor "who has mastered the art of gesture and movement (herein lies the power!) manipulates his masks in such a way that the spectator is never in any doubt about the character he is watching: whether he is the foolish buffoon from Bergamo or the Devil."[22]

Movement and gesture for Meyerhold included a specific form of choreographed pantomime which was controlled by musical rhythms. "Acting is melody, directing is harmony,"[23] he wrote, and added that a performance could only achieve perfection and precision if "the rhythm of the music and the rhythm on the stage are perfectly synchronized."[24] Typically, he rejected plays that consisted chiefly of ideological debates and used pantomime, controlled by music, as an alternative to words. "The mime stops the mouth of the rhetorician who belongs not on the stage but in the pulpit; the juggler reveals the total self-sufficiency of the actor's skill with the expressiveness of his gestures and the language of his movements -- not only in the dance but in his every step,"[25] he explained, emphasizing the need to depart from formally scripted plays. The audience of a pantomime becomes less interested in plot than in

> the manner in which the actor's free inspiration manifests itself through his sole desire *to dominate* the stage, which he himself has built, decorated and lit; to dominate, carried along by improvisations unexpected even to himself. What does it mean to transform oneself, to lose oneself in the character? What does it mean to reveal always oneself through a host of different characters? Pantomime excites not through what is concealed within it but by how it is created, by the framework which confines its heart, by the skill of the actor revealed through it.[26]

Meyerhold was equally fascinated with the grotesque, which to him implied a mocking attitude toward life, and the mixture of seemingly uncomplementary qualities with an exaggeration of the contrast between tragic and comic elements.[27] He wrote that the "grotesque does not recognize the *purely* debased or the *purely* exalted. The grotesque mixes opposites, consciously creating harsh incongruity and *relying solely on its own originality.*"[28] He found that his notion of the grotesque was inextricably mixed with his idea of theatricalism in the broadest sense.

In Meyerhold's view, the grotesque created the potential for the actor and director to add a level of commentary to the theatrical proceedings that would, presumably, deeply engage the audience. He sought inspirations for grotesque elements in commedia, and found them in the malicious and violent commedia figures and deformed dwarves drawn by Callot, the Venetian street comedies of Goldoni, and the *fiabe* of Gozzi. He also sensed the opportunity to deepen "life's outward appearance to the point where it ceases to appear merely natural."[29]   Meyerhold's understanding of the grotesque not only informed his productions, it also anticipated the *teatro grottesco* movement in Italy.

Meyerhold first met commedia in performance in 1903, when he performed in a circus melodrama called *The Acrobats*, by Austrian dramatist Franz von Schönthan.   This play impressed contemporary critics with its realistic depiction of backstage life. Meyerhold's performance as Landowski, a tragic clown, was judged outstanding. This character proved to be an embryonic vision of Meyerhold's Pierrot, which he brought to full flower in Blok's *The Fairground Booth* and later in *Carnaval*, Mikhail Fokine's ballet set to Robert Schumann's commedic music. The staging of *The Acrobats* featured a few elements which became Meyerholdian signatures. Most notable was his location of the action between two audiences: the actual theatre audience and an imaginary one for the circus-within-the-play. Throughout his career,

Meyerhold sought new ways to bring the actor and the spectator together, and he made the forestage a commonly shared place which belonged equally to performer and audience.

As many commedists would, Meyerhold viewed Pierrot as the butt of life's cruelest jokes. His use of numerous commedia masks in his productions, as well as his commedic transformation of characters into universal human symbols, however, had as much to do with his idea of the dichotomy existing between the actor and his role as it did with his imitation and interpretation of commedia. Here he foreshadows Brecht's *Verfremdungseffect* (theory of alienation or estrangement), the notion that the actor remains an actor who "shows" his character instead of becoming the character. Experimentation with many techniques assisted Meyerhold's actors to create the illusion of breaking down the barrier posed by fourth-wall Realism. He abolished the use of a front curtain in his 1906 production of Ibsen's *Ghosts*, and continued the practice in many productions. Beginning with *The Fairground Booth*, he regularly kept the house lights up in the auditorium during the entire performance, locating the audience directly in the play's milieu, and he also exposed as many of the working parts of the stage as possible. The flies, ropes, and lights were all visible, and the heavy stylization of the acting made it clear that extreme theatricality was its conscious intent. These techniques, as well, were later employed by Brecht.

Meyerhold stated that the "first impulse toward determining the path my art was to take"[30] came in *The Fairground Booth*, by poet Alexander Blok,[31] which opened on December 30, 1906, at Vera Komissarzhevskaya's Theatre in St. Petersburg.[32] The audience was vociferously divided over both this ironic little Pierrot play and its production -- some cheered loudly, others booed. Meyerhold recognized no such division. For him, *The Fairground Booth* was a coherent pastiche of grotesquerie, buffoonery, and irony played out by faithless and contradictory characters inspired by commedia.

It was Meyerhold himself who had read Blok's poem "The Fairground Booth" and persuaded the poet to make a play of it. Establishing a tone that has become characteristic for modern commedia, the poem effectively captures the sinister, grotesque, and playful elements of a child's fairy tale. With Meyerhold's help, Blok was able to maintain the essence of his poem in the play, which offered several fragmented scenes, filled with contradictory meanings and allusions. He respected Meyerhold's acting and directing skill, and dedicated *The Fairground Booth* to him, although he once sardonically wrote that modern directors treat written plays as mere *scenarii*, onto which the director imposes his vision, and to which the actor adds his improvisations.

Although similarities exist between Meyerhold's staging of *The Fairground Booth* and Craig's *The Masque of Love* and Barker and Housman's *Prunella*, neither of the two earlier English productions equals Meyerhold's blending of cynical irony and absurd buffoonery, to achieve an effect that became typical of modern commedia. Craig and Barker both used music to accentuate the mood and unify the elements of their productions, but Meyerhold went a step further. Using Mikhail Kuzmin's[33] music, he set a rhythmic tempo on which the entire performance floated. It is, however, the political and socially transforming qualities of the play and its production that give it its place in the new Russian theatre. In a letter written on December 22, 1906, Blok encouraged Meyerhold about these aspects:

> *Any* puppet show, mine not excluded, has ambitions to be a *battering ram*, to smash a breach in dead matter: the puppet show runs into, goes to meet, and shows up the dreadful, lewd embraces of this matter, as though offering itself as a bait, so that stupid, dull matter is lured on, begins to gain confidence, starts to make advances in its turn; and THIS is when "the hour or the mystery" should strike. Matter has been tricked and now she is weaker and submissive; in this sense I do "accept the world" -- the world with its dullness and immobility and dead, dry colours, but only in order to trick the bony old hag and to make her young again: in the embraces of a jester and puppet-master,

the old world grows prettier, younger, and its eyes become transparent, fathomless.[34]

In *The Fairground Booth*, Blok presents the typical commedia love triangle involving Harlequin, Pierrot and Columbine. As the plot unwinds, he also attacks the conventions of the realistic stage with its foundation in illusionism and the overly romanticized qualities of Symbolism. Blok's character, The Author, periodically forces his way onto the stage protesting the "improvisations" marring his script:

> I never dressed my characters up in buffoon's dress. Unbeknown to me they re-enacted some kind of ancient legend. I acknowledge neither legends, nor myths, nor other such vulgarities. And especially, the allegorical playing upon words: it is unseemly to call a woman's braid the scythe of Death! This will corrupt the female estate. Gracious ladies and gentlemen. . .
>
> [*A hand poked out from behind the curtain grabs the Author by the scruff of the neck. With a yelp, he disappears into the wings.*][35]

Meyerhold's own performance as Pierrot ousted many traditional aspects of the character. Retaining the sadness and universality of Pierrot, Meyerhold completely rid the character of the preciousness and delicacy that had often been incorporated in nineteenth century interpretations. He was detached, ironic, and impudent, yet totally engaging to his audience at the same time.

In the play, Pierrot awaits the coming of Columbine at a masked ball, but when she arrives, everyone except Pierrot recognizes her as the embodiment of Death. As the guests and a chorus of mystics flee, they warn Pierrot of Death's arrival, but Pierrot refuses to be frightened: "I don't listen to fairy tales. I am a simple man. You won't fool me. This is Columbine. This is my fiancée."[36] Actress Valentina Petrovna Verigina, a member of the cast, recalled that in response to Blok's stage direction, "Pierrot awakes from his reverie and brightens up," Meyerhold added the gesture of flapping his sleeves, expressing "the dawning hope of the clown."[37] The simple eloquence of this gesture made it appear that "he was listening to a song being sung by his heart of its own free will. He wore a strange expression, gazing intently into his own soul."[38] An even more powerful impression was made when Columbine/Death comes to claim Pierrot, but as they are about to embrace, the scenery flies away and the actors scamper into the wings. The curtain falls, leaving only Pierrot, who stares at the audience reproachfully before playing a sad tune on his pipe.

Meyerhold remained constant in his enthusiasm for commedia techniques as he had discovered and employed them in *The Fairground Booth*. But when the play was revived in 1914, Blok had fallen out of sympathy with both the traditions of commedia and Meyerhold's directing style, preferring instead the realistic theatre of Stanislavsky.

Four years after *The Fairground Booth*, Meyerhold staged Arthur Schnitzler's *The Veil of Pierrette* at the Interlude House in St. Petersburg, on October 9, 1910, under the title *Columbine's Scarf*. The change of title symbolizes the liberties Meyerhold took with Schnitzler's play. He had faithfully adhered to Blok's stage directions with *The Fairground Booth*, but with *Columbine's Scarf* he radically altered the original in an effort "to banish the cloying sweetness so often associated with pantomime and create a chilling grotesque in the manner of E.T.A. Hoffmann."[39] He emphasized the idea that human beings are puppets battered by the winds of Fate and other powers beyond their understanding. His adaptation, described here by an eyewitness, contains similarities with *The Fairground Booth*:

> The frivolous Columbine, betrothed to Harlequin, spends a last evening with her devoted Pierrot. As usual, she deceives him, swearing she loves him. Pierrot proposes a suicide pact and himself drinks poison. Columbine lacks the courage to follow him and flees in terror to the wedding ball where the guests await her impatiently. The ball begins, then whilst an old-fashioned quadrille is playing, Pierrot's flapping white sleeve is glimpsed first through the windows, then

LIVERPOOL JOHN MOORES UNIVERSITY
LEARNING SERVICES

through the doors. The dances, now fast, now slow, turn into an awful nightmare, with strange Hoffmanesque characters whirling to the time of a huge-headed Kapellmeister, who sits on a high stool and conducts four weird musicians. Columbine's terror reaches such a pitch that she can hide it no longer and she rushes back to Pierrot. Harlequin follows her and when he sees Pierrot's corpse he is convinced of his bride's infidelity. He forces her to dine before the corpse of the love-stricken Pierrot. Then he leaves, bolting the door fast. In vain Columbine tries to escape from her prison, from the ghastly dead body. Gradually, she succumbs to madness; she whirls in a frenzied dance, then finally drains the deadly cup and falls lifeless beside Pierrot.

The Hoffmannesque grotesquerie was heightened by the scene designs of Nikolai Sapunov, one of Meyerhold's most effective collaborators, who had previously designed *The Fairground Booth*. Music, composed by Ernst Dohnanyi, again played a significant unifying role, particularly in the ball scene.

Eugene Vakhtangov, a protege of Stanislavsky's whose mature style was as broadly theatrical as Meyerhold's, saw *Columbine's Scarf* and wrote in his diary: "What a genius is this director! Every one of his productions is new theater. Every one of his productions could launch a whole new trend."[40] Vakhtangov directed his definitive production, *Princess Turandot*, in 1922, and it clearly owed much to his admiration of Meyerhold's daring theatricality, as well as of commedia.

On November 9, 1910, within a month of the opening of *Columbine's Scarf*, Meyerhold presented Molière's *Don Juan* at the Alexandrinsky Theatre. In it Meyerhold "tried to interpret the character of Don Juan according to the principles of the theatre of the mask,"[41] since the character of Don Juan offered a multiplicity of contradictory attitudes and emotions. His face was a mask which "embodies all the dissoluteness, unbelief, cynicism and pretensions of a gallant of the court of Le Roi-Soleil; then we see the mask of the author-accuser; then the nightmarish mask which stifled the author himself, the agonizing mask he was forced to wear at court performances and in front of his perfidious wife."[42]

This production of *Don Juan* revealed Meyerhold's on-going experimentation with the relationship between audience and actor. Meyerhold's desire to abolish the front curtain was carried to an extreme by designer Alexander Golovin, who decorated the entire auditorium in decadent Baroque tapestries and ornament, making the entire theatre, in effect, an integral part of the action of the stage. He cast the popular character actor Konstantin Varlamov as Sganarelle because of his faith in the actor's considerable comic experience, which permitted especially rich opportunities for improvisation. Varlamov's asides, many made directly to individual audience members, brilliantly accentuated Meyerhold's idea of the closer relationship between the actor and his audience.

In the years prior to the Russian Revolution, Meyerhold never strayed from commedia experimentation for very long. *Harlequin, The Marriage Broker,* by Volmar Liustsinius (pseudonym of Vladimir Solovev), opened on November 8, 1911, at the Assembly Rooms of the Nobility in St. Petersburg. A pantomime written specifically to promote a revival of commedia, *Harlequin, The Marriage Broker* drew its visual inspiration from the drawings of Jacques Callot and the simple stages of traditional commedia. The crude but brightly-colored setting featured a backdrop roughly painted as a moonlit sky, with rooftop below, for a scene in which Harlequin climbed onto the roof to throw stars into the sky.

The choice of wordless pantomime in *Harlequin, The Marriage Broker* was a culmination for Meyerhold, a chance to combine many of the elements he had stressed for a decade in his theories. Uniquely, it was performed in three different styles. The first was an antiquarian recreation of commedia; the second, a charade in modern dress; and the third, an exotic mixture in which the conventions of commedia were ritualized into symbolic images. In this last variation, instead of traditional costumes, the actors appeared in tails, dinner jackets, and evening gowns. The only additions were the "essential props of the *commedia dell'arte*: a mask, a tambourine, a stick for Harlequin, a hat -- just enough to suggest the character in question."[43]

As with *The Fairground Booth*, *Harlequin, The Marriage Broker* featured commedia masks coupled with the appearance of The Author, who delivered a prologue and an epilogue. The Author also appeared in a scene in which he and Harlequin race through the auditorium, breaking through the fourth wall and stressing, once again, the connection between actor and audience. It was essential to Meyerhold to emphasize the theatrical; this emphasis was, for him, the only way to depict the complexities of life and the inner struggles of his characters: "To show life on the stage means *to perform* life; serious matters may become amusing and amusing matters may seem tragic."[44]

Shortly after he presented *Harlequin, The Marriage Broker*, Meyerhold opened his Studio Theatre school in St. Petersburg. The curriculum for the school included an emphasis on the techniques of commedia and its derivatives. During the first year, Vladimir Solovev taught a course on commedia, and it became a staple of the school's curriculum. The basic course of study for the Studio in 1916-1917, for example, included classes on stage movement, technical aspects of production, musical recitation in drama, application of traditional devices of the seventeenth and eighteenth centuries to the modern theatre, and the principles of Italian improvised comedy. Meyerhold's school, like his productions, aimed at defeating the predominance of the realistic theatre through the use of commedic techniques.

For his elaborate and mystical production, *Masquerade* by Mikhail Lermontov, which was produced on February 25, 1917, at the Alexandrinsky Theatre in St. Petersburg, Meyerhold continued his experimentation with masks, as he had in *Don Juan*. Although he typically exposed the tricks of the stage and stripped it down to its essentials, in *Masquerade* he demonstrated his equal mastery of spectacle. The elaborate and ominous settings by

Alexander Golovin were obviously inspired by the Venetian carnivals painted by Pietro Longhi. Meyerhold focused on the play's central character -- the sinister Unknown Man, who was dressed in a black cloak with a white mask, in the manner of eighteenth century street carnivals. The character became a demonic Pierrot lurking about the edges of the production providing ironic commentary on the proceedings.

At the outbreak of the Revolution, Meyerhold immediately joined the Communist Party, and put considerable effort into theatrical activity in support of the Revolution. He became head of the Theater Division of his People's Commissariat of Education in 1922, and for a year he taught acting and directing for several new theatre groups in Moscow.[45] One of his outstanding productions during this era was Vladimir Mayakovsky's *Mystery-Bouffe*, which opened on November 17, 1918, in Petrograd. The satire of contemporary life in the play did not prevent Meyerhold from employing clowning techniques and circus elements, to add a timeless universal slant to a pointedly contemporary political tract. His characters remained symbols, and though they were in modern dress, Norris Houghton observed that they were "completely depersonalized representatives of type. He wipes all expression from their faces, except the permanent stamp which their make-up gives to them. They are empty masked automatons. Here the Sovietized Commedia dell'Arte is most apparent."[46]

Meyerhold's definitive production of Fernand Crommelynck's[47] *The Magnanimous Cuckold* was staged on April 25, 1922, at his Moscow Workshop, against the backdrop of the memorable constructivist setting by L.S. Popova and V.V. Liutse. In it, Meyerhold solidified his acting theory that has since become known as biomechanics. This term, so typical of the Constructivists fascination with the relationship between man and machine, described an acting style that borrowed heavily from Meyerhold's understanding of the *cabotin*, ancient mimes, acrobats, jugglers, circus, and commedia.

In the same year, Meyerhold's production of the gloomy comedy *The Death of Tarelkin* by Alexander Sukhovo-Kobylin was staged in a circus environment, and mocked some of his most famous productions. He transformed the drab play into a tragic-farce in which Tarelkin, a minor and forgotten functionary, is accidentally reported dead. Focusing on Tarelkin's struggle through endless bureaucratic red tape to reinstate himself among the living, Meyerhold looks back at Gogol and anticipates Dario Fo's *Accidental Death of an Anarchist* when he interpreted Tarelkin as "a merry prankster who makes fools out of the police. He flies across the entire width of the stage on a cable, like an acrobat, in order to get away from the police."[48]

For the remaining fifteen years of his career, Meyerhold worked with his own company in Moscow, where a few of his remaining productions drew on the influence of commedia. Gogol's *The Inspector General*, adapted by Meyerhold and M. Korenev, opened on December 9, 1926. The production was something of a return to Meyerhold's earlier fascination with Hoffmannesque grotesque. Through his use of biomechanics and commedic elements, he was able to arouse emotional reactions through the audiences' associative powers: "A cigar or a fan in the hand of an actor is no longer simply a cigar or a fan, but a symbol for all the qualities which the observer can associate with those objects and their users."[49]

Although Meyerhold's productions became increasingly more contemporary and obvious in their political implications, they retained their emotional power through his use of the commedic notion that characters can be seen as depersonalized human symbols. The last of his productions to make striking use of this idea, as well as commedia, was Peter Illyich Tchaikovsky's opera, *Queen of Spades* (1890), with scenario and text, by Meyerhold and V. Stenich, after the Alexander Pushkin story. It opened on January 25, 1935, at the Maly Opera in Leningrad. In a scene set in a music room, guests at a party are being entertained by a pantomime with set and costumes inspired by Callot. Meyerhold juxtaposed the pantomime and the action of the play's characters in an absurd game truly worthy of commedia. He himself explained:

> During the pantomime in which the plot revolves around a note which the heroine, Smeraldina, gives to the hero, Tartaglia, we see Hermann, sitting behind Liza, press a note into her hand. Smeraldina passes the note to Tartaglia at the same time as Hermann passes his note to Liza. The episode is reflected as though in a mirror.[50]

Despite his extraordinary achievements, government initiated criticism of Meyerhold, and what were termed his "formalist" productions, mounted under Stalin's rule, and on January 8, 1938, his theatre was closed down by official decree. In a touching gesture of goodwill, Stanislavsky immediately offered his long-time artistic nemesis the opportunity to direct for the Stanislavsky Opera Theater. Meyerhold took the job, but it proved to be only a temporary reprieve. He was arrested on June 20, 1939, only days after giving a speech in which he is said to have forcefully defended his work and his theatre. Following his arrest, Meyerhold completely disappeared, and it was many years before it was revealed that he had been executed in prison on February 2, 1940. He was posthumously "rehabilitated" in 1955, and with the subsequent publication of many of his essays, as well as increased scholarly interest in his productions, his extraordinary theatre work has become familiar to contemporary theatre artists.

Commedia in Russia After Meyerhold

Although Meyerhold's commedic theatre dominated the Russian anti-realistic stage during the first thirty years of the twentieth century, many other Russian playwrights, actors, and directors found commedia similarly rejuvenating and enlivening. Commedists Alexander Blok and Mikhail Kuzmin, who had collaborated with Meyerhold, were part of the burgeoning

Symbolist movement which took root in Russia after 1900. Many Symbolists were drawn both to the spirit and the techniques suggested by commedia. Poet and dramatist Fyodor Sologub (1863-1927) influenced both Meyerhold and Blok, and was, in turn, influenced by them. He was fascinated by masks as symbolic embodiments of the tragedy and comedy of life, noting that every "earthly face and every earthly body is only a guise, only a marionette destined for one playing each, for an earthly tragicomedy -- a marionette set in motion for word, gesture, laughter, and tears."[51] The masked actor created for Sologub a mystical and ambiguous world, where

> Tragic horror and the laughter of the buffoon stir the fraying but still seductive veils of our world with equally irresistible force -- the world that seemed so familiar to us, all at once, in the fluidity of play, becomes astonishing, dreadful, overwhelming or repulsive. Neither the tragic nor the comic mask will deceive the attentive spectator any more than, in enchanting him, they have deceived the participant in the play, or will deceive, in admitting him to the sacrament, the participant in mystery.

Not all early twentieth century Russian writers,[52] even the Symbolists, however, were true believers in the anchoring influence of commedia. Leonid Andreyev (1871-1919) was an uneasy Symbolist and, along with Blok, one of the few defectors from the ranks of modern Russian commedia worshippers. He initially resisted the realistic theatre and what he viewed as the resultant impoverishment of dramatic literature. Proclaiming that the plays of Chekhov were being given an unwarranted realistic treatment at the Moscow Art Theatre, "which knows only *things*. Who needs things?"[53] He resisted the all-powerful director in Meyerhold's mode and called for a stylized drama. His plays -- *The Life of Man* (1906), *Tsar Hunger*(1907), *The Black Maskers* (1908), *Anathema* (1909), *The Ocean* (1910), and, *He Who Gets Slapped* (1915), which is set in a circus and uses the image of the clown symbolically -- all owe something to commedia. It is *He Who Gets Slapped* which most obviously combines commedic elements with traditions of Russian folk puppet theatre, ritualized Oriental drama, and circus. Despite this, however, Andreyev found the pervasive interest in commedia as deadly conventional as the "things" of the realistic stage:

> Note how the *commedia dell'arte* characters Harlequin and Pantaloon, congealed and set once and for all, have found a haven in our ordinary drama, hidden behind such immobile and frozen masks as *romantic lead, simpleton, ingenue, noble father, raisonneur,* etc. Always the same pack of cards, which can be used to play different games -- but the king is always king, the knave always knave, and the six of clubs never anything but the six of clubs. All conventional, all based on pretense, all acting![54]

In looking at what he considered the failure of the Symbolist movement, Andreyev pointed to a stage tradition that was loaded with "contraband." Both Realism and Theatricalism as they existed only compromised with existing stage traditions, instead of reforming them:

> stylized figures, barefoot dancers, nameless enigmatic personages, galvanized (but not resuscitated) Pierrots and Harlequins, symbolic blind men, symbolic deaf and dumb, symbolic devils, gnomes, fairies and frogs. The blind men tripped over the sets, the devils sank without trace, Harlequin groaned like a living being, barefoot dancers looked lugubrious, a very fat person tried unsuccessfully to turn into a shadow. . And the whole naive masquerade meant only one thing: thought is suffocating in your theatre! -- the soul is dying on those boards of yours![55]

Another Symbolist, Valery Bryusov (1873-1924), hoped that the theatre would take a step toward "the spiritualization of art, toward overcoming the fatal contradictions between the essence and the surface of art."[56] Although he was not truly a commedist, his "psychodrama," *The Wayfarer* (1910), paved the way for the commedic monodramas of Nikolai Evreinov (1879-1953).

Working in the theatres of pre-Revolutionary St. Petersburg, Evreinov viewed theatre as "illusion (lies like truth) and theatre as an event (a present-tense reality transcending the boundaries of art)."[57] In his own works, and in plays by others that he staged, he made use of highly theatrical elements from carnival and commedia. He identified strongly with the central characters of his own plays in whom he created a Christ-Harlequin duality similar to Craig's Zany-Priest.

Evreinov was especially touched by commedia and made a strong personal identification with it. At the age of thirteen he ran away from home to join the circus and as an adult he would dress as a clown for dinner parties in his home. "I am Harlequin and as Harlequin I shall die,"[58] he wrote, and his "Commedia of the Soul" evolved from his perception that elements of commedia, especially the mix of comic and tragic aspects, masks, and anarchic play, could inspire new revelations about the self. These commedic ideas could be seen clearly in Evreinov's concept of "monodrama," which meant that all actions and characters of the play are seen through the eyes of the hero/protagonist (the ego). The audience is the alter-ego, and all external and internal action blend in a way that makes it possible for the audience to identify itself with the protagonist. Thus, both the drama of the play and the drama of the spectator's personal life is transformed. He wrote that the "artist of the stage must on no occasion show objects on the *drama's* boards as they are in themselves -- only when represented as experienced by or reflecting someone's *ego*, his torment, his joy, his wrath or indifference, will they become organic parts of that desired whole which in truth we are right to call total drama."[59]

Like Craig and Meyerhold, Evreinov was impressed by the "barefoot dancer," Isadora Duncan. A central theme of his plays is the betrayal of love by Woman, which is also a typical theme of traditional commedia, and particularly the nineteenth century romantic vision of it. To Evreinov, Duncan was the embodiment of his understanding of "Woman" in the commedic tradition; she was a modern Columbine. He also made theatre itself a subject of his drama, and the idea of make-believe was essential in his plays:

Everything in the theatre is, and *must be*, conventional. There exists at the moment of theatrical perception a sort of silent agreement, a sort of *tacitus consensus*, between the spectator and the player whereby the former undertakes to assume a certain attitude, and no other, towards the "make-believe" acting, while the latter undertakes to live up to this assumed attitude as best he can.[60]

However, Evreinov felt that conventionalized "systems" of acting, particularly Stanislavsky's, undermined the instinctive and natural abilities of the actor. Acting, after all, was a basic human instinct: "Theatricality is pre-aesthetic, that is to say, more primitive and more fundamental than our aesthetic feeling, or feelings."

Holding that his soul was "nothing but an actor constantly changing his costumes and masks,"[61] he believed in dreams as the drama of an individual's life. Like Craig, who insisted that the theatre supply a "sense of being beyond reality,"[62] Evreinov proposed that

The dream is a drama of our own invention. It is a monodramatic theatre in which one sees oneself in an imaginary reality as if on some gigantic cinematographic film. And what thrilling plays are sometimes staged upon the ethereal boards of this playhouse! Indeed, it isn't for nothing that Maeterlinck drops in his "Death" the wise aphorism: "Each one of us, while dreaming, is a real Shakespeare."[63]

Like many of his contemporaries, Evreinov rejected the realistic stagings of the Moscow Art Theatre, and satirized them in his 1915 play *The Fourth Wall*. He proclaimed that "theatre has *its own truths, theatrical truths,* which have nothing to do with the everyday truths of our reality."[64] He called for a return to "theatricality," which meant for him a return to the earliest manifestations of theatricality: masks, rites, and rituals which liberate the artists of theatre from "the fetters of reality. . . .without theatricality we would have only a duplication of life. . . .But the aim of art is the creation of new values."[65]

Evreinov's earliest harlequinade, *The Power of Charms* (1899), was a primitive attempt at commedic theatre that led to his most important works, which were produced at The Ancient Theatre (1907-1912)[66] and The Crooked Mirror Theatre (1910-1917). At these theatres, he directed many of his own plays, as well as those of other authors. *The Merry Death* (1908), a bittersweet harlequinade, was staged for the first time on April 13, 1909, at the Gay Theatre (and revived in 1911 and 1912). Its plot deals with Harlequin, who is bedridden with an illness and has been informed by a fortune-teller that he will die at midnight. Having invited Columbine, the wife of Pierrot, to dinner, Harlequin attempts to persuade Pierrot not to be jealous. Pierrot is jealous, however, and decides to move the clock forward so that Harlequin will die sooner. When Columbine appears she is surprised at Pierrot's passive reaction. A lamp symbolizing the life force begins to flicker as Death appears in the guise of an attractive young girl. Harlequin gives her the flickering lamp, which blacks out, and in the remaining moonlight Pierrot declaims: "Let the curtain down; the farce is over!"

At about the time he wrote *The Merry Death*, Evreinov was influenced by the theories of Craig, which were becoming widely known in Russia. In 1908, Craig commenced work with Stanislavsky on a production of *Hamlet*, which was first performed in 1911. Despite the obvious differences between Craig's theories and Stanislavsky's methods, the production was, unconsciously, a tentative application of Evreinov's monodramatic theory, although missing any obvious connection to commedia. Craig's über-marionette and Nietzsche's superman also contributed to his understanding of monodrama. In his plays, the monodramatic was inherently theatrical and commedic, and his central character was Harlequin, the super-clown. The plays, which he called "tragi-farces," juxtaposed the images of Harlequin the trickster with Christ the Savior. In *The Presentation of Love* (1909) and *The Theatre of the Soul* (1912) he continued to experiment with his notion of monodrama. The latter is an interesting but didactic play, which begins with a professor explaining that the soul consists of three parts: reason, emotion, and the eternal (or subliminal). Evreinov's concepts culminated most effectively in his best-known play, *The Chief Thing* (1919). Life as a dream, or an illusion, was the core of *The Chief Thing*, as he explained in his preface to the published play:

> Since we are unable to give happiness to the unfortunate, we must at least give them the illusion of happiness.

> "This is the chief thing," teaches Paraclete, whose name means advocate, helper, comforter.

> "I am an actor myself," he says, "yet my field is not the stage of the theatre, but the stage of life, to which I call all masters in the art of creating illusions of happiness."

> "With all my heart do I believe in the mission of the actor who comes down from the boards into the impenetrable darkness of life with the weapons of his art. For it is my earnest conviction that the world will be regenerated through the actor and his magic art."

> The faith of Paraclete is the moving principle of my entire play "The Chief Thing." In the pragmatic conception of the hero of this play -- the final Truth demanded by Morality, cannot be incompatible with social justice. *Love for humanity requires a benevolent theatrilization of life*; the latter requires artistic masks, while masks are based on deception. But in this sort of deception is hidden the Truth which is identical with good. Above the stern laws of life there is the higher law of Love which is personified in Paraclete.[67]

The Chief Thing was a major success in the Soviet Union and it became one of the few plays by Evreinov to have a successful stage life outside of the Soviet Union. It was given major productions by Pirandello in Rome in 1924, at New York's Theatre Guild, and in Charles Dullin's Théâtre de l'Atelier in 1926.

Evreinov's productions at the Crooked Mirror included an extremely diverse collection of pantomimes, "grotesques," and vaudevilles, as well as classics and contemporary European dramas. In 1920, he wrote and staged an extraordinary production, *The Storming of the Winter Palace*, in which he experimented with reconstructing the role of the spectator, extending beyond

Meyerhold by using the audience as participants in the production. Using hundreds of audience members as revolutionaries, he recreated a well-known, emotionally-charged moment in Russian history. Evreinov emigrated to Paris in 1925, where he lived until his death, and contented himself with occasional foreign productions of his work and some theoretical writings.

Another contemporary of Meyerhold's and Evreinov's, Alexander Tairov (1885-1950), founded Moscow's Kamerny Theatre in 1914. With his wife, Alice Koonen, as leading lady, he staged a wide variety of modern and classic plays. He especially admired Craig, whom he called "the Pope," [68] but he was haunted by Craig's disappointments, and "his exasperated apotheosis of the marionette."[69] Like many commedists, Tairov resisted the over-emphasis placed on dramatic literature, which, he believed, had led to a crisis in acting by making the actor too obedient, even subservient, to the text.

The art of acting was the most difficult, Tairov reasoned, particulary in the contemporary theatre where "dilettantism" was rampant. He agreed with Craig's desire to limit the spread of the theatre's naturalistic tendencies, but he thought Craig went too far when he advocated throwing it out altogether. He also disagreed with Craig's notion of the master artist of the theatre. He thought it unrealistic to expect any single artist to master all of the necessary tasks of the theatre. He hoped, instead, for a collective art based on "Unity, without which of course any work of art is unthinkable."[70] He would work through the actor for the "development of the creative will and the creative fantasy, the ability to entice from it any scenic figure, to call up and control the necessary emotions -- these comprise the internal technique of the actor. The route to it lies for the most part through *improvisation*."[71] Improvisation meant freedom for the actor from the grip of the literary play, for, as he says, "the theatre does not depend organically on literature."[72] Tairov found the notion that literature creates theatre an absurd one:

> Was Meyerhold's beloved commedia dell'arte also created by literature? Or Molière, who really did create a theatre with his own literature (his plays), was he himself not in turn influenced to a significant degree by Scaramouche and his troupe?. . .And was not the literature of Goldoni himself engendered to a significant degree by the theatre of commedia dell'arte? How can one say after this that literature creates theatre?

Less concerned with the opposite poles of comedy and tragedy, Tairov was certain that genuine theatrical action could be found in "the *mystery* and the *harlequinade*. But between these poles it assumes special, original, and unique forms in every play, in every production."[73]

Tairov made use of many commedic elements in his productions. After working with several different companies, he was invited by Konstantin Mardzhanov[74] to stage Schnitzler's *The Veil of Pierrette* at the Free Theatre. In his adaptation of Schnitzler's play, Tairov sought to recreate the light-hearted elements of pantomime as a new and serious form of mime drama. This was a vivid contrast to Meyerhold's 1910 adaptation which played up the play's tragic elements. Seeking a method by which to stage "these flickering forms, these agitating harmonies, these enthralling rhythms,"[75] Tairov looked first to ancient forms of pantomime, but knew instinctively that any attempt at recreation would be hollow. Instead, he examined commedia history, searching for "that which was genuine and unchanging, and from there set out on our own unfamiliar and difficult path."[76]

With this in mind, he found Schnitzler's scenario unsettling in that it called for only "uninteresting illustrative gesture."[77] He aimed to transfer the work to "a plane of the most intense emotion. Then illustrative gestures, conventionalized informative actions, feelings, and words would not be needed. For in moments of maximum emotional strain, *silence* sets in."[78] Pointing out that emotional gesture, with its "power to reveal the true art of theatre, the art of pantomime,"[79] was the desired goal, he wrote that pantomime is a production of such scope, such spiritual revelation that *words die*, and in their stead genuine scenic *action* is born -- scenic action in its primary aspect, the form of which is saturated with intense creative *emotion*, seeking an outlet *in corresponding gesture*.

Tairov believed, as Meyerhold did, that musical accompaniment was necessary in order to achieve the emotional eloquence of pantomime. He used music as a guiding score for the pantomimic actor, who was controlled and supported by the tempo and rhythm of the music. This first commedic experiment "had accomplished only a very small part of what we were capable of."[80] In retrospect, he acknowledged the "significant influence both the naturalistic and the stylistic theatres"[81] had on the production, realizing the vast amount of internal work, which itself "required not months but years, we had further to master a new craft of acting. Only then would we be in a position actually to incarnate our feelings and visions."[82]

The Kamerny Theatre opened its doors for the first time on December 12, 1914, with a highly successful production of Kalidasa's Sanskrit drama, *Shakuntala*. The repertory soon included a highly diverse collection of works, with elements of commedia appearing in Tairov's productions of Goldoni's *The Fan* and Beaumarchais' *The Marriage of Figaro*, both produced in 1915, and Shakespeare's *The Merry Wives of Windsor*, appearing in 1916. *The Marriage of Figaro* particularly emphasized theatricality, virtually recreating the commedic spirit of Beaumarchais' time through the use of an elaborately Baroque environment. During the 1917-1918 season at the Kamerny, Tairov staged *King Harlequin* by R. Lothar and *The Toy Box*, with music by Claude Debussy, under the spell of commedia.

King Harlequin, which opened on November 29, 1917, was a tragi-comic commedia in which Harlequin kills a Prince by throwing him over a cliff during a fight over the affections of Columbine. Harlequin then takes the Prince's place in life, ultimately becoming King. Columbine, believing that Harlequin is gone, realizes that she loves him. Harlequin's band of players are equally unhappy over the apparent death of Harlequin and turn to the King for help. Taking Pantaloon as his servant, Harlequin reveals his true identity only to Pantaloon. The citizens are anxious to crown the new King and Harlequin is taken before the aged and blind Queen Gertrude, who realizes immediately that Harlequin is not her son. Sensing his basic goodness, however, and wishing no grief for her country, she continues the charade and crowns him King. Harlequin finds that being King is difficult, even though he proves to be a compassionate one, refusing to sign any decrees of execution and worrying over the well-being of the peasants. Columbine, having realized her undying love for Harlequin, plots to murder the new King, assuming that he had killed Harlequin. In the final scene, Harlequin returns to his role in a commedia being performed by Pantaloon's troupe at court, and enacts, through pantomime, his own life story beginning with his fight with the Prince. Columbine is overjoyed at the reappearance of Harlequin, and before they run off together, Harlequin declares that it is better to be a good Harlequin than a bad King. The use of extremely simple and grotesque Cubist settings by B.A. Ferdinandov, and an emphasis on the play-within-the-play commedia characters, were bold and saving strokes by Tairov. The sentimentality of the play was thereby lessened, especially the transformation of the commedia characters into timely universal symbols.

Tairov's staging of *The Toy Box,* another pantomime in which he used cubism and commedia, had a colorful, toy-filled setting that emphasized the childish simplicity of the harlequinade. This concept propelled "the artist toward an entirely different composition, sparkling and variegated like the cloak of Harlequin."[83] His memorable touches with the actors included having them move as puppets, in a stiff and awkward pattern typical of a child's doll. Occasional sound effects were used, but the stylized movement set to Debussy's music, and the environment and costumes created a sense of unified rhythm and harmony in the visual and aural elements. He even more successfully achieved this harmony in his next, and most important, commedic production, *Princess Brambilla*, based on the 1820 E.T.A. Hoffmann fable of the same name and visually influenced by Jacques Callot's drawings. *Princess Brambilla* opened on May 4, 1920, and combined elements of grotesque mysticism, carnival, and commedia, Tairov worked from a brief and simple scenario. Flickering chandeliers helped create an hypnotic and disorienting setting for the harlequinade, especially

> in the second act, where a fifteen-minute commedia dell'arte pantomime was integrated into the action of the play. Harlequin is transformed into a scarecrow, cut up into pieces by the Doctor, and his members scattered about the stage to be reassembled "by magic" into the living, dancing Harlequin.[84]

Pantomime was carefully orchestrated to music which, of "all the arts, . . .is the closest to the theatre,"[85] and which was prominently featured in all of Tairov's commedic productions. The light-hearted and highly expressionistic staging emphasized the actor-centered skills of juggling, clowning, and acrobatics, creating "a fantastic capriccio."[86] The visual elements, and the commedia characters, inspired by Callot's drawings, moved him closer to his visual goals. He especially sought modern counterparts for the immediately recognizable costumes of the characters of Pierrot and Harlequin, noting that their

> immortality lies in the fact that they are organically fused with their stage figures; it is as impossible to steal from Harlequin his costumes as it is to strip him of his skin. . . I am not at all suggesting that we restore them. The characters of the contemporary theatre and the theatre of the future are much more complicated than Pierrot and Harlequin, and the costumes for them must of course be different, but they must be constructed according to the same sure principle -- the principle of harmony with the dynamic essence of the scenic figure being created by the actor.[87]

Tairov's highly theatrical style generally led the Kamerny away from modern drama. It was 1923 before they produced any significant modern plays (they had considerable success with Eugene O'Neill's dramas) and it was 1929 before the Kamerny offered a contemporary Soviet play, *Natalia Tarpova*, and it failed. Perhaps this failure at the Kamerny resulted from a lack of commitment, for to Tairov, the time had come for a theatre of "genuine national festivals, for carnivals, for spontaneous and joyful playacting,"[88] and the artists of the theatre must be the first to welcome them "insofar as they touch upon our many-faceted art. But we must have firm knowledge that the means of the theatre, as a self-contained art, are on a completely different level and in different artistic situations."[89] During the mid-1930's, he ran into difficulties with the government and the theatre was placed under the control of a committee. Control was returned to him in 1939, and he continued to run the theatre until 1950, when it was closed permanently. Tairov died later that same year.

Another anti-realist drawn to commedia was actor and director Eugene Vakhtangov (1883-1922), who joined the Moscow Art Theatre company under Stanislavsky, but like Meyerhold, soon found himself at odds with Stanislavsky's methods. Vakhtangov believed that Stanislavsky's approach ended the era of theatrical artificiality because he "started creating a live human being, with a live heart beating and blood running. This man started living a real life and thus left theatre. . . .Now is the time to restore the theatre to theatre again. . . .What I do, I'd like to call *fantastic realism*."[90]

Vakhtangov was no cautious or conservative artist, but he attempted to bridge the highly theatrical concepts of Meyerhold and the realism inherent in Stanislavsky's approach, using elements of both. He envisioned a modern theatre of the common people, proclaiming that art must not be alienated in any way from the people and their ways. Here he parted company with intellectuals and political dramatists, believing that theatre should "seek the soul of the people. In the meeting of these two souls, that of the artist. . .and of the people, a truly national myth may be conceived."[91]

Like Meyerhold, Vakhtangov attempted to achieve his people's theatre through the renewed creativity of the actor, modeled on the improvisatory, movement-oriented style of commedia. Although he thought that it was not possible to "teach anybody how to create because the creative process is a subconscious one,"[92] he decided that the actor's education should supply his unconscious with a variety of skills including the "ability to free oneself, to concentrate, be serious, theatrical, artistic, active, expressive, observant, easily adaptable, etc. . . .The unconscious, armed with such an arsenal of means, will forge from the supplied material, an almost perfect product."[93] Vakhtangov claimed that the "conscious is never creative. The unconscious is,"[94] and it was the actor's unconscious inspiration communicated to the audience that he believed to be the heart of a truly vital theatre. He stressed that an actor who "consciously feeds the unconscious and unconsciously expresses the result -- he is a talent. He, who unconsciously interprets the unconscious, and equally unconsciously expresses the result -- he is a genius."[95].

Vakhtangov founded his own theatre in 1914 in Moscow. It was just another training studio (Studio 3) connected to the Moscow Art Theatre, and its inauspicious beginning, in March, 1914, with a production of Boris Zaitsev's *The Lanin Estate*, was followed by a few moderate successes. As early as 1914, he stated his interest in commedia, but the Moscow Art Theatre emphasized the need to develop in the areas of the realistic drama, and Vakhtangov, for a time, conformed. In 1918, however, with a production of *Macbeth*, in which he played the leading role himself, the theatre came into its own. That same year, he founded the Habimah Theatre, where he staged a memorable production of Solomon Ansky's *The Dybbuk* in 1922.

It was at the theatre bearing his name that Vakhtangov created his finest productions, including Maeterlinck's *The Miracle of St. Anthony* and Gogol's *The Marriage; An Utterly Incredible Occurrence*, and, his last, an uncompromisingly theatrical treatment of Gozzi's *Princess Turandot*. Although this was his only overtly commedic production, his unique vision of reality connected him instinctively to the immediacy and versatility of commedia: "The artist is merely the crystallizer and the perfector of these symbols treasured for him in the people's art depository."[96] Vakhtangov had become ill shortly before beginning work on *Princess Turandot*, and some preliminary work had been done by assistants while he was recuperating in a sanitarium.[97] It had initially been decided to use Schiller's version of *Turandot*, but upon returning to work, Vakhtangov was disappointed with it and decided to switch to Gozzi's original version.

The emphasis was not to be placed on the simple telling of the story of Princess Turandot, but on "one's contemporary attitude towards her, one's irony, and the smile provoked by the *tragic* contents of the tale."[98] Vakhtangov believed that this could only be accomplished through the ability of the actors to "enchant the audience by their expressiveness, ingenuity, and musicality."[99] He was, like Meyerhold, no mere antiquarian, but an eclectic who was not a rigid follower of any particular style or form. Each play dictated a unique style or form to him, and it was to be developed in concert with the designers and the actors. The essence of commedia, he believed, was its lack of restraint: "Let the theatre be filled with unconstrained joy, youth, laughter, improvisation, immediacy and closeness with human emotions side by side with irony and humor. Let it be the holiday of our fantasy, our pleasure in life and creation."[100]

Princess Turandot called for masks, but Vakhtangov did not use historically accurate ones; instead, he devised extremely exaggerated make-up that captured the spirit of the masked tradition while still permitting the actors a mobility of facial expression. In exploring the nature of the stock masks of commedia, he and his actors found themselves exploring their own natures. The play became their vehicle and the characters became the showcase of their beings. Some improvisation was used, leading to the development of a closely knit ensemble since the actors had to learn to trust each other. Surviving photographs and designs indicate that the production was a stunning visual feast of virtuoso acting staged with imaginative simplicity.

At the beginning of the play, the stage was covered with brightly colored strips of fabric. On a signal from the actor playing Truffaldino, the fabric was lifted by the actors who, in time to music, wrapped the strips around themselves. In seconds, the actors, who had first appeared in evening dress, transformed the fabric and a few props into the brightly colored costumes expected in commedia. The commedic spirit was truly evoked when the actors ad-libbed on topical matters, well-known personalities, and members of the audience.

The opening of *Princess Turandot*, on February 28, 1922, was a triumph, but Vakhtangov was too ill to attend the first night. Stanislavsky phoned him at intermission to inform him of its great success. Many members of the cast and audience carried flowers to Vakhtangov's bedside following the performance. He died on May 29, 1922, and as a permanent homage *Princess Turandot* has remained in the repertory of the Vakhtangov Theatre. It has been played well over a thousand times, and Vakhtangov anticipated its longevity when he noted that it was successful because "harmony was achieved in it."[101]

The pervasive influence of commedia in Russian theatre during the first thirty years of the twentieth century spread to the cabaret stage and back again. Kuzmin led the way, but undoubtedly the best known cabaret entertainer of the era was Nikita Baliev (1877-1936), a minor comic actor at the Moscow Art Theatre, who encouraged some of his fellow actors to join him in establishing a cabaret. Under Baliev's direction, they created a small stir before the Revolution with their cabaret *The Bat*. During the Revolution, Baliev left Moscow (where several other similar cabaret entertainments had appeared) for Paris, where he established an extraordinarily popular version of *The Bat*. His revues made use of commedic techniques as well as elements of music hall and vaudeville, and featured short burlesques on topical themes, mimed sketches based on old ballads, folk songs, and scenes with sets and costumes reminiscent of the richness of the Russian ballet at its height. All of this was presided over by Bailev himself, the animating genius of the troupe, as a genial master of ceremonies. He was often compared favorably with Charlie Chaplin for his ability to stand apart from everyday life and comment upon it, but it was also clear that he was a unique talent, as Brooks Atkinson observed in 1927:

> He reduces his expression to its bare essentials: to a melancholy drawl of the voice, to a slight nod of the head or a sly questioning of the eyes. Yet he is never vague. Through a long travestied opera he acts in pantomime from a box seat without being uncertain in a single detail. Or in the "Where is Meyer?" turn he bounces on with a dented derby hat for an innocuous whirl. He never loses identity. . . .It is his production, but he takes no part in the group entertainment. In his way he is a hero, a god of sardonic comedy, a genius in pantomime.[102]

Baliev's use of contemporary stock characters, which he and his cast continually invented, certainly followed the traditions of commedia in which the actors had also transformed themselves into absurdly exaggerated human types. The revue was so popular in Paris that it was brought to London in 1921 by producer C.B. Cochran and went on to New York in 1922, for the first of many extended visits. Baliev never returned to Russia, but his revue was perhaps the most visible and popular exemplar of modern Russian commedia internationally. Its popularity continued until the time of his death, when, despite efforts to keep it alive, the revue folded. A variety of other revues, cabarets, and music halls thrived in Russia during the first three decades of the twentieth century. Like Bailev's work, most of it was indebted to commedic traditions.

Constant Mic (Konstantin Miklashevsky), "the leading Russian authority on the Italian *commedia dell'arte*,"[103] published an important historical study of commedia during the 1920's which generated interest among theatre practitioners, but by this time commedia in performance survived mostly through the work of the students of Meyerhold, who carried forth the tradition in Russia and throughout Europe and America. Mic had been instrumental in encouraging Meyerhold's interest in commedia when they were both young actors.

Director Sergei Ernestovich Radlov (1892-1958), who had received his earliest training during the most intense period of Meyerhold's interest in commedia,[104] led a movement to merge the traditional folk theatre with a modern sensibility to create a new popular theatre. Borrowing from circus, silent film comedy, and commedia, he proclaimed that the actor's art consisted of the proper disposition of sound, movement, and emotion. During the early Soviet era, he experimented with improvisation, children's theatre, puppets, and simultaneous staging techniques. He also helped found the Theatre of Popular Comedy, where circus performers were employed for a variety of "circus-comedies" and pantomimes. He staged many plays by Molière and Shakespeare, and after the mid-1920's he worked on Shakespeare's plays almost exclusively.

Director Nikolai Okhlopkov (1900-1967), another disciple of Meyerhold's, worked mostly in the naturalistic vein, although he departed from this for a 1934-1935 season at the Moscow Realistic Theatre, where he directed *Aristocrats* by Nikolai Pogodin, a play about the building of the White Sea Canal. Okhlopov's version was a stylized Meyerholdian grotesque carnival, mixing elements of Oriental forms with commedic performance techniques. He even used actors as pieces of furniture and scenery in a modern variation of commedia's *zanni*, as had been done in various ways by Meyerhold and Vakhtangov in their productions. The production was revived in 1957, using

> attendants in blue masks and dominoes -- figures from the pages of
> Jacques Callot -- to serve as property men in the Chinese manner.
> They move about the stage in full light, distributing props: a telephone,
> for example, which one of them holds while a character makes a call;
> then, when the call is completed, takes off the stage. When a table is
> needed, two others bring on a rectangular piece of green baize;
> squatting on the floor, they hold it taut while characters gather around
> it in conference. By such means, Okhlopkov reminds the audience that
> no matter how realistic a picture of life in a labor camp this may be,
> it is still only a theatrical presentation and is to be accepted as
> such.[105]

In 1938, Okhlopkov's Realistic Theatre was closed by Stalin and his
company was forced to join with Tairov's Kamerny Theatre ensemble. He
produced only one play at the Kamerny before leaving with his actors to join
the Vakhtangov Theatre, which he found more compatible.

The Safonova Theatre (The Affiliated State and Academic Maly
Theatre) produced Jacinto Benavente's modern commedia, *The Bonds of
Interest*, in 1935, but shortly thereafter that theatre was also closed by
government decree. Beginning in the 1920's, and continuing through the early
1950's, a deliberately orchestrated attack on the non-realistic theatre took
shape in the Soviet Union. Marxist critics attacked theatres producing Elizabethan, Baroque, and eighteenth century comedies, as well as works inspired
by Hoffmann's grotesque characters and commedia. The Marxists believed
that these productions strove

> with the glitter of scenes, colors, costumes, and situations, to create a
> self-sufficient entertainment in the theater that was removed from life.
> They did not strive at all to reveal the class content included in the
> action of the play.
>
> The great ideals that inspired the working class do not consist of the
> contemplation, oblivion, and penetration into the other world. They
> are a concrete and practical program for changing the world.[106]

It was undoubtedly the inherently satiric view of power and the powerful that truly drove the Marxist opposition to theatrical theatre. This systematic attack on theatricality would eventually force the end of Meyerhold's career and the departure of other anti-realists from Russia. Despite these oppressions, however, the impact of the works of Meyerhold, Evreinov, Tairov, Vakhtangov, and others, was so powerful and widespread that commedic elements continued to show up in Soviet productions, albeit cautiously. *The Merry Wives of Windsor*, produced by Yuri Zavadski (1894-1977) at the Mossoviet Theatre, was an example of later day commedia in Russia. Zavadski, who had played Kalaf in Vakhtangov's *Princess Turandot*, attempted to combine some of Stanislavsky's principles with Vakhtangov's. He used commedia masks in *The Merry Wives of Windsor*, and staged other plays by Shakespeare and Goldoni, and Lermontov's *Masquerade*, with subtle commedic flourishes.

One striking contemporary example of the survival of commedia in the Russian theatre is Eugene Schwartz's *The Shadow*, an adaptation of Hans Christian Andersen's *The Man Who Lost His Shadow*, produced at the Leningrad Theatre of Comedy in 1960. Both the scene design by Nikolai P. Akimov and the production were said to be in commedic style. It was extremely popular and also presented by the Moscow Theatre of Young Spectators a decade later, demonstrating the resilience of commedic tradition even after years of Soviet-dictated performance guidelines.

The Theatre of Comedy, founded in 1935 under the direction of Akimov, promoted a theory of "elastic" theatre, wherein actors play an eclectic range of roles in plays from drama to comedy, farce, fairytale, West European classics, and Soviet domestic dramas. His productions of Schwartz's plays during the Stalin era were daring, since the political satire behind the fairytale surface was especially pointed. Commedia influences and satire were especially evident in productions of *Twelfth Night* and *As You Like It*, both produced in 1938, at the height of Stalin's oppressions.

The Theatre of Comedy continues as an important Russian theatre today, but except for it, a strong tradition of commedic elements in circus, and the fading echoes of Meyerhold's era, commedia, one of the strongest influences on the Golden Age of Russian theatre has fundamentally disappeared in the wake of Socialist Realism. Perhaps in the age of glasnost, it will reappear. .

Fig. 1.   Edward Gordon Craig's design for "Pierrot" in his 1901
production, *The Masque of Love*.

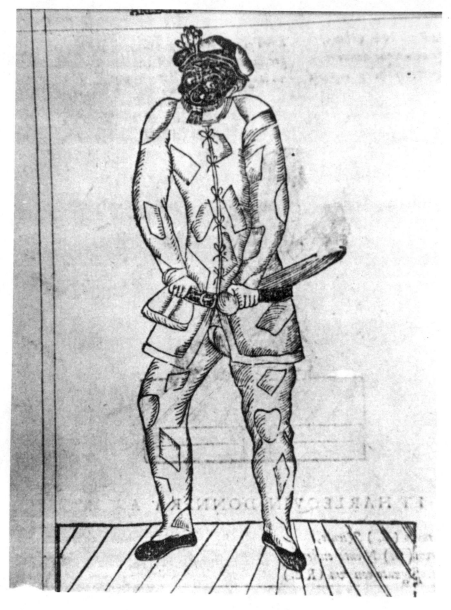

Fig. 2.　　Tristano Martinelli as Arlecchino, 1601.

Fig. 3.   A commedia dell'arte troupe.

Fig. 4.   Marcello Moretti as Arlecchino in the Piccolo Teatro di Milano's production of *The Servant of Two Masters*.

Fig. 5.   Eduardo De Filippo.

Fig. 6.   Dario Fo as "The Maniac" in his play, *Accidental Death of an Anarchist*.

Fig. 7.   Dario Fo as Arlecchino in his play, *Hellekin, Arlekin, Arlecchino* (1985).

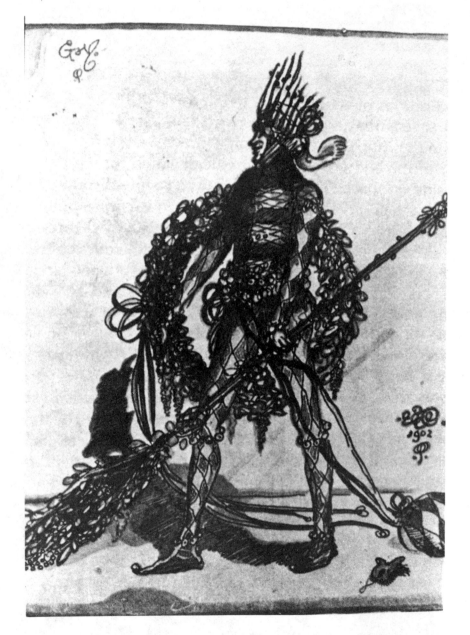

Fig. 8.   Edward Gordon Craig's design for "Harlequin" in his 1901
production, *The Masque of Love*.

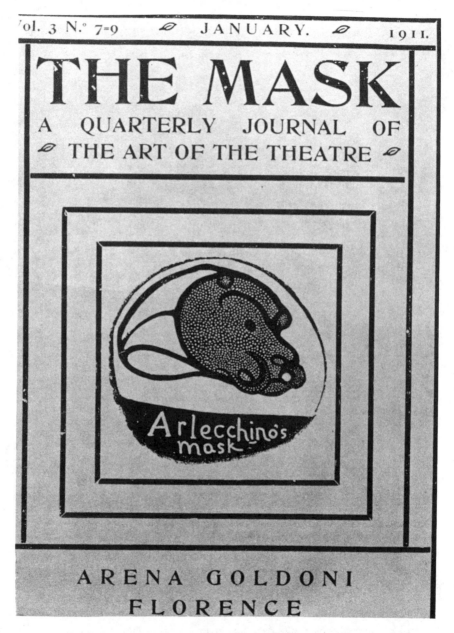

Fig. 9.   The January 1911 cover of *The Mask*, featuring Edward Gordon
            Craig's woodcut, "Arlecchino's Mask."

Fig. 10.   Edward Gordon Craig's 1911 woodcut, "La Commedia."

Fig. 11.   An illustration from a published version of Laurence
Housman's and Harley Granville Barker's 1904 play, *Prunella,
or Love in a Dutch Garden*.

Fig. 12.   A scene, featuring Lionel Atill (right), from Harley Granville
Barker's production of French playwright Sacha Guitry's play,
Deburau, produced on the New York stage by David Belasco.

Fig. 13.   Jim Dale in the title role of the Young Vic Theatre's production of *Scapino!*

Fig. 14.   A scene from Peter Brook's landmark production of *A Midsummer Night's Dream*.

Fig. 15. Vsevolod Meyerhold as Pierrot in his 1906 production of Alexander Blok's *The Fairground Booth*.

Fig. 16.   An illustration of the setting for the 1914 revival of Alexander
Blok's *The Fairground Booth*, staged by Vsevolod Meyerhold.

Fig. 17.   A scene from the Theatre Guild production of Nikolai
Evreinov's *The Chief Thing*, featuring Estelle Winwood as
Columbine.

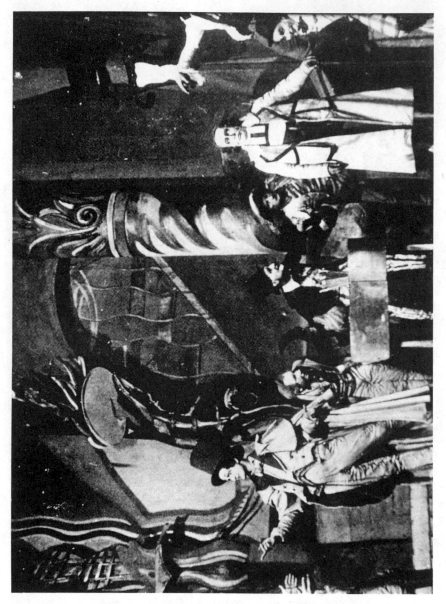

Fig. 18.   A scene from Alexander Tairov's production of *Princess Brambilla*.

Fig. 19.   The final scene from Eugene Vakhtangov's 1922 production of *Princess Turandot*, showing the four commedia characters on the far left and right sides framing the rest of the cast.

Fig. 20.   Helene and Hermann Thimig in Max Reinhardt's 1924 production of *The Servant of Two Masters*.

Fig. 21.   Hermann Thimig, as Truffaldino, gorges himself on spaghetti in an acclaimed scene from Max Reinhardt's 1924 production of *The Servant of Two Masters*.

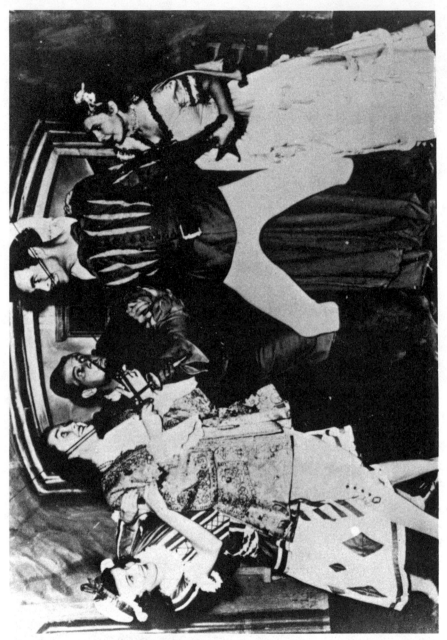

Fig. 22. Nanette Fabray (far left) and Robert Ryan (second from right) in Max Reinhardt's 1939 production of *The Servant of Two Masters*, retitled *At Your Service*, produced by Reinhardt's Hollywood Workshop.

Fig. 23.   Bertolt Brecht (left) performing with beerhall comedian Karl
Valentin.

Fig. 24.   Molière as Sganarelle.

Fig. 25.   The Théâtre des Funambules on the Boulevard of Crime in Paris.

Fig. 26.   Jacques Copeau, second from left, as Scapin in his production
of *The Tricks of Scapin*.

Fig. 27.   Copeau's actors in costume for a street performance.

Fig. 28.   Jean-Louis Barrault and Arletty in a scene from the classic film,
Les enfants du paradis.

Fig. 29.   Marcel Marceau as his legendary character, Bip.

Fig. 30.   Jacques Lecoq.

Fig. 31.   A scene from Vadim Uraneff's 1923 New York production of
Alexander Blok's *The Fairground Booth*, retitled *The Show
Booth*, with scene designs by Robert Edmond Jones.

Fig. 32.   A scene from the Detroit Arts Theatre production of Ben
Hecht's and Kenneth Sawyer Goodman's 1916 play, *The Wonder
Hat*.

Fig. 33.　　The San Francisco Mime Troupe performing in a San Francisco park in the 1960's.

Fig. 34.   The evening ritual from the 1991 Bread and Puppet Theatre
"Domestic Resurrection Circus" in Glover, Vermont.

A Fist in the Eye: Commedia in Eastern Europe and Scandinavia

Simultaneously, we discovered the stage of the primitive theater, the performances of a barker, children's games, circus pantomimes, the tavern theater of strolling players, the theater of masked celebrating villagers. The stage could arise anywhere -- any place could lend itself to theatrical fantasy.[1]

-- Jindřich Honzl

Commedia found its way onto the stages of Eastern Europe, as it had in virtually all European cultures, by the end of the eighteenth century. Theatrical influences similar to commedia can be found in Eastern Europe very early in the court performances of Byzantine entertainers and jugglers beginning around the twelfth century. After the arrival of the Turks in the fourteenth century, there were few entertainments except for clowns (called *pelivans*), dervish dances, and puppet plays.

In the early twentieth century, inspired by Russia's commedists, as well as those of Germany, France, and Italy, modern commedic techniques brought new energy to Eastern Europe's theatres following the first World War. Politics had certainly been on the minds of several of Russia's commedists, particularly between 1900 and 1935, but commedic theatre had a particularly political destiny to play out east of the Oder throughout the twentieth century. Commedia techniques and characters, as revived and reinvented by Eastern Europe's theatre artists, became a powerful tool for political resistance of repressive governments.

Yugoslavia

In Yugoslavia, commedic elements can first be seen in the plays of Croatian dramatist Marin Držić (1505-1567), an Italian-educated priest who wrote plays for a local theatre in Dubrovnik. He wrote many comedies, farces, and pastoral plays, most of which have been lost. His works were popular in Yugoslavia largely because of the influence of Plautus, Boccaccio, and commedic traditions apparent in his style. During the eighteenth century, free adaptations of Molière's commedic plays, changed to suit local conditions and translated into native dialects, were extremely popular in Dubrovnik, and are occasionally revived today. Beginning in the eighteenth century, mild satires of government inefficiency and pseudo-realistic comedies utilizing folkloric elements were the closest surviving commedic elements. Although commedia also lived on in circus and cabaret entertainments, little significant evidence of it can be found in Yugoslavian theatres in more recent times.

Hungary

Molière's works featuring elements of commedia found their way into Hungary during the eighteenth century. Protestant school plays were particularly noteworthy because a notable poet, Mihály Csokonai Vitéz (1773-1805), wrote satiric comedies for student performances, including *The Widow Karnyo and the Two Coxcombs* (1799), which employed commedic improvisational techniques. By the middle of the nineteenth century, Hungarian theatre found its native voice, but except for the popularity of social satires, until the early twentieth century any significant influence of commedia is difficult to detect.

The Hungarian theatre found itself in a period of new growth in the early twentieth century, due in large part to a few native playwrights who discovered some value in commedic traditions they had learned from the Russian stage. Lajos Ziláhy (1891-1974), born in a small town in western Transylvania, was the first important Hungarian dramatist in the post-World War I period. Although best known for his realistic dramas, Ziláhy wrote a satiric commedia play, *Musical Clowns* (1925), dealing with the relationship of a poet to his public. Other Hungarian playwrights, including Ferenc Molnar (1878-1952), were influenced by Pirandello's reality versus illusion plays, but could not be considered especially commedic.

The most important influence on the Hungarian stage in the first part of the century was director Sandor Hevesi (1873-1939) who sought to combine many of the best traits of Craig and Reinhardt in his work. As director and organizer of a modern repertory system in Hungary, Hevesi staged an impressive array of classical and modern plays. His involvement with the Hungarian National Theatre and Opera House, as well as with the Thalia Society, placed him at the forefront of Hungarian theatre. He gained international recognition as a promoter of innovative theatrical concepts after founding his own company in 1904. In the *The Mask* (July, 1912), Craig reported on Hevesi's National Theatre production of *The Defiant*, an improvised play based on an old commedia scenario preserved by Luigi Riccoboni. Craig's praise was lavish; Hevesi had succeeded in reviving "the splendid traditions of the *Commedia dell'Arte*."[2] *The Mask* reported several critical reactions from Hungarian newspaper critics who found that the production offered "So much real, and really felt, joy, so much cheerfulness. . ."[3] and that "without any learned high-browedness; one was permitted to forget history and to enjoy an enchanting spectacle."[4] For his part, Hevesi admired Craig, "the truest revolutionist I have ever known,"[5] and his devotion to Craig's concepts reveals much about Hevesi's approach to theatre: "He discovered for us that in a rope-dancer there may be more theatrical art than in an up-to-date actor reciting from his memory and depending on his prompter."[6] Unlike many East European theatrical figures of his time, Hevesi was more focused on commedia as a resource for developing new theatrical techniques, than he was in commedia's potency in addressing political matters. Aside from the considerable popularity of cabaret since World War I, little significant evidence of commedia can be found in Hungary after Hevesi's experiments.

Poland

It is unclear when commedia first reached Poland, although there is evidence of the appearance of an actor in the character of a *zanni* in Cracow in 1592. It is clear that in the 1590's, commedia influenced plays dealing with the adventures of the stock character Albertus, a village sexton sent to war as a recruit in place of the parish priest. *The Parish Priest's Expedition* (c.1590) and *Albertus Returns From War* (c.1596), are strikingly similar to Beolco's Ruzzante plays, and innumerable other commedia scenarios. The enormous popularity of Albertus gave rise to a flood of crude native farces in similar style. Its combination of commedia, ancient comedy, and Shrovetide entertainments produced a unique brand of native folk farce, that lacked commedia's sophisticated understanding of character, but shared its raucous and busy stage.

During the seventeenth century, commedia actors performed in markets and at fairs -- and toured throughout the country. The memoirs of Francesco Andreini, the leader of Italy's famed Gelosi troupe, were published in Polish in 1652, and Arlecchino made his first documented appearances in plays performed in Latin in schools. Italian commedia troupes played in Warsaw and at court theatres as early as the 1690's, when Gennaro Sacco and his troupe arrived from Italy. In the eighteenth century, commedia troupes continued to tour Poland, most notably Tommaso Ristori's, but commedic influences were in little evidence during the nineteenth century, except in the plays of Aleksander Fredro (1793-1876). Fredro's comedies, including *Ladies and Hussars* (1825), *Maiden Vows* (1833), and *Vengeance* (1834), were popularly produced in Lwów. In the style of Molière's commedic plays, Fredro's comedies featured broadly stereotypical characters and lively action.

After 1900, Craig's theories caught on in Poland, as they had in Hungary, especially in the work of designer and director Leon de Schildenfeld Schiller (1887-1954). Born in Cracow, he spent his early twenties in Paris, sometimes working as a cabaret singer and journalist. While there, he met Craig, who encouraged Schiller's interest in and ideas about theatre. In 1908 and 1909, he contributed articles on contemporary Polish theatre and grotesque characters in dramatic history, including those from commedia, to Craig's journal, *The Mask*. His commitment to "total theatre," as well as his love for both realistic and romantic drama, resulted equally from his admiration for Polish playwright and painter Stanisław Wyspianski,[7] Craig, and Stanislavsky.[8] Schiller also produced commedic plays by Molière, and wrote the libretto and staged composer Karol Szymanowski's (1882-1937) satiric commedia ballet, *Mandragora* (1920). The ballet concerns a bored royal court entertained by bizarre games created by a eunuch. A grotesque parody, *Mandragora* centrally features commedia characters during the eunuch's games, including a dance by Columbine to clarinet accompaniment and Harlequin performing mock Italian tenor's arias. The Doctor and Capitano also appear for comic effect in Szymanowski's ballet, which clearly owes much to Prokofiev's *Love for Three Oranges*.

Early in the century, some Polish writers had been attracted to commedia characters and pantomime. Bolesław Lesmian (1878-1937), a poet and Symbolist, wrote essays on the nature of pantomime drama in Poland. He was influenced by Blok and other Russian commedists, especially in two obscure pantomime plays, *Pierrot and Columbine* and *The Frenzied Fiddler*. In these two works he presents the theatrical, ironic and personally allegorical themes found in Blok's *The Fairground Booth*. *Pierrot and Columbine* is a typically modernist commedia, stressing "conventionality and artificiality"[9] in a harlequinade that reveals Pierrot as a "poet, [hiding] the despair of a skeptical sage and a creator."[10]

After the dreadful suffering in Poland during the Nazi occupation of World War II, theatre regenerated slowly and when it reappeared it was transformed. No longer restrained, theatre became direct and hard-hitting as the name of the leading new theatre conveys. Bim-Bom,[11] started in Gdansk in 1953 as a unique form of performers' theatre, emphasized physical action and mixed elements of cabaret, carnival, circus, and commedia. One of the guiding spirits of Bim-Bom, Jerzy Afanasjew, founded The Afanasjew Family Circus in 1958 as a follow-up to Bim-Bom, seeking, in part, a Polish theatrical form drawing on the old commedia tradition of family troupes. Folk performance traditions, fairs, and native Christmas pagaents were studied by Afanasjew, who determined that his family members would each play certain fixed characters. He appeared as Polichinella, the circus director, with his wife as Columbine, and his brother-in-law as a clown. He said that the simple and direct goal of his circus was "to make people laugh -- by gesture, facial expression, and music --so that *Circus* will be an experience for all: the child, the workman, the soldier and the finicky intellectual, and artist. We go about our work keeping in mind the paintings of Peter Breughel, the silent film, classic literature and music hall, Chaplin, Eisenstein, Pudovkin and Grock, cabaret and the Proletkult."[12] The troupe presented their *Comedy of Masks* commedia-style -- on a horse-drawn wagon in 1961 at the Gdansk City Carnival. Their final piece, *Good Evening, Clown* (1962), showing the clown and his family as "a dream of pictures never painted by Columbine, a dream inherent in Harlequin's everyday costume."[13] In the mid-1950's, Henryk Tomaszewski founded Wrocław's Mime Theatre on the principles of mime established by Marcel Marceau in France. Tomaszewski, whose works demonstrated a delightfully absurd view of the universe, scripted many of his performances and employed such commedic devices as masks in plays ranging from Gozzi to Ionesco.

Circus and mime are not the only forms of entertainment in Poland inspired by commedia. Puppet theatres have also drawn from commedic traditions, and are best exemplified by the Arlekin Puppet Theatre in Łódź. Their recent play, *Growing Up With Baby*, was replete with characters and situations out of commedia. There are over twenty-five puppet theatres operating in Poland at present, and most owe much to commedia's characters and techniques. Cabaret entertainments influenced by commedic elements became popular in Cracow at the turn of the century. Among the best was *Zielony Balonik* (Little Green Balloon), which opened in October, 1905, under the guiding spirit of Stanisław Przybyszewski. The Little Green Balloon became a center of artistic developments in Poland, prominently featuring the writings of Tadeusz Zelenski (1874-1942). It also had significant impact on the works of Polish commedists, including Schiller.

The contemporary Polish theatre has been dominated by Jerzy Grotowski (b. 1933), whose acting and production theories have become internationally known in recent decades. After studying drama in Cracow and Moscow, Grotowski founded the Theatre of 13 Rows in Opole, in 1959. There he staged productions of classics of the ancient and modern drama, in which his actors improvised in opposition to the text as a way of arguing with earlier cultural beliefs. Grotowski's experiments also involved attempts to transform the traditional actor-audience relationship. With his company, he moved to Wrocław in 1965 and they renamed themselves the Laboratory Theatre. Although not overtly commedic, Grotowski's simplified, audience-participatory, improvisatory performance style suggests the influence of commedic techniques. Once Grotowski published his theories in *Towards a Poor Theatre* (1968), the company began to gain international attention.

Contemporary Polish theatre is quite diverse -- and commedic entertainments including cabaret, broad political satire, and companies and collectives performing in streets, are much in evidence.

Czechoslovakia

During the Renaissance, the plays of Plautus and Terence were performed in schools and in public by students in Czechoslovakia. Touring Italian troupes, as well as those from Germany and England, appeared regularly in the sixteenth century. Folk entertainments, many with commedic elements, were performed at holidays, and most mixed farce with social satire. Crude native folk plays were popular from the mid-seventeenth century, but the first Czech professional theatres in the eighteenth century featured foreign companies, including commedia troupes and marionette theatres.

Early in the twentieth century, Czechoslovakian director Jaroslav Kvapil, impressed by the quality of productions he had seen in other European capitals, tried to raise the standards of production at the National Theatre in Prague, but found little support from his audience or fellow theatre artists. In 1918, Karel Hugo Hilar (1884-1935), a powerful and flamboyant director, accomplished what Kvapil had begun. Many Czech playwrights of this time, most of whom had their work produced in the National Theatre, were inspired by the commedic productions of Meyerhold, Tairov, and other Russian directors of their era. Prominent among them was Edmond Konrad (1889-1957), who held up the satiric mirror to post-World War I society in several comedies filled with commedic stereotypical characters and situations, including *Family Affair* (1927) and *Comedy Squared* (1925), which applied commedia characters and techniques in a satire of the post-World War I divorce epidemic.

Of all the Eastern Europeans, Czech directors took the greatest advantage of commedic forms. Emil Burian (1904-1959) founded the "D 34"

Theatre in 1934. He staged simplified productions of the classics, including Molière's commedic plays, with an emphasis on innovative lighting and music as a unifying force. After some years as a secondary school science teacher and theatre critic, Jindřich Honzl (1894-1953) began creating a theatre of the proletariat. As a communist, Honzl became particularly interested in artists and literary intellectuals who were turning away from Realism. In 1925, he published *The Spinning Stage*, a collection of theoretical essays stressing that everything "that makes up reality on the stage -- the playwright's text, the actor's acting, the stage lighting -- all these things in every case stand for other things. In other words, dramatic performance is a set of signs."[14] He stressed that the actor "*represents someone, that he signifies a role in a play. Hence it does not matter whether he is a human being; an actor could be a piece of wood, as well.*"[15] The Craigian notion of the actor as puppet led to a rediscovery of "the theater of the street,"[16] like commedia, and a diversity of informal performance traditions, which he foresaw transforming the Czech stage.

Honzl explained that each historical era has emphasized one particular component of theatrical expression without diminishing the overall effectiveness of a complete performance. He stated that there had been "theaters without authors (or without authors of note),"[17] as in commedia, as well as theatre "without actors or without great actors,"[18] and without directors. He wanted a theatre that was the sum total of a mixture of various arts (directing, design, music), but he was convinced that the art of the actor was supreme among them. There could be no theatre for Honzl without the actor, although the other components could, to a greater or lesser degree, be eliminated. An actor could interest an audience even as a "pantomime that is conducted in an empty circus ring solely by the actions of a player. There are numerous examples (such as the famous clowns Grock, Fratellini, and others) that the actor's actions by themselves can captivate the audience."[19]

In 1927, Honzl became director of Prague's avant-garde Liberated Theatre, where his productions boldly reflected Meyerhold's principles. Honzl's production of V.V. Klicpera's *Hadrian in Rome* (1929), staged in Brno, was an especially memorable application of his commedic staging techniques. After the fall of the First Republic in 1938, and the subsequent Nazi invasion, Honzl remained in Czechoslovakia, but was able to direct only a few staged readings of Czech literature during World War II.

Jiří Frejka (1904-1952), a protege of Hilar, remained fundamentally apolitical before, during, and after World War II. He was especially interested in creating a poetic theatre, but one based on improvisation and the techniques of commedia. His 1926 production, *Cirkus Dandin* (the previous year he had staged Molière's *Georges Dandin* with his own amateur Experimental Theatre), was, on a simpler scale, a distinctly Meyerholdian production. With the aid of scenic artist Antonin Heythum, he directed such modern commedic plays as Evreinov's *The Merry Death* and Goll's *Insurance Against Suicide*. Frejka believed that theatre "is not only *what* is played, but also *how* it is played."[20] For a time, he and Honzl worked in partnership at the Liberated Theatre, where he staged *Telegrams on Wheels* by V. Nezval, while Honzl presented works by Apollinaire, Marinetti, and Goll, among others. By mid-1927, however, they realized that their fundamental ideologies had become very different. Barbara Day writes that Frejka "saw himself as a practical man of the theatre, able to take any play from the traditional canon and turn it into spontaneous entertainment by the use of constructivist or *commedia dell'arte* techniques,"[21] while Honzl "considered that the choice of play was important: he wanted a studio-type theatre that would go beyond competitive styles toward a response to a specific text."[22]

After Frejka's departure, Honzl invited two young performers, Jiří Voskovec (1905-1981) and Jan Werich (1905-1980), to work at the Liberated Theatre. Voskovec and Werich, or V + W as they became known, opened the Liberated Theatre in 1926. Their first production, *The Vest-pocket Revue*, featured music and skits that became increasingly satiric as V + W observed the rise of Fascism. Their simply staged performances showcased V + W as actors and authors, both wearing clownish makeup and costume. Voskovec generally played straight man to Werich's more broadly conceived, riotous clowning, and both used American silent film comedians as their models. In 1932, Honzl directed V + W in *Caesar*, a revue in which their high-spirited clowning took on an especially sharp satiric edge, focusing on the rise of dictators like Hitler and Mussolini. Their very next revue, *Ass and Shadow* (1933), focused even more directly on Hitler, eliciting an official protest from the German embassy in Prague. Riots between Fascist sympathizers and the majority of the audience broke out at their production of *The Hangman and the Fool* in 1934, in which V + W savagely satirized Fascist leaders with their memorable comparison of past leaders to present. In the past, kings needed to have hangmen and fools. In the present, demonstrated V + W, leaders are fools who were themselves both hangmen and kings.

V + W continued with their anti-Hitler, anti-Fascist attacks until well into 1938. Their last two productions, *Heavy Barbora* and *A Fist in the Eye*, satirized events surrounding the Sudeten crisis. When the First Republic collapsed, their license was denied, and they emigrated to the United States. After the war they returned to Czechoslovakia, but they never reopened their theatre. In 1948, Voskovec returned permanently to the United States to work in films and theatre, while Werich continued performing at Prague's Theatre of Satire until his retirement in 1968.

After World War II, director Otomar Krejča (b. 1921) began his career in Prague, and ran the city's most successful theatre, The Gate, from 1965 to 1972. It was an actor's theatre founded on principles of psychological realism. Despite this, he depended on the use of masks "as a natural outgrowth of carnival."[23] In productions of Schnitzler's *The Green Cockatoo*, Josef Topol's

The End of the Carnival, or Michel de Ghelderode's *The Masquers of Ostend*, produced in 1965, Krejča depicted the spirit of carnival, "as a move toward a purer theatricality."[24]   In these and other productions, he was able to "multiply the impact of the residual magic and wonder latent in the masked performer by taking advantage of the inherently histrionic, ritual element of carnival celebrations."[25]   Government censorship prevented Krejča from working in Czechoslovakian theatres between 1972 and 1990, but with the sweeping political changes recently in Eastern Europe, Krejča went back to work.   His recent French production of Beckett's *Waiting for Godot* emphasized the play's most theatrical elements, and, as he strives to start a new company in Prague, commedic elements will surely appear in his productions since he plans to draw from the canon of Shakespeare, Beckett, and Chekhov.

Cabaret and music hall have been popular in Czechoslovakia since the nineteenth century. Prague's semi-professional cabaret, *The Seven of Hearts*, like many music halls throughout Europe, includes fresh and innovative performances of topical sketches, many using dance and improvisational techniques clearly inspired by commedia. Pantomime had been consistently popular in music halls and the smaller theatres in Prague; mime, improvisation, fools and clowns, and satire continue to dominate. Most notable among these anti-naturalistic theatres is The Prague Pantomime Theatre, founded in 1958 in a medieval church building on the banks of the Moldau, under the direction of Ladislav Fialka (b. 1931). Fialka, who had trained as a ballet dancer, specificially uses commedic characters and techniques in the development of his actors' pantomimic skills. When they played New York in August, 1964, their production, *Pierrot's Journey*, a pantomime about pantomime, seemed to critics to pale beside the traditions of Chaplin, and more recently, Marceau. Fialka, who himself performs as the white-faced Pierrot, borrows from Deburau, silent film comedies, Shakespeare, commedia scenarios, and a variety of sources in the creation of his pantomimes.

Most recently, playwright Daniela Fischerová (b. 1948) used commedic elements in her play, *Princezna T* (1986), which had its premiere in Prague in 1988. Inspired by Gozzi's *Turandot*, the play focuses on times when humans must choose between evils, and when ideals are superfluous, or worse. Fischerová uses three commedic *zannis* who move in and out of the stage reality, introducing the play, changing scenes, creating transitions, and adding to the mood and atmosphere by embodying and speaking what otherwise would be unspeakable. The *zannis* are "only occasionally charming; most of the time they provide a sharply ironic, even cynical perspective on the action; their comments and actions often become grotesque, malicious, and, at times, sadistic."[26] Also, Ctibor Turba, a member of the Prague Faculty of Dramatic Arts, recently staged a puppet play inspired by commedia called *Commedia dell'arte Wardrobe Commedy*.

Commedic elements similar to those in Hungary, Poland, Yugoslavia, and Czechoslovakia found their way into the theatres other Eastern European nations, including Albania, Bulgaria, and Rumania. Bulgaria's Theatre of Satire, founded in 1957 in Sofia, managed to develop an ensemble-style acting company and to present a varied repertory, including commedic plays and productions, despite strict government supervision. Their productions also owed much to Russian stage traditions, particularly those of the early twentieth century. Rumania's Comedy Theatre of Bucharest featured highly theatrical productions in the commedic tradition, but more importantly, Rumania produced an internationally significant director, Liviu Ciulei (b. 1923). Ciulei worked from 1948 until the late 1970's as an actor, director, and scene designer for the Lucia Sturza Bulandra Theatre in Bucharest where he made his mark directing the classics in highly original interpretations. Beginning in the 1970's, Ciulei began accepting guest directorships at theatres in Germany, Australia, Canada, and the United States. He was appointed artistic director of the Guthrie Theatre in 1981, and held the position until 1985. In 1984, his production of *Twelfth Night* at the Guthrie prominently featured elements of commedia, circus, and Fellini's commedic film, *The Clowns*.

Censorship and political repression slowed the development of Eastern European theatres in the middle of the twentieth century, just as the arts had been stifled in Russia by Stalin during the late 1930's. Literature was a significant outlet for political thought during these repressions, but political theatre was genuinely quelled, at least, in part, because repressive governments have accurately understood theatres to be breeding grounds for revolutionary sentiments and resistance. Open and unrestrained theatre has been a sign of a relatively healthy society, and since the recent political upheavals in Eastern Europe, including playwright Vaclav Havel's[27] rise to the presidency of Czechoslovakia, theatre has once again begun to flourish on the stages of Eastern Europe.

Scandinavia

Sophisticated theatre arrived late in Scandinavia. Folk entertainments had existed early and most evolved out of Scandinavian history and myth, but during the eighteenth century a few playwrights of note, influenced by European drama and theatrical techniques, appeared. Some were drawn to commedic elements, particularly in Denmark, Norway, and Sweden.

Theatre in Denmark began with church-related dramas during the Middle Ages, followed by elaborate festivals featuring Italiante scenic spectacle. The first important Danish playwright was Norwegian-born Ludvig Holberg (1684-1754), who borrowed freely from ancient Roman comedy, Ben Jonson, Molière, and commedia, and invented some new characters of his own for his native comedies. When Copenhagen opened its first Danish-speaking theatre in 1722, Holberg supplied it with nearly thirty comedies by 1728, his first was an adaptation of Molière's *The Imaginary Invalid* (1722). Holberg ultimately became known as the "Molière of the North," and his variant plays include those which focus on an ironic vision of human irrationality, others featuring much social satire, and still others driven by commedic intrigues. One of Holberg's contemporaries, Pieter Langendijk (1683-1756), was similarly influenced by commedic tradition, particularly in his play *Arlequin as a Shareholder* (1720). Johannes Ewald (1743-1781), Denmark's first important tragic playwright, wrote a few comedies, and one, *Harlequin the Patriot* (1772), featured commedia characters and a farcical plot; it was first produced twenty-five years after Ewald's death. By the middle of the nineteenth century, commedia pervaded Danish culture. Even the beloved storyteller Hans Christian Andersen (1805-1875) included commedia characters in some of his tales. One Andersen story from *What the Moon Saw* featured a tragic love triangle featuring Harlequin, Columbine, and Pierrot; it attracted the attention of Edward Gordon Craig who made a little drama of it in hopes of performing it himself as a young actor. Commedia has had little impact in modern Denmark, although playwright Sven Clausen (1893-1961) wrote a popular play, *Among Garlands of Roses* (1933), which is a playful marital comedy that uses modern counterparts for the commedia characters of Pierrot, Harlequin, and Columbine. There has been much political street theatre in Denmark since the 1970's, but little can be seen as being directly inspired by commedic traditions.

Although theatre has existed in Norway for at least four centuries, its first permanent playhouses featuring Norwegian-born actors were not built until the early nineteenth century. Among early Norwegian playwrights, Henrik Wergeland (1808-1845), the poet and social critic, wrote theatre pieces ranging from vaudevilles to serious dramas on contemporary issues. One of his vaudevilles, *Harlequin Virtuos* (1830), was distinctly commedic in its characters and situations. Norway's greatest dramatist, Henrik Ibsen (1828-1906), seemed to avoid anything remotely like the theatricality typical of commedia, even in his highly symbolic last plays. More recently, Italian director Eugenio Barba's (b. 1936) *Kasparina* (1967), staged at Oslo's Odin Teatret, which he founded, was based on the Kaspar Hauser legend. In this case, the Hauser legend, most famously dramatized by German dramatist Peter Handke, owed more to Greek tragedy than to the commedic elements which inspired Handke. Few other commedic manifestations can be identified in the contemporary Norwegian theatre.

Sweden's theatrical development began with medieval liturgical dramas, but by the seventeenth century, the Swedish stage became distinctly secular. Short burlesque plays, presumably in imitation of German touring players, became popular. Court entertainments featured the requisite elaborate Italianate scenery, and in 1628, Gustav II Adolf set up the first permanent acting troupe at his court. A few years later, Christina encouraged Swedish culture through performances of foreign companies, including commedia troupes. French companies took up residence, including harlequinades in their repertories, but few native dramatists of any significance emerged until the late nineteenth century. Sweden's greatest playwright, August Strindberg (1849-1912), although making no overt use of commedic elements in his plays, applauded and encouraged a return to commedic improvisation in his preface to *Miss Julie* (1889):

> Some theatres in Italy have, as we know, returned to the art of improvisation and have thereby trained actors who are truly inventive -- without, however, violating the intentions of the author. This seems to be a step in the right direction and possibly the beginning of a new, fertile form of art that will be genuinely productive.[28]

The freedom from device in Strindberg's *The Dream Play* (1901) and *The Ghost Sonata* (1908) could be said to derive from commedia, but there is no evidence to suggest that Strindberg consciously looked to commedia. He did, however, serve as an inspiration for such later dramatic movements as Absurdism, which was distinctly commedic. A bit later, Hjalmar Frederik Bergman (1883-1931) demonstrated a mild interest in commedia. Under the spell of Strindberg, Maeterlinck, and Ibsen, he wrote realistic and poetic works appraising man's nature and the forces that guide him. His commedic interest is seen most clearly in the trilogy entitled *The Marionette Plays* (1917), which includes *Death's Harlequin, A Shadow,* and *Mr. Sleeman is Coming.*

Despite the contribution of commedic tradition to the early development of Scandinavian theatre, and the occasional manifestation of it in native forms, commedia failed to contribute as profoundly to Scandinavian culture as it had to so many others. Recently, however, the work Barba and his Odin Teatret, founded in Oslo in 1964 (and which has transformed itself into the Nordick Teaterlaboratorium in Holtstebro, Denmark), has focused on a comparative study of acting traditions and techniques with emphasis placed on an intercultural perspective. Like such forerunners as Craig and Meyerhold, and especially Decroux, and, more recently, Fo, Barba has turned to the traditions of Oriental and commedic theatre. Regarding the rise of commedia as "One of the most important phenomena in the history of modern theatre,"[29] and noting its base in anarchic, anti-social behavior demonstrated by the desire of the actors, through improvisation, to break "out of their social confinement, to discover beyond discrimination a form of sociality without having to accept the norms of recognized morality."[30]

Barba founded the International School of Theatre Anthropology in 1979, and using Denmark as his base, disseminates new thought on diverse matters related to acting, from Kathakali to commedia, attracting new interest in a commedic theatre on an international basis.

CHAPTER SIX

From Hanswurst to Handke: Commedia in Germany and Austria

Today and for all time, man must stand at the centre of all theatrical art, man as actor. Where the actor is also a dramatic writer, he has the power to create a world according to his own image, thus awakening the drama to its highest form of life, like Shakespeare and Molière. Whosoever has anything to do with the theatre should be an actor. Whether or not he practices the art of acting is of secondary importance. Many great playwrights, teachers of the dramatic art, theatre managers, were actors without ever having played on the stage. Only when the director, the stage manager, the poet, the dramatic teacher, the scenic artist, the musician, are all actors, when everyone on the stage and everyone in the audience is an actor, and joins in the play, then, and only then, the theatre fulfils its highest mission.[1]

-- Max Reinhardt

The German culture poses a complex mixture of theatrical, literary, and philosophical backgrounds, making it difficult to separate out the theatre strain. Italian plays were given at the Bavarian court as early as 1568, about the time some extraordinary frescos of commedia scenes and characters were painted on the walls of Trausnitz Castle, leaving unique iconographic evidence of commedia's influence. Commedia troupes from Italy began appearing in Germany and Austria as early as the 1680's, and were a powerful force in the development of indigenous theatre forms. Crude folk entertainments evolved into a strong native drama by the dawn of the eighteenth century, due in considerable part to this influence of commedia. Out of these local entertainments came a variation on commedia's *zanni* called Hanswurst. Bearing the stamp of his place of origin, Hanswurst was a pot-bellied, beer-swilling peasant. This stock character likely rose to such prominence because of exceptional acting performances, most notably those of Joseph Anton Stranitzky (1676-1726) who popularized the character. Hanswurst soon appeared in all improvised comedies and even contributed comic turns in most serious works. He was similar to Beolco's Ruzzante; a clever knave with the uncanny ability to work his way out of even the most troublesome situations. The character was always recognizable by his red jacket, yellow pantaloons, cone-shaped green hat, and wooden sword. Hanswurst remained influential well into the nineteenth century, and he even had an alter-ego, Kasperl,[2] a puppet similar to Punch, which took on many of the characteristics of the typical Hanswurst,[3] and ultimately eclipsed him in popularity. It is clear that Hanswurst, and his many manifestations, led to stock rustic and working class characters who peopled nineteenth and early twentieth century comedies.

For some time, the extreme popularity of Hanswurst postponed any serious changes in German drama. The works of Kaspar von Stieler (1632-1707), an early German poet and nobleman, were commedic. His plays were mostly written for Thuringian and Saxon court performances and featured Scaramutza, his particular derivative of the commedia mask, Scarmuccia. Beginning in the 1720's, Johann Christoph Gottsched and Carolina Neuber began an active reform of the German theatre by encouraging a completely new repertory of plays that aimed, in part, at the complete banishment of Hanswurst and his ilk.[4] Gottsched and Neuber fundamentally succeeded, but folk and commedic traditions continued to intrigue even the most significant of Germany's artists.

The influence of commedia lingered, especially in its impact on the slowly evolving literary drama. Germany's greatest poet and dramatist,

Johann Wolfgang von Goethe (1749-1832), spent twenty-six years, from 1791 to 1817, as artistic director of the Hoftheater in Weimar, where, along with his many innovations, he experimented with commedic techniques. His novel, *Wilhelm Meister's Apprenticeship* (1795-1796), focuses on a man who loves theatre at its most theatrical, but, more significantly, Goethe used improvisation and half-masks in a production of Terence's *The Brothers*, and experimented with some commedia *scenarii*. Goethe later wrote of his visit to Rome when he had been dazzled by carnivals, commedia characters and actors, and street entertainers of all sorts, regarding them as extraordinarily effective symbolic human images. He was especially enamored of masks,

> which in our country have as little life and meaning for us as mummies, here seem sympathitic and characteristic expressions of the country: every age, character type and profession is embodied in some extraordinary costume, and since people run around in fancy dress for the greater part of the year, nothing seems more natural than to see faces in dominoes on the stage as well.[5]

Goethe's contemporary, Friedrich Schiller (1759-1805), mostly remembered for his tragedies, turned out a highly polished tragicomic adaptation of Gozzi's *Turandot*, which he called *Turandot, Princess of China* (1802). Giacomo Puccini made use of Schiller's treatment for his opera Turandot, which retains some of the commedic elements introduced by Gozzi. Although it is clear that commedia had marginal impact on Schiller's work, he was touched by it. Heinrich von Kleist's (1777-1811) plays typically offer an existential view of the fragility of humans and their world. His essay, "About the Marionette Theatre," is a commedic statement suggesting that until man understands his nature he is a puppet unable to comprehend his world and its forces. He was influenced by Molière, as seen in his play *Amphitryon* (1807), and some of his other works, particularly *Cathy from Heilbron* (1810), are also influenced by fairytale elements. Austrian dramatist Ferdinand Raimund (1790-1836) was more indebted to commedia than any of his contemporaries. He interpreted commedic traditions, with an emphasis on fairytales. Raimund transformed traditional Viennese fairytale plays by weaving bittersweet pain and doubt into fanciful and graceful commedic farces. In Raimund's moralistic plays, the movement from illusion, to a recognition of a deeper human reality, mirrored the slow changes that were to push commedia further out of the limelight in the nineteenth century, especially as the realistic theatre began to take shape. His best plays, *The Girl from Fairyland; or, The Farmer as Millionaire* (1826), *The King of the Alps and the Enemy of Man* (1828), and *The Spendthrift* (1834), all reflect a persuasive blending of illusionism with his own particular brand of idealistic and conservative realism. Johann Nestroy (1801-1862) may be perceived as a link between the commedic folk theatre of Hanswurst or Raimund and such modern German and Austrian commedists as Brecht and Horváth. His earliest plays obviously reflected folk and fairytale elements, but his later satiric plays became increasingly realistic and political. Nestroy also acted in his plays, including *The Talisman* (1840) and *Freedom Comes to Krähwinkel* (1848).

Diverse commedic elements appeared in many other plays and entertainments throughout the nineteenth century, but when modern commedic plays and techniques arrived on German and Austrian stages they arrived via the influence of other modern European theatre artists. Although commedia had a powerful impact in Germany and Austria on cabaret[6] and other popular entertainments, and occasional literary figures, in the theatre between 1900 and 1930 it was most visible in the work of a single director.

Max Reinhardt

Craig's theories were more original and controversial; Meyerhold was more political and theatrically daring; but, if there was one stage artist who became the international symbol of the new staging practices at the beginning of the twentieth century it was Max Reinhardt (1873-1943). Reinhardt was born in Baden, near Vienna, and while still in his teens he began to study acting. His whole life was the theatre, and by the early 1890's he was playing small roles at the Neue Volkstheater in Vienna and in summer theatre. His first full season was spent at the Stadttheater in Salzburg in 1893-94, after which he was engaged by Otto Brahm for the Deutsches Theater in Berlin. Brahm became his most significant mentor, although the pupil quickly outdistanced the teacher.

In 1901, while still serving a dutiful apprenticeship with Brahm, Reinhardt opened a cabaret, *Schall und Rauch*, which evolved into the Kleine Theater in 1903. Slowly resisting the German theatre's movement toward Realism, he staged a variety of controversial contemporary works there, including dramas by Strindberg, Gorky, Wilde, and Wedekind. By 1903, Reinhardt had left Brahm's ensemble and officially became artistic manager of the Kleines and Neue theatres. When in 1905 the Deutsches Theatre also fell under his management, he had emerged as a dominant figure of the German stage, maintaining a repertory of German and European classics while also producing an array of new works. Not content to keep his company in Berlin or Vienna, beginning in 1909, he made almost continuous tours of German cities, as well as of the capitals of Europe and, ultimately, the United States. His preeminence can be assumed from Arthur Schnitzler's comment that "If God ever came to Berlin, he'd make sure he got tickets to see Reinhardt."[7]

As an extremely eclectic director, Reinhardt found inspiration in many places. In 1903, he attended an exhibition of Craig's designs, which "impressed him deeply and decisively,"[8] and he sought to learn more about the newest production concepts emanating from London and other European capitals. He borrowed openly from the work of his contemporaries, particularly Craig, much to the Englishman's intense annoyance. Craig had received numerous offers from Reinhardt to produce in Berlin as early as 1904, but negotiations typically broke down over finances or play selection. In later years, Craig bitterly criticized Reinhardt's methods, and the inevitable comparisons between them never failed to infuriate Craig, who felt that Reinhardt and his troupe had "a touch of genius," but that they were "without originality and without art. They exhibit to the audience all the evidences of their hard labor, but beauty stubbornly refuses to come upon their stage."[9] Craig's reaction is undoubtedly self-serving and biased. Reinhardt's prolific involvement in numerous theatres and tours, and his unprecedented commercial and critical success, were a source of frustration and envy for Craig, who had achieved so little production work. Looking at the two from a more objective standpoint, Sheldon Cheney commended Reinhardt's "prodigious energy,"[10] but qualified his praise by pointing out that he "worked too fast to be the deep thinker and original creator that Craig is."[11]

Perhaps so, but Reinhardt had a genius for theatrical production that was, despite its debt to many identifiable influences, fully his own. Margaret Dietrich notes that he led what was for a time an inconceivable revolution "precisely because its origin lay in the spirit of music, of rhythm, and in the sensual qualities of the scene. He was a magician of the stage, inexhaustible in finding ways of staging the visions of his dream-world."[12] Reinhardt's "dream world" was filled with characters, visions, and techniques from a stunning variety of sources. Like Craig and Meyerhold, he found traditional Oriental theatre, ancient ritual drama, and commedia to be rich sources of inspiration. He was less interested in using commedia as a political battering ram than Blok and Meyerhold were, or as a tool for recreating performance techniques, as both Meyerhold and Craig had done. Reinhardt was an antiquarian, seeking to recapture the childlike joy of clowns, carnival, and fairytales, freed from the radical performance theories of Craig or the ironic grotesquerie and political cynicism of Meyerhold. He sought to make what he perceived as the original commedic spirit alive to a modern audience. This desire had its source in Reinhardt's love of clowns and comics.

Theatrical tradition generated something of a religious fervor and respect in Reinhardt. Leopoldskron, his home in Salzburg, was a miniature museum of theatrical art and commedia emphemera, with a special emphasis on eighteenth century items. Commedia's broadly theatrical, anarchic energy attracted Reinhardt, and he hoped to introduce it to the modern German stage. It is likely that he first became interested in commedia through his knowledge of the Austrian folk theatre where the commedic Hanswurst character ruled supreme. Although Reinhardt shared a distrust of the realistic stage with Craig and Meyerhold, he was less a revolutionary iconoclast than he was an iconographic theatricalist who believed in

> the deathlessness of the theatre. It is the happiest loophole of escape for those who have secretly put their childhood in their pockets and have gone off with it to play to the end of their days. The art of the stage affords also liberation from the conventional drama of life, for it is not dissimulation that is the business of the play but revelation. Only the actor who cannot lie, who is himself undisguised, and who profoundly unlocks his heart deserves the laurel. The supreme goal of the theatre is truth, not the outward, naturalistic truth of everyday, but the ultimate truth of the soul.[13]

His love of the actor was similar to Craig's and Meyerhold's, although he particularly favored the magical clowns associated with the play of childhood rather than the ironic dualities of Meyerhold's Pierrot, or the rigidly controlled movements and gestures of Craig's über-marionette. Centrally, Reinhardt was an actor, and he directed his actors as substitutes for himself, instead of as creative collaborators. Nevertheless, he did consider the actor the dominant theatrical artist and his ideal actor, like Craig's, was a master artist:

> It is to the actor and to no one else that the theater belongs. When I say this, I do not mean, of course, the professional actor alone. I mean, first and foremost, the actor as poet. All the great dramatists

have been and are today born actors, whether or not they have formally adopted this calling, and whatever success they have had in it. I mean likewise the actor as director, stage-manager, musician, stage-designer, painter, and certainly not least of all, the actor as spectator.[14]

Reinhardt lamented the cautiousness of modern actors compared to performers of earlier periods. Commedia clowns, he alluded, as they

wandered about like gypsies. . .developed stronger, rarer personalities. They were more unbridled in their passion; their outbursts were more powerful, the spirits that possessed them, more masterful. They had no outside interests. They were actors, body and soul. Today the body is willing, but the spirit is weak, and their interests are divided.[15]

He eloquently redefined the myth of the evolution of theatre and acting to parallel childlike play, suggesting that early man

had an irresistible desire to throw himself into a fantastic play of changing one form into another, one fate into another, one effect into another. These were the first attempts to fly above his narrow material existence. The possibilities inherent in him but not brought to full growth by his life thus unfolded their shadowy wings and carried him far over his knowledge and away into the heart of a strange experience. He discovered all the delights of transformation, all the ecstasy of passion, all the illusive life of dreams.[16]

Reinhardt hoped, as Craig had hoped, for the appearance of the ideal actor who could create while maintaining complete control of his being and the forms and genres of the stage. He fancied that this actor would be "at once sculptor and sculpture; he is man at the farthest borderline between reality and dream, and he stands with both feet in both realms. The actor's power of self-suggestion is so great that he can bring about in his body not only inner and psychological but even outer and physical changes."[17] Reinhardt's love of the actor, and his own experience at acting, did not hamper his directing ability: he was an inventive and dominating maestro of the stage. Actors who worked with him recalled his eye for visual elements, for the rhythm of the entire performance, and for the unyielding force of his directing style. He was remembered as a benevolent dictator, the master puppeteer of his productions. To catch the director's strong vision and the guiding rhythm associated with it, was the actors' ultimate goal:

> The essential task of the director is to interpret the dreams of others in his own fashion and to render his interpretation effective and real. The essential character of his work consists primarily in clearly comprehending the meaning of the work to be produced; in developing the action in plastic fashion; in getting his own image of the dramatic characters, which naturally must be humanly rounded out beyond the individual plot; and above all, determining the inner melody of the production.[18]

His sometime collaborator, playwright Hugo von Hofmannsthal, described how Reinhardt's control worked: he managed to combine his interest in many of the individual production elements with a fascination for the endless possibilities of visual design and for the actors' art. As Hofmannsthal remembered:

> Reinhardt greatly loves all these elements of the play. He will not be without them; his hand holds them in a firm grip. He needs them, and makes use of the all; the magic spell cast by the great actor, as well as by the clown's grimace and by the painter's craft. But he subordinates them all to a higher end -- to the organized whole.[19]

Borrowing from the theories of Swiss designer and theorist Adolphe Appia, Reinhardt found two essential unifying elements: music and light. His most memorable productions became spectacular theatrical symphonies. With *The Comedy of Errors*, for example, he used music in much the way a film director scores a movie, with music setting the rhythm and the emotional scheme of the entire performance. Here he is closer to Craig, whose early productions made the unification of music and movement dominant over words. Reinhardt's productions often centrally included movement, especially silent movement, accompanied by music.

It is important to note that although he is remembered today primarily for his huge symphonic productions, Reinhardt was at least as equally interested in small scale productions which de-emphasized state-of-the-art technology. He remodeled the Redoutensaal at the Imperial Palace in Vienna in 1922, and began producing plays by such writers as Goethe, Molière, Calderon, and Hofmannsthal. American producer and scene designer Kenneth Macgowan, an admirer of Reinhardt's work, recalled that the stage of the Redoutensaal went

> beyond even Copeau's Vieux-Colombier in the attempt to re-establish in our century that active relationship between actor and spectator which existed in the great theatres of other centuries, and towards which the finest minds of the theatre have been striving. Here is a stage freed from all the associations of modern stage-setting, innocent of machinery or illusions, essentially theatrical. Actors must be actors upon its boards. They can not try to represent actual people; they can only present themselves to the audience as artists who will try to give them a vision of reality.[20]

Macgowan might have added that the Redoutensaal was perfect for those Reinhardt productions most influenced by commedia. He could also capture the commedic spirit in any theatre, since it was such an integral part of his style, both as an actor and as a director. His productions owed much to his innate "sense of play, which was so strong in childhood and can not be dispensed with in art and especially not in the theatre."[21] Rejecting naturalistic acting, he worried that the vivid style of acting and dramatic elements "found in the old Austrian and Bavarian theatre, such as the commedia dell'arte,"[22] would find little nourishment on the realistic stage. Literature, he feared, "has tyrannised [sic] too much over the theatre and carried it too far away from its starting-point."[23]

While Reinhardt believed literary theatre stifled the creativity of both director and actor, his commedic productions did not, as a rule, depend on any significant improvisation. Although he occasionally permitted an especially gifted comic actor latitude while rehearsing a role, Reinhardt preferred to maintain the illusion of spontaneity and improvisation within a studied performance. He emphasized the carnivalesque visual aspects of eighteenth century commedia, and was also drawn to the rambunctious clowning of earlier commedia, but his intention was that all clowning be well-rehearsed and perfected for performance.

The earliest evidence of commedia in a Reinhardt production was in Schnitzler's one-act play-within-a-play, *The Green Cockatoo* (1899), which he produced at the Kleines Theater in November, 1904. The play is an interesting mixture of Schnitzler's themes of sexual politics as reflected by the theatre as metaphor. It was the emphasis on theatricality in Schnitzler's play, which focuses on actors during the French Revolution, that obviously attracted Reinhardt. After this time, his productions of Shakespeare's and Molière's comedies began with the actors approaching the stage as travelling players, who then began to perform the play. Theatricality and artifice were thereby foremost in an audience's mind.

Reinhardt's two greatest comic productions, *A Midsummer Night's Dream* (first staged at the Neues Theater in Berlin in January, 1905), and *The Servant of Two Masters* (first produced at the Kammerspiele Theater in Berlin in October, 1907), were mounted again and again throughout his career, and the later versions often varied substantially from earlier treatments. Typically, these productions became increasingly commedic.

Reinhardt's earliest versions of *A Midsummer Night's Dream* were performed in period costumes before a realistic set. Eventually, like most of his other works, this play was presented with increasing simplicity and symbolism. This was due, in part, to the conceptions of scene designer Ernst Stern, who had worked as a cartoonist and artist before Reinhardt invited him to collaborate. The two staged a variety of productions between 1906 and 1920. In Reinhardt's first treatments of *A Midsummer Night's Dream*, the trees were realistic models of papier-mache, and time passed by careful changes in light and shadow. In later productions of the play, however, Reinhardt and

Stern strove to conceive the play freshly by cutting away the props requisite to the realistic stage. They wished to see the play within a simpler "spiritual" context and created a dream-like atmosphere on a recreated ornately detailed Baroque stage.

In a dozen productions between the first in 1905 and the 1935 Hollywood film version, Reinhardt's conception of *A Midsummer Night's Dream* moved away from Realism. In later versions, the play's magic, its fairytale qualities, and low comedy came to the fore.[24] As director, Reinhardt took seemingly antithetical qualities, and permitted them a sympathetic and complementary coexistence. His son and biographer, Gottfried Reinhardt, remembered that all of Reinhardt's versions of *A Midsummer Night's Dream* succeeded because each became "a conceptual whole."[25] Gottfried Reinhardt points out that in one early version the

> woods *acted*. The actors were a botanical part of the woods. Trees, shrubbery, mist, moonlight intermingled with the lovers, the rehearsing artisans, the trolls, the elfs, the spirits. The music, the wind, the breathless running, the clowning, the fighting were all of one key and come from one and the same source. So did the calm, the sweep, the dream, the poetry. Nothing was background, nothing foreground. Passion, humor, lyricism, bawdiness, nobility, fantasy did not have their allotted moments side by side or consecutively. They were ever-present, simultaneous, feeding on one another in multiple symbiosis.[26]

Reinhardt's early biographer Huntley Carter pointed out, for example, that the childlike and theatrical treatment of *A Midsummer Night's Dream* Reinhardt employed brought out the "Commedia element of broad humanity in Shakespeare's plays, and [reminded us that] the plays themselves appealed to the ordinary public, the man of culture, and to the actor."[27]

The 1935 Warner Brothers' film version, directed by Reinhardt and William Dieterle, offers rare tangible evidence of Reinhardt's conception of *A Midsummer Night's Dream*. The film ties a somewhat realistic visual scheme (a concession to Hollywood, perhaps) to a more mature view of the characters typical of his later versions. The childlike fantasy of the arcadian scenes, the passion of the lovers, and the nobility of the court are attended to. However, the farcical, low comedy of Shakespeare's "rude mechanicals" performing their play-within-a-play, and the high-jinks of the denizens of the fairy kingdom, are the most memorable features of the film. This achievement owes much to Shakespeare's appreciation of clowns and to Reinhardt's love of commedia.

Gottfried Reinhardt points out that his father failed to get the cast he most desired for the film. Aside from being a film buff's wildest fantasy, Reinhardt's cast choices reveal much about the broad spectrum that he applied to *A Midsummer Night's Dream*. His ideal cast would have included Clark Gable (Demetrius), Gary Cooper (Lysander), Myrna Loy (Helena), Joan Crawford (Hermia), John Barrymore (Oberon), Greta Garbo (Titania), Fred Astaire (Puck), Walter Huston (Theseus), Charlie Chaplin (Bottom), W.C. Fields (Thisbe), and Wallace Beery (Lion). His choice of Hollywood's most popular romantic leading men and women for the lovers, the grandly theatrical Barrymore and the ethereal Garbo for the fairy king and queen, the distinguished Walter Huston as Theseus, the lithe Astaire as the fairy sprite, and the film era's greatest clowns, Chaplin and Fields, for the leading rustics, suggests a grandiose wedding of the sublime and the ridiculous that Brooks Atkinson described, in his review of Reinhardt's 1927 New York production of the play, as "a symphonic pageant in imaginative beauty unrelated to anything in our daily lives."[28] The cast that actually appeared in the film was decidedly less exciting. The lovers, with the exception of the youthful and lovely Olivia da Havilland as Hermia, were weak, or disastrously miscast, and on film, despite state-of-the-art special effects, the magical qualities of the fairy scenes seem routine. Reinhardt's commedic touch is most vividly present in the inspired clowning of Mickey Rooney's Puck and the rustics, with filmdom's leading hoodlum actor, James Cagney, as Bottom, and character actors Joe E. Brown, Frank McHugh, and Hugh Herbert in support.

Reinhardt's adeptness with the low comedy scenes had been noted by critics in his earliest productions of the play:

> the lovers were not particularly impressive on opening night; nor did Titania and Oberon do full justice to the poetry of Shakespeare. Fortunately, the clowns made up for these flaws; under the leadership of Hermann Thimig they saved the evening with their refreshing humor. Bottom's awakening after his adventure with Titania was a brilliant pantomime loudly applauded by the spectators.[29]

A Midsummer Night's Dream was (if one counts the film version) the most widely seen of Reinhardt's productions. It has become the definitive modern version of the play, replaced only in 1970 by Peter Brook's exhilarating production which owes even more to the techniques of commedia and clowning. Though Brook's *A Midsummer Night's Dream* has replaced Reinhardt's, it pays it homage as well.

During his career, Reinhardt, at one time or another, directed most of Shakespeare's comedies. These were generally well-received, but few achieved the acclaim of *A Midsummer Night's Dream*, although a particularly acclaimed production was Reinhardt's *Twelfth Night*, which he first staged in Budapest in May, 1909.[30] Part of his ambitious Shakespeare cycle, the play was revived often. Lively performances, "full of burlesque gaiety,"[31] showcased Reinhardt's love of clowns and commedic moments. In the commedia tradition, he used cast members to perform short pantomimes during set changes. These little scenes became regular features of Reinhardtian theatre. Like Meyerhold, he kept audience members mindful of their involvement in the performance, ever aware that actors were players on the stage, not characters come to realistic life.

Specific commedic touches were incorporated in the actual performance of Reinhardt's *The Taming of the Shrew*, which opened December 15, 1909, at the Deutsches Theater in Berlin. It later played in Budapest and London, where it was presented by John Martin-Harvey. Aside from Craig's simple, symbolic setting for *Much Ado About Nothing* in 1903, London had rarely seen Shakespeare staged with the simplicity employed by Reinhardt. To emphasize the play's farcical qualities, Reinhardt made use of a small group of players separate from the actors themselves. They were dressed as commedia types, and they changed scenes, did acrobatics, and otherwise diverted the audience. In the case of *The Taming of the Shrew*, this was not just technique for its own sake, but an aesthetic interpretation of the play. As the designer Ernst Stern said, the

> piece was less a comedy than a farce, hard tack for primitive tastes, and thus to play it as a piece of barnstorming was right. After all, argued Reinhardt, for whom was the piece intended? For Christopher Sly, the drunken tinker. It was not high comedy, but typical low comedy, a rambunctious farce. Only so interpreted did Petruchio's coarse brutalities become at all tolerable.[32]

With this in mind, Reinhardt set the action before a tavern from which the drunken Christopher Sly has been ejected. Stern dressed the actors in "the striking and colourful costumes of the clowns, harlequins, columbines and pantaloons of the Italian *Commedia dell'Arte*, after the engraving of the great French master, Callot."[33]

Reinhardt's love of farce, especially as it is understood within commedia tradition, marked all of his Shakespearean productions. Even the darker themes of *The Merchant of Venice* (first staged by him in Vienna in May, 1910) were played against "the impetuous festive spirit of the early Renaissance,"[34] according to the preeminent Danish critic George Brandes. The setting was a "sumptuous, irresponsible, reckless Venice, with the young men caparisoned in extravagant costumes and the flirtatious women displaying their Oriental jewels."[35] Like Shakespeare, Reinhardt was enamored of the spirit of Venice itself, and he "never wearied of putting her on the stage (in his many *Merchants of Venice*, *Othellos*, in *Tales of Hoffmann* and the revivals of Gozzi and Goldoni) or on the screen (in his second film, *Venetian*

Nights)."[36] The particular effect of focusing on the joy-filled and colorful street life of Venice was that the appearance of Shylock produced a "disturbing dissonance in the atmosphere of light-hearted Venetian cheer."[37]

Venice's carnival spirit also was put to good use in Reinhardt's production of *Much Ado About Nothing*, first presented on February 23, 1912, at the Deutsches Theatre. [38] Here he played out the farcical, light-hearted aspects of the play against the decadent wonders of the Italian city. One witness recalled that the production was as "Light as a feather, you keep time with Beatrice's blithe love dance, joyful and grateful to the artist who makes you see life so optimistically. Relying on himself alone, Reinhardt wiped the dust off that comedy and revealed its immortal face."[39]

Reinhardt's inspired production of Goldoni's *The Servant of Two Masters*, staged regularly between the years 1907 and 1940, was more profoundly commedic than any of his other productions.[40] As Augusta Adler recounts of the 1924 version, Reinhardt

> wanted to play Goldoni's comedy in the simplest way possible, as it had been enacted on stages at fairs in the poet's time. The stage was of utmost simplicity: a scaffold of boards and trestles on which the scenery was placed by actors during the change of scenes. A small orchestra conducted by Bernhardt Paumgartner accompanied the play and the interpolated dances. The Viennese cast, Hugo, Hermann and Helene Thimig, Paul Hermann, Sybille Binder and Dagny Servaes acted in true Commedia dell'Arte tradition on these boards. It was a perfect performance.[41]

Reinhardt instinctively understood the nature of commedia, particularly in his use of the script, which he was able to see as a scenario. Critics have suggested that Reinhardt overstepped his role as director, usurping the work of both the playwright and the actor. It seems more the case, however, that Reinhardt was perfectly in his element as a director, particularly when he loosened the script to bring forth a comic atmosphere so rich that his actors found their own work nearly magically transmogrified. In support of

Reinhardt's focus on the actors, Otto Preminger, the well-known film director and character actor, played a minor role in Reinhardt's *The Servant of Two Masters*, and recalled that the director was drawn to the play's "rich opportunity for actors, and while he would never permit an actor to overact, he also did not make them underact."[42]

Reinhardt was particularly lucky that the 1924 production of *The Servant of Two Masters* was anchored by the performances of the Thimig family, a remarkable group of actors experienced in all forms of drama, but particularly adept in broad comedy. Like a traditional commedia troupe, they had the almost unique experience in modern theatre of working together on stages for most of their lives. Galvanized by the manic pace set by Reinhardt, Hermann Thimig as Truffaldino, Hugo Thimig as Pantalone, and Helene Thimig as Smeraldina, pulled together memorable performances, and formed the nucleus of an extraordinary ensemble cast.[43] Subsequent productions nearly always featured at least one Thimig; the 1926 Salzburg revival had four Thimigs in the cast, thanks to the addition of the youngest sibling, Hans Thimig, in the role of Florindo.

Hermann Thimig dominated the performance with his "brilliant, overflowing impersonation of Truffaldino."[44] Judging from many contemporary accounts, he gave that rare and unforgettable performance during which an actor of genius elevates farce to art. He understood, as his commedia forebears had, that this sort of lunatic acting requires complete conviction and a total, unswerving commitment to all actions, even the most insignificant. His most memorable moment came in the scene in which the half-starved Truffaldino gorges himself on an overflowing bowl of pasta, an extended pantomime which must have come very close to the spirit of traditional commedia *lazzi*.

Apart from his ability to inspire extraordinary performances from his cast, Reinhardt invariably made changes in the play itself. He asked

LIVERPOOL JOHN MOORES UNIVERSITY
LEARNING SERVICES

Hofmannsthal to contribute a new prologue in which all of the characters, except Truffaldino, came forward to introduce themselves to the audience. The search for the missing actor which followed permitted the audience to see a controlled form of anarchy amid the improvisation; they knew from the outset what the evening's lunatic mood was to be. Reinhardt also commissioned a new translation of the play's text, and added commedic passages from the plays of the eighteenth century playwright, and occasional Hanswurst, Johann Josef Felix von Kurz,[45] but the play's language was clearly secondary to Reinhardt's interpolated clowning.

The addition of conductor Bernhardt Paumgartner's varied selection of music and songs, some drawn from Austrian folk music as well as from Mozart, were an integral part of the production, beginning with the 1924 version. Reinhardt worked for a consistent and unified whole, with scenery and costumes in the spirit of Baroque commedia, inspired by the works of several Venetian painters, including Giovanni Canaletto. Relying on the painterly influence, Reinhardt insisted that all of the scenery be flat and obviously one-dimensional. The set was constructed so it appeared that the actors were completely responsible for changing and rearranging the scenery. Preminger recalled that Reinhardt "didn't use the curtain. The scene changes were effected by just changing the furniture; and the furniture was changed by us young actors carrying out little tables and chairs in a dance step."[46] Actors entered and exited through swinging doors, and the audience could see them as they waited offstage for their cues.

Reinhardt's scene and costume designer, Oskar Laske, created costumes that were accurate antiquarian recreations. Bright and vibrant colors were used, set against the lighter, pastel background of the highly artificial setting. Laske's design depicted a bit of the fanciful background of eighteenth century Venice, but the scenic panels were scrambled absurdly into a random order in performance. Reinhardt was so pleased with Laske's scenery and costumes that they were used for the 1924 production, the 1928 American tour, and the 1930 and 1931 Salzburg versions.[47] Although the scenery was theatrically artificial, Reinhardt insisted on real props, especially for the scenes involving food. Aware that a major characteristic of several commedia characters was gluttony, he believed that the appeal of the food itself was a fundamental element in the creation of Truffaldino's character. Hermann Thimig always gorged himself on real spaghetti in performance.

Reinhardt's last *The Servant of Two Masters* was presented as part of his Los Angeles Actors' Workshop in 1939-1940. Retitled *At Your Service*, this version differed considerably from his earlier treatments of the play. Here he was working with young and relatively inexperienced actors, including Robert Ryan and Nanette Fabray at the beginning of their careers. Changes were made to address the tastes of an American audience. For example, a song sung by Truffaldino and Smeraldina in the German version was based on Austrian folk music, while in the American version a comically stereotypical Italian love song replaced it. Again demonstrating an instinctive understanding of commedia characters, Reinhardt sought new comic business suited to the particular abilities and mannerisms of his new cast. He was especially impressed with the musical talents of Fabray, who, in the role of Smeraldina, was a hit with her performance of "Smeraldina's Song." Its first verse was an ironic commentary on the falseness of men, but the second dropped the cynicism and offered practical advice on flirtation.

Looking back, Ryan thought that it was unfortunate that Reinhardt was mostly remembered for such spectacular productions as *The Miracle* and *Everyman*, "only one part of a multi-faceted genius."[48] For Ryan, the center of Reinhardt's work was his obsession with "the inner life of man, the mysterious spirit that both flickers and flames in all of us. How to release it was his artistic dedication and the creative purpose of his life. Two people sitting in a hovel served his purpose as well (and often better) than a giant stage jammed with battalions of actors and Everests of scenery."[49]

Despite the implied simplicity of commedia, however, Reinhardt brought much spectacle to his commedic productions, including his elaborate staging of Gozzi's *Turandot*, which was first presented on October 27, 1911, at the Deutsches Theater. It is not surprising that Gozzi's Chinese fairytale, which includes four commedia characters, appealed to him, for it contained elements of commedia, Oriental theatre, and the movement and pantomime implied by both. Not satisfied with Schiller's translation, the only existing German version of *Turandot* at that time, Reinhardt commissioned a new version by Karl Vollmoeller, who was able to create an adaptation freer, more mobile, and generally closer to Gozzi's commedic spirit than Schiller's Enlightenment era verse treatment. In Vollmoeller's prose, Reinhardt found the opportunity for a wilder and more comic improvisational style. Although he used much dialogue from the original play in the scenes between commedia characters, he worked with his actors in rehearsals to improvise business and dialogue. The commedia characters were especially successful, and played lightly before Ernst Stern's fantastical setting, which emphasized the mystical and mythical Oriental background of the play. The simple costumes for the commedia characters were in effective contrast to the bright and ornate colors of the Chinese scenes. Reinhardt emphasized the fantasy in the play, and used the evocative music by Ferruccio Busoni[50] as a score

> adapted to tell the story. The prelude introduced us to the scene and the principal characters were given their themes. The entrances were announced; the emperor's by a fanfare, Turandot's being given out by the cellos and bases and so on. The music thus moving and acting throughout the play. Much of the music is indeed worthy of quotation as an example of its successful application of the needs of the drama.[51]

The 1926 production of *Turandot* at the Salzburg Festival was quite different from the 1911 version. The scenery and costumes were modified for the outdoor Salzburg Theatre in designs by Oskar Strnad, and this time the music was composed and directed by Bernhardt Paumgartner. Despite its fundamental workability, especially in permitting comic interpolations by the commedia characters, Reinhardt felt that Vollmoeller's 1911 translation had not gone far enough. For the 1926 production, he asked Alfred Polgar to make whatever changes he regarded as necessary, and to add some new material. The loose and improvisatory quality of Polgar's new passages emphasized still more the commedic aspects of the play. This pleased Reinhardt, who wished to focus even more attention on the play's four commedia characters this time. Polgar's extensions and simplifications of Vollmoeller's version created a lighter and more playable style, allowing occasional opportunities for the actors themselves to interpolate. Reinhardt hoped to heighten the ensemble playing by setting up acting duels among the four commedia characters. According to critics, the idea backfired when it became apparent to the audience that the actors "spent their energy trying to top each other."[52]

Reinhardt may have hoped for too much. The confines of early twentieth century training for actors conspired to defeat any true recreation of commedic improvisation. Not only were rehearsal periods relatively brief, but actors were not brought up in the close-knit ensemble tradition of commedia at its height. When Reinhardt put four leading comedians together, he invited the kind of competition and jealousy the critics describe. Furthermore, even the most gifted modern actors were ill-equipped to excel in the art of improvisation, even under Reinhardt's tutelage. By over-emphasizing the comedians, the play was distorted, and the lyrical Chinese fairytale that is its framework, was pushed too far into the background.

Reinhardt also produced plays from the canon of the French classical theatre. He staged Beaumarchais' *The Marriage of Figaro* at the Deutsches Theater in December, 1916, but it was Molière's plays that especially intrigued him. A Molière play, *The Bourgeois Gentleman*, led him into an extraordinary collaboration with Hofmannsthal and Richard Strauss. Although Gottfried Reinhardt recalled that his father considered his opera productions as "marginal efforts,"[53] this was an exception. Reinhardt had asked Hofmannsthal to adapt the work, and Strauss to write incidental music, but

> Hofmannsthal conceived the notion that he would substitute for the Turkish ceremony an entertainment that Monsieur Jourdain presents for Count Dorante and the Marquise Dorimene -- a little chamber opera, no longer than thirty minutes. There Hofmannsthal wished to contrast, "heroic mythological figures in eighteenth century costumes, dressed in crinolines and ostrich feathers, with figures from the commedia dell'arte." The chamber opera was to be called *Ariadne auf Naxos*.[54]

Ernst Stern's scene design, in concert with Reinhardt's staging, emphasized the mythological aspects of the opera and what Stern considered its "delightful and charming anachronisms."[55] The scene was set in a grotto in a palm grove where "Ariadne and Bacchus (as a young man) sing, and the supporting cast consists of various nymphs and a number of familiar figures, such as Zerbinetta, Harlequin, Truffaldino and others from the *Commedia dell'Arte*."[56] Molière's Jourdain, the bourgeois gentleman, played by Viktor Arnold, was used by Reinhardt as a spectator, much as he had used Christopher Sly in *The Taming of the Shrew*. Commedia characters, whose rambunctious and earthy love affairs served as counterpoint to the grand passions of Ariadne and Bacchus, made it possible to combine *opera seria* and *opera buffa* in an effective manner that brought new life to both forms.

In the libretto of *Ariadne auf Naxos*, commedia characters, led by Zerbinetta, brought an amusing and touching simplicity and humanity to the effete posturings of the mythical Ariadne and Bacchus. Hofmannsthal used aspects of Austrian popular comedy, as well as his understanding of commedia via Molière. In the opera scene, when Zerbinetta and her commedia troupe descend on the opera depicting the love of Bacchus and Ariadne, Hofmannsthal suggests through the mythical characters that love can transport lovers to a higher plane; and, in counterpoint, shows that earthly love abides always in the numerous partner-changing affairs of the commedia characters. This was a delicate combination, as Hofmannsthal pointed out in a letter to Strauss in 1911:

> Even if I think. . .only of the two groups, Ariadne-Bacchus, Zerbinetta and the four men -- even then I must tell myself that they need a mysterious power higher than music alone in order to reveal their ultimate significance at all. The subtly conceived exiguity of this play, these two groups acting beside each other in the narrowest space, this most careful calculation of each gesture, each step, the whole like a concert and at the same time like a ballet -- it will be lost, meaningless, a tattered rag, in incompetent hands; only in Reinhardt's, yours and mine can it grow into a singing flower, the incarnation of dance. *Love* is what it needs, enthusiasm, improvisation. . . .[57]

While no genuine improvisation occurred in the performance of the opera, Reinhardt proved a master of creating the illusion of spontaneity and improvisation even within the confining symphonic structure of an opera.

Ariadne auf Naxos opened at the Royal Opera House in Stuttgart on October 25, 1912, and Reinhardt's contribution was significant. His most effective touches were seen in Molière's play, which served as prologue to the opera. He had hired Viennese dancer Grete Wiesenthal to help bring the comedians to an especially ambitious level of movement. It was typical of a Reinhardt production, however, that the leading comic actor dominated the performance, and this was certainly true of Viktor Arnold as Jordain. Walther Volbach recalled that

> Never before and never thereafter have I witnessed such comic acting. I laughed when Jordain tried to learn how to dance, to dress, and to fence, yet I had so much pity for him that I felt like warning him when those aristocrats deceived him. And one had to cry and to laugh at the same time when, after the opera, unhappy, disappointed, alone on the stage, he said he would give his little finger to be a nobleman.[58]

The combination of Molière's play and the opera caused the initial performance to last nearly four hours. Despite impressive work in all areas, audience members complained, and in subsequent productions, Molière's comedy was dropped and replaced by a shorter operatic act, which established and explained the combining of the *opera seria* and *opera buffa* characters and which maintained the sense of the clashing of two worlds and two genres. This is how the opera is typically staged today, but, as Volbach wrote, "I must confess I still prefer the original form. I am happy I had the privilege to see and hear that unforgettable production by Strauss and Reinhardt."[59]

Reinhardt's numerous other productions of Molière's plays[60] were all influenced to some degree by his interest in commedia, but none more than his production of Molière's last play, *The Imaginary Invalid*, staged first at the Kammerspiele in March, 1916.[61] In typical Reinhardtian fashion, the leading comic actor dominated the proceedings. In this case, it was the small, rotund actor, Max Pallenberg, who had joined Reinhardt's company in 1915, following success in comic roles in operetta. As Argan, the ultimate hypochondriac, Pallenberg was permitted a freedom of improvisation in performance that was extraordinary. Reinhardt was delighted, but Pallenberg's fellow actors often feared his departures from the text, since he was inclined to also omit their cue lines. Oliver Sayler, who saw the 1923 revival at Leopoldskron (Reinhardt's palatial home) recalled that Pallenberg "swung the lariat of his wit in the carefree manner of the *commedia dell'arte* and ensnared with it not only the rest of the players but the last of a hundred spectators seated luxuriously in Archbishop Firmian's golden chairs round the great blaze in the fireplace of the marble hall at Leopoldskron."[62]

The production's stage decor was simple, and Reinhardt again made use of "a small band, who wore the costume of the period, [and] accompanied the short intermission scenes, in which Commedia dell'Arte figures floated past as in a colorful dream: Colombine, Harlequin, Polichinelle, Il Dottore and Zerbinetta."[63] The beginning of the performance was an ingenious mixture of reality and theatre, as Pallenberg, in character as Argan, served as host, offering improvised greetings to audience members as they were being seated. He talked about his various aches, pains, and imagined diseases, and introduced other characters as well, allowing the rest of the cast an opportunity to improvise, and demonstrate their individual skills at acrobatics or word-play.

The effect of commedia on Reinhardt was also visible in many of the contemporary plays he produced. Viktor Arnold, who ended a successful career when he committed suicide in despair over the outbreak of World War I, wrote a play entitled *Pierrot's Last Adventure*, which opened on March 19, 1912, at the Kammerspiele in a production directed by Reinhardt. Arnold himself was described as "a comedian of fantastic grotesqueness"[64] and "a master in giving expression to his most foolhardy fantasies."[65] He stood out as a modern Pierrot in a play that was otherwise a pallid imitation of the heavily ironic commedic plays that found an enthusiastic audience in Russia. It achieved only modest success, and never reappeared in Reinhardt's repertory after its initial production.

Karl Vollmoeller, who had adapted *Turandot* for Reinhardt the previous year, wrote a play called *A Venetian Night* which was first staged by Reinhardt in London in November, 1912.[66] It was a mime play intended to capitalize on the great international success of Reinhardt's earlier production of the mime play *Sumurun* in 1910. Ernst Stern supervised the installation of a revolving stage at London's Palace Theatre, but the Lord Chamberlain found *A Venetian Night*, which told the story of the adventurous love affairs of a rich and beautiful Venetian lady, "too dangerous to public morals to be permitted to be played as it stood."[67] Changes were made to secure the Lord Chamberlain's reluctant approval, but the play failed after three weeks. It was not especially commedic in any of its obvious elements, but Reinhardt did emphasize the carnival spirit in his depiction of Venice. Other contemporary plays Reinhardt staged with commedic features include

Pirandello's *Six Characters in Search of an Author* and Somerset Maugham's *Victoria*.

Reinhardt's successes continued through the 1920's, but as the Nazis rose to power, Reinhardt, a Jew, found himself in a precarious position. By 1933, the Nazi Regime had forced him to deed his theatres in Berlin to "the German people," and the following year, he gave up his theatres in Vienna and his home, Leopoldskron. After staging *The Merchant of Venice* with Italian actors at the Campo San Trovaso in Venice, Reinhardt left Europe for the United States, where he spent the remainder of his career.

Commedia in Germany and Austria After Reinhardt

Modern commedic theatre did not catch on in German and Austrian theatres as it had in Russia, despite Reinhardt's talent for using its techniques and traditions, and the great success many of his productions enjoyed during the first third of the twentieth century. A few of his contemporaries, however, and especially playwrights of the subsequent two generations, did continue to experiment with it.

Hugo von Hofmannsthal (1874-1929), Reinhardt's sometime collaborator, was interested in bringing features of other dramatic forms into his poetic plays. He wrote plays and operas inspired by classical myths and the Symbolist movement. As early as 1895, he recognized that audiences were tired of the emphasis placed on literary drama, and, in Michael Hamburger's words, were eager to turn to "all those arts which are executed without speech: for music, for the dance, and all the skills of acrobats and jugglers."[68] Among other traditions, Hofmannsthal recognized the importance of acrobatics, carnival, and circus on theatre. The image of the fool was especially influential on Hofmannsthal, and his early one-act play, *Death and the Fool*, blends his interest in commedia and medieval drama. Claudio, the "fool" of the title, at the point of his death, reminds one of both Everyman and Harlequin. In Hiram K. Moderwell's account of the play,

> The fool is called upon by Death, the Fiddler, to depart this life. He is unwilling. Then to the sound of the fiddle comes first his dead mother, then his former sweetheart, then his old friend. Each lived only for the Fool, and what has the Fool done with this costly life of his? Yes, he is ready to die. And Death, while taking him, marvels at these beings, who explain what cannot be explained, who read what is not written, and chart paths in the eternal darkness.[69]

Hofmannsthal uses elements of the medieval and commedic image of the fool for his dark allegorical vision of humankind's failure to live life to the fullest. His fool can only hope that having failed to live fully during his life, he will find in death a new life.

Hofmannsthal's most significant involvement with a commedic work was his libretto for Reinhardt's staging of Strauss's *Ariadne auf Naxos*, and, to a lesser degree, in his librettos for *Der Rosenkavalier* (1911) and *Arabella* (1929), as well as his three-act comedy, *The Difficult Man* (1921), which makes many references to clowns and circuses. Although he was not a true commedist like Craig, Meyerhold, or Reinhardt, he was able to realize in operatic form the deeply-dimensioned human qualities which the seemingly one-dimensional masks of commedia could provide.

Austrian dramatist Arthur Schnitzler (1862-1931), best known as the author of *Anatol* (1893) and *The Round Dance* (1902), included commedic touches in several works. Typically, his characters drift aimlessly, at times yearning for deeper love (often with tragic consequences), while making do with a variety of fleeting sexual encounters. In a sense, life and love is improvised play to Schnitzler's drifters.

One of Schnitzler's earliest commedic plays, *The Green Cockatoo* (1899), is set in Paris on the eve of the French Revolution. The star of a company of actors performing in a tavern is playing a jealous lover. He discovers that his wife is having an affair with one of the noblemen watching the play. In a rage of jealousy, he kills the nobleman, shattering the high-spirited gaiety of the tavern. At the same moment, the French Revolution begins in the streets outside the tavern. Schnitzler's use of a commedic jealous lover whose true jealousy is initially masked, and the juxtapositon of the gaiety of the tavern and the play-within-the-play, with a depiction of a cataclysmic historic event, are typical modern uses of commedic elements. Schnitzler also wrote such overtly commedic plays as *The Transformation of Pierrot* (1908), a brief play in six scenes, and *The Veil of Pierrette* (1910), a "soft-edged, sentimental, and morbid"[70] play that was notably produced in an almost completely transformed adaptation by Meyerhold in 1910.

German dramatist Paul Ernst (1866-1933) wrote several successful comedies, including *A Night in Florence* (1904), *Saint Crispin* (1910), and *Pantaloon and His Son* (1916), which show commedic characters from a fresh angle. In these plays, the comic situation, often arising out of a confusion of identity, provokes reflection rather than laughter. Unlike Hofmannsthal, who found commedia through indirect sources (Molière), Ernst seems to have looked directly at traditional Italian commedia, to which he brought a distinct and specific reality. Ernst's commedic plays, set during carnival time in Venice around 1700, posit a dual existence for his characters, who are typically involved in a lover's triangle. The characters usually enter the scene wearing masks, which they remove to speak. The ambivalence and duality of the characters created by the use of masks is central to Ernst's plot and themes. Masks are the main cause of mistaken identity and various plot confusions, as well as a protection from complete revelation of self.

Traditional commedia *lazzi* are reworked by Ernst who makes the humor more subtle. The clowning pays homage to original commedia style while transforming it for a contemporary audience. His humor is never rambunctious yet it hints at traditional commedia. Ernst worked to create a comedy of ideas, emphasizing verbal play rather than physical slapstick. He focuses on the problem of identity, not only in the masks and other superficialities, but in the very nature of the characters, and the transforming and confusing effect love has on them. Commedia techniques are used by his characters to reveal the evils of bourgeois society.[71]

The dominant figure in twentieth century German drama was Bertolt Brecht (1898-1956), whose plays and epic theatre concepts have radically influenced the course of the modern stage. Brecht's techniques were partially indebted to commedia. His early dramas, inspired by Expressionism, led to the epic theatre style developed by Brecht and by director Erwin Piscator. In his *Verfremdungseffekt* (theory of alienation or estrangement), which held that an audience should not be emotionally engaged in the unfolding drama, but, instead, intellectually inspired by its political and social statements to act upon the wrong portrayed, Brecht called for the creation of highly theatrical means to avoid any realistic treatment of the subject matter whatsoever.

In the late 1920's, Brecht began writing what are now his most acclaimed works.[72] Some of his earlier plays and sketches used clowns as central images, and he started a version of Gozzi's *Turandot* in 1930, under the title *Turandot or the Congress of Whitewashers*. He worked on it again in 1953, but left it unfinished at his death (Brecht intended eleven scenes; a ten scene version has been produced). In some of his plays, commedic central characters are battered by the harshness of the world and the cruelty and self-absorption of those around them. Explaining his reaction to the established theatre of his day, he clearly described his notion of a significant comic theatre:

> in a comedy such base human characteristics as avarice, swank, stupidity, ignorance, disputatiousness; in a serious play the dehumanized social setting. White-washing is in itself something unquestionably ignoble, love of truth unquestionably noble. Art is in a position to represent the ugly man's ugliness in a beautiful manner, the base man's baseness in a noble manner, for the artist can also show ungraciousness graciously and meekness with power. There is no reason why the subject matter of a comedy portraying "life as it is" should not be ennobled. The theatre has at its command delicate

colours, agreeable and significant grouping, original gests -- in short, *style* --; it has humour, imagination and wisdom with which to overcome ugliness.[73]

Although he often strove for naturalness from his actors, Brecht also worked in a "sharply caricaturing manner, partly learned from *commedia dell'arte* techniques, which required the actors to make their stylisation of speech and movement very evident."[74] Brecht found an historical parallel for his alienation effect in the stylized gestures of Chinese actors and various kinds of folk theatre, of which commedia was, for him, an important example. On the subject of folk plays, he explained that they are

> normally a crude and humble kind of theatre which academic critics pass over in silence or treat with condescension. In the second case they prefer it to be what it is, just as some regimes prefer their "Volk" crude and humble. It is a mixture of earthy humour and sentimentality, homespun morality and cheap sex. The wicked get punished and the good get married off; the industrious get left legacies and the idle get left in the lurch. The technique of people who write these plays is more or less international; it hardly ever varies. To act in them all that is needed is a capacity for speaking unnaturally and a smoothly conceited manner on the stage. A good helping of superficial slickness is enough.[75]

Brecht was by no means calling for a revival of the old Volk plays, which he considered "utterly bogged down,"[76] but he felt that interest in reviving them in the modern theatre "proved the existence of certain needs, even though it cannot satisfy them. It can in fact be assumed that there is a need for naive but not primitive, poetic but not romantic, realistic but not ephemerally political theatre."[77]

To achieve his ends, Brecht dissected the differences between truth and artifice in theatrical performance. He pointed to the value of masks, finding that "actors can do without (or with the minimum of) makeup, appearing *natural*, and the whole thing can be fake; they can wear grotesque masks and represent the truth."[78] In an unpublished note for his play *Man is Man*

(1924-1925), Brecht anticipated a theatre like that of Vermont's The Bread and Puppet Theatre, when he scribbled "masks stilts gigantic hands,"[79] which would serve

> both the parable-like clarity of the transformation and the depersonalization of the actors, who were thereby forced to bring to the surface through external gestures through most obvious behaviour emotions that otherwise remain hidden. In this way the "natural face" of the lead actor could be used effectively at a certain point in the action.[80]

Brecht's interest in "depersonalizing" actors led him to clowns and clowning. He admired the films of Charlie Chaplin, but he was most influenced by Munich beerhall comedian Karl Valentin, "an authentic heir of the harlequins of the *Commedia dell'arte*."[81] His admiration of clowns found its way into *Man is Man*, in which Pierrot-style white make-up was worn by the soldiers. In the original 1926 production of *Man is Man*, he had been particularly unhappy with the treatment of the soldiers in early rehearsals of the play and asked Valentin for advice. Valentin observed that

> "They're scared, they look pale" ("Furcht hams, blass sans"). This matter-of-fact answer gave Brecht the clue he was seeking: he made the soldiers up white, a characteristically theatrical metaphor for a psychological condition. So Peter Lorre as Galy Gay whitened his face after recovering from his mock-execution in preparation for his transformation into a soldier. Brecht and he discussed the possibility of whitening the face earlier to indicate his fear of death, but "between fear of death and fear of life he chose to treat the latter as more profound."[82]

The commedic technique of working his cast with only a scenario in mind assisted him in developing much of the play in rehearsal. Influenced by Reinhardt's established convention of almost continual use of commedia characters during scene breaks, and by Valentin's performances (in which he occasionally participated), Brecht made notes in 1920 suggesting ideas for "cooling off emotional scenes on the stage, including tragic scenes. He ultimately insisted that if he were in charge of a theater, he would engage two clowns, who would appear during intermission and mock the play, its heroes, and its performance style."[83] Brecht was certainly no slavish imitator of other theatrical traditions and forms, but, like Meyerhold, he transformed elements of many forms, including commedia, through his genius.[84]

One of Brecht's contemporaries, playwright Ödön von Horváth (1901-1938), combined elements from commedia in a recreated form of Viennese popular comedy based on plays by Raimund and Nestroy. Horváth was a moralist. Human beings, in his view, need improvement: if man wishes to do away with evil, he must fundamentally change. Horváth's characters were drawn accordingly. For such plays as *Italian Night* (1931) and *Figaro is Getting Divorced* (1937) he used commedia characters to clarify Viennese comic types, who had become too worn out to offer much inspiration. In both these plays, as in most modern commedia performances, the central theme is love and its confusions. Raw lust drives the characters, preventing the appropriate matches from being made until the gratuitous happy resolution. Horváth uses the well-worn lunatic occurrences of commedia to represent fundamental human lunacies, that extend to suggest the absurdity of existence. To him, humans are pretentious animals living in a society driven by greed and licentiousness; the commedic elements he employs emphasize this. The fundamental changes characters undergo in the final scenes appear extraneous.

Friedrich Dürrenmatt (1921-1990), the post-Brechtian German dramatist best known in the English-speaking theatre, wrote in his essay *Problems of the Theater* (1955) that our disintegrating world and society is a subject for comedy rather than tragedy because "Comedy is the only thing that can still reach us. Our world has led to the grotesque as well as to the atom bomb. . . .And yet, the grotesque is only a way of expressing in a tangible manner, of making us perceive physically the paradoxical; it is the form of the unformed, the visage of a faceless world."[85]

His plays, *The Visit* (1956) and *The Physicists* (1962), could hardly be described as overtly comic, since they take a fundamentally pessimistic view. By reflecting the harrowing anxieties of their time, though, they are similar to other modern commedia plays. Dürrenmatt, like Brecht, is a master at making harrowing anxieties into comic theatre, and at creating characters who are grotesquely absurd. These aspects are traceable in part to commedia. For example, in *The Physicists*, Dürrenmatt creates a grotesque world in which rationality is seen as madness. His characters disguise their madness with rational masks; in this way, Dürrenmatt reflects not only the plays of Brecht, but the commedic theatre of Pirandello.

Several of Dürrenmatt's contemporaries made a similar marriage between pessimism and commedic techniques. In his play *Philoktet*, Heiner Müller (b. 1928) combines commedic elements with the traditions of Greek tragedy, using comedy as a contrasting foundation to support the tragedy. He purposely undermines any possibility of taking the tragedy very seriously, and thereby makes his play a stinging satire on the insanity of war. An absurd and deceitful society which corrupts its young, gives his characters little hope of escape from the confinements of society.

Peter Handke (b. 1942) aims for a form of total theatre by employing commedia *lazzi* to view human relations, as well as the relation of humans to objects. In *Kaspar* (1968), Handke pointedly uses a name that evokes the memory of the legendary character of Viennese comedy, Kasperl. The play is loosely based on the real life of a young man who was found wandering on a street in Nuremburg in the nineteenth century. He had experienced virtually no contact with human beings or the ways of society, having been kept in a locked closet all his life. Handke explores the changes his character undergoes when people try to teach him language, and the manners and fashions necessary to survive in a bourgeois society. Kaspar is dressed as a clown, although Handke does not view him as solely comic. In Handke's view, Kaspar becomes a transcendent universal fool in the manner of Arlecchino, Pierrot, or Chaplin. He shows how language is political manipulation; it becomes a constant pummeling of cliches that have been drummed into humans in all times. In Handke's plays, society has reformed man into a creature under full social control. Instinctively, humans are highly skeptical about this, and rebel against its confines through commedic business and gestures, reminding the audience again and again that human beings cannot be completely controlled.

Italian-born director Robert Ciulli studied philosophy and worked in Italian and French theatres before moving to Germany and founding the Theater an der Ruhr in 1981. Ciulli has gathered a company that functions as a true ensemble and aims to be a truly international theatre. His productions, ranging from Shakespeare's *A Midsummer Night's Dream* (1982) to Handke's *Kaspar* (1987), are Meyerholdian in their extreme theatricality and political intent. With Shakespeare and Handke, as well as with his many other productions,[86] especially *The Flea* (1984; based on Ruzzante) and a series of sketches drawn from the works of De Filippo called *Clowns* (1989), Ciulli has made use of such commedic elements as masks, puppets, clowns, and the traditional stock characters of commedia.

Recently, the Volksstück (Folk Play), appearing in the works of Franz Xaver Kroetz (b. 1946) and Martin Sperr (b. 1944), among others, has risen as yet another commedic expression in German drama. Growing out of early German folk traditions, and particularly shaped by Horváth's work, Volksstücke are written for audiences in local dialect. Currently, they focus on the absurdities of a consumer culture and other aspects of contemporary life. Even the popular German Documentary Drama has turned away from a photographically realistic style in favor of a cartoon-like quality, that is certainly at least partly inspired by commedic impulses.

Other contemporary German dramatists were, and continue to be, influenced by commedia and its traditions which they passed down through the ages in popular comedy. The Germans and Austrians have been particularly adept at using the old tools, commedic and otherwise, to explain an increasingly bewildering world to itself.

CHAPTER SEVEN

The Tricks of Scapin: Commedia in France

There is in art a renewing of eternal forces which is accomplished. . . through a periodic return to the original source, to the maternal bosom. If it is a question, for future authors, of establishing a New Comedy, a universal comedy, and of writing them out very legibly, in terms which everyone would find intelligible, they would perhaps find it necessary to once again study a theatrical form that we consider archaic, but which never ceased trying to return to ancient sources before fertilizing, for several centuries, all of Western theatre, right up to Molière, who exhausted its meaning, its essence, and its warmth. I'm speaking of this comedy of the Italian Renaissance known as the commedia dell'arte.[1]

-- Jacques Copeau

Italian commedia troupes first appeared in Paris between 1571 and 1604, and performed there frequently after 1599 (the Italian players seemed to be in permanent residence by the 1640's). They inspired a hearty interest in the form and encouraged French writers to develop native farces. French actors of the period emulated the Italians by creating variations on commedia stereotypes. Henri LeGrand (c.1587-c.1637) created Turlupin, a clever servant similar to commedia's Brighella. As other actors of the period, he played a stock character recognizable by his costume and stage tricks; he improvised dialogue from a scenario as the Italians did. Early French dramatists, such as Jean de Rotrou (1609-1650), wrote commedia characters into their plays. In *Clarice* (1641), Rotrou created the Spanish captain, Rhinoceronte, a version of commedia's Capitano.

With the triumph of Neoclassicism, and the solidifying of acting companies in seventeenth century France, dramatic literature flowered. Among the leading dramatists, Pierre Corneille (1606-1684) wrote plays influenced by commedia, most especially *The Comic Illusion* (1635 or 1636), which includes Matamore, a braggart soldier traditional in both ancient Roman comedy and commedia, along with a pair of lovers, several clever servants, and a magician. Despite the explosion of literary drama, commedia remained popular in France. Italian troupes were in continual residence in Paris, and toured throughout the provinces during the seventeenth century. Commedia, however, made its most significant mark on the greatest comic playwright of the age.

Jean-Baptiste Poquelin, known as Molière, was born in 1622, the son of a prosperous upholsterer. The boy was well educated, and expected to move into a court position, before his interests turned to the theatre. In 1643, he helped form the Illustre Théâtre with a small troupe that included members of a struggling band of performers, the Béjart family. They failed in Paris, and subsequently took to the provinces. Molière ultimately headed the troupe, which performed a variety of plays and absorbed many commedia traditions. His first major work, *The Blunderer*, was successfully performed at Lyons in 1655, and three years later, the troupe was invited to perform in Paris by the king's brother. More importantly, they were given the use of the Théâtre du Petit Bourbon, which they shared with an Italian commedia company headed by Tiberio Fiorilli, the legendary Scaramouche. Once again, however, the French company was not well received, until Molière's comedy *The Affected Ladies* was performed in 1659. After this success, the company soon moved to the Palais-Royal. For the next fourteen years, they performed Molière's greatest plays, many of which were farces modeled on commedia scenarios, including *Sganarelle* (1660), *The Doctor in Spite of Himself* (1666), and *The Tricks of Scapin* (1671). Even Molière's more sophisticated comedies, *The School for Wives* (1662), *The Misanthrope* (1666), *Tartuffe* (1667), *The Miser* (1668), and *The Imaginary Invalid* (1673), are populated by cheeky and manipulative servants, foolish and vain masters, quack doctors, young lovers, and other commedic types. Molière often played leading roles in his own plays, and as head and central artistic force of his company, he enjoyed a status that must have been similar to that of the leaders of early Italian commedia troupes.

In 1680, seven years after Molière's death, the Comédie-Française was formed. At the same time, the Italian commedia actors, with an aging but still active Scaramouche at their head, took over the Hôtel de Bourgogne, expanding their already enormous popularity. Despite a varied repertory that included French and Italian plays, the acting style remained similar to that found in commedia, and even the most literary plays of the day allowed for improvisatory liberties. The great age of Italian commedia in France came to an abrupt end in 1697, when the Italian players were expelled from the country for a period of about twenty years, for offending Louis XIV's mistress, Mme. de Maintenon.[2]

Sentimental comedy became increasingly popular in the early eighteenth century, and with it came a subtle variation on commedia in the plays of Pierre Carlet de Chamblain de Marivaux (1688-1763). His commedic play, *Arlequin Refined by Love* (1720), was performed by the Italian troupe of Luigi Riccoboni (1676-1753). Known onstage as Lélio, Riccoboni achieved prominence performing in Marivaux's plays after the Italians were reinstated in Paris. Marivaux projected delicate emotions, fantasy, and psychological probing through the stock characters and situations of commedia, though the highly sentimental nature of his works has made them of little interest in more recent times. Commedia characters and situations were also present in Pierre-Augustin Caron de Beaumarchais' (1732-1799) plays *The Barber of*

Seville (1775) and *The Marriage of Figaro* (1783).

One of the great actors performing in France during this period was Evaristo Gherardi (1663-1700). He was a famous Arlecchino with the Italian players, and also compiled an important compendium of scenarios. In *Le Théâtre Italien*, Gherardi describes more than forty scenarios that combine elements from French and Italian commedia. Riccoboni, who had arrived in Paris in 1716 with some of the actors from the expelled Comédie-Italienne, led the troupe to become a state theatre by 1723. His attempts to revive the old improvised comedy met with mixed results, and the Italians began to depend increasingly on written texts, which accelerated their assimilation into the mainstream French theatre. Although playwrights demonstrated a continued willingness to write for the Italians, changes in taste and acting styles ultimately succeeded in a final ouster of the Italians.[3]

In the early nineteenth century, a new dramatic form which derived from commedic elements developed in France. The Grand Guignol, were brief horror plays very popular with nineteenth century audiences. They derived from an outdoor marionette theatre in Lyon around 1815, under the direction of puppet master Laurent Mourquet (1744-1844). Mourquet's puppet hero, Guignol, was based on commedia's Polichinelle, but with added local characteristics. He was jolly, not too bright, easy to trick, yet quite cunning at times, and possessed a sinister touch of cruelty. The puppet Guignol inspired the Grand Guignol, the name chosen for a series of plays which featured live actors in place of puppets. The Grand Guignol was founded in Paris by Oscar Metenier (1859-1913), and its performances featured a fairly even distribution of farcical and horrific short pieces. Ultimately the bloodcurdling and extremely graphic horror plays the Grand Guignol produced achieved greater popularity than the humorous works.[4]

Commedia was at a low ebb in European theatres at the beginning of the nineteenth century, its characters and traditions surviving mostly in pantomime, and revivals of Molière and Goldoni. The appearance of Jean-Gaspard Deburau (1796-1846), however, revitalized wordless French pantomime, which, at the time was popular, but considered a nefarious entertainment aimed at the lower classes. Deburau brought Pierrot, a variation of the Italian *zanni* Pedrolino, to the stage of the disreputable Théâtre des Funambules on Paris' Boulevard of Crime.[5] From 1825 until his death, Deburau perfected the pale, love-sick Pierrot, and the audiences at Funambules, as well as most of the intellectuals identified with the Romantic movement in France, made the character an indelible part of the culture of their day.[6]

Despite the fact that he lacked his father's genius, Charles Deburau (1829-1873) was instrumental in continuing the Pierrot tradition, and solidifying it as a powerful theatrical image. Writers during the Age of Romanticism were drawn to the melancholy qualities of the masks of commedia, particularly Deburau's Pierrot. They created a variety of plays featuring subtle variations on the character Pierrot, changing him from the familiar gentle clown into a grotesque and often sinister figure, as in Paul Margueritte's (1860-1918) *Pierrot Assassin of His Wife* (1881). The play became enormously popular, and Sarah Bernhardt played Pierrot in one production. Her performance, and those of many lesser actors of the age, began a tradition of Pierrot being played as often by women as by men.

Champfleury (Jules Husson; 1821-1889), Charles Nodier (1780-1844), Charles Baudelaire (1821-1867), Théophile Gautier (1811-1872), Théodore de Banville (1823-1891), Gustave Flaubert (1821-1880), Edmond de Goncourt (1822-1896), Jules de Goncourt (1830-1870), Joris-Karl Huysmans (1848-1907), Paul Verlaine (1844-1896), and Stéphane Mallarmé (1842-1898), in addition to Margueritte, were among the French critics, poets, and playwrights of the nineteenth century who were fascinated by variations on Deburau's Pierrot, and used their individual ideas of the character often in their own works. The most internationally known of these was *The Prodigal Son* by Michel Carre *fils* (b.1865), produced in Europe and America, beginning in the early 1890's. In this play, Pierrot is thrown out of his bourgeois family, and lives a dissolute life pursuing a relationship with the faithless Phrynette. Disillusioned by his lover's infidelity, Pierrot returns to the bosom of his family, where he is forgiven and finds acceptance and peace. In this production, Pierrot was played by a woman, and from that time forward the character has retained a tone of sexual ambiguity. Later, such French Symbolists as the poet Jules Laforgue (1860-1887), who identified with Pierrot, turned to commedia. Laforgue's poetry, and that of many lesser writers, was laced with commedic imagery.

Although the direct influence of commedia on playwright Alfred Jarry (1873-1907) is unclear, his Ubu plays were certainly forerunners of the Theatre of the Absurd, which is indebted to many commedic influences. *King Ubu*, written as a marionette play in 1888 (when Jarry was only fifteen years old), and first produced in 1896, is a savagely comic, revolutionary work, incorporating masks, cartoon settings, pantomime, and broad slapstick. Its first production, staged with puppets by Firman Gémier, created considerable controversy because of its anarchic tone and radical departure from recognizable theatrical genres.[7] Jarry's other *Ubu* plays lacked the revolutionary impact of the original, although they contained many commedic elements. He later articulated his theory of "Pata-physics" (the science of imaginary solutions), and it was subsequently adopted by the Surrealists, who often created brutal farces from the incongruities of human reality. Later still, Absurdists made use of it as well.

At the turn of the century, Roman-born French writer Guillaume Apollinaire (1880-1918) wrote mostly poetry, setting the scene for the Surrealist movement. His theatrical work did not begin until within a year of his death from injuries received in World War I. At the time of his death,

Apollinaire had been working on an *opera buffa* piece, *Casanova*, which is set in an Italian piazza at carnival time. The story begins with the arrival of strolling players intending to perform a work by Gozzi. Although the main plot focuses on Casanova, the second act includes a performance on a booth stage by the actors in commedia costumes acting for an audience also dressed as commedia characters.

Perhaps the most striking influence on the explosion of French commedia at the beginning of the twentieth century was the result of the experimental commedia productions of George Sand (Lucile-Aurore Dupin, baronne Dudevant; 1804-1876). Although best known as a novelist, many of Sand's plays were produced in Paris between 1840 and 1872, and, of greater significance to the study of commedia, many others were staged at her private Nohant Theatre between 1846 and 1863. Unlike most of her commedic predecessors, Sand was not interested in commedia solely for its rich collection of plots, characters, and easily identifiable images. Her experiments anticipated the great artists of the twentieth century who would rediscover the form in attempts to change the very nature of theatre.

Sand's first documented experiment with commedia at Nohant was her play *Lélio* (later called *Marielle*), first performed in 1850, and improvised from her own scenario. Impressed with the outcome, she began to study commedia history in earnest. She was not particularly interested in reforming acting, but she did hope to revive what she viewed as the unique style of commedia acting, and again anticipating twentieth century commedists, she wanted to see a three-dimensional human being behind the mask, with the purpose of "appreciating the serious and sober artist behind the farcical buffoonery."[8] For Sand, the improvisational qualities of commedia had some shortcomings but much to recommend it. For example, she recognized that commedia actors

> got confused, repeated themselves or cut things too short. Some

scenes were totally lacking in any appeal, but the audience would wait indulgently, knowing that at one moment or another the actor's inspiration would return and make up to them the damages. And in effect, when that inspiration came it was incomparable, and impassioned the audience more than the greatest interpreters of the greatest writers could ever do.[9]

Sand continued her experimentation into a second season at Nohant, which she devoted completely to commedia. With the assistance of her son, Maurice (1823-1889), author of an interesting commedia study, *Masques et bouffons*, she revived Beolco's short plays, assisting in the translation of two: *Ruzzante Returns from the Wars* and *Bilora, or the Second Rustic Play*. *Bilora* was first produced at Nohant with a specially written prologue by Sand in 1859, with revivals in 1860 and 1861. Although her other interests distracted her from commedia experimentation, her emphasis on the complex nature of the form and its potential value to theatre practice were easily decades ahead of their time. Her definition of commedia remains a clear and articulate statement of its significance in all times:

> The *commedia dell'arte* is not only a study of the grotesque and facetious,. . .but also a portrayal of real characters traced from remote antiquity down to the present day, in an uninterrupted tradition of fantastic humour which is in essence quite serious and, one might almost say, even sad, like every satire which lays bare the spiritual poverty of mankind.[10]

Jacques Copeau

Aside from the Italian theatre, where commedia was born, the French stage had perhaps the most immediate connections with earlier commedic traditions, through the popularity of Deburau, and Pierrot plays inspired by his interpretation, George Sand's experiments with commedia performance techniques, and Jarry's *Ubu* plays. Few modern theatrical artists, with the exception of cabaret and variety entertainers, were aware of its great potential until actor, director, and teacher Jacques Copeau (1879-1949) turned to it in the second decade of the twentieth century.

Copeau began his career at the beginning of the century as a drama critic for a number of Parisian periodicals. In his articles, he relentlessly attacked the tired conventions of Europe's *fin-de-siècle* stage. To him, it was clear that theatrical art in France had exhausted traditions it was still practicing. He strenuously resisted the "leniency" with which critics and public alike seemed to accept a theatre, which had become to him, empty and antiquated. He felt driven to "tell the truth about the theatre."[11] He vehemently rejected commercial plays and practices, and the guiding precepts of the contemporary theatre, looking instead to what he regarded as the unchanging truths about the theatre of the past to create an as yet unknown future theatre.

Copeau realized early on that it would be necessary to become a practitioner himself, to truly understand and change the French stage. His first major step toward that goal came when he founded the Théâtre du Vieux Colombier in 1913. At the Vieux Colombier, Copeau actively worked against the proliferation of Realism in the theatre, and began to promote his theories, which were based, in part, on those of André Antoine,[12] Appia, and Craig. He decided that it was his mission to bring beauty and poetry back into the theatre, a task which he said "was vast and would be laborious."[13] Feeling a deeply moral sense of the responsibility of theatre to its society, he set about to create a company which would "form this little nucleus from which life will radiate, around which the future will bring its gifts."[14] The theatre's repertory was drawn mostly from the plays of Molière and Shakespeare, but Copeau's performance techniques were derived directly and almost exclusively from commedic traditions.

Directly inspired by Craig, Copeau sought theatrical artifice not photographic realism. He stated his ambitious intentions in a prospectus published in September, 1913, in which he quickly asserted the contempt which he and his followers held for the current condition of the French stage: it was weak, disorganized, frivolous, and filled with vanity. Because theatre critics had become too acquiescent, the public was misguided. Although some of the artists Copeau rejected, including farceurs like Feydeau, could also be connected to commedia, it is important to note that Copeau was a classicist. He insisted that the Vieux-Colombier repertory would demonstrate "a particular veneration to the classics, ancient and modern, French and foreign."[15] His company would also familiarize itself with the best contemporary techniques and movements, which he identified as the innovations of French director Jacques Rouché, as well as the work of Meyerhold, Stanislavsky, Nemirovich-Danchenko, Reinhardt, Craig, Barker, and other iconoclasts of the modern stage. Like Craig, Meyerhold, and Reinhardt, Copeau was inspired by a diverse array of dramatic forms and sources. His nephew and student, Michel Saint-Denis, recalled that his models were "the Greeks, the sixteenth-century Spaniards, and above all the Elizabethans, the Commedia dell'arte, the classical theatre of France."[16] Copeau also turned to the remnants of earlier traditions of the French stage in working-class theatres, taverns, and, as Craig and Meyerhold, in music halls, cabarets, and fairgrounds. His study of Molière led to an examination of "Italian comedy. I caught a glimpse of the style of farce and, in order to respect its movements, I brought it back,"[17] usually in plays by Molière or Shakespeare.

Significantly, there was also inspiration to be found on the modern stages of other countries, at that time largely unknown by other French theatrical artists. For instance, following a pilgrimage to Florence to talk with Craig, Copeau visited Émile Jacques-Dalcroze at his School of Eurythmics in Geneva:

I remember, one day that Craig repeated to me his famous "You believe in the actor, I do not," replying: "I do not know if I believe in the actor. But I do believe in a new spirit which will transform the art of the actor. I believe in something which I know, and have tested, something which was established between a group of young actors and myself through daily work which lasted a year. On that something I have started to build." Well here, in the very first session, I have found that something between Dalcroze and his students that exists between me and mine.[18]

Léon Chancerel[19] points out that it was probably Craig who convinced Copeau of the value commedia held for the contemporary theatre artist. After visiting Craig, Copeau began to visualize a modern improvisational comic form, with the power to elicit laughter and recognition from an audience, regardless of the boundaries of language. He decided that "modern comedy, being literary, intellectual, indulging in conversation or discussion, has strangely reduced the physical resources of actors."[20] He believed that modern comedy must be created from models taken from comedy at its highest level of achievement, and he concluded that commedia was the definitive model (for tragedy, he felt that the artist must return to ancient Greek tragedy).

Realistic dramas, especially those by Ibsen, had gained a foothold in France, but like Craig, Meyerhold, and Reinhardt, Copeau rejected them as models. The term "Ibsenesque," he said, had become "synonymous with incoherence, hermeticism and moroseness."[21] His rejection of realistic drama undoubtedly had more to do with his ideas about acting than anything else. He insisted that "acting should be simple rather than natural, because acting should seem natural but not be so. The question is how to make it appear that way."[22]

In selecting the first Vieux-Colombier company, Copeau was less concerned with finding experienced performers, than discovering individuals with an instinctive understanding of his brand of theatricality. He committed himself and his troupe to a rigorous training program in which they would develop an *"awareness and experience of the human body."*[23] The actor, he believed, was to "give himself. In order to give himself, he must first possess himself."[24] In this, Copeau is close to Meyerhold, who insisted on the predominance of the actor as a completely controlled and diversely skilled instrument. Copeau was not a Reinhardtian antiquarian when it came to commedia. There was to be no Baroque splendor or rolling carts of merry clowns at the Vieux-Colombier. The simplicity, the direct communication (and communion) with the audience, the universality of the commedia stock characters were the elements he wished to rediscover for the modern stage from commedia. On January 21, 1916, novelist and playwright André Gide recorded in his diary a significant discussion with Copeau about:

> the possibility of forming a small troupe of actors, with enough intelligence, ability and training, to be able to improvise on a given scenario, to be capable of reviving the *commedia dell'arte* in the Italian style, but with new stock characters: the bourgeois, the nobleman, the wine merchant, the suffragette, would replace *Arlequin*, *Pierrot* and *Columbine*. Each one of these characters would have its own costume and way of speaking, walking and thinking. And each of the actors would only impersonate one such character, and would never change from it, but would enrich and amplify it continually. If this project were to get off the ground, I can see it needing, and I would welcome this, a complementary theatre, one which would both excite and exalt the performer.[25]

Although it is clear that such a theatre was never created in any pure state by Copeau, his productions, as Meyerhold's, demonstrate that the stock characters of commedia, especially as he used them in the plays of Molière and Shakespeare, were powerful archetypal human symbols. Of equal significance, performance techniques learned from commedia traditions guided his work in training his actors. He placed the emphasis on the actor, first and last, and he intended to create a theatre in which "his actors would escape the realisms and pretences of the modern theatre, and would play to and with the audience as their spirit demanded."[26] Copeau was sympathetic to Appia's desire to use light and music as harmonizing forces, but, ultimately, he rejected spectacle, and insisted that the actor must carry it all. In his aim to create an acting technique that incorporated simplicity (rejecting the affectations of theatricality as well as naturalness in acting), emphasis was placed on the play's action as a result of character motivation. Thorough training would create an actor able to perform in any genre, and would lead to the development of a strong ensemble style. As Michel Saint-Denis recalled, Copeau's actors "received a very detailed training of voice, body and imagination, which fitted them to act in the sort of modern plays which would demand of them the same difficult standards as the old classics had done."[27]

Copeau agreed with Craig that the state of acting had degenerated, and that most modern actors were "vain and arrogant,"[28] which made them incapable of subordinating their personalities to their roles. His emphasis on the importance of ensemble playing entailed for his actors "*No affectation* of any kind whatsoever, whether of the body, the mind, or the voice. What we are seeking is headlong harmony."[29] He wanted to develop a brotherhood among actors, yet he was not an elitist. He believed that "our art only gives and takes its virtue through contact with a large number, and that it only flowers in a form that can be called popular."[30] Like Grotowski, Copeau's love of acting bordered on the religious, and his respect for the audience was that of a priest for his congregation. His great strength was unquestionably in working with actors. Saint-Denis recalled that the

> actors would rehearse *sotto voce*, without any eloquence, careful not to force the text, just sketching tempo and rhythm without trying to achieve anything too early. During rehearsals Copeau would move ceaselessly from the auditorium to the stage; if an actor was in difficulty, he would talk to him freely but confidentially at the back of the stage. As an actor himself he instinctively knew when to grant freedom to an actor and when to apply the right kind of pressure during the successive stages of rehearsals.[31]

Once the actor's vocal, mental, and physical equipment was

harmonized, the actor could let the character take over. Copeau did not believe that the actor enters a role, but that the character "approaches that actor, who demands of him all that he needs, who little by little replaces him in his skin. The actor applies himself to leave him a free field."[32] Copeau helped each of his actors find a specific stock character directly inspired by commedia masks, with the intention that each actor would play a basic stereotype regardless of the particular play being produced. The actor could add elements of his own personality and other embellishments, without undermining the simplicity and clarity of his or her stock character. These characters represented basic human behaviors (good and bad), and also suggested various classes and professions. It seemed to him that such characters could serve, as they had originally in commedia, as human symbols playing out the ultimate comedy of life. He explained this in a 1916 letter to one of his actors, Louis Jouvet:

> It's the rebirth of satire and gaiety -- There you are! It's no more difficult than that. . .(no scenery, you always have the same accessories with their immutable physiognomy, just like that of the actors). I already see three of these personages. . .the *Intellectual* (doctor, philosopher, professor, etc.), the *Agent* (or representative) (deputy, minister, electoral agent, grocery merchant, etc.), the *Adolescent* (the child in his family, the schoolboy, the suitor, the artist, the soldier, in short the "idealist," Pierrot's grandson, with a powder-white face, etc.).[33]

From the beginning of the Vieux-Colombier experiment, Copeau used masks for performances of Molière's comedies and commedic farces. In 1921, partly inspired by his visit to Florence, where he had been impressed by Craig's collection of masks, Copeau introduced masks as a training device for his actors. The mask eliminated facial expressions, forcing the actors instead to develop full use of their bodies and voices. After considerable exploration and experimentation, he and his actors reached the conclusion that a neutral mask, lacking any definitive expression, was required for an actor to rechannel his expressiveness into movement. This emphasis on movement pushed Copeau toward commedic "play" and improvisation. Although he admired Dalcroze's eurythmics, he found some of the stock gestures used stiff and unnatural. Animal movements, musical rhythms, and gymnastics seemed more effective to Copeau, and he studied them in depth. During his 1922-23 season, he arranged for some instruction from the famous Italian clowns, the Fratellini Brothers.[34] They impressed upon the Vieux-Colombier company that the art of clowning required almost unlimited physical skill, ranging from juggling and tumbling to trapeze work.

Copeau's emphasis on the art of the actor, which came to include significant clowning training, prevailed over virtually every aspect of his productions. Not surprisingly, his company spawned an unprecedented number of distinguished actors who were to carry Copeau's ideas into theatres of their own making. Jouvet, Saint-Denis, Charles Dullin, Gaston Baty, Georges Pitoëff, and Etienne Decroux were only some of the students of Copeau who, at various times, fell strongly under his spell before striking out on their own. Perhaps his impression on others is his greatest legacy, for these artists, as well as *their* followers, including Jean-Louis Barrault, Jacques Lecoq, and Marcel Marceau, revolutionized the performance techniques of the modern French theatre. Whatever ultimate departures from Copeau's ideas they later made, they all seemed to agree upon his extraordinary skill as a director, and the validity of his general approach to actor training. He was, preeminently, a teacher who inspired actors with his almost religious devotion to theatre.

Copeau's desire to re-theatricalize the theatre with the spirit and techniques of commedia led him to actually consider discarding the literary texts of plays. He considered turning them into rough scenarios, but he found that even traditional commedia *scenarii* were "not very funny. The *spirit* is in the movement."[35] In any event, the use of the *scenarii* seemed to be the place to begin, as he explained in a letter to Jouvet:

> Don't you think that certain texts could be revitalized, regenerated, by an exercise consisting of *reducing them to outlines*, resumés, sort of skeletons of action that the actor would preliminarily have to improvise, animate, and dress by himself. Thus one could put the actor on his own with these texts full of influences and thus could one more easily rejuvenate the classic?. . .[36]

He was certain that only "the stage makes the actor, as it alone makes the author. But it undoes them too. From time to time, it may be good to take them away from the stage,"[37] and so

> our scenes, almost improvised, matched the circumstances, the season, the locality, the audience. They were healthy, vigorous, almost completely free of the theatre's dust. They sketched boldly but incompletely, poorly but sincerely freer, airier styles. They have often obtained, *naturally*, this audience adhesion, these moments of perfect communion between the stage and the house, which are the height of the theatre, and which so many aesthetes and theorists seek to attain through sophisticated means.[38]

Explaining his interest in Molière's farces, Copeau stated that these were plays "with a lot of movement in them, because they are the ones that are least suited to the cold, congealed, half-dead interpretation that is inflicted on them on the official stages."[39] His respect for Molière knew no bounds, and focused on the great playwright's seemingly innate understanding of commedia:

> Molière had something ready to hand, a precedent, a *comedic substance*, behind him. He uses it in his endeavours both as a point of attack, and of departure. Recipes were handed down to him which he needed only to make use of in order to bring them to a point of perfection. . . .The comedy, or rather the *theatre* he had before him -- the theatre of the Italians -- had been extant for so long, had reached such a point of development that, if taken as a *starting-point*, any surpassing of it would at once constitute greatness.[40]

No doubt, Copeau's interest in Molière's farces had to do with their compatibility with his own understanding of commedia. They offered sophisticated and dimensioned treatments of commedia's stock characters, with clear motivations, and unprecedented freedom for the improvising comic actor. At the Vieux-Colombier from the very beginning, and throughout his career, Copeau experimented with every variable of commedic theatre he could find. He adapted Molière and Shakespeare, as well as the plays of lesser classical playwrights and modernist commedia plays.[41] His greatest period of achievement was between 1913 and 1924, although he continued to have a profound influence on matters in the French theatre until well into the 1940's. Covering all of Copeau's major productions making use of commedia would require a book-length study, but several, especially Molière's *The Tricks of Scapin* and Shakespeare's *Twelfth Night*, are especially illuminating. Norman Marshall wrote that what he remembered most about these productions was

> their lightness, their grace, and their gaiety. Pictorially they were exquisite because of the skill with which Copeau composed his grouping and movement on the various levels of his stage. . .But one was never conscious of a producer composing effective groupings for their own sake; they seemed the natural result of the action of the play, just as the movement about the stage had an ease and fluidity which gave the impression that it had been spontaneously created by the actors themselves instead of being the work of the producer.[42]

He rarely brought his commedic skills to the comedies of Shakespeare, but did have particular success with *Twelfth Night*, which was first performed at the Vieux-Colombier on May 22, 1914.[43] Jean Villard-Gilles recalled that "we were afforded some of those rare moments when mind and soul have one accord; and as if touched by a kind of grace we felt ourselves transported by one single flap of a wing towards the eternal peaks."[44]

Jouvet, who gave one of his most memorable performances as Sir Andrew Aguecheek, assisted Copeau with the set design for the production, which, characteristically, was a predominantly bare stage. It was decorated simply and colorfully with a few furnishings, and its use, as Copeau later acknowledged, "clarified for me the idea of making an architectural expedient out of the stage."[45] Saint-Denis, noting both the influence of commedia and the utter originality of the treatment, remembered that the production "*drew curved lines; it was fluid, free, as if improvised. The comedians seemed to be inflated by air, or as if stuffed with straw -- creatures of their imagination; they had neither hair, hats, nor swords of ordinary historical reality, and their acting had a peculiar, floating lightness.*"[46] Copeau's methods actually accentuated the values that were most central to Shakespearean comedy: poetic charm, lightness, and subtle variations in mood. Waldo Frank observed that physically the play

> moved from four levels: the balcony, the main stage, the proscenium doors on either wing, the dungeon underneath the apron where Malvolio was imprisoned. From these four planes, the characters wove a design of fantastic movement. It lifted and wafted in the fore-ground of the play. And in the background, from out the shadows under the balcony of the Countess, roared the laughter of the tippling clowns -- Sir Toby Belch, Sir Andrew Aguecheek and their fellows -- whose antics are the true motivation of the piece.[47]

Copeau accentuated the commedic aspects of *Twelfth Night*; the elements of the carnival masque, the disguises, the love of folly and lampooning of pretension, all lent themselves perfectly to commedic treatment. Although the play also offered much subtlety and gentleness in its comedy, he did not forget that "its inspiration is as Saturnalian as the music-hall's. It is of the season in which bonds are loosed; it loosens all laces, it tugs at all stays, it cup-crowns its companions, it cross-garters its foes."[48]

When *Twelfth Night* was presented during the two seasons (1917-1919) that the Vieux-Colombier troupe spent in New York, away from the turmoil and deprivation of World War I, it was among the most popular of their presentations. Realizing that the plot of the comedy "gathers round a jest,"[49] one critic was impressed with Copeau's alchemy in changing the traditional tone of the play, while also remaining faithful to the text. He had slanted the play from "a poetic romance of unrequited love to a romping farce of invariable good-humoured grace, in which a practical joke plays the star role."[50] John Corbin of the *The New York Times* was impressed with "how much the play gains when a full text is spoken under stage conditions approximating those for which it was written."[51] He acknowledged that the action was better paced, the development of the characters more sustained, and the combination of both subtle, while broad humor was maintained. All of this was achieved despite the fact that the play's emphasis on language, so typical in English-speaking productions was, for Copeau's troupe, alien.

It was, of course, with Molière's plays that Copeau always found the best opportunities for the exploitation of his commedic concepts. From the very beginning of the Vieux-Colombier, Molière's farcical plays were a staple of the repertory. *Love's the Best Medicine*, which opened on October 23, 1913,[52] was, as one American critic noted, "one of the farcical entertainments with which Molière varied his labors in high comedy, falling between *Don Juan* and *Le Misanthrope*."[53] Commedic inspiration was present in brightly colored costumes, grotesque make-up, and an emphasis on movement and slapstick.

The Miser, which opened exactly one month later, on November 23, 1913,[54] was, by its very nature, less farcical than *Love's the Best Medicine*. One of Molière's greatest masterpieces, it "was a test of unusual severity"[55] for the fledgling Vieux-Colombier company. It offered deeper, richer roles and, judging at least by the staging of the New York version a few years later, the result achieved was "most fortunate. There are a full dozen parts that require the touch of an artist, and each of them stood out distinctly in itself, yet remained always in its due relation to the work as a whole."[56] Charles Dullin, one of the finest actors in the company, excelled as Harpagon.

The Jealousy of Bourbouillé, first presented on January 1, 1914, at the Vieux-Colombier,[57] offered a return to a broader style. Copeau, as usual, emphasized the farcical elements, and made "no attempt at reality. The characters are types or puppets, not individuals."[58] He further exaggerated the one-dimensional nature of the stock characters of the sharp-tongued wife, the jealous husband, and the pompous doctor, by enlivening the play with an especially fast-paced and highly physical production. In the New York revival, Louis Jouvet was especially praised for his performance as the loquacious doctor.[59]

The most definitive Copeau production, and the most commedic, was *The Tricks of Scapin*, staged as the first presentation of the two American seasons, opening on November 27, 1917, at New York's Garrick Theatre.[60] Copeau had been appalled by most contemporary productions of Molière's plays, which to him were theatrical fossils adhering to outmoded traditions, performed without vigor or conviction by actors who often interpolated extra - dialogue in a half-hearted attempt to sound natural. For *The Tricks of Scapin*, in addition to a recreation of the Vieux-Colombier stage at the Garrick Theatre, Copeau made use of a *treteau*, a square raised platform with stairs off the front, sides, and back, as well as a small raised level between two sets of steps at the front. It proved to be the most controversial aspect of the production, but Copeau explained that the "*treteau* is in itself action, it makes the form of the play materialise and, when the *treteau* is occupied by actors, when it is penetrated by the action itself -- it disappears."[61]

Wishing to strip the stage of virtually all scenery, realistic or not, he felt that most of the modern anti-realist movements were really about "scenery, that is all. And I am most of all against scenery."[62] The *treteau* added another level of distance from any sort of realistic detail, but, more than anything, it recalled the simple raised platform or wagon, typical of traditional commedia performances. It was a "stage" in a very theatrical sense, one that was infinitely flexible by nature of its extraordinary simplicity. *The Tricks of Scapin* was only one of several productions in which Copeau used the *treteau*, and Waldo Frank recalled its particular benefits:

> Observe how the methods of Copeau contrive to meet its problem. The play is a mass, but not without grace: it has the solidity of the mental acrobat measuring his prowess upon volatile trapezes and flimsy paper rings. The design of the play is this: Scapin, an irrepressible unit -- and two pairs of lovers and two fathers as the fragile and flighty accessories to prove him. Copeau does not temporize with his design. He sets a naked platform upon the center of his stage. And at once, in its bold, sharp prominence that part of Scapin has a marvelous symbol. This platform stands for Scapin quite as clearly as Scapin, in his pied garment, stands on it. About it move the victims: shifting, uncertain, forever in the shadows:-- waves beating against a rock and thrown upon it merely to fall back diminished. Molière stands forth, created. His farce has never been seen in this form; and yet he has not been belied. He has been simply more faithfully, more completely *brought* upon the stage. In the bluff blocking of the scene, in the unceasing body movement of the actors, it is his words that live.[63]

John Corbin cited Copeau's awareness that actors of "the old comedy of masques"[64] were agile and athletic. The *treteau* permitted the actors to approximate the skill of their forebears, by requiring great speed and grace, as well as by providing a flexible obstacle, demonstrating that his addition of this "seemingly purposeless erection is thus the result of an artistic perception as subtly intelligent as it is original."[65]

Perhaps encouraged by the *treteau*, *The Tricks of Scapin* was one of Copeau's most physical productions, played broadly and in a totally presentational fashion. Convinced that comedy and movement were inseparable, his treatment of the work permitted an endless stream of physical business, with an emphasis on its connection to character motivation. Comedy was, for him, the dramatic equivalent of ballet. Copeau played Scapin himself in his definitive stage characterization; he excelled at the very things he strove to create in the entire production, and he was particularly adept at wringing all possibilities from the *treteau*:

Here Scapin may disport himself at his pleasure; he may lie down on this platform or sit cross-legged playing dice with Silvestre; he is always in full view of the audience, and, what is more, without assuming a dignity untrue to his role, he can dominate the other characters, who, for the time being, stand on the stage floor below. And when these other characters mount in their turn upon the platform, they are, as it were, hemmed in; the edge prevents them from moving away, a fact which renders very much more effective all the scenes of fruitless flight and bodily encounter.[66]

Critics found his performance to be "a marvel of agility and grace,"[67] in which he revealed "a virtuosity in broad farce which, in a man of such high intelligence and delicate sensibility, is astonishing."[68]

Despite the success of *The Tricks of Scapin*, Copeau perceived the Vieux-Colombier seasons in New York as a failure. He had hoped to provide a positive influence on the maturing American theatre at an important moment in its development, as well as to achieve some financial security for his company. It seemed, however, that New York theatregoers expected Copeau's troupe to be an extension of either the Parisian boulevard theatres or the Comédie-Française. Worse yet, Copeau's elimination of visual realism in his productions disoriented audiences who had become accustomed to it, and the company's eclectic and largely classic repertory seemed far too esoteric.

Despite the immediate disappointments, this was an important visit. Although some aspects of the "new stagecraft" of the European theatres had trickled onto American stages, influencing the designs of Robert Edmond Jones and the writings of Kenneth Macgowan and Sheldon Cheney, who expounded the theories of Craig, Appia, and the Russians, *The Tricks of Scapin* was the first highly visible, clearly articulated view of many of their principles to be seen in America. Many American directors, designers, and stage historians have written of Copeau's American seasons, but few have made any direct reference to the use of commedia in his productions. He ultimately realized that the American seasons had been "a senseless project.

Think about it: in the middle of war, to transplant, without any previous acclimitization, into the milieu most unfavorable to its growth, and even to its cohesion -- not a tried organization, but a dream hardly even hatched, whose value is completely spiritual."[69]

Some of Copeau's most interesting commedic experiments were done when he retreated to Burgundy with a young company (*les Copiaus*) in 1924. Here he wrote and staged a one-act version of Goldoni's *The Mistress of the Inn*, which he called *Mirandoline*. It was first performed on May 24, 1925, with his son-in-law, Jean Dasté, appearing in the cast. The bill also included Thomas de Gueulette's *Parade*, which contained exaggerated variations of commedia characters. Copeau even adapted three traditional commedia *scenarii*, all of which emphasized masks, movement, pantomime, and music, with a minimum of plot complexity or dialogue: *Harlequin the Magician* (1925), *The Illusion* (1926), and Ruzzante's *The Woman of Ancona* (1927). *The Illusion*, as he recalled, came very close to an historically accurate recreation of Medieval and Renaissance traditions of street theatre when it was performed in Basel. Here the actors could be seen

> stopping and singing on a village square, making a game of mounting their portable stage. And the comedy, or rather, the mystery play, took place with masks, a little music, ghosts, an old peasant, a witch, a princess, assassins and demons. Finally, the dream dissipated, the little company would roll up its mats and its curtains, gather up its props, put out its lanterns and then move on, all the while singing its refrain. . .[70]

He attempted a variety of different commedic pieces with *les Copiaus*, for along with *Harlequin the Magician*, *The Illusion*, and *The Woman of Ancona*, plays by Molière and Beaumarchais were also experimented with during this time, although never publicly performed.

Copeau continued his experimentation for many years, wrestling with frustrations which included the departures of his best students, who sought the critical and commercial rewards which he himself disdained. When *les*

Copiaus disbanded in May, 1929, Copeau went on to produce a few plays in Italy and for the Comédie-Française. His great era of experimentation had ended, but he continued to rethink and revise his theories for the rest of his life, maintaining his commitment to a modern theatre erected on the traditions of commedia.

Commedia in France After Copeau

Copeau's rediscovery and recreation of commedia was among the seminal theatrical developments of the early twentieth century in France. Although commedia had its greatest effect on actors and directors, modern French playwrights[71] also found specific aspects of commedia useful.

Antonin Artaud (1896-1948), an impassioned surrealist, was, in a sense, a link between Absurdist playwrights and the practitioners of the French stage who sought departures from realistic drama. Artaud began his theatrical life as an apprentice actor in Charles Dullin's Atelier from 1921 to 1923, where he played eleven roles, beginning with a small one in Henri de Régnier's *The Scruples of Sganarelle*. He went through Dullin's commedic training, which included emphasis on improvisation, pantomime, and masks, and he was impressed:

> It seems to be by far the most interesting experiment now being made in the theatre. It is all based on such desire for moral *purity*, both in behavior and in the acting profession, and on such highly developed artistic principles that it can really be considered an *innovation* of our time. Hearing Dullin teach, I feel that *I'm rediscovering ancient secrets and a whole forgotten mystique of production.*[72]

A few years after leaving Dullin, Artaud, with fellow surrealist Roger Vitrac, founded the Théâtre Alfred Jarry, which opened on June 1, 1927, with a program including Artaud's one-act play, *Upset Stomach, or The Mad Mother*. Drawn to Balinese dance, but also to music hall and to the films of the Marx Brothers, he wanted to revive the language of movement and gesture, and to animate scenic elements and props, bringing them into the action of the play. Elements of pantomime were part of all the forms he admired, and he wanted to revitalize it in order to create an "unperverted" pantomime:

> I mean direct Pantomime where gestures -- instead of representing words or sentences, as in our European Pantomime (a mere fifty years old!) which is merely a distortion of the mute roles of Italian comedy -- represent ideas, attitudes of mind, aspects of nature, all in an effective, concrete manner, i.e., by constantly evoking objects or natural details, like Oriental language which represents night by a tree on which a bird that has already closed one eye is beginning to close the other.[73]

He anticipated Ionesco in his belief that comedy required the addition of "something disquieting and tragic,"[74] and, as well, absurd. Artaud longed for a transformational theatre:

> In a Marx Brothers' film a man thinks he is going to take a woman in his arms but instead gets a cow, which moos. And through a conjunction of circumstances which it would take too long to analyze here, that moo, at just that moment, assumes an intellectual dignity equal to any woman's cry.

> Such a situation, possible in the cinema, is no less possible in the theater as it exists: it would take very little -- for instance, replace the cow with an animated manikin, a kind of monster endowed with speech, or a man disguised as an animal -- to rediscover the street of an objective poetry at the root of humor, which the theater has renounced and abandoned to the Music Hall, and which the Cinema later adopted.[75]

Like Copeau, Artaud was distressed by much of what he saw on the contemporary stage, and he condemned it as decadent, because "it has broken away from the spirit of profound anarchy which is at the root of all poetry."[76] His new theatre would employ ordinary actions and gestures as a springboard, and "in the same way that HUMOR AS DESTRUCTION can serve to reconcile the corrosive nature of laughter to the habits of reason."[77] Artaud's notion of comedy as anarchy and his love of pantomime's grotesque and ridiculous elements was fundamentally commedic, although he cautioned that his ideas and plays "have nothing to do with Copeau's improvisations."[78]

The rise of the Theatre of the Absurd movement after World War II, especially in France, and partly inspired by Artaud, meant not only new directions for modern drama, but another kind of commedia revival. This was, perhaps, inevitable. As Martin Esslin has suggested, the appeal of commedia and its derivatives through the ages has demonstrated a power that other forms were not able to reach: "The tradition of the commedia dell'arte reappears in a number of other guises. Its characters have survived in the puppet theatre and the Punch and Judy shows, which also, in their own way, have influenced the writer of the Theatre of the Absurd."[79] Referring to the various popular entertainments inspired by commedia, including Elizabethan clowns, Hanswurst, harlequinades, pantomimes, music hall, vaudeville, and silent film comedy, Esslin writes that the greatest performers of these genres "reached heights of tragicomic pathos that left much of the contemporary legitimate theatre far behind."[80] Absurdism mixed and overlapped the clowning of commedia, carnival, and circus, and elements of fantasy and symbolism. Esslin stresses, moreover, that the abstraction of Absurdism comes from an "anti-literary attitude."[81] Here the Absurdists can be connected to Craig, Meyerhold, Reinhardt, Copeau, and their contemporaries, who struggled to move the theatre away from its almost total dependency on literature. Esslin sensed a connection between Roman mimes and the actors of commedia, and concluded that although the verifiable connection between them was difficult to prove, "the deep *inner* connection of all these forms remains a self-evident fact."[82] A profound understanding of the meaning of these ancient clowns, and a deep sense of the grotesque and nonsensical, as well as an emphasis on mime, nurtured the Absurdist playwrights. They were also drawn to the icons of silent film comedy, and many of their plays feature clowns and tramps intended as universal symbols of man, in the manner of

Harlequin, Pierrot, and Chaplin's "Little Tramp."

Samuel Beckett (1906-1989), author of *Waiting for Godot* (1953), the quintessential Absurdist play, makes use of elements from the entire spectrum of comic genres. In *Waiting for Godot*, he creates the illusion that his tramps[83] are improvising, and, this in itself, suggests the endless word games and nonsensical misunderstandings typical of commedia scenarios. There is no immediately discernible plot, or even any tangible sense of reality to impinge on the characters' comic digressions, although its atmosphere is carefully crafted by the playwright, instead of being invented by the actors, as it would have been in traditional commedia. For example, in a brief interlude in which commedic derivatives are mentioned, the seemingly inane banter of Vladimir and Estragon has an improvised quality:

> VLADIMIR: Charming evening we're having.
> ESTRAGON: Unforgettable.
> VLADIMIR: And it's not over.
> ESTRAGON: Apparently not.
> VLADIMIR: It's only the beginning.
> ESTRAGON: It's awful.
> VLADIMIR: It's worse than being at the theatre.
> ESTRAGON: The circus.
> VLADIMIR: The music hall.
> ESTRAGON: The circus.[84]

Beckett does not literally use any recognizable commedic traditions. There is no genuine improvisation suggested by the author, although in the first American production, comic Bert Lahr ad-libbed repeatedly. Also, in a recent New York production with Steve Martin and Robin Williams, improvised embellishments were added by Williams to the delight of some audiences, but to the outrage of many critics. There are no obvious commedia characters, no historically reconstructed *lazzi*, no commedic staging conventions in the play, yet Beckett does create an *illusion* of spontaneity and improvisation which parallels commedia. The action in Beckett's plays includes much nonsensical business which often resembles *lazzi*. Language is devalued, and there is a lack of realistic illusion, which is replaced by a grotesque improbability, similar to the anarchic environment associated with commedia.

Beckett borrowed on the traditions of some commedia derivatives to create his tramps, who are, in a sense, existential stock characters (for example, Hamm in *Endgame* is depicted as a grotesque actor, always fighting to be in the spotlight). Their ridiculous actions and pratfalls are in the spirit of commedia *lazzi*, and the plays' grotesque other-worldliness is, like commedia, a theatre of the imagination, converting life into a vaudeville performance or a circus act. French mime and acting teacher Jacques Lecoq has said that Beckett "brought a new dimension to the clown by having him expose the depths of existence. Tragic heroes having become inaccessible, the clowns replace them in *Waiting for Godot.*"[85]

Eugène Ionesco (b. 1910), a Rumanian whose career has been mostly spent in France, was a major exponent of the Theatre of the Absurd. He vehemently rejected Realism and traditional literary drama. His plays examine the impotence of language and human communication, the virulence of physical objects, and humanity's loss of control over its world. Beginning with *The Bald Soprano* (1950), he attempted to scramble and reconstruct the forms of drama, and he labelled plays with contradictory terms, emphasizing his disdain for the value of language and labels. For example, he called *The Chairs* (1957) a "tragic farce," and it is one of the most vivid examples of the influence of commedia, and its derivatives, on his work. Like Artaud, he especially longed to have available to him the means to bring the transformational scenes, typical of English pantomime, to his play:

> I personally would like to bring a tortoise on to the stage, turn it into a race horse, then into a hat, a song, a dragoon, and a fountain of water. One can dare anything in the theatre, and it is the place where one dares the least. I want no other limits than the technical limits of stage machinery. People will say that my plays are music-hall turns or circus acts. So much the better -- let's include the circus in the

theatre! Let the playwright be accused of being arbitrary. Yes, the theatre is the place where one can be arbitrary. As a matter of fact, it is not arbitrary. The imagination is not arbitrary, it is revealing. . . .I have decided not to recognize any laws except those of my imagination, and since the imagination obeys its own laws, this is further proof that in the last resort it is not arbitrary.[86]

He most effectively managed something of this in *Rhinocéros* (1960), wherein several characters change from humans to rhinoceroses during the action of the play.[87]

Despite the strong influence of commedia on French playwrights, its impact was greatest on actors and directors, many of whom were also caught up in the Existentialist and Absurdist movements. Copeau's fascination with commedia spread to his students, and they, in turn, passed it along to their followers. By the middle of the twentieth century, many major actors and directors in France were working to some degree within the commedic tradition.

After leaving the Vieux-Colombier, Copeau's nephew, Michel Saint-Denis (1897-1971), started the Compagnie des Quinze in 1930 with many former *Copiaus*. They achieved critical success for a time, but subsequently disbanded, and Saint-Denis moved to London to continue his work there. Although he adhered to many of Copeau's principles, he was considerably less interested than his uncle in a revival of commedia.

Copeau's son-in-law, Jean Dasté (b. 1904), who studied under Saint-Denis, and worked with the Compagnie des Quinze, put considerable energy into continuing to work toward Copeau's commedic theatre. In 1933, the Compagnie des Quinze performed several innovative theatre pieces, including Jean Variot's adaptation of Plautus's *The Twin Menaechmi*, in commedia style. When the Compagnie disbanded later that year, Dasté worked and studied at Dullin's Théâtre de l'Atelier, where he came to believe in theatricality for its own sake. Dasté believed that Copeau had made his actors understand "what *commedia dell'arte* must have been on the planks of the public squares."[88] Later, he and his wife, Marie-Hélène Copeau (b. 1902), headed several theatre companies which relied on pantomimic techniques. Having played leading roles in Copeau's most commedic productions, he was at home staging productions of commedic plays, including Molière's *The Flying Doctor* (1937) and *The Tricks of Scapin* (1943), Marivaux's *Harlequin Tamed by Love* (1942), and Eugène Labiche's *The Jackpot* (1949). Typical among their productions was *Exodus* (1946), a masked mime piece in which the actors transformed themselves, in Artaudian fashion, into animals, buildings, planes, chariots, sounds, bells, and clocks. They also revived Copeau's *Harlequin the Magician*, in 1941, and *The Illusion*, in 1950, both of which relied heavily on commedic techniques.[89]

Two other Copeau students, Charles Dullin and Louis Jouvet, had significant impact on the French stage. Dullin (1885-1949), like Copeau, was interested in a popular theatre that would serve as "a source of spiritual enrichment for the people."[90] He joined the Vieux-Colombier company in 1913, and after acquiring a firm grounding in Copeau's techniques, as well as a personal triumph in *The Miser*, left to form his own troupe. From 1921 to 1939, Dullin headed the Théâtre de l'Atelier, which also functioned as a school and a laboratory for experimental theatre. Here he intended to "return to the great traditions of dramatic art"[91] by applying the techniques of commedia he had learned from Copeau, especially an understanding of pantomime as an essential tool of the actor's craft, to the plays of Molière. Almost from the beginning of his career, even before his work with Copeau, Dullin experimented with commedia, but initially the results were disappointing. At the Neuilly Fair, he attempted a revival of commedia, which, although it failed, was significant to him in that "it gave a foretaste of my *improvisational* method of teaching young students; a tendency toward a people's theatre, yet not a *populist* one; a tendency to introduce plastic elements into the performance; a tendency to seek after a new kind of ordering of the spectacle."[92] Dullin, as most modern commedists, viewed commedia as a living thing, but added his belief that it was anarchic, an art that was "a primal scream into a state of semi-consciousness, an impetuous adolescence, irresistible in its spirit and momentum, a maturity conscious of the power obtained through the acquisition of wisdom, then old age. . .the old age of the dying clown."[93]

Dullin made virtuoso use of his understanding of commedic acting in his superb performance as Harpagon in *The Miser*, a role he first played under Copeau, and later in his own production. When it was produced as part of Copeau's New York seasons in 1918, some critics were surprised that Dullin aimed for a subtler, more psychological interpretation, down-playing Harpagon's venemous ranting and raving. *The New York Times* conceded, however, that "within its limits it was a finely modulated, deeply-imagined creation, sharp in its theatric effects and inerrantly comic."[94] Dullin had added an ingratiating shrewdness that leavened the character's greed, and heightened the light-hearted effects created by Copeau, becoming a "little broken old man, this man *of all humans the least humane*."[95]

Following his break with Copeau during the American seasons, Dullin turned to staging his own productions at the Théâtre de l'Atelier. He directed nearly seventy productions there, covering the full dramatic spectrum from Aristophanes to Pirandello. Many of these, such as his production of Ben Jonson's *Volpone*, were, like his Harpagon, lightened and softened in tone by his gentle humanity. Few of the Atelier's productions were commerical successes, for, as Norman Marshall wrote, Dullin's "view of life was too personal, too individual to make him a good interpreter of the works of those who saw life from a different viewpoint."[96]

Like Copeau, Dullin emphasized the importance of the actor. His company included Artaud at the beginning, and Jean-Louis Barrault later.

Long after he had established himself as one of the finest actors and directors in France, Barrault recalled that Dullin was like a sorcerer who

> conjured up for us the mystery of those long words like: Commedia dell'Arte (with two m's), improvisation, Zani, Pulcinella, etc. It would be excessive to say that he gave us the secret of these things, we probably did not deserve it, but he made us grasp the poetry which emanated from them, and to which he added his own personal poetry, which I shall never forget.[97]

At the Atelier, Dullin emphasized the importance of commedic improvisation, and instructed his actors, as Copeau had instructed him, in various techniques for mastering it to achieve a transformational style of acting. More a teacher than a director, more an actor than a manager, Dullin became increasingly disinterested in the commerical stage. When *Volpone* became popular, he ended the play's run, fearing that he and his company would be seduced away from their desire to experiment and explore. Like Copeau, he was not interested in scenic spectacle, and although he occasionally used stage machinery, he more typically avoided it. He did, however, admire Appia's theories, and believed that lighting was the most suitable visual element because it was a fluid, living medium like the actor.[98]

Louis Jouvet (1887-1951), a member of Copeau's original Vieux-Colombier company, appeared as Geronte opposite Copeau's Scapin in *The Tricks of Scapin*. His Geronte, "physically decrepit and a victim of contending emotions -- avarice, terror, rage, and humiliation,"[99] worked in perfect counterpoint to Copeau's energetic and youthful Scapin. Their relentless interplay contributed to both the electrifying pace and commedic spirit of the production. After gaining a sophisticated understanding of Copeau's technique, Jouvet headed his own troupes, beginning in 1922 as director of the Théâtre des Champs Elysées and in 1934 at the Théâtre de l'Athénée. As Arnolphe in Molière's *The School for Wives* in 1937, perhaps his definitive performance, Jouvet demonstrated his mastery of pantomime, learned, at least in part, from Copeau. Jouvet felt that pantomime was a fundamental human instinct evident from early childhood, and that the "perfect comedian would be one who developed this instinct to its maximum."[100] The major difference between the actor and the comedian, he believed, was in the area of pantomime, which was more developed in the comedian. A comedian differed from other actors by virtue of the process required to create a characterization: "The actor substitutes himself for the character, the comedian operates by means of penetration and insinuation."[101]

As Copeau, Jouvet felt that pantomime and gesture were "another language -- a universal language."[102] He did resist some of Copeau's ideas, and was increasingly less inclined to emphasize the farcical elements of a play, seeking, instead, the darker qualities inherent to the desperation of the character at the center of the farce. His comic actor was no clown, and he believed a "comedian can play several types,"[103] and was not restricted to one type of character as many comic actors were. Unlike Copeau, Jouvet emphasized the importance of speech:

> In training his voice, the comedian must first *pitch* it as singers do; then he must get to know its exact register. Once he has acquired good diction, he must study elocution. In the seventeenth century, that constituted almost the entire art of the comedian. For a long time acting, properly speaking, was reserved to pantomimists and actors of the *commedia dell'arte*. Once when he was asked his advice, Henry Irving said: "Speak clearly!" He answered all such questions with this motto: "Speak clearly!" and added: "Be human."[104]

Jouvet retained from Copeau an interest in harmonizing the performance with the audience. He promoted Copeau's emphasis on creating an ensemble, but added a touch of mysticism to his comprehension of the actor's art: "Before an audience one may say that the comedian has a density -- the quality of his presence. The comedian must learn to make use of this dynamism, this kind of *aura* that surrounds him."[105]

Following a lengthy period in which he worked mostly with

contemporary plays, Jouvet turned back to the classics, and Molière in particular, after World War II. After producing *The School for Wives*, and appearing in numerous plays by Molière for Copeau, he decided to tackle *Don Juan* and *Tartuffe*. The character of Don Juan particularly fascinated Jouvet, who resisted traditional views of the play, and down-played the more romantic and lightly comic tones. His Don Juan was an extremist, who hated social hypocrisy, throwing away positive values along with the negative elements he saw around him. Jouvet portrayed a haunted adventurer at the end of the line; he had seen it all and done it all. The interpretation was a revelation to audiences and critics when the production opened on December 24, 1947; they were unprepared for a performance of Molière's play demonstrating such depth and complexity. One critic proclaimed that by "breathing life into Molière's masterpiece, after waiting almost three centuries, Louis Jouvet gave us something close to a masterpiece as actor and director."[106]

Jouvet later directed *The Tricks of Scapin* for Barrault's company at the Théâtre Marigny, veering away from the broad farce of Copeau's version, to emphasize the play's lyrical qualities. He "conceived Scapin to be a lazy but comic knave, who, armed with many startling tricks, finally carried them too far, and was caught in his own snares."[107] On a permanent setting made up of several levels, Jouvet splashed colorful lighting, and set his actors free to leap and dance among them. At least in this respect, the production was reminiscent of Copeau's commedia. Borrowing one particular commedic tradition, Jouvet incorporated mime and dance interludes during the intermissions, keeping the light-hearted spirit of the performance alive.

During the run of *The Tricks of Scapin*, Jouvet turned his attention to another Molière masterpiece, *Tartuffe*, which he opened on December 28, 1950. He sought to make a deeply personal connection with Tartuffe as he had with Don Juan. Rejecting the traditional unctuous and sensuous fat man, his Tartuffe was an attractive, well-mannered aesthete: cold, calculating, and supremely self-aware. This interpretation led to the elimination of many of the play's lighter moments, leading some critics to complain that he was working against the play's specific directions. Explaining his view of the character, however, Jouvet claimed that Tartuffe's behavior is enigmatic and that "It is difficult, I say, to find the place, the passage where Tartuffe deliberately acts as an impostor."[108] As this indicates, Jouvet's later versions of Molière were far from commedic, but it is clear that his work with Copeau, and much of his own understanding of the comic art, owes a considerable debt to commedia.

A third generation of commedic actors and directors descending from Copeau emerged from the students of Dullin and Jouvet. Jean-Louis Barrault (b. 1910) began his career at Dullin's Atelier in 1931, where he acted a wide range of roles, mostly from the plays of Racine and Molière. While with Dullin, he met Etienne Decroux and they agreed to work together to develop a mime grammar, although they eventually disagreed about its application. Barrault saw mime as a valuable actor's tool, which could aid in the interpretation of a text, or be used as an innovative stage technique. He also promoted the "total theatre" concept advocated by Artaud, which presumed that theatre was a form in which all arts could be integrated to maximum effect. The mixture of the arts and the various elements of production succeeded for him in "humanizing itself to such an extent that it virtually becomes part of the action, that it succeeds, in short, in serving the theatre in its totality -- at this moment, total theatre finds its *unity*."[109] Barrault was, of course, influenced by Copeau through the teachings of Dullin, and Copeau observed of Barrault that he "is from the same school and is inspired by the same principles, but he pushes their consequences further because his technique is more perfect. He respects the text. . .but never misses an opportunity to develop an action or to add an episode of invention."[110] Barrault himself was unable, and unwilling, to separate the influences on him:

"There was no succession of influences; it all worked inside of me simultaneously."[111]   Barrault recalled that while studying with Dullin, commedia was emphasized. He especially remembered that:

> we used to peer at the prints representing figures which defied the law of gravity; we weaved strange characters into our dreams; we should have loved to have had feet slim and pointed like those rubber-like dancers, the exuberant gusto of their fat old men or the lightning wit of the first Zani. We should have loved, above all, to share the nomadic life of these pleasant, philosophical scoundrels. More than twenty years have elapsed since those days, and we have never stopped exploring documents and reading books on this subject. Above all we have shed our clothes, donned the slip and practised our exercises in practically every theatre where we have been.[112]

Extensive experimentation with masks and acrobatics led to an attempt to define and grasp the intangible techniques of commedia. Barrault also tried to understand the content of commedic performances which consisted "essentially in representing life, only by using the human body. There is in my opinion a kind of performance which consists in taking four barrels, in fixing up on them planks in the shape of an apron-stage, climbing on these planks, and with the help of one's body, breath, voice, face and hands, recreating the world."[113]   Despite this allegiance, Barrault claimed that "Commedia dell'Arte remained for me an enchanting but closed world which I hoped to visit one day."[114] In the eyes of knowing observers, he did visit that world. His efforts to find a link between physical gesture and the psyche culminated in his theory of tragic mime, first demonstrated in his own adaptation of William Faulkner's *As I Lay Dying* (1935). When he later played Deburau in Marcel Carné's film masterpiece, *Les enfants du paradis* (1945), Barrault was able to demonstrate the expressive power of modern mime to a large international audience. Aside from Copeau, Barrault was the French theatrical artist most profoundly influenced by commedia and its characters. He recognized commedia's universal attributes and the symbolic significance of its stereotypical characters. He saw commedia as the "true art of the theatre,"[115] which

> denounces the absurdity of life and endeavours to restore its equilibrium. The Commedia dell'Arte, which I cannot claim to know fully, seems to me just as old as man. How many "doctors" do we not meet in life, and is the second Zani with the white mask not the modern lamplighter? Don't we meet everywhere these extraordinary characters which Callot had already fixed on copper? But in the end it is the actor who, through his technique, transposes these characters into his magic world which has done away with gravity, and in which imagination is free to move about and to enjoy itself.[116]

Barrault saw two purposes in theatre: escape and illusion. Theatre "is the realm of dreams, and this is why the art of the theatre is specifically the art of dreams."[117] The dream-maker was the actor, and commedia represented to him, as it had to so many other modern commedists, the pinnacle of the actor's art. His actor became completely familiar with his character over a long period of time, and physically trained to the limit of his powers and the peak of control. He had to have a sharp mind with "an encyclopedia of tirades with which he could meet any dramatic situation."[118] The commedia actor skilled at improvisation, could achieve "the kind of theatre which compels the actor to get to the pitch of his *own true personality*. It is the kind of art which shows that freedom lies beyond silence and not within. An ignorant actor could not improvise for long; only somebody who knows a lot can invent new words."[119]

Pantomime was the key, and the modern actor had to learn the language of gestures which have

> a side which is both charming and obsolete, belonging to comedy. This is the difference between comedy and tragedy. The new silent mime has a cosmic bearing. . .it is direct, there are no detours. . .death is faced head on. However, in comedy, you can resort to frills and pirouettes. . . .This is not pejorative, but it is a distinction. In the Commedia dell'Arte, for instance, things take place which are not only tragic but atrocious; yet they are always treated with pirouettes and light-hearted spirit.[120]

Pantomime was "the recreation of life by gesture,"[121] and to Barrault an important tool in the training of a commedic actor was the mask which

> confers upon a given expression the maximum of intensity together with an impression of absence. A mask expresses at the same time the maximum of life and the maximum of death; it partakes of the visible and of the invisible, of the apparent and absolute. The mask exteriorizes a deep aspect of life, and in so doing, it helps to rediscover instinct.[122]

Above all, the true strength of commedic acting technique was the increased value placed on gesture and movement. Pantomime was originally, "a deaf and dumb art -- modern pantomime is the Art of Silence."[123] The possibility that a mime could "reach up to tragedy"[124] would elevate not only the power and technique of pantomime, but at the same time, recreate the entire art of theatre. Barrault viewed theatre as communion between actor and spectator, and although he was an expert mime, he did not wish to specialize purely in that area. He increasingly moved toward topical political relevance in his work. After *Les enfants du paradis* (and a stage production, *Baptiste*, elaborating on his character from the film), he hoped to create many more sketches for the character of Baptiste, an amalgam of Pierrot and Arlecchino, but without success: "What a pity, for so many important things could have been expressed through Baptiste, who is surely related to Kafka and to Hamlet. What a splendid satire of our age could take place through him. . . .One need not confine oneself to the old pantomime. . . .Baptiste was something special."[125] Barrault saw in Baptiste both universal and immediate relevance. The pantomimic scenes in *Les enfants du paradis* vary between rambunctious comedy and heart-breaking poignancy. Like commedia's Arlecchino, and Deburau's Pierrot, "Baptiste is a primitive, a child. . . . Naughty at his strongest moments, he can only fight and kill in a dream."[126] After World War II, Barrault rarely returned to the commedic pantomime he had performed so brilliantly before and during the war. He believed that "a good mime should not be the caricature of an actor, but on the contrary, he should be more capable than all others to act in a realistic drama, as he will know how to use simple and true gesture."[127]

Barrault's commedic mime techniques were absorbed into his productions of Molière's plays. In explaining the effect of Molière on French drama, he astutely identified a key reason for the proliferation of commedia in the modern era. Molière, he wrote, "is ourselves, quotations from his plays are part of our minds since our earliest age; we have grown up with him,"[128] and his plays were successful, then and now, because "they are artificial. They are spectacular pirouettes."[129] In a fruitful stage partnership with his wife, actress Madelaine Renaud, Barrault produced highly successful productions of several of Molière's plays throughout the remainder of his career, including *Amphitryon* (1947 and 1961), *The Tricks of Scapin* (1949 and 1963), *The Misanthrope* (1954), *The Affected Ladies* (1961), and *The Bourgeois Gentleman* (1972). These, as well as several works by Marivaux and Beaumarchais, were all informed by Barrault's complex understanding of commedia.

Etienne Decroux (1898-1991), Barrault's early partner in the movement toward modern mime, began his career as a protege of Copeau. He literally created his own artistic genre out of the acting exercises Copeau had developed for the Vieux-Colombier. "Copeau had ignited us so well that those who left him took the fire with them,"[130] Decroux said, and using Copeau's techniques as a departure point, he set out to create a new, autonomous art form emphasizing movement. After parting company with Barrault, Decroux developed it as a separate and unique genre. Aside from Copeau, Decroux was also inspired by Craig, and especially Craig's theory of the über-marionette. With his actors, he sought to achieve the physical and mental control he felt Craig had called for:

> I personally wish for the birth of this actor made of wood. I envision this large-scale marionette arousing, but its appearance and its movements, a feeling of seriousness and not of condescension. The

marionette that we desire must not make us laugh or feel moved as does the playing of a young child. It must inspire terror and pity and, from there, rise to the level of the waking dream.[131]

Decroux's admiration for Craig was great, and he wondered if any of the great Russian experiments would "have ever seen the light of day if Craig's ideas had not spread across Europe at the beginning of the century?"[132] Like Craig, he rejected Realism, exclaiming that "Art should not be too present. Poetry is absence. That is why memory is a good poet. Memory is at a distance, subtracting, adding, assembling. Art is like a dream."[133] He developed a system of codified gestures and aesthetic principles which he believed established the viability of a "new" mime. In the process, he resurrected mime as a form of popular entertainment, although he had also recreated it as "statuary mime," which attempted to present the illusion of mobile sculpture. Unlike traditional pantomimic forms which combined movement with dialogue or music, he sought the eloquence of movement in silence. He was opposed to the broad facial expressions and physical gestures typical of nineteenth century pantomime: "I detested this form. . . .An art is first of all serious and adds the comic aspect later. And this pantomime seemed to me to be systematically comic, even before one knew what the subject was."[134]

Decroux developed a strict and elaborate system of physical training, and he used masks inspired by Cubist or other abstract sculpture, which helped to train the eye of the viewer on the movement of the torso (an example of his style can be seen in the now traditional mime movement of "walking in place"). Barrault referred to pirouettes and dance in his conception of mime, but Decroux saw dance and mime as opposites: "Dance is abstract and based on music. Mime is concrete and based on life."[135] He encountered mask exercises while with Copeau, but he extended the mask's value to include its ability to obscure individual and psychological traits. By masking the actor's face, the expression offered by the body was necessarily heightened. The actor thus became an abstract human symbol, removed from any realistic detail or measurable time. The mask "permits not only justice, since justice is not universally respected, but it permits use of talent that otherwise would be lost, talent like gold hidden in the earth, or like a little child lost in the ocean."[136]

The differences between literary drama and pantomime were clear to Decroux. "In the course of an evening with friends, you can read Baudelaire sitting down, but in order to do justice to Corneille you must take off your jacket; and in order to play a text in *commedia dell'arte* style, you must strip down to your shorts,"[137] he wrote, and added that even Molière with his brilliant comic muse demanded that "the actor must behave modestly, although he can still determine speed and force."[138] Decroux, in contrast, imagined "what fullness, what fantasy, what sudden displays of fireworks, what caressing or sinuous voice, what machine-gun delivery, what wail of feline love, what whimper of a dog, run over and lingering in death; in short, what vocal wonders an actor could allow himself with an absolutely poor text."[139] Commedia, and some of its derivatives, were central to Decroux's approach. He copied six words from an old music hall poster that, for him, epitomized the fundamental elements of a mime's performance: gaiety, laughter, rhythm, dynamism, charm, and emotion. He and his disciples gave relatively few public performances, but one of his students conquered the popular stage as a mime without peer.

Marcel Marceau (b.1923) joined Dullin's Atelier in 1944 as a young actor. Decroux spotted his extraordinary ability as a mime, and recruited him to help refine the mime grammar. After two years, he had mastered Decroux's techniques, but being more interested in performance than in further study, he broke away. In 1946, he joined Barrault's company to perform in the pantomimes *Baptiste* and *Arlequin*, but by this time Barrault had relegated mime to a relatively minor place in his repertory, so Marceau broke away again, to perform independently. Along with his immediate predecessors, he instinctively understood that mime sprang from non-verbal commedic characters, and particularly Deburau's Pierrot, "the key character in the art of mime,. . .I wanted to revive him. Preserving the essential characteristics of classical pantomime and placing him in the period of Daumier and Lautrec."[140]

In *Dead Before Dawn* (1948), a mimo-drama (an adaptation of a play or short story), Marceau used the Pierrot character and a dark theme reminiscent of late nineteenth century Pierrot plays. His character, Ghoe, is seen hanging dead from a lamppost, but he revives and tells of his unfortunate past life which he hopes to conquer. When the moonlit night dies, he is again seen hanging. The entire piece was staged as a symbolic and lyrical dream. This poetic form of mime, mixing lyricism and tragedy, was certainly no innovation on Marceau's part. It had been part of the Pierrot repertory for at least a century, but this version featured a unique characteristic. Roger Blin narrated the story while Marceau and his cast mimed the action. Unlike Decroux and Barrault, and certainly Deburau, he was willing to rely, at least to a certain extent, on a text.

In another piece, *The Coat*, suggested by a Gogol short story, he juxtaposed the somber drabness of a low-level Russian civil servant's world with the bright colors of Montmartre, creating a grotesque commentary on human existence. Here the use of Meyerholdian duality grotesquerie connects Marceau to a different brand of modern commedia. He did not restrict himself, however, to one statement. In *The Fair*, another mimo-drama, he used the familiar world of carnivals and fairs to capture the feeling of joy derived from such entertainments, with no particular reference to any theme.

Marceau's legendary "Bip" character first appeared in 1947 and has remained the pivotal part of his program since then. Until 1956, his performances consisted of multi-character, silent mimo-dramas and dramas written specifically for mime performance. After 1956, he has devoted himself to solo Bip numbers and romantic or comic pantomimes, which were virtuoso renderings of the Decroux technique. With the creation of Bip, he moved away from mimo-drama to shorter, and perhaps purer, pantomimes. Bip, a twentieth century Pierrot, liberated him to "create a new style of mime using his adventures."[141] Unlike traditional commedic clowns, Bip was divorced from the self-generated anarchy and manipulative mischief, that a Harlequin or a Pedrolino might create. Bip was even more passive than Chaplin's "Little Tramp," who seemed swept up by forces out of his control. Bip was a dreamy child drifting, with an element of wonder, from one discovery to another. Marceau himself stated that mime on the modern stage is about "the poor fellow who is out of the general scheme of things. This conflict is the condition of his existence."[142] Bip was a watcher, even observing his audience, and a romantic, "listening with a timid ear and a wistful face to the laughter, tears and applause of the people who identify themselves with him."[143] In film and on television, as well as on concert stages, Bip has become an instantly recognized figure. Several generations of actors have profited from mime techniques inspired by Marceau, but, nonetheless, his style of mime has had little direct influence on the course of modern theatrical practice, or the proliferation of commedia.

An important contemporary of Marceau's is Jacques Lecoq (b. 1921), an athlete who was introduced to mime in the company of Jean Dasté, where he was inspired by the experimental work being done in mime. He viewed mime quite differently from Decroux, feeling that a highly defined system of gestures worked against the achievement of natural movement. Mime, he firmly believed, should express primal needs rather than studied aesthetics. He acknowledged that Decroux had been a necessary step in the development of the modern revival of mime, but came to feel that mime must explore new avenues of expression, rather than be limited by a fixed code of gesture. Lecoq developed a training system aimed at freeing mime from artificial gesture, developing an approach that was more direct and visceral. The outcome, ironically, was that his methods rarely achieved naturalistic effects. In his school, founded in 1956, he aimed at a physical expression of environment and character through use of masks which, like Decroux's, focused attention on the body. He pointed to the evolution of the clown characters in the Absurdist plays of Beckett and Ionesco as validation of his theories, and placed emphasis on each mime's liberation of a personal clown.

Mime, Lecoq believed, should reveal the inner life and emotions of the character portrayed. His use of acrobatics extended beyond any mere visual "gag" to expose the emotions and attitudes of characters. For example, "Pantalon, in a rage, would make a dangerous reverse somersault, without performing a demonstration of an acrobatic exercise. The somersault was not visible in and of itself, but it was part of the architecture of anger, and the audience only felt the overwhelming rage of Pantalon."[144] In his school, he rejected any restrictive notions imposed on mime training, stressing that

> It is the gesture behind the gesture, in the gesture behind the word, in the movement of material objects, in sounds, colors, and lights, that the school finds its origins. Man understands that which moves by his ability to "mimic" it; that is, to identify himself with the world by re-enacting it with his entire being. Beginning in the silent body of man the impulses toward expression take shape -- dramatic impulse and then dramatic creation.[145]

Lecoq attempted to understand bodily expression, finding essences while creating "bodily impressions." Imitating the "people, elements, animals, plants, trees, colors, lights, material objects, sounds"[146] discovered in everyday life, he and his students attempted to bring together gesture and word to explore "the point where they are merged. A word must be charged with the impression of the body, and not defined by itself."[147] Their study included looking to past performance traditions, like commedia, "wherein the action is the act, and Greek tragedy wherein the speech is substance: these are theatre forms which engage the whole being: pelvis, solar plexus, and head."[148]

Clowning in such various styles as Chaplin, Beckett, and Ionesco, became a central focus, for the "clown in the spirit of today has replaced the hero, who no longer exists in the theatre. We emphasize the exploration for one's own clown, the one who has grown up within us and which society does not permit us to express."[149] Along with commedia, Lecoq studied the techniques of the Greek chorus and the Roman mime, and he became convinced that the mime must understand the notion of Aristotelian imitation on an immediate and personal level. He was certain that "man knows only what he receives and plays back. It is the gestural playback mechanism of knowledge."[150] He insisted, however, that anyone can *imitate* without being able to *act*: "The difference comes from what the talented, skilled, and trained actor extracts consciously and intuitively from what he observes -- a common point of gesture among all men, a sort of common denominator."[151] Gesture, Lecoq believed, was the most basic and earliest form of human communication. It preceded knowledge, thought, and verbal language. Mime evolved in silence, and "gesture engages action in silence. When gesture replaces the word, it is called pantomime; such was the case with Roman pantomime and with the white pantomime (Pierrot)."[152] Although he emphasized mime, Lecoq does not ignore the written word as a valuable source. Of the balance between actor and script, he decided that the actor "should be able to dominate, to transpose his orchestration."[153]

Masks (five basic types: neutral, expressive, larval, commedia, and red clown's nose) were used as a training tool to "facilitate the discovery of the central point, the essence of a relationship, or a conflict, the discovery of the gesture which is the sum of all gestures, the word which represents all words."[154] Lecoq's masked mime learned to direct his expression into his body, to learn to play the emotions and character indicated by the mask, to play the opposite of the emotions and character indicated by the mask, and, most importantly, as a stimulus for his imagination. In Lecoq's conception of commedia "all passions are pushed to an extreme, and the question is not that of life but of survival."[155] The word is joined to the gesture in his commedia, and his mimes developed expertise and rapport with masks; they used gesture to create character, they improvised dialogue, used rhythm and movement as integrated elements, and achieved clarity and simplicity in both word and gesture.[156]

By the mid-1950's, the influence of commedia on French theatre artists was less immediately visible, but still ingrained deeply in their style.[157] Significant among current French directors is Ariane Mnouchkine (b. 1939), who has made considerable use of commedia techniques, and has attempted "to try as far as possible to give the actors control over their art, so that they will be as prepared and ready as possible to use it in the service of what people need -- not by asking them what they want but by representing their experience of life."[158] Her Théâtre du Soleil productions emphasize the social implications of the stage, from both an historical and a contemporary viewpoint. She is not interested in psychologically motivated characters, but instead uses characters as theatrical constructions. With her company, she has experimented with the language of the stage under the influence of ritualized Oriental styles (including Kathakali, Bunraku, and, most importantly, Noh) and commedia.

The Théâtre du Soliel began in 1964, as an off-shoot of a university group. Originally set up as a cooperative venture, Mnouchkine's company, like the actors of traditional commedia, became, in a very real sense, a family. Preparing communal meals and participating in all aspects of production work are part of her actor's work. The company has presented plays by Gorky, Wesker, and Shakespeare in a manner that critics refer to as Artaudian. They prepared themselves in ways that are similar to the techniques employed by Copeau:

> The actors improvised every day in various village meeting places, both outdoors and indoors, around themes proposed by the people, who were very receptive to the masks, costumes and physical movements of the performers, as well as to the accuracy of what was expressed about their lives.[159]

The company hit its stride with *Les Clowns* (1969), written as direct commentary on the 1968 political upheaval in France, and with a production of *A Midsummer Night's Dream* in a circus-setting that anticipates Peter Brook's landmark 1970 staging. Mnouchkine concluded that the purpose of theatre was to arouse the audience's interest in existing social conditions and to make suggestions for change. She believed that the emotional and intellectual engagement of the audience was possible only through the audience's ability to recognize themselves in the play. *Les Clowns*, a series of improvised sketches, was a logical step for a company that emphasized improvisation in actor training and represented a solidifying of the Théâtre du Soleil's social goals. The image of the clown mirrored the artist and his place in society, and was seen in sketches that examined the creative process, and also permitted actors to make statements about prevailing social conditions. In preparation for *Les Clowns*, Mnouchkine and her company worked intensively on the physical aspects of performance, including gymnastic skills, and, beginning with no script at all, the actors were allowed a level of improvisation that truly freed them to freshly create their characters and the play. In rehearsal, costumes, props, and masks were readily available for experimentation, and, like her predecessors, Mnouchkine emphasized masks in actor training with the ultimate goal of achieving a seamless ensemble.

The Théâtre du Soleil's next important production was *1789* (1970), another improvised performance, based on the revolutionary historical and political events in France during that cataclysmic year. A much larger production than *Les Clowns, 1789* was a theatrical spectacle, and made use of commedia, music, gymnastics, readings of historical documents, puppets, tableux showing traditional renderings of historical events, and commedic techniques. It was, in a sense, a play-within-a-play: what the audience saw was *1789* performed by a troupe of eighteenth century actors on small platform stages as in commedia. Mnouchkine was thereby able to create an immediacy that avoided any conventional narrative of historical events or a realistic drama of life in that era. Her device made it possible for the audience to feel it was seeing a contemporary story told by those who were actually living it.

1789 was the Théâtre du Soleil's first unqualified success, and it even occasioned two sequels of sorts: *1793*, which chronicled the apocalyptic events of the French Revolution, and *L'Age d'or*, which examined the effect of that era on modern life. For *L'Age d'or*, the company adopted commedic masks and argued that the best way to achieve a popular theatre was through improvisation. They were able to create obvious parallels between traditional commedia characters and modern counterparts, and while this was nothing new, it was especially effective in performance. With an emphasis on the ideas of Copeau and Meyerhold, Mnouchkine proclaimed that her actors "long to dive into the study of the fabulous techniques of earlier epochs when theatre was theatrical."[160]

In 1977, Mnouchkine wrote and directed *Molière*, a film offering a revisionist biographical treatment. In keeping with her theatrical aesthetic, Mnouchkine's recreations of seventeenth century performance traditions emphasized commedic techniques, and brought out the struggle of the artist to contribute to society. She turned to the classics in the 1980's and 90's with a cycle of Shakespeare's plays, including *Richard II* (1981), *Twelfth Night* (1982), and *Henry IV, Part One* (1984), emphasizing the political machinations in the plays, *Sihanouk* (1985), a more overtly contemporary political play, and Aeschylus' *Oresteia* (1990). For these productions, Mnouchkine mingled elements of Noh, Kabuki, and Kathakali, and also many commedic techniques. Elements of German cabaret, French *bateleurs*, Grand Guignol, and Chinese opera have also found their way into Théâtre du Soleil productions.

The French stage has come full circle. Mnouchkine has acknowledged that in the manner Copeau returned to commedia and Molière for inspiration, she and her company are looking to Shakespeare, the traditions of Oriental theatre, and commedia for the inspiration to find new relevance in classic drama, and to recreate the modern stage. Copeau would approve.

CHAPTER EIGHT

The Show Booth: Commedia in the United States

This brings us to comedy, which is inherently subversive and visionary, always has a moral, and has always been popular. The traditional class connections of the dramatic genres are conventionally explained in terms of relative sophistication: only the aristocracy has leisure and refinement to consider the great issues propounded by tragedy; realism appeals to the no-nonsense outlook of the bustling middle class; comedy delights the childlike hedonism of the masses. Another way of putting it is to say that each genre carries a different subliminal message, and each class knows which message it wants to hear. Tragedy says there is an immutable order which it is idle to resist (our tragedy is the theater of the absurd, which says it is an immutable disorder); realism says the game is to the strong; comedy says you can have what you are being denied.[1]

-- Joan Holden, The San Francisco Mime Troupe

Although commedia found vital new life on most of Europe's stages in the first three decades of the twentieth century, the work of the modern commedists did not readily cross the Atlantic. Despite numerous attempts and experiments with commedic productions and techniques, particularly in New York, it was not until the appearance of politically driven street theatre groups in the 1960's that twentieth century commedia came into its own in the United States. Before American commedia came wildly alive in the streets of San Francisco around 1960, it could only be found in antiquarian experiments and on variety stages.

American theatre began developing native forms and producing original plays midway through the eighteenth century. At that time, commedia was at its lowest ebb on Europe's stages; when it was seen at all, it was in derivative harlequinades and pierrot shows. One of the first original plays staged in New York, was, in fact, one of these plays, *The Adventures of Harlequin and Scaramouch, or the Spaniard Trick'd*, a pantomime with "grotesque characters," which was presented at Henry Holt's Long Room in February, 1738/9. From all reports, it was little more than a pale imitation of European harlequinades. Most American theatrical bills in the eighteenth century were accompanied by afterpieces consisting of "comic operas," burlesques of well-known plays, or a pantomime which often featured commedic characters and incorporated music, dialogue, slapstick, and impressive scenic effects. Elements of these pantomimes did creep into developing native forms.

In 1868, the immensely popular pantomime *Humpty Dumpty* by actor G.L. Fox (1825-1877) began its astounding run of over one thousand performances. Fox himself appeared as the Clown, a broadly conceived amalgam of Grimaldi,[2] Pierrot, Punch, Pulcinella, and the new American stereotype, the rough-and-tumble Bowery mischief-maker. Fox had been a moderately successful actor and had the distinction of appearing in the original production of *Uncle Tom's Cabin*,[3] but Humpty Dumpty became his whole career, and led to numerous spinoffs consisting of, as Laurence Senelick writes, "a strong admixture of high-jinks and physical stunts, with Clown, Pantaloon, Harlequin, and Columbine comprising the low-comedy element."[4] Fox sponsored a group of five English acrobats, The Hanlon-Lees troupe, who, teamed with a French clown, Agoust, performed daring tricks, elaborate sight gags, and acrobatic stunts that were a forerunner to the silent film comedies of Georges Mélies and Mack Sennett. This type of pantomime entertainment was slowly but steadily eclipsed by the growing popularity of minstrels and musical comedy toward the end of the nineteenth century.

In 1829, when Thomas "Daddy" Rice (1808-1860) introduced his eccentric blackface character and "Jump Jim Crow" dance, American popular entertainments (including minstrels, vaudeville, musical comedy, and ultimately film and television) began to employ a vast array of commedic elements. The popularity of Rice's dance led to entire productions he named "Ethiopian Operas," which were basically short skits that permitted him ample opportunity for broad clowning. With the first appearance of the Virginia Minstrels in 1843, blackface minstrel entertainments modelled on Rice's began to dominate popular entertainment. Various grotesques, buffoons and fools, from Jim Crow and Zip Coon to "Bones" and "Tambo," became the first popular American commedic folk characters.

The blackfaced clown, most often portrayed by whites and less often by blacks, reigned on American stages until the middle of the twentieth century, when heightened awareness of the offensiveness of racial stereotypes signalled its demise. Until that time, however, comic blackface characters appeared not only in minstrel shows, but in musicals, straight plays, and films as well. In an article on minstrelsy, Richard Moody succinctly characterizes the similarities between American minstrels and commedia performers:

> As in the *Commedia* the special talents of the acting company determined the specific nature of the performance. Any limitations suggested by the script were followed only if compatible with the creative desires of the particular players. The Negro minstrel show never developed as many distinct comedy types as the *Commedia*, but certainly the Tambo, Bones, Interlocutor, and *wench* performers belong to the same theatrical family as the *Commedia's* Doctor, Captain, and Harlequin.[5]

Another Rice, circus clown Dan Rice (1823-1900), was a memorable American zanni of his day. Often dressed as the personification of Uncle Sam, Rice filled his circus tent with animals named for politicians and celebrities, setting a tone for topical satire that continues to the present.

Following minstrels, other commedic characters appeared in various light entertainments, from "Mose," the Yankee fireman first portrayed by F.S. Chanfrau, to the characters of Edward Harrigan's (1845-1911) Mulligan series of musical burlesques. On the musical and variety stages, a broad spectrum of ethnic stereotypical characters (Irish, German, Jewish) appeared as comic masks in the manner of commedia. Critic, novelist, and playwright William Dean Howells was quick to spot the similarity between such types and the characters of commedia. Harrigan's Mulligan series, which began in 1879 with *The Mulligan Guards' Ball*, reminded Howells favorably of Goldoni's commedic Venetian plays which similarly featured simplistic plots emphasizing colorful stereotypical characters. Harrigan approached the creation of his plays in the same manner as Goldoni, noting that "In constructing a plot I use one that is simple and natural -- just like what happens around us every day."[6] Howells compared Harrigan's plays to eighteenth-century commedia, noting that they were "like Shakespeare's plays, like Molière's plays, in being the work of a dramatist who is at the same time a manager and an actor. Possibly this is the only way we can have a drama of our own; it is not a bad way; and it is at least a very natural way."[7] Howells points out that

> The old Venetian filled his scene with the gondoliers, the serving-folk, the fish-women, the trades-people, the quacks, the idlers, the gamesters, of his city; and Mr. Harrigan shows us the street-clearners and contractors, the grocery-men, the shysters, the politicians, the washer-women, the servant-girls, the truckmen, the policemen, the risen Irishman and Irish woman, of contemporary New York.[8]

Harrigan played the feisty Dan Mulligan in *The Mulligan Guards' Ball* (1879), and its many sequels, including *The Mulligan Guards' Surprise* (1880), *The Mulligans' Silver Wedding* (1880), and *Cordelia's Aspirations* (1883). His stage partner, Tony Hart (1855-1891), played his son and the Mulligans' outrageous and rowdy black maid, Rebecca. Harrigan and Hart created comic characters that served them well, just as the stock masks of commedia had served Italian actors during the Renaissance. Howells found in their work "the spring of a true American comedy, the beginning of things which may be great things."[9] Although other writers and performers created similar American stereotypes, it was the vaudeville stages after 1900 that supported Harrigan's descendants: they virtually exploded with native commedic images.

In contrast to the growing reliance of popular entertainment on commedic forms, serious theatre expressed little interest in commedia. Modern European commedic plays staged in New York had to brave the critical and commercial indifference of critics and audience alike.[10] J.M. Barrie's one-act play *Pantaloon*,[11] Barker and Housman's *Prunella*,[12] Barker and Calthrop's *The Harlequinade*,[13] and Guitry's *Deburau*,[14] among others, all had modestly successful runs in New York in the years around World War I. None of these efforts, despite some individual successes,[15] seemed to promote interest in commedia, despite the fact that between 1910 and 1930, there were attempts each season to produce avant-garde commedic plays from Europe.[16] When the prestigious Theatre Guild began its operation at the Garrick Theatre on a shoe string budget in 1919, they surprisingly chose Jacinto Benavente's modern commedia, *The Bonds of Interest*, in a translation by John Garrett Underhill, as their first production. Staged for less than two thousand dollars, the Guild production, with direction and scene designs cleverly created from discarded scenery and modest materials by Rollo Peters, who also played Leander, opened on April 14, 1919. Although it was respectfully received by critics, it chalked up a disappointing run of only thirty-two performances.[17] The Guild did not find its footing until its second production, St. John Ervine's *John Ferguson*, an unqualified critical and commercial success. Nonetheless even after the Guild was well established, it periodically elected to attempt other commedic productions despite the near disaster of *The Bonds of Interest*.[18]

Ironically it was the revolutionary turmoil in Russia which indirectly let Americans know how original modern commedia could be. Many Russian

artists, poets, playwrights, and novelists emigrated to New York in the wake
of the 1905 and 1917 revolutions, and the impact of these working artists was
varied and significant. The first modern Russian commedia play to appear in
New York was Evreinov's one-act harlequinade, *The Merry Death*, produced
by the Washington Square Players[19] on October 2, 1916, under the direction
of Philip Moeller, with settings by Robert Edmond Jones. Critics, however,
failed to see its import, finding it merely a light novelty. Meyerhold's brand
of commedia found its way onto the American stage via *The Fairground Booth*
in 1923, through the work of his former pupil, actor and director Vadim
Uraneff. One of many Russian expatriate artists who crowded into New York
in the early 1920's, Uraneff had appeared opposite Blanche Yurka in the 1920
Broadway production of *Musk*, and as Lucianus in the celebrated 1922 Arthur
Hopkins production of *Hamlet* with John Barrymore. Uraneff's energy led
him to forcefully state a commitment to bringing commedia to the American
stage. To accomplish his mission he founded a producing organization he
called "American Commedia dell'arte, Inc. (*The Theatre*)."[20] Their first, and
apparently last, production was a bill presented in the "non-representational"
manner which included *The Song of Songs*, based on the King James text of
psalms, and arranged as a drama by Patrick Kearney, and Blok's *The
Fairground Booth*, translated as *The Show Booth*. Uraneff explained his notion
of the "non-representational" method as "not a *representation* of life, but a
spectacle or *show*. Originated by Meyerhold, in Petrograd, as a revolt against
the naturalism of the Moscow Art Theatre, it is really a return, in principle,
to the methods of the earlier theatres, notably the Commedia dell'arte of
Italy."[21] In an article, "Commedia dell'arte and American Vaudeville,"
published in *Theatre Arts Monthly* later that same year, Uraneff quoted Craig's
call for a revival of commedia, which could give "to future generations a hint
as to the possibilities of the Art of the Theatre."[22] Certain conditions must
exist in a particular culture for such a revival to occur, Uraneff believed:

It must be evident from what has been said that America has every requisite for a brilliant revival of Commedia dell'Arte. All that is required to complete it are native American productions with scenarios constructed from the material now in use in American vaudeville stylized to meet the stylization of character and supplied with a stylized *mise-en-scène* in the spirit of the whole.[23]

He proposed five fundamental concerns largely drawn from Meyerhold's theories, including dominance of the production by the actor who never steps out of character, stylization in all aspects of the production, and an emphasis on interaction with the audience. More specifically, he reminded directors that the acting style does "not aim to give the illusion of life on the stage,"[24] but is "in a style of exaggerated parody."[25] Uraneff pointed to Eddie Cantor, Bert Williams, Fred Stone, James Barton, and Charlie Chaplin as embodiments of American commedia types, and he believed it was necessary to develop other contemporary characters that paralleled commedic masks in all forms of popular culture:

To assemble a complete collection of American theatrical types already fixed in the mind of the primitive spectator, to complete the parallel with Commedia dell'Arte, one must not limit oneself to vaudeville, but include other forms of the commercial theatre -- musical comedy, farce, burlesque, the moving picture. There we find the business man, the sailor, the black face comedian, the sweetheart, the chorus girl, the "sissy." Just as in Commedia dell'Arte, each type has its characteristic appearance; its characteristic walk, costume, gestures, and movements. Its traditional make-up, as, for instance, that of the black-face, is quite as artifical as the mask of the Italian. Some of these types are almost identical with the personages of Commedia, others have been transformed under the influence of our more complex modern life among sky scrapers, aeroplanes, electric signs, and machinery. Others have disappeared, and new ones have taken their places.[26]

The Show Booth opened for what turned out to be a run of ten special matinee performances at the Booth Theatre on April 3, 1923,[27] with Uraneff directing, translating (with Padraic Colum), and, borrowing heavily from his memory of Meyerhold's work, as he conceived the *mise-en-scène*. Although the program indicates that Robert Edmond Jones only designed the costumes for the production, he was apparently also responsible for the arrangement of the scenery within the confines of Uraneff's recollections of the Meyerhold production. In *The Theatre of Robert Edmond Jones*, Ralph Pendleton writes that "Jones apparently designed the Uraneff production of Blok's *The Show Booth*; but his designs were accidentally destroyed, and no other information seems to be available."[28] In fact, the New York Public Library has a file on Uraneff and his production *The Show Booth* which, although missing Jones' designs, does include a set of interesting production photographs. Jones led American designers after World War I toward the techniques and concepts of Europe's "New Stagecraft" as epitomized by the concepts of Craig, Appia, and especially Copeau, when he wrote that the stage "will be presented frankly for what it is, a stage."[29] This could be realized, he believed, through a focus on

> the traditional, ancient stage, the platform, the *treteau*, the boards that actors have trod from time out of mind. What we need in the theatre is a space for actors to act in, a space reserved for them where they may practice their immemorial art of holding the mirror up to nature. They will be able to move with ease to and from this space, they will be able to make their appropriate exits and entrances. We shall find a way to bathe these actors in expressive and dramatic light. And that is all.[30]

Jones clearly adhered to this principle in his designs for *The Show Booth*. A small stage platform, similar to both the flat-bed wagons used as stages by medieval and commedia performers, and Copeau's *treteau*, was placed in the center of the Booth Theatre's proscenium stage. It was decorated along the front with a drape of lightly colored triangles, and capped with a gauzy fabric suggesting the inside of a small circus tent. The platform stage was framed to create a small false proscenium, and two sets of steps on either side of the front of the platform led from the actual stage floor to the top of the platform stage. A light curtain inside the false proscenium could be opened (as it was for the mystics' scene) to reveal an inner stage shaped by two angled side walls and a back wall. Only a few props and furnishings were used, acknowledging the visual simplicity typical of commedia. Surviving photographs of the actors in the setting show a striking similarity to illustrations of Sapunov's design and Meyerhold's staging of the original Russian production.

The critical and box office response to *The Show Booth* was less than enthusiastic. Although *The New York Tribune* critic "B.F." found the production to be "exceedingly well done,"[31] *The New York Times* critic John Corbin's response was, unfortunately, more typical:

> Seldom has any ostensibly radical movement been more backward looking. Alexander Blok's "Show Booth" centres in a revival of the ancient Commedia dell'arte. Its modernity consists in the fact that the supposed author of the play rushes on the stage from time to time to protest that his piece was written as realism and has been metamorphosed by the non-representational producers. He is an exponent of Stanislavsky's school, and is eventually lynched by the Clown and hurled bodily off stage.[32]

The Show Booth seems, at least in part, to have been a victim of a nationalistic backlash against the extravagant attention paid to the numerous Russian artists working in the arts in New York in the early 1920's. Corbin cynically added that "having had the Moscow players, it is well to have also *The Commedia dell'arte, Inc.* At least the Inc. is modern."[33] More importantly, Uraneff was not Meyerhold, and the production seems to have been a faithful but pale imitation rather than a freshly conceived creation. In the Russia of 1906, *The Fairground Booth* had caused a near riot in its audience over the social and artistic implications it represented, but in America seventeen years later, the play offered no connection to contemporary concerns and seemed, at best, a quaint novelty. The mere passage of time made Uraneff's outspoken rejection of realistic theatre seem hollow and out of place.

Between the early 1920's and the appearance of the San Francisco Mime Troupe and other politically-inspired improvisatory groups in the 1960's, no overt attempt was made in the American theatre to establish a modern form of commedia that attemped to use its techniques as Blok's and Meyerhold's "battering ram." Nonetheless, echoes and shadows of commedia could be heard and seen on many American stages.

Uraneff had noted in his 1923 *Theatre Arts Monthly* article "Commedia dell'arte and American Vaudeville" that contemporary stage comedians and vaudevillians were of a type. He made this observation in an era when silent film comedies and variety bills filled theatres with enthusiastic audiences. Many of the stage comedians appearing in musical comedy, revues, and vaudeville between 1900 and 1930, followed the tradition of minstrels and the plays of Edward Harrigan, by creating distinctively commedic stereotypes. Bert Williams, Al Jolson, and Eddie Cantor stood out among those artists who continued to perform in the blackface minstrel tradition. Williams' forlorn hobo sang the unforgettable "Nobody," Jolson's incorrigible "Gus" searched for his mammy on Southern plantations, and Cantor's bespectacled skipping sissy brought the minstrel images into modern times. The broad ethnic caricatures of such artists as Fanny Brice, James Barton, and Smith and Dale, were examples of similarly outlandish stereotypes, and were only a few of the many commedic types that peopled the book musicals and revues of the first three decades of the century. Modern stereotypical characters, often representing life's underdogs and misfits, emerged from vaudeville too. W.C. Fields' juggling misanthrope, Will Rogers' laconic and satiric cowboy, and Ed Wynn's "perfect fool" were some of the best known variations on commedic themes.

Commedic elements proliferated on variety stages and were apparent in film, radio, and television. Commedia itself, however, was rarely seen in serious American drama. European commedic plays had not been enthusiastically received, and only a few early twentieth century American playwrights and poets were drawn toward commedic traditions.[34] Although Eugene O'Neill, certainly the American theatre's most ambitious experimenter of the era, used masks (inspired by classical drama, not commedia), he regarded revivals of commedia with disdain: "A return to the fluid, impromptu drama of the *commedia dell'arte*? On that day we might also just as well resume our old ancestral impromptu gesture of scratching for fleas."[35] Other dramatists, though, borrowed freely from its traditions.[36] One interesting early experiment was *The Wonder Hat*, a popular one-act play by Kenneth Sawyer Goodman (1883-1918)[37] and Ben Hecht (1894-1964), which was first produced at Detroit's Arts and Crafts Theatre in 1916. Also in 1916, Percy Mackaye's (1875-1956) *Caliban of the Yellow Sands*, an elaborate masque in celebration of Shakespeare's tercentenary featured scenes inspired by many earlier forms, including commedia, as well as such commedic elements as clowns and grotesquerie.

The setting for the play is an enchanted park where the world-weary chums Harlequin and Pierrot smugly avoid the flirtations of women, especially Columbine. Both, however, are enamored of her. She loves Harlequin, and lurks about the park hoping to attract his attention, although both are too proud to admit their feelings for each other. Columbine encounters a seller of dreams, old Punchinello, who gives her a magic slipper that, when worn, makes the wearer irresistible. Harlequin also meets Punchinello and acquires a hat which makes its wearer invisible -- the wonder hat. In a mild comedy of confusions, Pierrot sees Columbine in her slipper and falls in love with her, arousing Harlequin's jealousy. Columbine becomes aware of Harlequin's invisible presence, and he observes the power of her slipper. Both stubbornly refuse to give up their charms, and the play ends with the opinion of Columbine's maid, Margot, that "the question can't be answered to suit everybody, so it's my advice that we ring down right here, and allow everyone to go home and fix up an ending to conform to the state of his own indigestion."[38] *The Wonder Hat* had a modestly successful life on amateur stages, but proved to be little more than a curio.

American poet and novelist Edna St. Vincent Millay (1892-1950), who had appeared as Columbine in the Theatre Guild's production of *The Bonds of Interest*, was remembered by Brooks Atkinson as an artist who "liked anything that was impractical."[39] She herself wrote one memorable commedic play, *Aria da Capo*, a symbolic parable of war and the human instinct for conflict. It was first produced by the Provincetown Players on December 5, 1919.[40] Millay's title borrows the musical term for a song in three parts, with the third part a repetition of the first. She creates a striking counterpoint between the frivolity of commedia farce and the bitterness of her theme through an effective mingling of satire and lyricism, symbolism and expressionism, and elements of harlequinade and pastoral plays. Her characters sustain a delicate balance between a comparatively realistic treatment of the shepherds and the stylized theatricality of Harlequin and Columbine. Millay manages, despite the use of commedia characters, to explore a serious theme that is rarely handled as lightly as she manages it. Certainly war was not to be depicted as comic, and Millay

> endeavored to do violence to that attitude. Within a Harlequinade setting she placed Cothurnus, a stock figure of Greek and Rome tragic drama, as the prompter for Corydon and Thyrsis, the protagonists in a war conflict. The tragedy on stage represents the human incapacity for a real confrontation with death -- death is treated with playful disdain, maximum distance, with the "audience-will-forget" attitude. The insertion of the war tragedy into the *commedia dell'arte* setting is the very core and center of the play.[41]

The use of commedia masks permitted Millay an opportunity for making simple and eloquent statements with a childlike directness about the nature of human conflict:

> . . .I know a game worth two of that!
> Let's gather rocks, and build a wall between us;
> And say that over there belongs to me,

And over here to you![42]

In November, 1919, Millay wrote her mother that *Aria da Capo* was "one of the best things I've ever done."[43] The universality of both the themes and the characters of the play have kept it one of the most often produced one-act plays of the twentieth century.[44]

American actors and theatre companies have frequently been compared frequently to commedia players.[45] Actors from Mrs. Fiske to the Lunts were identified as commedia types by various critics. Eva Le Gallienne's (1899-1991) ambitious Civic Repertory Company, founded in 1926, recognized classic and contemporary commedia in a staggering repertory of plays. While still a drama student in 1915, Le Gallienne played Pierrot in Théodore de Banville's *Le Baiser*. She recalled that she copied her make-up for the character "from a picture of Sarah [Bernhardt] in *Pierrot Assassin*."[46] As director and leading actress of the Civic Repertory Company, Le Gallienne staged a few productions -- including Benavente's *Saturday Night*, Schnitzler's *The Green Cockatoo*, and plays by Goldoni and Molière. Shakespeare's *Twelfth Night* was presented in an especially broad comic interpretation -- suggesting more than a passing interest in commedia, particularly in her emphasis on slapstick, and the carefully created illusion of improvisation.[47]

Although The Group Theatre is now remembered mostly for its productions of the naturalistic dramas of Clifford Odets, members of the group were interested in commedia techniques. Lee Strasberg (1901-1982) talked often to his students about the history of acting, and especially admired such Russian commedic productions as Vakhtangov's *Princess Turandot*. The Group Theatre experimented with improvisation in both acting training and in rehearsals, using exercises based on one word or the use of gibberish. One improvisation for a scene from *Twelfth Night* had Beany Barker and Sanford Meisner borrowing commedia figures to superimpose over Shakespeare's characters. Although none of their productions was obviously commedic, The

Group Theatre was nonetheless importantly influenced by commedia.

The Federal Theatre Project, under the direction of Hallie Flanagan (1890-1969), produced a wide array of classic and contemporary plays and experimented with new forms, many of which were inspired by Europe's theatrical avant-garde. Flanagan believed that the 1936 "living newspaper," *Triple-A Plowed Under*, was performed using techniques derived from many cultures, "from Aristophanes, from the Commedia dell'Arte, from Shakespearean soliloquy, from the pantomime of Mei Lan Fang."[48] She had also seen some of Meyerhold's productions on a trip to Russia in 1926, and recalled that a typical Federal Theatre Project performance, such as one in Omaha in May, 1936, was, in many respects, a modern counterpart to the sort of excitement and carnival spirit generated by commedia:

> Red, white, and blue bunting hung from office buildings, bands played, fifty store windows of *Made in Omaha* goods were unveiled, a special train took visitors on a tour of industrial plants, and around brightly lighted stages on street corners crowds gathered to see Federal Theatre players do their part in *Know Omaha* week. This was Commedia dell'Arte playing to the crowd, talking to the crowd, laughing with the crowd, this was midwest carnival performance -- roping and whip-snapping acts, circus bicycle-riding acts, strong man acts, rapid fire dancing.[49]

The demise of the controversial Federal Theatre Project in 1939, at the hands of an ultra-conservative U.S. Congress, ended a period of fascinating experimentation and the hope that an American brand of folk theatre, similar to commedia, might proliferate.[50]

Several antiquarian commedic productions were produced between the 1930's and the 1950's, but an angrier spirit of socially-conscious commedia emerged during the turbulent 1960's. Various forms of improvisatory, satiric, and overtly political theatre emerged as part of the varied protest movements caused by such issues as civil rights, sexual liberation, feminism, consumerism, corruption in government, protests against damage to the environment, the military-industrial complex, the nuclear build-up, and especially America's involvement in Vietnam. These issues inspired and charged radical street entertainments with an exhilarating energy. Artists, as they have in many eras, reacted to a variety of social, political, and moral issues through their art. Turning to streets and alleys, empty garages and abandoned theatres, they wrote plays and improvised, they used masks and shouted obscenities. Theatre -- serious, living, comic, rude theatre -- had once again taken to the streets. Quite simply, commedia was reinventing itself again to suit the needs of its time.

Typical of the 1960's were "Happenings," a form that owed much to the commedic tradition of improvisation, but extended beyond it by making its action completely random, permitting the actor the ultimate freedom of acting "only functionally, and not esthetically or creatively."[51] When the radical social and political energies of the 1960's cooled, many of these groups and forms passed from the scene, but those that survived have become stronger and keep improvisational theatre alive around the edges of mainstream American theatre. This continuity suggests that in a troubled world, American artists will give their art in service of social change. For many of those so inclined, such as Peter Schumann (b. 1934), founder of The Bread and Puppet Theatre, all arts must be political:

> whether they like it or not. If they stay in their own realm, preoccupied with their proper problems, the arts support the status quo, which in itself is highly political. Or they scream and kick and participate in our own country's struggle for liberation in whatever haphazard way they can, probably at the expense of some of their sensitive craftmanship, but definitely for their own soul's sake.[52]

Dario Fo -- the Italian counterpart of the politicized American actors and troupes of the last thirty years -- believes that it is his mission "to advance certain democratic appeals, to form public opinion, to stimulate, to create moments of dialectical conflict,"[53] and this is clearly the mission of the radical American theatre artists inspired by commedia.

It was soon after World War II that the Italian theatre began to rediscover the political power of commedia and its performance techniques. Such ideas first reached America in the work of Carlo Mazzone-Clementi. After performing in Italy, where he was born, and in France, where he came under the influence of Lecoq and Marceau, Mazzone-Clementi emigrated to America in 1957. Specializing in mime and commedia (playing the role of Brighella), he started his own school, The Dell'Arte School of Mime and Comedy, in California in 1971. Here, he and his successors grapple with the idea of commedia and its techniques, realizing that although it was possible to "conjecture about *commedia* in a historical framework, we cannot *know* what it was like,"[54] and explained that the "magnetic appeal of *commedia*, for me, has been to rediscover the magic of the performer; how he worked, what he did, and to some extent, why he did it, consciously or not."[55]

Attempting to understand the problems of the application of commedic techniques to the twentieth century stage, Mazzone-Clementi began with mime as exemplified by Marceau, who, he said, was a catalyst for his own work. His knowledge of the theories and practices of Decroux, Barrault, Lecoq, and Marceau emphasized for him the visual and pantomimic traditions of a form that was "earthy, fertile, alive, and ready to fly. It is *popular* theatre in terms of what it depicts and to whom it appeals."[56] He believes it is impossible to "talk of *commedia*, or my approach to it, without discussing both mime and silent movies,"[57] but, more significantly, he views commedia as a form of theatre

> that points out our human frailties and foibles in such an honest, unpretentious way, a theatre in which actors are skillful, perceptive, inventive, united, and generous, seems to me to be much needed today. In a world gone mad, who has more to say to us than the zanies? Well, the Venetians have a proverb, "If they aren't crazy, we don't want them." And *commedia*, after all, is not a theatrical form, it is a way of life.[58]

The complexities and basic human impulses inherent in commedia have always made the audience an active part of the production. When the Dell'Arte troupe toured with a Gozzi play filled with magic and commedia characters, Mazzone-Clementi was impressed with the effect different audiences had on the performance:

> We first performed for six people in a barn in a rural area of northern California. We then took it to the Firehouse Theatre in San Francisco, where the audience, mostly young intellectuals, were delighted by the play's comments on intellectual pretensions. Our next performances were at a small theatre in Berkeley, attended mostly by college students. They responded warmly to the elements of fantasy and comic business. We then played the city parks of Berkeley, attracting young people, old people, children, and dogs. The play changed considerably, became broader, more directly involved with the audience, as the audience itself became an "improviso" element, shifting, moving, and responding.[59]

The company's first important production, *The Loon's Rage* (1977), was mounted with the support of a National Endowment for the Arts grant which permitted the troupe to perform a play dealing with Native American themes expressed through the techniques of commedia. The play's themes included one that has continually appeared in Mazzone-Clementi's productions: nature versus modern technology. The Dell'Arte Players' 1980 production, *Whiteman Meets Bigfoot*, generated considerable controversy over a plot element involving a man making love to an ape. Performances were picketed by groups protesting the depiction of an "ungodly, unnatural and immoral act."[60] *Performance Anxiety* (1982) featured a combination of a traditional commedia plot involving Isabella, Pantalone, and Arlecchino, with a contemporary backstage story about egotistical actors performing at a dinner theatre. With the addition of a few backstage plot twists, the separation between "actors" and "characters" blurred, and the backstage concerns of the actors spilled into the "onstage" action and the plot of the commedia, with such issues as birth control and suicide overtaking the light-hearted machinations of the commedia characters.

Mazzone-Clementi prefers to refer to commedia characters as "comic prototypes" and insists that traditional commedia masks are a valuable study in contrasts, since the "immobile upper half is in counterpoint with the mobile lower jaw of the actor, which somehow becomes an extension of the mask itself."[61] Through experimentation, he discovered that the mask "hides and reveals at the same time. To work with a mask one must be aware of its implications. A mask puts one immediately on a tightrope between poetry and prose."[62] Character masks served as metaphors for him and supported his belief that "life, too, must be discovered and united with the life and visions of the actor."[63] During the 1960's, similar groups appeared emphasizing topical comedy and satire. The natural language of such a theatre includes distorted elements drawn from contemporary popular culture, aggressive recruitment of a working-class audience, collective creation of works (which are extensively researched, highly topical, and seldom "finished" or definitive), and avoidance of any similarity with conservative and bourgeois theatre forms. Many of these ideals are, of course, to be found in traditional commedia, and it is not surprising that these artists and groups continued to look toward commedia for inspiration.

One of the first and most celebrated of such groups is The San Francisco Mime Troupe. Initially under the leadership of R.G. Davis, a disciple and student of the mime techniques of Decroux and Paul Curtis. Davis, who has written a book about the tumultuous first ten years of the troupe, beginning in 1959 with staged productions featuring commedic techniques and masks infused with topical and highly controversial political material. Until 1970, under Davis' guidance, they produced their most overtly commedic work. Their productions during these years included *The Dowry* (adapted from Molière and Goldoni; 1961), *The Root* (adapted from Machiavelli's *Mandragola*; 1963), *Ruzzante's Maneuver* (written by Milton

Loan Receipt
Liverpool John Moores University
Learning and Information Services

Borrower ID: 27111045001 29
Loan Date: 06/02/2009
Loan Time: 12:47 pm

Shakespeare :
31411012520175
Due Date: 27/02/2009 23:59

Commedia dell'Arte :
31110069165 46
Due Date: 27/02/2009 23:59

The theatre of yesterday and tomorrow :
31110072398 31
Due Date: 13/02/2009 23:59

Shakespearian comedy /
31110034762494
Due Date: 27/02/2009 23:59

Please keep your receipt

in case of dispute

Savage; 1963), *Chorizos* (adapted by Tom Lopez from a Saul Landau scenario; 1964), *Tartuffe* (adapted from Molière by Richard Sassoon; 1964), *A Minstrel Show, or Civil Rights in a Cracker Barrel* (by Saul Landau and R.G. Davis; 1965), *Il Candelaio* (adapted from Giordano Bruno by Peter Berg; 1965), *Olive Pits* (adapted from Lope de Vega by Peter Berg and Peter Cohon; 1966), *The Miser* (adapted from Molière by Frank Bardacke; 1966), *L'Amant Militaire* (adapted from Goldoni by Joan Holden; 1967), a revised version of *Olive Pits* (1967), *Ruzzante, or the Veteran* (adapted from Beolco's plays by Joan Holden, 1968), *The Farce of Pathelin* (adapted by R.G. Davis and Joel Weisman from the French classic; 1968), and many cabarets, vaudevilles, and skits, as well as adaptations of Brecht and Jarry. Davis left the troupe in 1970, when the majority of the company decided to make a greater commitment to collective creation of their works. After his departure, commedic elements became less overt in the troupe's productions, but the use of broad stereotypes, improvisation, and interaction with the audience in a rough form of revolutionary theatre remain central to their style.

There was, from the beginning, a strong commitment on the part of the troupe to reach the "American Everyman" for, as Davis pointed out, "The intrinsic nature of commedia dell'arte is its working-class viewpoint."[64] In 1968, Davis articulated the revolutionary nature of the troupe when he proclaimed that "We try in our humble way to destroy the United States."[65] Current artistic director Joan Holden, who views the troupe's mission as "inherently subversive,"[66] tends to agree with him. In action, the performance "always measures an unsatisfactory reality against its corresponding ideal, and whose form demands that solutions be invented for problems raised, may be the revolutionary art form *par excellence.*"[67]

When the troupe moved away from traditional commedia stock characters, it created modern counterparts, like the Lawyer, the Politician, the College Student, and the Feminist, creating a wider range for addressing contemporary topics. This approach heightened the political satire that has always been the troupe's hallmark while maintaining an improvisatory style coupled with pre-planned lazzi reminiscent of commedia. Beginning with plays on the Vietnam War (*The Rape of the Eagle*) or the "Chicago Seven" (*The Trial of Huey Newton*), and continuing through present day works satirizing the Reagans, George Bush, Dan Quayle, steel plant closings, U.S. government support of repressive Third World leaders, American involvement in Nicaragua, and opposition to civil rights for minorities and women, the San Francisco Mime Troupe has charged the traditions of commedia with a powerful "agit-prop" approach in the tradition of Dario Fo. When preparing a production, the entire troupe selects a major political issue as the basis for a play. They maintain a firm focus on the news of the day, while experimenting with commedia performance techniques as a way of expressing their particular slant on the news:

> We improvised from old scenarios and plays by Molière and Goldoni; we wrote our own scenes; tried different characters. We discovered that the stereotypical characters operated both an an escape valve for irritation and as an integrating force. To the liberal, they often appear to show prejudice. However, if you dig the people and the contradictions, the stereotypes are more accurate in describing social conditions than bland generalities. We eventually learned in commedia, and later in the Minstrel Show, how to make stereotypes carry the burden of social satire.[68]

Commedia implied that the actor was the all-important element, and Davis believes that the actor is completely dependent on the audience, who "is master. If your joke works, they laugh. If it doesn't, they don't. A simple formula that anyone can live by."[69] Davis searched for ways to gain audience involvement: "In our commedia the performer had to be totally involved. There was no open fourth wall, in fact, there were no walls. Therefore, the performer had to keep his thoughts way ahead of the action. This commedia was *Brechtian* in that the stage play was a game."[70]

The troupe often performs outdoors, and manages the delicate balance of radical politics with art. The upbeat, good-humored style of the troupe has often tempered the razor-sharp satire in their productions, but it has also created considerable controversy. Their earliest productions were obviously commedic, since the troupe played commedia characters in traditional masks and costumes. More recent productions focus on contemporary stereotypes in much the same way that they had used commedia masks. Each year, a new production keeps the issues examined immediate and controversial:

> We have to get that combination of political comprehension and artistic creation. And as an artistic group, we have to put the balance on aesthetics. If a performer doesn't make it then he's no good. The performance is important. The political position is important to develop the kind of performance because you won't do certain things in the mime troupe unless you have that certain political-social aspect. That is, we're free swinging and demand a lot of freedom and justice for ourselves as well as other people.[71]

The prominence of The San Francisco Mime Troupe continues with the group perpetuating its modern commedia and street theatre approach in outdoor performances made particularly lively by incisive topical content.[72] Other theatre troupes have adopted approaches similar to The San Francisco Mime Troupe. El Teatro Campesino, founded in California by Luis Valdez (b. 1940) in 1965, found its political energy and commedic style as a result of Valdez's stint as an actor with The San Francisco Mime Troupe and his interest in the commedic plays of Ben Jonson. Valdez emphasizes improvisation in the creation of his *actos*, one-act revolutionary commedic skits. He believes that "Art is communication. The more artful you are, the more straight-telling you are."[73] El Teatro Campesino encourages audience involvement because, as Valdez put it, "society does not allow us to make noise."[74] To attract the interest and attention of farm workers, he found it necessary to develop a lively and informal outdoor style, making liberal use of slapstick, bawdy humor, and satire in the most raw commedic style. The earliest performances of El Teatro Campesino were crudely constructed and acted sketches that examined, in an obvious fashion, the political and economic realities of the lives of migrant farm workers. In more recent years, their works have broadened in scope to include diverse issues of particular significance for Mexican Americans.

Schumann's The Bread and Puppet Theatre, founded in 1960, vehemently opposed America's military involvement in Vietnam, supported Cesar Chavez's Mexican-American grape pickers, and lobbied on behalf of ghetto children. In New York City slums the group ran workshops to teach children to make puppets. The Bread and Puppet Theatre eventually established a permanent home base on a farm in Glover, Vermont, where they give their annual "Domestic Resurrection Circus." They perform outdoors, use satire, carnival and circus techniques, occasional improvisation, and stereotypical commedic characters to create redemptive visual symbols and images, through the use of astoundingly oversized puppets. Their sidewalk shows and puppet plays, including a revisionist *Punch and Judy* (1967), make up only part of their efforts to reach a wide public not usually drawn to the commercial stages. Schumann looks to commedic traditions for inspiration, especially Kasperl, and, of course, marionette theatre.

The Compass Players, founded in the late 1950's by David Shepherd, who had been inspired by Viola Spolin and Paul Sills, attempted to "create a contemporary version of *commedia*, a popular theater which, working improvisationally from scenarios, would deal in comic terms with present-day society."[75] Shepherd combined his notion of commedia with techniques drawn from Brecht. The Compass was without an official playwright, used no scripted play, and worked from a scenario backstage which was "as we fondly imagined -- the Commedia dell'arte idea. We wrote a story out, usually eight to twelve scenes written out on a sheet of paper, and we'd follow through the scenes by rehearsing."[76] Other groups, including Snake Theatre, Second City,

The Committee, The Establishment, Uncommon Denominator, The Session, Third City, The Living Premise, Stewed Prunes, The Third Ear, and The Fourth Wall, were among the many improvisational comedy troupes that rose to prominence during the 1960's and 1970's (some had formed as early as the 1950's). Commedic techniques offered inspiration to all of these groups: performers from many of them have gone on to lead other troupes or develop careers as solo artists.[77]

More recently, American theatre artists have absorbed commedic elements into innovative revivals of classics, or in new works reflecting changing moral, social, and political values.[78] Theatre of the Ridiculous was articulated by Ronald Tavel, a 1960's playwright inspired by Andy Warhol, for whom Tavel wrote several screenplays. Tavel was inspired by commedia, noting Theatre of the Ridiculous writers and performers "had passed beyond the absurd. Our position is absolutely preposterous."[79] The Theatre of the Ridiculous is "both clownish and foolish"[80] and exists to expose the utter ridiculousness of institutionalized society."[81] It also features elements of grotesque, burlesque, acrobatics, mask-like makeup and broad stylization of all elements, and particularly emphasizes a campy destruction of traditional sexual stereotypes and conventional morality. Dan Issac writes that while viewing Tavel's *The Life of Lady Godiva* (1966), he felt he "was watching *commedia dell'arte* as a joyous celebration of homosexuality, a revelatory and liberating experience for actors and audience alike."[82] Other commedic plays by Tavel include *Screen Test* (1966), *Kitchenette* (1967), and *Gorilla Queen* (1967). Tavel's centrality as playwright of the Theatre of the Ridiculous was eclipsed by Charles Ludlam's rise to prominence. Ludlam (1940-1987), founder of the successful and controversial Ridiculous Theatrical Company, had an extravagant and flamboyant comic flair as an actor, director, and playwright, and his "camp" sensibility could clearly be seen in his first important play, *When Queens Collide* (1967). This work abounds in puns, raffish satire, perverse manifestations of logic, and a range of attitudes and issues dealing with homosexuality. He viewed commedia as valuable to his style, but misleading to the modern theatre artist attempting to embody the late twentieth century worldview

> as a sentimental thing, where you are trying to recreate a sense of what had gone on before, or you use those discoveries in a collision of techniques which create a new thing that means more to us. The thing about *commedia* is that it is all resolved at the end -- marriage is a happy ending, and no one feels that way now. That's one of the problem's with modern comedy, to restore harmony at the end when so many values have been toppled down. So asymmetrical and irregular works have to be produced in order even to begin to evoke reality. But I'm more interested in the collisions of aesthetics.[83]

His commedic playwriting and performing continued unabated through such works as *Big Hotel* (1967), *Bluebeard* (1970), *Eunuchs of the Forbidden City* (1972), *Stage Blood* (1974), *Hot Ice* (1974), *The Enchanted Pig* (1979), *The Mystery of Irma Vep* (1984), *Salammbô* (1985), and *The Artificial Jungle* (1986). Before his untimely death from AIDS, Ludlam also appeared regularly in his own plays and in works by others, including a notable production of Ibsen's *Hedda Gabler*, in which he played Hedda.

Commedia even found its way into contemporary performance art in the 1980's. Martha Clarke (b. 1944), one of the co-founders of the mime troupe Pilobolus, presented her hour-long piece *Miracolo d'Amore* (1988), first at the Spoleto Festival, and later in New York. As her other works, *Vienna: Lusthaus*, *The Hunger Artist*, and *Endangered Species*, it merged music, dance, theatre, and opera, and featured an Italianate setting populated with commedia clowns. The production combined earthiness, humor, music, and poetry to create images celebrating the miracle of love and life. Although some images of male and female nudity created controversy, *Miracolo d'Amore* was inspired by Italo Calvino's Italian folktales and, as Clarke explains, her use of commedia's Pulcinella was inspired by Tiepolo while demonstrating a striking similarity with the commedic figures painted by David Hockney: "The image is very Venetian. In Tiepolo's drawings, sometimes there are three Pulcinella's on a page or twenty of them -- all identical in dress -- except that they're each very different personalities. They became the model for the men in the piece."[84]

Bill Irwin's recent *Largely New York*, which opened on Broadway in May, 1989, to generally laudatory reviews, is as connected to commedia as it is to circus and Chaplin. Irwin's work is certainly less overtly political than many of his contemporaries, but his light-hearted view of the difficulties of life in an increasingly technological age, is reminiscent of Chaplin's *Modern Times*, and it has found an appreciative audience. His completely mimed performance as the "Post-Modern Hoofer," with a supporting cast of clowns and dancers serving as all-purpose *zanni*, demonstrated the power that commedic movement and gesture continues to wield. Ron Jenkins writes that Irwin, like other post-modern clowns in America, are in constant threat from forces that

> reflect the complexity of our cultural environment. In addition to fighting such traditional adversaries as the pull of gravity and the constraints of authority, modern comics must confront the tryanny of mass media, technological dehumanization, political subterfuge, social alienation, rampant consumerism. Consequently they must draw on all the mental and physical resources at their disposal to emerge from the battlefield with their self-respect intact.[85]

Irwin himself puts it simply, as certainly his commedia predecessors would have, when he states that the "heart of clowning for me is how to get yourself into dilemmas. I don't have to look for them. They come my way."[86] Irwin is one of many contemporary entertainers depending on performance techniques borrowed from such popular and enduring street entertainments as circus, carnival, medicine shows, vaudeville, 1960's counter-culture experimental forms, and of course, commedia. Some, like Geoff Hoyle, who refers to commedia as the "sit-com" of the Renaissance, have come full circle. After acting in several American productions of Fo's plays and performing with Irwin in The Pickle Family Circus, Hoyle's one-man show, *Feast of Fools* (1990), has attracted audiences because of its emphasis on the basic human comedy of the stock characters of commedia; like Irwin he includes little obvious political content.

Whatever the particular slant of an individual artist, post-modern clowns and entertainers (or "new vaudevillians") offer a liberating and liberated form of comedy that is fired by a profound level of ingenuity and virtuosity that easily parallels the skill of the greatest artists in earlier popular forms. Non-traditional theatre forms and visionary artists have been drawn to the clown, improvisation, and a direct assault on the audience's sensibilities that must have evolved from earlier styles. Commedia and street theatre techniques break down barriers between the audience and the performer, and the clown's traditional role as a battered survivor of a harsh and demoralizing world serves to increase both the intimacy and potency of the performance. Despite the extraordinary and diverse skill of these great commedic performers, they share a special tenaciousness that results from their ability to illuminate "the conflicts between ordinary people and the forces that victimize them."[87] As original commedia actors must have been in their own place and time, contemporary clowns are inspired to focus on the perils of surviving the multitude of lunacies which make up life in modern America.

The "intellectual striptease"[88] of con men and magicians Penn and Teller, the scathing political satire of monologist Spalding Gray, the restlessness and eccentricity of musician and oral historian Stephen Wade, the spontaneous bungling of Avner the Eccentric, the wickedly anti-consumer "theatre of trash" of Paul Zaloom, and more traditional clowns such as Larry Pisoni ("Lorenzo Pickle"), Frank Oliver, Ronn Lucas, and George Carl, emphasize how elements of verbal satire can be combined with virtuoso physical dexterity. Significantly, in 1991, the Ringling Brothers and Barnum and Bailey circus for the first time in over one hundred twenty years, named a clown as its headliner. Italian-born clown David Larible, from a seven generation circus family led the circus on a year-long tour of the United States. Whether through verbal satire, slapstick clowning, music, acrobatics, magic, or mime, these performers reach for, and repeatedly act out, a profound and often unsettling strain of human absurdity. They amuse us while they also unsettle us about our shared fates, much in the way the original commedia performers must have done for their audiences.

Although it is true that the influence of commedia on the twentieth century American stage has taken many forms, it has only rarely achieved anything that could be said to mirror the explosive creativity and popularity of commedia at its height. That heritage in all its multitudinous diversity has spread itself everywhere. As Martin Green and John Swan wrote in *The Triumph of Pierrot*,[89] it is impossible to fully comprehend the pervasive impact of a form whose "images are all around us."[90] It is obvious that these images have found an impressively diverse set of meanings when played out on the modern and post-modern stages of Europe and America.

APPENDIX

The influence of *commedia dell'arte* on the twentieth century stage has been profound and far-reaching. Commedia has had a similar impact on other aspects of contemporary culture, particularly the fine arts, film and television, literature, and music. This appendix offers a brief survey of the influence of commedia on these art forms.

Art

From the earliest days of commedia, artists have captured its spirit and characters in drawings, paintings, and sculpture. In the sixteenth and seventeenth centuries, most commedia artists offered crude and literal images. Jacques Callot (c.1592-1635) was the first to truly capture the vibrant spirit and vulgar nature of commedia in his twenty-four engravings, *Balli di Sfessania*, probably made after a visit to Italy in 1621. Milanese gardener Dionisio Minaggio's "bird feather pictures" of commedia characters are cruder than Callot's engravings, but through his unusual medium, Minaggio expresses the colorful and vital life of commedia's characters.

The eighteenth century artists of France were especially drawn to commedia via the Théâtre Italien. The works of Claude Gillot (1673-1722), and his student, Antoine Watteau (1684-1721), offer exquisite Rococo images reflecting, through detail and color, the simple humanity of commedia. By the eighteenth century, commedia iconography was everywhere, deeply ingrained in most European cultures, especially Italy, France, and Germany. In Italy,

Alessandro Magnasco (1667-1749), Giovanni Domenico Ferretti (1692-1768), Marco Marcola (1740-1793), Giovanni Battista Tiepolo (1696-1770), and his son, Domenico (1727-1804), were paramount among artists who captured diverse images of commedia and its characters.

During the Age of Romanticism, French artists and writers were especially attracted to the image of Deburau's Pierrot. While writers constructed plays and poems featuring commedia characters, artists increasingly viewed them as romanticized icons of humanity. Gavarni (Guillaume-Sulpice Chevalier; 1804-1866) featured images of carnival using subtle gradations of tone and texture to create subdued and realistic portraits of the stock types. Honoré Daumier (1808-1879) turned to caricatures of Pierrot, who is typically seen in Daumier's works as a melancholy victim of life's caprices.

In the mid-nineteenth century, Thomas Couture (1815-1879) made a series of seven paintings of commedia masks, elevating them, through his themes, to tragic proportions, especially in his "Duel After the Masquerade," painted between 1857 and 1859. Couture's student, Edouard Manet (1832-1883), made a satiric lithograph portrait of Marshall MacMahon, then president of the French Republic, in the likeness of Polichinelle. Police confiscated and destroyed many of the fifteen hundred copies of the lithograph.

The many visions of commedia characters through the centuries seem to culminate in the work of Pablo Picasso (1881-1973), who featured commedia characters in many of his drawings, sculptures, and paintings, particularly during his "rose period" (1904-1905) when he focused on varied depictions of comic performers (saltimbanques). In 1916, Picasso was invited to design scenery and costumes for the Ballet Russes production of Jean Cocteau's and Erik Satie's commedic ballet *Parade*, produced to great acclaim in 1917.

Commedia characters were a popular subject for the artists of the Cubist movement, which had been sparked by Picasso. Dating from Watteau, artists identified themselves with the actors/masks of commedia, carnival, and circus, and this trend continued unabated into the twentieth century in the works of Picasso, the Cubists, the Futurists, and many others. Among Picasso's contemporaries and followers influenced by commedia are Georges Braque (1882-1963), Juan Gris (1887-1927), and Georges Rouault (1871-1958), whose many works feature clowns, often in Christ-like poses. David Hockney (b. 1937) reinvented Picasso's scene and costume designs for a new production of *Parade*, in 1981, also inspired by the Punchinello drawings of Tiepolo, as were his designs for *Turandot* in 1991.

Film And Television

The proliferation and popularity of film after 1900 created the twentieth century's greatest art form. Thomas Alva Edison's kinetoscope and Louis Lumière's *cinématographe* were barely viable instruments when the earliest comic moments appeared on film. The first comic genius of the film medium was French magician and director Georges Méliès (1861-1938), whose bizarre and hilarious images were essentially filmed theatre. His 1902 masterpiece, *A Trip to the Moon*, demonstrates Méliès understanding of the power of absurdity and incongruity on film, but the static placement of the camera and his emphasis on spectacle over character was to be supplanted by the great silent film comics of the next decade.

Silent film comedies, so popular between 1910 and the appearance of sound films in the late 1920's, provided one of the richest media for the extension of commedic traditions in the twentieth century. Mack Sennett's (1880-1960) early comic films featured the Keystone Kops, a riotous brotherhood of *zanni* led by the inimitable Ford Sterling (1883-1939), and Sennett's star, Mabel Normand (1894-1930), as effective a modern Columbine as could be imagined. Sennett and his actors probably never heard of commedia, but they had certainly heard of music hall, vaudeville, and burlesque, where the commedic spirit survived during their formative years. Among Sennett's many "discoveries" was the definitive silent screen comic, Charlie Chaplin (1889-1977), whose film persona, "The Little Tramp," became as familiar to movie audiences as Arlecchino had been to Renaissance theatre audiences.

"The Little Tramp" combined the rambunctious, knock-about aspects of Arlecchino with the winsome sadness of Pierrot. Other film comedians of the era, including Max Linder (1883-1925), Buster Keaton (1895-1966), Harold Lloyd (1893-1971), John Bunny (1863-1915), and Harry Langdon (1884-1944), were similarly commedic in the intensely personal stereotypes they developed. Virtuosos of physical comedy, and athletes adept at expressing feelings and ideas with every part of their bodies, they appealed to audiences as powerfully as their commedia forebears. The arrival of sound films did not end the film comedy boom, although sound took away the pure exploration of physical comedy which the silent films raised to high art in the commedic tradition. Chaplin made a few post-sound era films, but in them he stubbornly refused to give in to "talk." He often used sound for its purely comic possibilities, making his soundtrack a confusion of endless babble or rude noises. The poetic pantomime perfected by Chaplin and Keaton was lost to the age of sound films. Although he never mentions commedia by name, Chaplin wrote of the significance of pantomime in an article in *The New York Times* when his classic *City Lights* was released in 1931. Chaplin resisted the rapid movement toward sound, proclaiming, "My screen character remains speechless from choice."[1] He stressed the importance of "pantomimic art" which "has always been the universal means of communication. It existed as the universal tool long before language was born. Pantomime serves well where languages are in the conflict of a common ignorance. Primitive folk used the sign language before they were able to form an intelligible word."[2] Like more formal commedia afficianados, Chaplin was convinced of the primacy of movement which served "to effect the gradual transition from farce to pathos or from comedy to tragedy much more smoothly and with less effort than speech can ever do."[3]

Despite Chaplin's resistance, sound films came, and other comedians who had similarly paid their dues in music halls, vaudeville, and musical comedy, populated the screen of the talkies. In the 1920's, The Marx Brothers, Groucho (1890-1977), Harpo (1893-1964), Chico (1891-1961), Zeppo (1900-1979), and Gummo (1894-1977), rose from vaudeville to become stars of a uniquely anarchic brand of musical comedy in *I'll Say She Is* (1924), *The Cocoanuts* (1925), and *Animal Crackers* (1928). In the early 1930's, sans Gummo, the remaining four brothers became major film stars in a series of classic comedies, including *The Cocoanuts* (1929), *Animal Crackers* (1930), *Monkey Business* (1931), *Horse Feathers* (1932), and *Duck Soup* (1933). Without Zeppo, they continued to make films as a team until the late 1940's. This one comedy team contained a spectrum of commedic types: the wise-cracking Groucho was Pantalone, the silent Harpo combined elements of Pulcinella and Pierrot, the crafty Chico mixed aspects of Brighella and several other *zanni*, and Zeppo was an especially bland *innamorato*. Their best films featured an improvisatory quality and absurd, decidedly surrealistic, sight gags and slapstick.

Oliver Hardy (1892-1957) and Stan Laurel (1890-1965) each had separate successful careers in silent films before teaming up in early sound films. Hardy, fat and self-important, is a direct descendant of Il Dottore, and Laurel, soft-spoken and meek, is kin to Pulcinella and Pierrot. A similar commedic odd couple can be seen in Bud Abbott's (1895-1974) city slicker and Lou Costello's (1906-1959) babyish, pudgy clown. By the late 1940's, the universal qualities of these great comedies had faded, leaving only pale generic burlesques full of worked-over formulas.

A kind of comic anarchy returned to film in the outrageously vulgar and occasionally sublimely lunatic film farces of Mel Brooks (b. 1926), a loose-cannon of savage satire and broad ethnic, sexual, and social stereotypes. Brooks was particularly effective in his earliest films, *The Producers* (1968) and *Blazing Saddles* (1973), in which he satirized film and show business stereotypes, reinventing them as symbols of human vice.

European films were also drawn to commedia, often in more overt ways. Marcel Carné's (b. 1906) and Jacques Prévert's (b. 1900) classic *Les enfants du paradis* (1945) featured commedic elements in the sublime performance of Jean-Louis Barrault and its fictionalized depiction of the on and off stage life of the great French Pierrot, Deburau. Many European filmmakers were drawn to the images of commedia, including master director Jean Renoir (1894-1979), whose many films demonstrate commedic influences, although they are particularly overt in *The Golden Coach* (1952). Other great European filmmakers inspired by commedia include Ingmar Bergman (b. 1918), whose many films feature clowns and commedic influences, especially *Sawdust and Tinsel* (1953), and Federico Fellini (b. 1921), whose *La Strada* (1954) is filled with clowns and circus performers and a tragic commedic love triangle. All of them feature commedic characters, situations, and carnivalesque settings. Performers out of the vaudeville and music hall traditions were popular in European films. The stock company of England's "Carry On" films offered the broadest comedy, but the true heirs to commedia in English film comedy are Monty Python, whose outrageous anarchy, scatalogical humor, and savagely satiric contemporary stereotypes attracted audiences in both film and television. American television, too, had its commedic parallels in the madcap clowning of Lucille Ball's (1911-1989) scatterbrained housewife, and in the inspired, improvisatory interplay of Jackie Gleason's (1916-1987) pompous

Ralph Kramden and Art Carney's (b. 1918) slow-witted Ed Norton. The many characters created by Sid Caesar (b. 1922), Imogene Coca (b. 1908), and their supporting cast, on the early 1950's *Your Show of Shows* paved the way for *Saturday Night Live* and *Second City Television*, two television shows featuring a small ensemble cast in highly improvisatory satiric sketches. Ron Jenkins has identified late-night television's Johnny Carson (b. 1925) as a modern Arlecchino, bringing to his perennial monologues "a microcosm of America's obsessions."[4] Focused on scathing satire of celebrities and politicians of the moment, Carson's carefully crafted cool, detached persona renders his attack palatable to a huge viewing audience. Truly improvising comedians, however, remain few and far between. Jonathan Winters (b. 1925), Richard Pryor (b. 1940), Lily Tomlin (b. 1939), and Robin Williams (b. 1952) stand out among improvisatory performers who have created a gallery of characters who expose different levels of contemporary society, as commedia actors have done for centuries.

Literature

Commedia's influence on literature has been significant from the beginning. Aside from its incalculable impact on playwrights, commedia also inspired many writers of novels, short stories, and poetry. The characters of commedia became models to writers who expanded the limits of these models to enrich them. The commedic love triangle can be found in the works of many eighteenth and nineteenth century writers. Robert Storey has chronicled commedia's profound impact, via Pierrot, on the French Romantics of the nineteenth century, but commedia's presence can be identified in a wide range of novels, stories, and poems since the middle of the nineteenth century, and most writers seem to have encountered commedic influences on some level. In Martin Green's and John Swan's *The Triumph of Pierrot*, the authors identify commedic influences on the works of Vladimir Nabakov

(1899-1977), Evelyn Waugh (1903-1966), Edith Sitwell (1887-1964), T.S. Eliot (1888-1965), Wallace Stevens (1879-1955), F. Scott Fitzgerald (1896-1940), Ernest Hemingway (1899-1961), D.H. Lawrence (1885-1930), Marcel Proust (1871-1922), Franz Kafka (1883-1924), and Jean-Paul Sartre (1905-1980), among others.

Music

 Music has found many useful elements in commedia. As early as the sixteenth century, Adriano Banchieri's (1568-1634) and Orazio Vecchi's (1550-1605) madrigal comedies demonstrate commedic inspiration, especially Vecchi's *L'Amfiparnaso* (1594). But the earliest concrete evidence of commedia's influence on music can be found in *intermezzi*, comic interludes performed between the acts or scenes of an *opera seria*. *Intermezzi* contributed to the widespread familiarity with Italian comedy in France, where they became popular. Authors of *intermezzi* took many inspirations from the characters and situations typical of commedia. The loosely constructed plots, the illusion of improvisatory dialogue, disguises, slapstick comedy, and the employment of dialects for comic purposes are among the many elements of commedia found in *intermezzi*. Commedia characters appear exactly as they are found in traditional commedia (Pantalone in *La finta tedesca* and Capitano in *La fantesca*) in numerous *intermezzi*, including Giovanni Battista Pergolesi's (1710-1736) *La Serva Padrona* (1733), which is a significant example of the genre.

 Filled with old fools, comic servants, and young lovers, *opera buffa*, full-length comic operas, were commedic entertainments which became popular on the eighteenth century musical stage. Wolfgang Amadeus Mozart's (1756-1791) *The Marriage of Figaro* (1786) and, to some extent, *Don Giovanni* (1787), *Così Fan Tutte* (1790), and *The Magic Flute* (1791), feature commedic characters and situations.

Commedia's influence on instrumental works appears later and can be found as early as the mid-nineteenth century in Robert Schumann's (1810-1856) suite for solo piano, *Carnaval. Scènes mignonnes composées pour quatre notes* (1833-1835). Twentieth century composers drawn to commedia include Kurt Weill (1900-1950), Maurice Ravel (1875-1937), Francis Poulenc (1899-1963), Paul Hindemith (1895-1963), Bohuslav Martinu (1890-1959), and Carl August Nielsen (1865-1931). Among the most overtly commedic are Darius Milhaud's (1892-1974) suite for two pianos, *Scaramouche* (1943), Claude Debussy's (1862-1918) composition for piano, *Suite Bergamasque* (1890), and several works by Arnold Schönberg (1874-1951). Schönberg was influenced by commedia through cabaret entertainments and Grand Guignol in his musical revolt against Wagner and the Symbolist movement. His *Pierrot Lunaire* (1912) is of particular commedic interest for its instrumental color, spirit of improvisation, and parody. Featuring twenty-one poems set for speaker and chamber ensemble, *Pierrot Lunaire* is self-contradicting as its focus continually shifts at random, as in a dream, from the bizarre activities of the clown to the poet in the first person to the self-absorbed artist. On one hand, it is grotesque, macabre, and filled with biting mockery; one the other hand, it is consciously sentimental, good humored and genuinely touching in its pathos. Other instrumental pieces, which have been importantly performed as ballets, include Erik Satie's (1866-1925) *Parade* (1917), Max Reger's (1873-1916) *Balletsuite* (1913), and Igor Stravinsky's (1882-1971) *Petrushka* (1911) and *Pulcinella* (1920, revised 1947), influenced by Pergolesi's *La Serva Padrona* as well as commedia. *Petrushka*, choreographed by Mikhail Fokine (and danced by Vaclav Nijinksky) as a reflection of his desire to elevate ballet from mere spectacle to a composite theatrical art, features an impressionistic use of music, borrowing elements from Russian folk music and popular tunes of the fairground. Ballets featuring commedia elements have been common in the twentieth century. Notable among these is Szymanowski's *Mandragora*, which featured a libretto by Leon Schiller and was premiered in 1920 at the Teatr Polski following a performance of Molière's commedic play, *The Bourgeois Gentleman*.

Other contemporary commedic compositions include Peter Schickele's (b. 1935) *Commedia* (1979) for wind instruments, Oscar van Hemel's (b. 1892) *About Commedia dell'Arte* (1967), and Richard Rodney Bennett's (b. 1936) *Commedia* (1972-1973). More recently, German composer Karl-Heinz Stockhaüsen (b. 1928) composed a clarinet solo, *Harlekin* (1975), featuring the clarinetist dressed as Harlequin and inviting movement for the musician and improvisation.

Among modern serious operas featuring commedic characters or situations are Ruggiero Leoncavallo's (1858-1919) *I Pagliacci* (1892), Richard Strauss' (1864-1949) *Der Rosenkavalier* (1911), *Ariadne auf Naxos* (1912), and *Arabella* (1929), Ferruccio Busoni's (1866-1924) *Arlecchino* and *Turandot* (both 1917), Giacomo Puccini's (1858-1924) *Turandot* (produced after his death in 1926), Alban Berg's (1885-1935) *Lulu* (1935), Serge Prokofiev's (1891-1953) *Love for Three Oranges* (1919) and *Chout* (or *The Buffoon*; 1915), and Harrison Birtwistle's (b. 1934) *Punch and Judy* (1966-1967).

BIBLIOGRAPHY

Books:

Amico, Silvio d'. *Storia del teatro drammatico.* new and rev. ed. Milano: Garzanti, 1958.

_____. *Storia del teatro italiano.* Milano: V. Bompiani, 1936.

Anderson, Reed. *Federico Garcia Lorca.* New York: Grove Press, 1984.

Apollinaire, Guillaume. *Le Théâtre italien.* Paris: L. Michaud, 1910.

Apollonio, Mario. *Storia della commedia dell'arte.* Roma: Augustea, 1930.

_____. *Storia del teatro italiano.* Firenze: Sansoni, 1981.

Artaud, Antonin. *The Theatre and Its Double.* Translated from the French by Mary Caroline Richards. New York: Grove Press, Inc., 1958.

Aslan, Odette. *Roger Blin and Twentieth-Century Playwrights.* Translated by Ruby Cohn. Cambridge: Cambridge University Press, 1988.

Atkinson, Brooks. *Broadway.* New York: Macmillan Publishing Company, Inc., 1974.

Aubert, Charles. *The Art of Pantomime.* Translated from the French by Edith Sears. New York: Henry Holt and Company, 1927.

Bablet, Denis. *Edward Gordon Craig.* Translated by Daphne Woodward. London: Eyre Methuen, 1981.

Baer, Nancy Van Norman. *The Art of Enchantment. Diaghilev's Ballets Russes 1909-1929.* San Francisco, California: Universe Books, 1988.

Bakshy, Alexander. *The Theater Unbound.* New York/London: Benjamin Blom, 1969.

Banham, Martin, ed. *The Cambridge Guide to World Theatre.* Cambridge: Cambridge University Press, 1988.

Banning, Kenneth, ed. *Mon Ami Pierrot. Songs and Fantasies.* Chicago, Illinois:

Brothers of the Book, 1917.

Barba, Evgenio. *Beyond The Floating Islands.*. With a postscript by Ferdinando Taviani. Translations by Judy Barba, Richard Fowler, Jerrold C. Rodesh, Sawl Shapiro. New York: PAJ Publications, 1986.

Barba, Eugenio, and Nicola Savarese. *A Dictionary of Theatre Anthropology. The Secret Art of the Performer.* London and New York: Routledge, 1991.

Barker, Granville, and Dion Clayton Calthrop. *The Harlequinade. An Excursion,* Boston, Little, Brown, and Company, 1918.

Barker, Harley Granville. *On Dramatic Method.* London: Sidgwick & Jackson, 1931.

Barrault, Jean-Louis. *Reflections on the Theatre.* London: Rockcliff, 1951.

_____. *The Theatre of Jean-Louis Barrault.* Translated by Joseph Chiari. New York: Hill and Wang, 1959.

Barrie, J.M. *The Plays of J.M. Barrie.* New York: Charles Scribner's Sons, 1929.

_____. *What Every Woman Knows and Other Plays.* New York: Charles Scribner's Sons, 1930.

Barrymore, Ethel. *Memories.* New York: Harper and Brothers, 1955.

Bartow, Arthur. *The Director's Voice. Twenty-One Questions.* New York: Theatre Communications Group, Inc., 1988.

Bassnett-McGuire, Susan. *Luigi Pirandello.* New York: Grove Press, 1983.

Beaumont, Cyril W. *The History of Harlequin.* London: Beaumont, 1926.

Beerbohm, Max. *Around Theatres.* London: Rupert Hart-Davis, 1953.

Bentley, Eric, ed. *The Classic Theatre.* Garden City, New York: Doubleday and Company, Inc., 1958.

_____. ed. *The Genius of the Italian Theatre.* New York: Mentor Books, 1964.

_____ ed. and trans., *Naked Masks. Five Plays by Luigi Pirandello*. New York: E.P. Dutton and Company, Inc., 1952.

_____ . *The Pirandello Commentaries*. Evanston, Illinois: Northwestern University Press, 1986.

_____ . *What is Theatre? Incorporating The Dramatic Event and Other Reviews 1944-1967*. New York: Atheneum, 1968.

Bentley, Nicolas. *The History of the Circus*. London: Michael Joseph Ltd., 1977.

Billington, Michael, ed. *Performing Arts: A Guide to Practice and Appreciation*. New York: Facts on File, 1980.

Bishop, George. *The World of Clowns*. Los Angeles, California: Brooke House Publishers, 1976.

Bloom, Harold, ed. *Luigi Pirandello*. New York and Philadelphia: Chelsea House Publishers, 1989.

Bordman, Gerald. *The Oxford Companion to American Theatre*. Oxford: Oxford University Press, 1984.

Bogard, Travis, ed. *The Unknown O'Neill*. New Haven and London: Yale University Press, 1988.

Bond, Richard Warwick. *Early Plays from the Italian*. Oxford, 1911.

Boughner, Daniel. *The Braggart in Renaissance Comedy*. Minneapolis, Minnesota, 1954.

Bradby, David. *Modern French Drama 1940-1990*. Cambridge: Cambridge University Press, 1991.

Brady, David, and David Williams. *Director's Theatre*. New York: St. Martin's Press, 1988.

Bragaglia, Anton Giulio. *La commedia dell'arte: canovacci della gloriosa commedia dell'arte italiana raccolti e presentati da Anton Giulio Bragaglia*. Torino: Ed. "Il Dramma", 1943.

_____. *Pulcinella*. Rome: Gherardo Casini Editore, 1953.

Braun, Edward. *The Director and the Stage*. New York: Holmes and Meier, 1982.

_____, ed. *Meyerhold on Theatre*. New York: Hill and Wang, 1969.

_____. *The Theatre of Meyerhold*. New York: Drama Book Specialists, 1979.

Brecht, Stefan. *The Bread and Puppet Theatre*. Two volumes. London and New York: Routledge/Methuen, 1988.

Brenner, Clarence D. *The Theatre Italien: Its Repertory*, 1716-1793. Berkeley, California: 1961.

Brook, Peter. *The Empty Space*. New York: Avon Books, 1969.

_____. *The Shifting Point, 1946-1987*. New York: Harper and Row, 1987.

Brown, Frederick. *Theatre and Revolution. The Culture of the French Stage*. New York: The Viking Press, 1980.

Brown, Maria Ward. *The Life of Dan Rice*. Long Branch, New Jersey, 1901.

Bucknell, Peter. *Commedia dell'arte at the Court of Louis XIV. A Soft Sculpture Representation*. London: Stainer and Bell, 1980.

Bührer, Michel. *Mummenschanz*. New York: Rizzoli Books, 1986.

Burckhardt, Jacob. *The Civilization of the Renaissance in Italy*. New York, 1958.

Burdick, Jacques. *Theater*. New York: Newsweek Books, 1974.

Cairns, Christopher, ed. *The Commedia dell'Arte from the Renaissance to Dario Fo*. Lewiston/Queenstown/Lampeter: The Edwin Mellen Press, 1989.

Calendoli, Giovanni. *L'attore: storia di un arte*. Roma: Ediz. dell'Ateneo, 1959.

Caputi, Anthony. *Buffo: the genius of vulgar comedy*. Detroit: Wayne State University, 1978.

Carlson, Marvin. *The Italian Stage. From Goldoni to D'Annunzio.* Jefferson City, North Carolina and London: McFarland and Company, Inc., 1981.

_____ . *Theories of the Theatre.* Ithaca and London: Cornell University Press, 1984.

Carnicke, Sharon Marie. *The Theatrical Instinct. Nikolai Evreinov and the Russian Theatre of the Early Twentieth Century.* New York: Peter Lang, 1989.

Carter, Huntley. *The Theatre of Max Reinhardt.* New York: Mitchell Kennerley, 1914.

Castle, Charles. *Noël.* Garden City, New York: Doubleday and Co., 1973.

Cataldo, Antonio. *Il Ruzzante.* Milan, 1933.

Cerf, Bennett, and Van H. Cartmell, eds. *Thirty Famous One-Act Plays.* New York: The Modern Library, 1943.

Chambers, E.K. *The Medieval Stage.* Oxford: Oxford University Press, 1904.

Champagne, Lenora. *French Theatre Experiment Since 1968.* Ann Arbor, Michigan: UMI Research Press, 1984.

Chancerel, Léon. *Panorama du théâtre des origines à nos jours.* Paris: Leclerc, 1955.

Chessé, Ralph. *The Marionette Actor.* Fairfax, Virginia: George Mason University Press, 1987.

Cheney, Sheldon. *The New Movement in the Theatre.* New York: Mitchell Kennerley, 1914.

_____ . *The Theatre. Three Thousand Years of Drama, Acting, and Stagecraft.* New York: David McKay Company, Inc., 1967.

Clark, Barrett H., and George Freedley, eds. *A History of Modern Drama.* New York and London: D. Appleton-Century Company, Inc., 1947.

Clubb, Louise George. *Giambattista Della Porta Dramatist.* Princeton, New Jersey: Princeton University Press, 1965.

294

_____. *Italian Drama in Shakespeare's Time*. New Haven and London: Yale University Press, 1989.

Cole, Toby, and Helen Krich Chinoy, eds. *Actors on Acting*. New York: Crown Publishers, Inc., 1970.

_____, eds. *Directors on Directing*. New York: The Bobbs- Merrill Company, Inc., 1953.

Cooper, Douglas. *Picasso Theatre*. New York: Harry N. Abrams, 1987.

Cope, Jackson I. *Dramaturgy of the Daemonic. Studies in Antigeneric Theater from Ruzzante to Grimaldi*. Baltimore and London: Johns Hopkins University Press, 1984.

Copeau, Jacques. *Texts on Theatre*. Translated and edited by John Rudlin and Norman H. Paul. London: Routledge, 1990.

Cowan, Louise, ed. *The Terrain of Comedy*. Dallas: Dallas Institute of Humanities and Culture, 1984.

Craig, Edward. *Gordon Craig. The Story of His Life*. New York: Alfred A. Knopf, 1968.

Craig, Edward Gordon. *Books and Theatres*. New York: E.P. Dutton and Company, Inc., 1925.

_____. *Commedia dell'arte*. Unpublished manuscript, 1910-11. Bibliotheque Nationale, Paris.

_____. *Daybooks. 1909, 1910, 1911, 1912*. Unpublished daybooks. Hoblitzelle Library, University of Texas at Austin.

_____. *European Theatre from 1500-1900*. Unpublished manuscript. Bibliotheque Nationale, Paris.

_____. *Index to the Story of My Days*. New York: The Viking Press, 1957.

_____. *The Mask*. Sixteen volumes. New York: Benjamin A. Blom, 1967.

_____. *On the Art of the Theatre*. New York: Theatre Arts Books, 1980.

_____ . *Scene*. London: Oxford University Press, 1923.

_____ . *The Theatre - Advancing*. Boston: Little, Brown, 1919.

_____ . *Woodcuts and Some Words*. London and Toronto: J.M. Dent and Sons, Ltd., 1924.

Czerwinski, E.J. *Contemporary Polish Theater and Drama (1956-1984)*. Westport, Connecticut: Greenwood Press, 1988.

DaLuiso, Florence S., ed. *La Commedia dell'arte. An Exhibition*. Buffalo, New York: State University of New York at Buffalo, 1980.

Daniel, Howard, ed. *Callot's Etchings*. New York: Dover Publications, 1974.

Dario Fo and Franca Rame Theatre Workshops at Riverside Studios, London, April 28th, May 5th, 12th, 13th & 19th, 1983. London: Red Notes, 1983.

Davis, R.G. *The San Francisco Mime Troupe: The First Ten Years*. Palo Alto: Ramparts Press, 1975.

Decroux, Etienne. *Words on Mime*. Translated by Thomas Leabhart. Claremont, California: The Mime Journal, 1985.

Dick, Kay. *Pierrot*. London: Hutchinson and Co., 1960.

Disher, M. Willson. *Clowns and Pantomimes*. New York: Benjamin Blom, 1968.

Dixon, Michael Bigelow, and Michelle Y. Togami, eds. *Commedia dell'arte and the Comic Spirit. Classics in Context 1990*. Louisville, Kentucky: Actors Theatre of Louisville Monograph, 1990.

Dorcy, Jean. *The Mime*. New York: Robert Speller and Sons, Publishers, Inc., 1961.

Dorn, Karen. *Players and Painted Stage: The Theatre of W.B. Yeats*. Sussex, New Jersey: Harvester Press, 1984.

Drama and Symbolism (proceedings of the *Themes in Drama Conference*). Cambridge: Cambridge University Press, 1982.

Duchartre, Pierre Louis. *The Italian Comedy*. Translated by R.T. Weaver. New York: Dover Publications, Inc., 1966.

Dukore, Bernard F., ed. *Dramatic Theory and Criticism*. New York: Holt, Rinehart, and Winston, 1974.

Dunlop, Frank, and Jim Dale. *Scapino!* Chicago, Illinois: The Dramatic Publishing Company, Inc., 1975.

Dürrenmatt, Friedrich. *Plays and Essays*. Edited by Volkmar Sander. New York: Continuum, 1982.

Eaton, Katherine B. *The Theatre of Meyerhold and Brecht*. Westport, Connecticut: Greenwood Press, 1985.

Einstein, L. *The Italian Renaissance in England*. New York, 1902.

Eisner, Lotte. *The Haunted Screen: Expressionism in the German Cinema and the Influence of Max Reinhardt*. London, 1969.

Ekelof, Gunnar. *Commedia dell'arte*. Stockholm: Sallskapet Bokvannerna, 1984.

Erenstein, Robert L. *De geschiedenis van de Commedia dell'Arte*. Amsterdam: International Theatre Bookshop, 1985.

Esslin, Martin, ed. *The Encyclopedia of World Theater*. New York: Charles Scribner's Sons, 1977.

_____ . *The Theatre of the Absurd*. Harmonsworth: Penguin, 1980.

Evreinoff, Nicholas. *The Theatre in Life*. Translated by Alexander I. Nazaroff. New York: Brentano's 1927.

Fasso, Luigi. *Teatro dialettale del seicento: scenari della commedia dell'arte*. Torino: Einaudi, 1979.

Felner, Mira. *Apostles of Silence. The Modern French Mimes*. Rutherford, New Jersey: Fairleigh-Dickinson, 1985.

Filler, Witold. *Contemporary Polish Theatre*. Warsaw: Interpress Publishers, 1977.

Fido, Martin. *Shakespeare*. Maplewood, New Jersey: Hammond, 1978.

Flanagan, Hallie. *Arena. The History of the Federal Theatre*. New York: Benjamin Blom, 1965.

Fo, Dario. *Accidental Death of an Anarchist*. Adapted by Gavin Richards from a translation by Gillian Hanna. Introducted by Stuart Hood. London: Methuen, 1987.

_____. *The Tricks of the Trade*. Translated by Joe Farrell. Edited and with notes by Stuart Hood. New York: Routledge/Theatre Arts Books, 1991.

Forsyth, Karen. *Ariadne auf Naxos by Hugo von Hofmannsthal and Richard Strauss. Its Genesis and Meaning*. Oxford: Oxford University Press, 1982.

Four Plays by Lope de Vega, in English Versions and a Critical Essay by Jacinto Benavente. New York: C. Scribner's Sons, 1936.

Fowler, James, ed. *Images of Show Business from the Theatre Museum, V&A*. London: Methuen, 1982.

Frank, Waldo. *Salvos. An Informal Book About Books and Plays*. New York: Boni Liveright, 1924.

Frow, Gerald. *"Oh, Yes It Is!" A History of Pantomime*. London: BBC, 1985.

Gassner, John, and Edward Quinn, eds. *The Reader's Encyclopedia of World Drama*. New York: Thomas Y. Crowell Company, 1969.

Gehring, Wes D. *Charlie Chaplin. A Bio-Bibliography*. Westport, Connecticut: Greenwood Press, 1983.

Gilder, Rosamund. *Enter the Actress*. New York: Theatre Arts Books, 1960.

Gleijeses, Vittorio. *Le maschere e il teatro nel tempo*. Napoli: Società editrice napoletana, 1981.

Goldberg, Rose Lee. *Performance Art. From Futurism to the Present*. New York: Harry N. Abrams, Inc., 1988.

Goldoni, Carlo. *The Comic Theatre*. Translated from the Italian by John W. Miller. Lincoln, Nebraska: University of Nebraska Press, 1969.

_____. *The Servant of Two Masters and Other Italian Classics*. Edited by Eric Bentley. New York: Applause Theatre Book Publishers, 1986.

Golub, Spencer. *Evreinov. The Theatre of Paradox and Transformation*. Ann Arbor, Michigan: UMI Research Press, 1984.

Goodman, Kenneth Sawyer, and Ben Hecht. *The Wonder Hat and Other One-Act Plays*. New York: Appleton, 1925.

Goorney, Howard, and Ewan MacColl, eds. *Agit-Prop to Theatre Workshop. Political Playscripts 1930-1950*. Manchester: Manchester University Press, 1986.

Gorchakov, Nikolai. *The Theater in Soviet Russia*. Translated by Edgar Lehrman. New York: Columbia University Press, 1957.

_____. *The Vakhtangov School of Stage Art*. Moscow: Foreign Languages Publishing House, n.d.

Gordon, Mel. *The Grand Guignol. Theatre of Fear and Terror*. New York: Amok Press, 1988.

_____. *Lazzi: The Comic Routines of the Commedia dell'arte*. New York: Performance Arts Journal Publications, 1983.

Gottfried, Martin. *In Person. The Great Entertainers*. New York: Harry N. Abrams, 1985.

Gozzi, Carlo. *Five Tales for the Theatre*. Edited and translated by Albert Bermel and Ted Emery. Chicago and London: The University of Chicago Press, 1989.

Grabher, Carlo. *Ruzzante*. Milan, 1953.

Green, Benny, ed. *The Last Empires. A Music Hall Companion*. London: Pavillion Books, Ltd., 1986.

Green, Martin, and John Swan. *The Triumph of Pierrot*. New York: Macmillan, 1986.

Green, Michael, ed. and trans. *The Russian Symbolist Theatre*. Ann Arbor, Michigan: Ardis, 1986.

Green, Stanley. *The Great Clowns of Broadway*. New York: Oxford University Press, 1984.

Greenfield, Jeff. *Television. The First Fifty Years*. New York: Crescent Books, 1981.

Guitry, Sacha. *Deburau*. New York and London: G.P. Putnam's Sons, 1921.

Hamburger, Michael, ed. *Selected Plays and Libretti of Hugo von Hofmannsthal*. London: Routledge & Kegan Paul, 1964.

Hartmann, Rudolf. *Richard Strauss. The Staging of His Operas and Ballets*. New York: Oxford University Press, 1981.

Hartnoll, Phyllis, ed. *The Oxford Companion to the Theatre*. Oxford: Oxford University Press, 1983.

Heck, Thomas F. *Commedia dell'arte. A Guide to the Primary and Secondary Literature*. New York and London: Garland Publishing Company, 1988.

Hernández, Guillermo E. *Chicano Satire: A study in Literary Culture*. Austin, Texas: University of Texas Press, 1991.

Herrick, Marvin T. *Comic Theory in the Sixteenth Century*. Urbana, Illinois, 1950.

_____. *Italian Comedy in the Renaissance*. Urbana and London: Illini Books, 1960.

_____. *Italian Plays, 1500-1700, in the University of Illinois Library*. Urbana and London: University of Illinois Press, 1966.

Hewitt, Barnard. *Theatre U.S.A. 1668-1957*. New York: McGraw-Hill Book Co., Inc., 1959.

Hirst, David L. *Dario Fo and Franca Rame*. New York: St. Martin's Press, 1989.

Hobson, Harold. *French Theatre Since 1830*. London: John Calder, 1978.

Holme, Timothy. *The Servant of Many Masters. The Life and Times of Carlo Goldoni*. London: Jupiter, 1976.

Holt, Marion P. *The Contemporary Spanish Theater (1949-1972)*. Boston: Twayne Publishers, 1975.

Hoover, Marjorie L. *Meyerhold and His Set Designers*. New York: Peter Lang, 1988.

_____ . *Meyerhold. The Art of Conscious Theatre*. Amherst, Massachusetts: University of Massachusetts Press, 1974.

Houghton, Norris. *Moscow Rehearsals. The Golden Age of the Soviet Theatre*. New York: Grove Press, Inc., 1962.

_____ . *Return Engagement. A Postscript to 'Moscow Rehearsals'*. New York: Holt, Rinehart and Winston, 1962.

Housman, Laurence, and Harley Granville Barker. *Prunella, or Love in a Dutch Garden*. Boston: Little, Brown, and Company, 1937.

Housman, Laurence. *The Unexpected Years*. New York and Indianapolis: The Bobbs-Merrill Company, 1936.

Hsü, Tao-Ching. *The Chinese Conception of the Theatre*. Seattle and London: University of Washington Press, 1985.

Hughes, Glenn. *A History of the American Theatre. 1770-1950*. New York: Samuel French, 1951.

Innes, Christopher. *Edward Gordon Craig*. Cambridge: Cambridge University Press, 1983.

Jeffrey, Brian. *French Renaissance Comedy 1552-1630*. London: Oxford University Press, 1969.

Jenkins, Ron. *Acrobats of the Soul*. New York: Theatre Communications Group, 1988.

Johnson, Roger, Jr., Editha S. Neumann, and Guy T. Trail, eds. *Molière and the Commonwealth of Letters: Patrimony and Posterity*. Jackson, Mississippi: University Press of Mississippi, 1975.

Jones, David Richard. *Great Directors at Work*. Berkeley: University of California Press, 1986.

Jones, Edward Trostle. *Following Directions: A Study of Peter Brook*. New York: P. Lang, 1985.

Jones, Louisa E. *Sad Clowns and Pale Pierrots. Literature and the Popular Comic Arts in 19th-Century France*. Lexington, Kentucky: French Forum, Publishers, 1984.

Jones, Robert Edmond. *The Dramatic Imagination*. New York: Theatre Arts Books, 1941.

Kelly, Catriona. *Petrushka. The Russian Carnival Puppet Theatre*. Cambridge: Cambridge University Press, 1990.

Kennard, Joseph Spencer. *The Italian Theatre*. Two volumes. New York: William Edwin Rudge, 1932.

_____ . *Masks and Marionettes*. Port Washington, New York: Kennikat Press, 1967.

Kennedy, Dennis. *Granville Barker and the Dream of the Theatre*. Cambridge: Cambridge University Press, 1985.

Kerr, Walter. *The Silent Clowns*. New York: Alfred A. Knopf Inc., 1975.

Kirby, E.T., ed. *Total Theatre*. New York: E.P. Dutton & Company, 1969.

Kirby, Michael, and Victoria Nes Kirby. *Futurist Performance*. New York: Performing Arts Journal Publications, 1986.

Knapp, Bettina L. *French Theatre 1918-1939*. New York: Grove Press, 1985.

_____ . *Louis Jouvet. Man of the Theatre*. New York: Columbia University Press, 1957.

_____ . *The Reign of the Theatrical Director: French Theatre, 1887-1924*. Troy, N.Y.: Whitston Pub. Co., 1988.

Komisarjevsky, Theodore. *The Theatre and a Changing Civilisation*. London: John Lane The Bodley Head, Ltd., 1935.

Kott, Jan. *The Bottom Translation*. Evanston, Illinois: Northwestern University Press, 1984.

_____ . *Theatre Notebook, 1947-1967*. Translated from the Polish by Boleslaw Taborski. New York: Doubleday, 1968.

LaValley, Albert J., ed. *The New Consciousness*. Cambridge, Massachusetts: Winthrop Publishers, Inc., 1972.

Lea, Kathleen M. *Italian Popular Comedy*. New York: Russell and Russell, 1962.

Leabhart, Thomas. *Modern and Post-Modern Mime*. New York: St. Martin's Press, 1989.

Leach, Robert. *Vsevolod Meyerhold*. Cambridge: Cambridge University Press, 1989.

Le Gallienne, Eva. *At 33*. New York and Toronto: Longmans, Green and Co., 1934.

Leisler, Edda, and Gisela Prossnitz. *Max Reinhardt und die Welt der Commedia dell'arte*. Otto Muller Verlag Salzburg, 1970.

Leslie, Peter. *A Hard Act to Follow. A Music Hall Review*. New York and London: Paddington Press, 1978.

Lesnick, Henry, ed. *Guerilla Street Theatre*. New York: Avon, 1973.

Lindsay, Frank Whiteman. *Dramatic Parody by Marionettes in Eighteenth Century Paris*. New York: 1946.

Littlewood, Samuel Robinson. *The Story of Pierrot*. London: Herbert & Daniel, 1911.

Lievsay, John L. *The Elizabethan Image of Italy*. Ithaca, New York: Cornell University Press, 1964.

Lucas, F.L. *The Drama of Chekhov, Synge, Yeats, and Pirandello*. London: Cassell and Co., 1963.

Luciani, Vincent. *A Concise History of the Italian Theater*. New York: S.F. Vanni, 1961.

Luciano, Eleonora, ed. *The Mask of Comedy: The Art of Italian Commedia*. Louisville, Kentucky: J.B. Speed Art Museum, 1990.

Lyon, John. *The Theatre of Valle-Inclán*. Cambridge: Cambridge University Press, 1983.

Macdougall, Allan Ross, ed. *Letters of Edna St. Vincent Millay*. New York: Harper & Brothers, 1952.

Macgowan, Kenneth. *Continental Stagecraft*. London: Benn Brothers, 1923.

_____ . *The Theatre of Tomorrow*. New York: Boni and Liveright, 1921.

Machiavelli, Niccoló. *Clizia*. Introduction and translation by Oliver Evans. Great Neck, New York: Barron's Educational Series, Inc., 1962.

_____ . *The Mandrake*. Translated by Luigi Ricci. New York and Scarborough, Ontario: New American Library, 1980.

Madden, David. *Harlequin's Stick -- Charlie's Cane*. Ohio: Bowling Green University Popular Press, 1975.

Maltin, Leonard. *The Great Movie Comedians*. New York: Crown Publishers, Inc., 1978.

Manchel, Frank. *The Talking Clowns*. New York: Franklin Watts, 1976.

Mander, Raymond, and Joe Mitchenson. *Victorian and Edwardian Entertainments from Old Photographs*. London: B.T. Batsford, 1975.

Manifold, Gay. *George Sand's Theatre Career*. Ann Arbor, Michigan: UMI Research Press, 1985.

Mantzius, Karl. *A History of Theatrical Art*. (Volume 2: *The Middle Ages and the Renaissance*). London, 1903.

Marcia, Alberto. *The Commedia dell'arte and the Masks of Amleto and Donato Sartori*. Florence: Conti Tipocolor Calenzano, 1980.

Marker, Frederick and Lise-Lone. *Edward Gordon Craig and "The Pretenders." A Production Revisited*. Carbondale and Edwardsville, Illinois: Southern Illinois University Press, 1981.

Marranca, Bonnie, and Gautam Dasgupta, eds. *Theatre of the Ridiculous*. New York: Performing Arts Journal Publications, 1979.

Marshall, Norman. *The Producer and the Play*. London: Davis-Poynter, 1975.

Matejka, Ladislav, and Irwin R. Titunik, eds. *Semiotics of Art*. Cambridge: MIT Press, 1977.

Matthaei, Renate. *Luigi Pirandello*. New York: Frederick Ungar Publishing Co., 1973.

Max Reinhardt, The Oxford Symposium. Oxford: Oxfrod Polytechnic, 1986.

Mayer, David. *Harlequin in His Element: The English Pantomime,1806-1836*. Cambridge: Harvard University Press, 1969.

McKendrick, Melveena. *Theatre in Spain, 1490-1700*. Cambridge: Cambridge University Press, 1989.

Miclashevsky, Konstantin (Constant Mic). *La Commedia dell'arte*. Paris: J. Schifirin Editions de la Pleiades, 1927.

Mitchell, John D. *Theatre: The Search for Style*. Midland, Michigan: Northwood Institute Press, 1982.

Mitchell, Tony. *Dario Fo. The People's Court Jester*. London: Methuen, 1984.

_____ ed. *File on Fo*. London: Methuen Drama, 1989.

Moderwell, Hiram K. *The Theatre of To-Day*. New York: John Lane Company, 1914.

Molinari, Cesare. *La commedia dell'arte*. Milano: Mondadori, 1985.

Murray, William, trans. *Pirandello's One-Act Plays*. New York: Minerva Press, 1970.

Nathan, George Jean. *The Magic Mirror. Selected Writings on the Theatre*. Edited, together with an introduction, by Thomas Quinn Curtiss. New York: Alfred A. Knopf, 1960.

Newberry, Wilma. *The Pirandellian Mode in Spanish Literature from Cervantes to Sastre*. Albany, New York: State University of New York Press, 1973.

Nicoll, Allardyce. *A History of English Drama, 1660-1900*. Six volumes. Cambridge, England: 1952-1959.

_____ . *Masks, Mimes and Miracles*. New York: Cooper Square, 1963.

_____ . *The World of Harlequin: A Critical Study of the Commedia dell'Arte*. Cambridge: Cambridge University Press, 1963.

Niklaus, Thelma. *Harlequin Phoenix*. London: The Bodley Head, 1956.

Oreglia, Giacomo. *The Commedia dell'arte*. Translated by Lovett F. Edwards. New York: Hill and Wang, 1968.

Paget, V. (Vernon Lee). *Studies of the Eighteenth Century in Italy*. Chicago, 1908.

Pandolfi, Vito. *Il teatro del rinascimento e la commedia dell'arte*. Roma: Lerici, 1969.

Patterson, Michael. *The Revolution in German Theatre 1900-1933*. Boston, London and Henley: Routledge and Kegan Paul, 1981.

Peabody, Ruth E. *Commedia Works*. Lanham, Maryland: University Press of America, 1984.

Pendleton, Ralph, ed. *The Theatre of Robert Edmond Jones*. Middletown, Connecticut: Wesleyan University Press, 1958.

Peñuelas, Marcelino C. *Jacinto Benavente*. Translated by Kay Engler. New York: Twayne Publishers, Inc., 1968.

Piccolo teatro di Milano, 1947-1967. Milano: Ufficio stampa del Comune di Milano, 1967.

Pirandello, Luigi. *On Humor*. Translated by Antonio Illiano and Daniel P. Testa. Chapel Hill, N.C.: The University of North Carolina Press, 1960.

_____ . *Right You Are*. A Stage Version with an Introduction and Notes by Eric Bentley. New York: Columbia University Press, 1954.

_____ . *Sicilian Comedies. "Cap and Bells" and "Man, Beast and Virtue."* Two Plays by Luigi Pirandello. New York: Performing Arts Journal Publications, 1983.

306

_____ . *Three Plays. The Rules of the Game, Six Characters in Search of an Author, Henry IV*. Translated by Robert Rietty and Noel Creegan, John Linstrum, Julian Mitchell. London: Methuen, 1985.

_____ . *To-Night We Improvise*. Translated from the Italian, and with an Introductino by Samuel Putnam. New York: E.P. Dutton & Co., 1932.

Prideaux, Tom. *World Theatre in Pictures*. New York: Greenberg Publishers, 1953.

Proffer, Ellendea. *Evreinov*. Ann Arbor, Michigan: Ardis, 1981.

Purdom, C.B. *Harley Granville Barker*. London: Salisbury Square, 1955.

Pyman, Avril. *The Life of Aleksandr Blok. Volume 1. The Distant Thunder. 1880-1908*. Oxford: Oxford University Press, 1979.

Radcliff-Umstead, Douglas. *The Birth of Modern Comedy in Renaissance Italy*. Chicago and London: University of Chicago Press, 1969.

Redmond, James, ed. *Themes in Drama*. Cambridge: Cambridge University Press, 1982.

Reidt, Heinz. *Carlo Goldoni*. New York: Frederick Ungar Publishing, 1974.

Reinhardt, Gottfried. *The Genius. A Memoir of Max Reinhardt*. New York: Alfred A. Knopf, 1979.

Reinhardt, Max. *The Part of the Director*. Binghamton, New York: Max Reinhardt Archive, State University of New York at Binghamton, n.d.

Remy, Tristan. *Jean-Gaspard Deburau*. Paris: L'Arden, 1954.

Rennert, H.A. *The Spanish Stage in the Time of Lope de Vega*. New York, 1909.

Richards, Kenneth and Laura. *The Commedia dell'arte. A Documentary History*. Oxford: Basil Blackwell for The Shakespeare Head Press, 1990.

Ritter, Naomi. *Art as Spectacle. Images of the Entertainer Since Romanticism*. Columbia, Missouri: University of Missouri Press, 1989.

Robertson, Pamela E.C. *The Commedia dell'arte*. Natal: The University Press, 1960.

Rolfe, Bari. *Commedia dell'Arte, A Scene Study Book*. Oakland: Personabooks, 1977.

_____ . *Farces, Italian Style*. Oakland: Personabooks, 1978.

_____ , ed. *Mimes on Miming*. London: Millington Books, 1979.

Rose, Enid. *Gordon Craig and the Theatre*. London: Sampson Low, Marston & Co., 1931.

Rosenfeld, Sybil. *Foreign Theatrical Companies in Great Britain in the 17th and 18th Centuries*. London: 1955.

_____ . *The Theatre of the London Fairs in the 18th Century*. Cambridge, England: 1960.

Rowen, Shirley and David. *Carnival in Venice*. New York: Harry N. Abrams, Inc., 1989.

Rudlin, John. *Jacques Copeau*. Cambridge: Cambridge University Press, 1986.

Rudnitsky, Konstantin. *Meyerhold the Director*. Translated by George Petrov. Ann Arbor, Michigan: Ardis, 1981.

_____ . *Russian and Soviet Theater 1905-1932*. New York: Harry N. Abrams, 1988.

Saint-Denis, Michel. *Training for the Theatre*. New York: Theatre Arts Books, 1982.

Sainz de Robles, Federico Carlos. *Jacinto Benavente, Apuntes para una Bibliografia*. Madrid: Instituto de Estudios Madrilenos, 1954.

Salerno, Henry F., ed. *Scenarios of the Commedia dell'arte: Flaminio Scala's Il teatro delle favole rappresentative*. New York: New York University Press, 1967.

Salmon, Eric, ed. *Granville Barker and His Correspondents*. Detroit: Wayne State University Press, 1986.

Samson, Jim. *The Music of Szymanowski*. New York: Taplinger Publishing Co., 1981.

Sand, Maurice. *The History of the Harlequinade*. Two volumes. London: Benjamin Blom, 1968.

Sanesi, Ireneo. *La commedia.* 2d ed. Milano: Vallardi, 1954.

Sayler, Oliver. *Max Reinhardt and His Theatre*. New York: Brentano's, 1926.

_____ . *The Russian Theatre*. New York: Brentano's, 1922.

Schechter, Joel. *Durov's Pig. Clowns, Politics and Theatre*. New York: Theatre Communications Group, 1985.

Schmidt, Paul, ed. *Meyerhold at Work*. Austin, Texas: University of Texas Press, 1980.

Schouvaloff, Alexander, ed. *The Theatre Museum. Victoria and Albert*. London: Scala Books, 1987.

Schumacher, Claude. *Alfred Jarry and Guillaume Apollinaire*. New York: Grove Press, 1985.

Schwartz, Isadore A. *The Commedia dell'arte and its Influence on French Comedy in the Seventeenth Century*. New York: Columbia, 1933.

Segel, Harold B. *Turn of the Century Cabaret*. New York: Columbia University Press, 1987.

Selbourne, David. *The Making of "A Midsummer Night's Dream."* London: Methuen, 1982.

Senelick, Laurence. *The Age and Stage of George L. Fox, 1825-1877*. Hanover and London: University Presses of New England, 1988.

_____ . *Cabaret Performance. Vol. I: Europe 1890-1920. Sketches, Songs, Monologues, Memoirs*. New York: Performing Arts Journal Publications, 1989.

_____ . *Gordon Craig's Moscow "Hamlet"*. Westport, Connecticut: Greenwood Press, 1982.

_____ ed. *Russian Satiric Comedy*. New York: Performing Arts Journal Publications, 1983.

_____ . *Russian Dramatic Theory from Pushkin to the Symbolists*. Austin, Texas: University of Texas Press, 1981.

Shank, Theodore. *American Alternative Theatre*. London and Basingstoke: Macmillan, 1982.

Shaw, Bernard. *Three Plays for Puritans*. New York: Brentano's, 1929.

_____ . *Our Theatres in the Nineties*. London: Constable, 1932.

Shaw, Martin. *Up to Now*. London: Oxford University Humphrey Milford Press, 1929.

Simonson, Lee. *The Stage is Set*. New York: Theatre Arts Books, 1970.

Slonim, Marc. *Russian Theater. From the Empire to the Soviets*. New York: Collier Books, 1962.

Smith, Bill. *The Vaudevillians*. New York: Macmillan Publishing Co., Inc., 1976.

Smith, Susan Valeria Harris. *Masks in Modern Drama*. Berkeley, California: University of California Press, 1984.

Smith, Winifred. *Commedia dell'arte*. New York: Columbia University Press, 1912.

_____ . *Italian Actors of the Renaissance*. New York: Coward-McCann, Inc., 1930.

Sogliuzzo, A. Richard. *Luigi Pirandello: The Playwright in the Theatre*. Metuchen, New Jersey and London: The Scarecrow Press, 1982.

Speaight, George. *The History of the English Puppet Theatre*. London: 1955.

_____ . *Punch and Judy*. Boston: Plays, Inc., 1970.

Spiers, Ronald. *Bertolt Brecht*. New York: St. Martin's Press, 1987.

310

Starkie, Walter. *Jacinto Benavente*. London, New York: Humphrey Milford Oxford University Press, 1924.

_____ . *Luigi Pirandello 1867-1936*. Berkeley and Los Angeles, California, 1965.

Stein, Charles W., ed. *American Vaudeville As Seen By Its Contemporaries*. New York: Alfred A. Knopf, 1984.

Stern, Ernst. *My Life, My Stage*. London: Victor Gollancz Ltd., 1951.

Storey, Robert F. *Pierrot: A Critical History of a Mask*. Princeton: Princeton University Press, 1978.

_____ . *Pierrots on the Stage of Desire. Nineteenth Century French Literary Artists and the Comic Pantomime*. Princeton: Princeton University Press, 1985.

Styan, J.L. *Max Reinhardt*. Cambridge: Cambridge University Press, 1982.

_____ . *Modern Drama in Theory and Practice. II. Symbolism, Surrealism and the Absurd*. Cambridge: Cambridge University Press, 1981.

Swortzell, Lowell. *Here Come the Clowns*. New York: The Viking Press, 1978.

Symons, James M. *Meyerhold's Theatre of the Grotesque. The Post-Revolutionary Productions, 1920-1932*. Coral Gables, Florida: University of Miami Press, 1971.

Symonds, John Addington. *Renaissance in Italy*. New York, 1935.

Tairov, Alexander. *Notes of a Director*. Translated, and with an introduction by William Kuhlke. Coral Gables, Florida: University of Miami Press, 1969.

Taviani, Ferdinando and Mirella Schino. *Il segreto della commedia dell'arte: la memoria delle compagnie italiane del XVI, XVII e XVIII secolo*. Firenze: Casa Usher, 1982.

Taylor, Rogan. *The Death and Resurrection Show*. London: Blond, 1985.

Tessari, Roberto. *Commedia dell'arte: la maschera e l'ombra*. Milano: Mursia, 1984.

Therault, Suzanne. *Commedia dell'arte*. Paris: Centre National de la Recherche Scientifique, 1965.

Toll, Robert C. *On With the Show*. New York: Oxford University Press, 1976.

Tonelli, Luigi. *Il teatro italiano dalle origini ai giorni nostri*. Milano: Modernissima, 1924.

Towsen, John H. *Clowns*. New York: Hawthorn Books, Inc., 1976.

Ungar-Middleton, Clive. *The Entertainers*. New York: St. Martin's Press, 1980.

van Erven, Eugène. *Radical People's Theatre*. Bloomington and Indianapolis: Indiana University Press, 1988.

Varneke, B.V. *History of the Russian Theatre. Seventeenth Through Nineteenth Century*. New York: The Macmillan Company, 1951.

Wade, Allan, ed. *The Letters of W.B. Yeats*. New York: The Macmillan Company, 1955.

Wadsworth, Philip A. *Molière and the Italian Theatrical Tradition*. French Literature Publications Company, 1977.

Waldau, Roy S. *Vintage Years of the Theatre Guild, 1928-1939*. Cleveland and London: The Press of Case Western Reserve University, 1972.

Walton, J. Michael, ed. *Craig on Theatre*. London: Methuen, 1983.

Wellwarth, George E., and Alfred G. Brooks, eds. *Max Reinhardt 1873-1973*. Binghamton, New York: Max Reinhardt Archive, 1973.

Wilson, A.E. *King Panto*. New York: E.P. Dutton and Co., Inc., 1935.

Wilson, Garff B. *Three Hundred Years of American Drama and Theatre From 'Ye Bare and Ye Cubb' to Chorus Line*. Englewood Cliffs, New Jersey: Prentice-Hall, Inc., 1982.

Weinberg, Bernard. *A History of Literary Criticism in the Italian Renaissance*. Chicago, 1961.

Welleford, William. *The Fool and His Scepter: A Study in Clowns and Jesters and Their Audience*. Evanston, Illinois: 1969.

Welsford, Enid. *The Fool: His Social and Literary History.* New York: 1936.

Whitton, David. *Stage Directors in Modern France.* Manchester: Manchester University Press, 1987.

Willett, John, ed. *Brecht on Theatre. The Development of an Aesthetic.* New York: Hill and Wang, 1964.

Wilson, Albert E. *The Story of Pantomime.* London: Home & Van Thal, 1949.

Worrall, Nick. *Modernism to Realism on the Soviet Stage. Tairov -- Vakhtangov -- Okhlopkov.* Cambridge: Cambridge University Press, 1989.

Young, Stark. *Immortal Shadows.* New York: Charles Scribner's Sons, 1948.

Articles:

Alba, Manuel Sito. "The Commedia dell'Arte: Key to the Source of *Don Quixote*," *The Theatre Annual*, 1982, Vol. XXXVII.

Ambrose, G.B. [pseudonym for Gordon Craig] "Real Acting or, Can the Actor Create? Some Evidence He Can," *The Mask*, 1923, Vol. IX.

"Art de la comédie, comédie de l'art. Entretien avec Carlo Boso," *Jeu*, 1985, Vol. 35: 1.

"The Artist of the Theater: A Colloquy Between Eugene O'Neill and Oliver M. Sayler," *Shadowland*, 1922, Vol. 7, No. 2.

Atkinson, Brooks. "According to Reinhardt," *The New York Times*, November 18, 1927.

_____ . "Dutch to Russian," *The New York Times*, October 23, 1927, Section VIII.

_____ . "Guitry et Femme," *The New York Times*, December 28, 1926.

_____ . "The Play," *The New York Times*, October 17, 1933.

_____ . "Theatre -- Marcel Marceau," *The New York Times*, September 22, 1955.

_____ . "Intellectual Comedy at the Guild," *The New York Times*, March 23, 1926.

Avery, Emmett L. "Dancing and Pantomime on the English Stage, 1700-1737," *Studies in Philology*, July 1934, Vol. XXXI.

B.F. "*Song of Songs* and *The Show Booth* at Matinees," *The New York Tribune*, April 4, 1923.

Bader, A.L. "The Modena Troupe in England," *Modern Language Notes*, June 1935.

Ballerini, Luigi, and Giuseppe Risso. "Dario Fo Explains. An Interview," *The Drama Review*, March 1978, Vol. 22, No. 1 (T77).

Baretti, Joseph. "Carlo Gozzi and His Plays: An Extract from the *Manners and Customes of Italy*," *The Mask*, January 1911, Vol. III, Nos. 7-9.

Bargainnier, Earl F. "Davidson and Hofmannsthal on Naxos," *Theatre Research International*, Winter 1979/80.

Barker, Harley Granville. "Letter to Jacques Copeau," *Theatre Arts Monthly*, October 1929, Vol. 13.

Barnes, Clive. "Theater: Historic Staging of *Dream*," *The New York Times*, August 28, 1970.

Barrault, Jean-Louis. "Four Directors," Theatre Quarterly, April-June 1973, Vol. III, No. 10.

Baxanall, Lee. "The San Francisco Mime Troupe Perform Brecht," *Praxis*, 1975, Vol. I.

Bazzoni, Jana O'Keefe. "The Carnival Motif in Pirandello's Drama," *Modern Drama*, September 1987, Vol. XXX, No. 3.

"Benavente in the Round," *The New York Times*, December 1, 1951.

Bentley, Eric. "Copeau and the Chimera," *Theatre Arts Monthly*, January 1950.

_____ . "The Italian Theatre," *The New Republic*, October 5, 1953.

_____ . "Pirandello and Performance," *Theatre Three*, Fall 1987, No. 3.

LIVERPOOL JOHN MOORES UNIVERSITY
LEARNING SERVICES

314

Berson, Misha. "Dell'Arte Players of Blue Lake, California," *Drama Review*, June 1983, Vol. 27, No. 2, (T98).

Blau, Herbert. "Comedy Since the Absurd," *Modern Drama*, Vol. 25, 1982.

Bonner, Geraldine. "M. Copeau's Players," *The New York Times*, March 17, 1918, Section IV.

Boughner, Daniel C. "The Braggart in Italian Renaissance Comedy," *Publication of the Modern Language Association*, March 1943.

_____. "Don Armado and the Commedia dell'arte," *Studies in Philology*, April 1940.

Burian, Jarka. "Czech Theatre, 1988: Neo-Glasnost and Perestroika," *Theatre Journal*, Vol. 41, No. 3, October 1989.

_____. "Otomar Kreyca's Use of the Mask," *The Drama Review*, September 1972.

Busi, Frederick. "Cervantes' Use of Character Names and the *Commedia dell'arte*," *Romance Notes*, 1977, Vol. 25, No. 3.

E.G.C. [Gordon Craig] "Harlequin, A Note and Some Dates by E.G.C.," *The Mask*, 1927, Vol. XIII, No. 3.

Calendoli, Giovanni. "The Theatre of the Grotesque," *The Drama Review*, March 1978, Vol. 22, No. 1 (T77).

Camerlain, Lorraine. "Art de la comédie, comédie de l'art: entretien avec Carlo Boso," *Jeu*, 1985, Vol. 35, No.1

Campbell, O.J. "The Italianate Background of *The Merry Wives of Windsor*," *Essays and Studies in English and Comparative Literature*, 1932, Vol. VIII.

"Can the *Fool* Be Revived?" *The Nation*, December 25, 1913, Vol. 97, No. 2530.

Chamfleury, Jules. "Jean Gaspard Deburau. Some Notes on a Celebrated Pierrot, with an introductory word by Pierre Rames [pseudonym for Dorothy Nevile Lees]," *The Mask*, July 1914, Vol. VII, No. 1.

Chanceral, Léon. "Permanence et reveil de la Commedia dell'arte en France," *Rivista di studi teatrali*, 1954, Nos. 9/10.

Chaplin, Charlie. "Pantomime and Comedy," *The New York Times*, January 25, 1931, Section VIII.

Chatfield-Taylor, H.C. "Birthplace of the Modern Drama," *Drama*, February 1913, No. 9.

Chesley, Brent. "Correcting Errors Concerning Messink's *The Choice of Harlequin* (1781)," *Restoration and 18th Century Theatre Research*, Second Series, Winter 1988, Vol. III, No. 2.

Chiari, J. "Jacques Copeau," *World Review*, January-June 1952.

Clark, Barrett H. "The Last of the Pierrots," The Drama, August-September 1923, Vol. XIII.

_____ . "Strindberg, Reinhardt and Berlin," *Drama*, May 1914, Vol. 14.

Clubb, Louise George. "Italian Comedy and *The Comedy of Errors*," *Comparative Literature*, Fall 1967.

Cope, Jackson I. "Goldoni's Secret," *Theatre Survey*, Vol. 31, No. 2, November 1990.

Copeau, Jacques. "An Essay of Dramatic Renovation: The Théâtre du Vieux-Colombier," translated by Richard Hiatt. *Educational Theatre Journal*, December 1967, Vol. XIX, No. 4.

Corbin, John. "Barrieized Pinero," *The New York Times*, April 8, 1923, Section VIII.

_____ . "Molière Reborn," *The New York Times*, December 2, 1917, Section IX.

_____ . "Shakespeare's *Twelfth Night*, *The New York Times*, February 25, 1919.

Corrigan, Beatrice. "Harlequin in America," *The Canadian Forum*, November 1933.

Cox, Rebecca. "Marcel Marceau Speaks," *Prompt*, 1968, No. 11.

"Craig on Reinhardt," *The New York Times*, February 24, 1931.

Craig, Edward A. "Gordon Craig at Home," *Adam International Review*, 1966, Nos. 307-8-9.

_____ . "The Actor and the Über-marionette," *The Mask*, April 1908, Vol. 1, No. 2.

_____ . "Editorial Notes," *The Mask*, July 1910, Vol. III, Nos. 1-3.

_____ . "Letter to the Editor," *Theatre Arts Monthly*, October 1924, Vol. VIII.

_____ . "Memories of Isadora Duncan," *The Listener*, June 5, 1952, Vol. XLVII, No. 1214.

_____ . "Masks and Mimes," *The Observer*, November 1, 1931.

_____ . "A Plea for Two Theatres," *The Mask*, September 1918, Vol. VIII, No. 6.

_____ . "The Characters of the Commedia dell'arte; A List Compiled by Gordon Craig," *The Mask*, January 1912, Vol. IV, No. 3.

_____ . "The Commedia dell'arte Ascending," *The Mask*, October 1912, Vol. V, No. 2.

_____ . "Conversations with My Real Friends," *The Mask*, January 1913, Vol. V, No. 3.

_____ . "A Letter from Gordon Craig," *The Mask*, April 1911, Vol. III, Nos. 10-12.

_____ . "Letters to the Editor. The Music Hall and the Church," *The Mask*, January 1914, Vol. VI, No. 3.

_____ . "A Note on Italian and English Theatres," *Anglo-Italian Review*, April 1919.

_____ . "Shakespeare's Plays," *The Mask*, October 1913, Vol. VI, No. 2.

_____ . "To the Beggars and Despised Persons," *The Mask*, October 1913, Vol. VI, No. 2.

_____ . "To the Editor of Theatre Arts Monthly," *Theatre Arts Monthly*, October 1924, Vol. VIII, No. 10.

Creigh, G. "Zelauto and Italian Comedy: A Study in Sources," *Modern Language Quarterly*, June 1968, Vol. 29.

"Critics Criticized -- A Revival in Italy," *The Mask*, October 1912, Vol. V, No. 2.

Croce, Benedetto. "Commedia dell'arte," *Theatre Arts Monthly*, December 1933, Vol. 17.

Cummings, Scott. "Commedia's Essence is Survival (with Gusto)," *American Theatre*, December 1990.

Curtis, Jerry. "Echos de la *commedia dell'arte* dans *L'Amédée* de Eugène Ionesco," *Romance Notes*, 1974, Vol. 16.

D'Amico, Silvio. "Petrolini," *Theatre Arts Monthly*, November 1935.

_____ . "Reinhardt, Goldoni e la Commedia dell'Arte," *Nuovo Antologia*, June 1, 1932, Vol. 361.

"Dario Fo: Andiamo a Ridere," *A.R.T. News*, May 1987, Vol. 7, No. 4.

Day, Barbara. "Czech Theatre from the National Revival to the Present Day," *New Theatre Quarterly*, August 1986, Vol. II, No. 7.

Deak, Frantisek. "Antonin Artaud and Charles Dullin: Artaud's Apprenticeship in Theatre," *Educational Theatre Journal*, October 1977.

Defries, Amelia. "Origins and Social Significance of Harlequin and of the Commedia dell'arte," *Sociological Review*, October 1927.

Despot, Adriane. "Jean-Gaspard Deburau and the Pantomime at the Theatre des Funambules," *Educational Theatre Journal*, October 1975, Vol. XXVII, No. 3.

"Domenico Biancolelli. A Biographical Note," *The Mask*, April 1912, Vol. IV, No. 4.

318

"Double Bill at the Vieux Colombier," *The New York Times*, March 6, 1918.

Dukes, Ashley. "The Mask of Comedy," *Theatre Arts Monthly*, August 1925.

Ecnk, John J. "Stevens' Crispin as the Clown," *Texas Studies in Literature and Language*, Autumn 1961, Vol. III.

Esslin, Martin. "Max Reinhardt. High Priest of Theatricality," *The Drama Review*, 1974 (T74).

"Exquisite Fantasy of Rhapsodic Love," *The New York Times*, October 27, 1913.

F. "The Commedia dell'arte," *The Mask*, October 1912, Vol. V, No. 2.

Fido, Franco. "Myth and Reality in the *Commedia dell'arte*," *Italian Quarterly*, Spring 1968, Vol. II, No. 44.

Fisher, Ben. "Jarry and Florian: Ubu's Debt to Harlequin," *Nottingham French Studies*, 1988, Vol. 27.

Fisher, James. "Edward Gordon Craig and the Commedia dell'arte in the Twentieth Century," *From the Bard to Broadway*. Ed. by Karelisa V. Hartigan. Lanham, Maryland: University Press of America, 1987.

_____ . "Harlequinade: Commedia dell'Arte on the Early Twentieth Century British Stage," *Theatre Journal*, March 1989, Vol. 41, No. 1.

_____ . "*The Show Booth*: Commedia dell'Arte on the Twentieth Century American Stage," *New England Theatre Journal*, 1990, Vol. 1, No. 1.

Fletcher, Ifan Kyrle. "Italian Comedians in England in the Seventeenth Century," *Theatre Notebook*, 1954, Vol. VIII.

Fo, Dario. "Dialogue with an Audience," *Theatre Quarterly*, Autumn 1979, Vol. IX, No. 35.

_____ . "Some Aspects of Popular Theatre," translated by Tony Mitchell. *New Theatre Quarterly*, May 1985, Vol. 1, No. 2.

Freeman, Donald. "News of Reinhardt," *The New York Times*, November 30, 1924, Section VIII.

"French Company in Molière Farce," *The New York Times*, November 28, 1917, Section II.

G.N. [pseudonym for Gordon Craig] "Foreign Notes," *The Mask*, January 1911, Vol. III, Nos. 7-9.

Gardner, Paul. "Theater: *Chief Thing*," *The New York Times*, April 30, 1963.

Gaw, A. "The Evolution of *The Comedy of Errors*," *Publication of the Modern Language Association of America*, 1926.

George, David. "The *commedia dell'arte* and the Circus in the Work of Jacinto Benavente," *Theatre Research International*, Spring 1981.

_____ . "Harlequin Comes to Court: Valle-Inclán's *La marquesa Rosalinda*," *Forum for Modern Language Studies*, October 1983, Vol. 19, No. 4.

Gerould, Daniel. "Bim-Bom and the Afanasjew Family Circus," *The Drama Review*, March 1974, Vol. 18, No. 1 (T61).

_____ . "Paul Margueritte and *Pierrot Assassin of His Wife*," *The Drama Review*, March 1979, Vol. 23, No. 1 (T81).

Gherardi, Evaristo. "The Introduction to *Le Theatre Italien* of Evaristo Gherardi, Written by himself; Translated, with a Biographical Note Upon the Author by Dorothy Nevile Lees," *The Mask*, April 1911, Vol. III, Nos. 10-12.

_____ . "The Preface to *Le Theatre Italien*," *The Mask*, April 1911, Vol. III, Nos. 10-12.

Goggio, Emilio. "Dramatic Theories in the Prologues to the Commedie Erudite of the Sixteenth Century," *Publication of the Modern Language Association*, June 1943.

Goldsmith, R.H. "Wild Man on the English Stage [and in Italy]," *Modern Language Review*, October 1958, Vol. 53.

Golub, Spencer. "Mysteries of the Self: The Visionary Theatre of Nikolai Evreinov," *Theatre History Studies*, 1982, Vol. II.

Gordon, Mel. "Meyerhold's Biomechanics," *The Drama Review*, September 1974, Vol. 18, No. 3 (T-63).

Grassi, Paolo. "The Milan Piccolo Teatro," *World Theatre*, 1962, Vol. XI, No. 2.

Grassi, Paolo, and Giorgio Strehler, "Sixteen Years of the Piccolo Teatro," *Tulane Drama Review*, Spring 1984, Vol. 8.

Gray, H.D. "The Sources of *The Tempest*," *Modern Language Notes*, 1921, Vol. xxxv.

Green, Martin. "Evelyn Waugh and the Commedia dell'arte," *New York Arts Journal*, 1976, Vol. 1, Nos. iii-iv.

"Guerilla Theatre," *Time*, October 18, 1968.

Gundolf, Cordelia. "Molière and the Commedia dell'arte," *A.U.M.L.A.: Journal of the Australasian Universities Modern Language Association*, 1973, Vol. 39.

"Hampden Harlequinade," *The New York Times*, October 15, 1929.

Harrigan, Edward. "American Playwrights on the American Drama," *Harper's Weekly*, February 2, 1889, Vol. 33.

Herrick, Marvin T. "New Drama of the Sixteenth Century," *Journal of English and Germanic Philology*, October 1955, Vol. 54.

Hobson, H. "Copeau on Molière," *Drama*, Winter 1978, No. 123.

Holden, Joan. "Comedy and Revolution," *Arts in Society*, 1969, Vol. 6, No. 3.

Hoover, Marjorie L. "The Meyerhold Centennial," *The Drama Review*, September 1974, Vol. 18, No. 3 (T-63).

Houghton, Norris. "Theory into Practice: A Reappraisal of Meierhold," *Educational Theatre Journal*, October 1968, Vol. XX, No. 3.

Howells, William Dean. "Editor's Study," *Harper's New Monthly Magazine*, June-November 1886, Vol. 73.

Hulbert, Dan. "A Rare Old Play Comes to Light," *The New York Times*, April 25, 1982, Section II.

"Interview: Jean Giraudoux," *The New York Herald Tribune*, November 7, 1937.

"Interview: Charles Ludlam," *Performing Arts Journal*, Spring/Summer 1978, Vol. III, No. 1.

J.S. [pseudonym for Gordon Craig] "The Commedia dell'Arte or Professional Comedy," *The Mask*, January 1911, Vol. III, Nos. 7-9.

_____ . [pseudonym for Gordon Craig] "The Commedia dell'Arte or Professional Comedy," *The Mask*, April 1911, Vol. III, Nos. 10-12.

_____ . [pseudonym for Gordon Craig], "Madame Bernhardt and Variety," *The Mask*, January 1911, Vol. III, Nos. 7-9.

Jent, Deanna. "Colombaioni Present *I Saltimbanchi,*" *Theater*, Summer/Fall 1987.

Kahane, H. "Arthur Kahane, Reinhardt's Dramaturge," *Theatre Research International*, October 1978, Vol. 4.

Katz, Albert M. "The Genesis of the Vieux Colombier: The Aesthetic Background of Jacques Copeau," *Educational Theatre Journal*, December 1967, Vol. XIX, No. 4.

Kaufman, H.A. "Trappolin supposed a prince and *Measure for Measure,*" *Modern Language Quarterly*, June 1957, Vol. 18.

Kern, Edith. "Beckett and the Spirit of the Commedia dell'arte," *Modern Drama*, September 1966.

Kiernander, Adrian. "The Théâtre du Soleil, Part One: A Brief History of the Company," *New Theatre Quarterly*, Vol. II, No. 7, August 1986.

Kirby, E.T. "Mask: Abstract Theatre Modern and Primitive," *Drama Review*, September 1972.

Kueppus, B. "Max Reinhardt's *Sumurun,*" *Drama Review*, March 1980, Vol. 24.

L.C. "A Go at Commedia Dell'Arte," *The New York Times*, November 22, 1951.

Lamont, Rosette. "Reviews of *La Tempesta* and *Minna von Barnhelm,*" *Performing Arts Journal*, 1984, Vol. VIII, No. 2 (23).

Lanson, Gustave. "Molière and Farce," translated by Ruby Cohn. *Tulane Drama Review*, Winter 1963, Vol. 8 (T22).

Lea, Kathleen M. "Connections and Contrasts between the Commedia dell'arte and English Drama," *Rivista di studi teatrali*, 1954, Nos. 9/10.

_____ . "Sir Ashton Cokayne and the Commedia dell'arte," *Modern Language Review*, January 1928.

Leabhart, Thomas. "An Interview with Etienne Decroux," *Mime Journal*, 1974, Vol. 1.

_____ . "Etienne Decroux on Masks," *Mime Journal*, 1975, Vol. 2.

_____ . ed. *Mime Journal*, Nos. 9-10, 1979, Allendale, Michigan: The Performing Arts Center. (Issue devoted to Jacques Copeau).

Lehmann, A.G. "Pierrot and *fin de siecle,"* *Romantic Mythologies*. Edited by Ian Fletcher. London, 1967.

Lelièvre, Renée. "La Commedia dell'arte vue par George et Maurice Sand," *Cahiers de l'association internationale des études françaises*, 1963, No. 15.

Levi, Cesare. "Signor Brighella," *The Mask*, July 1912, Vol. V, No. 1.

Lima, Robert. "The *Commedia dell'Arte* and *La Marquesa Rosalinda,"* *Ramón del Valle-Inclán*. Edited by Anthony N. Zahareas. New York: Las Americas Publishing Co., 1968.

Listerman, Randall W. "Some Material Contributions of the 'Commedia dell'arte' to the Spanish Theatre," *Romance Notes*, 1976.

Longman, Stanley Vincent. "The Modern Maschere of Ettore Petrolini," *Educational Theatre Journal*, October 1975.

"M. Dullin Acts *The Miser*," *The New York Times*, January 7, 1919.

Madden, David. "Harlequin's Stick, Charlie's Cane," *Film Quarterly*, Fall 1968.

Matthews, Brander. "The Rise and Fall of Negro Minstrelsy," *Scribner's*, 1915, Vol. 58.

Mayer, David. "The Sexuality of Pantomime," *Theatre Quarterly*, February-April 1974, Vol. IV.

Mayor, A. Hyatt. "Gordon Craig's Ideas of Drama," *Hound and Horn*, April/June 1929, Vol. 2, No. 3.

Mazzone-Clementi, Carlo. "Commedia and the Actor," *Drama Review*, March 1974, Vol. 18 (T61).

McDowell, John H. "Some Pictorial Aspects of Early Commedia dell'arte Acting," *Studies in Philology*, January 1942, Vol. 39.

_____ . "Some Pictorial Aspects of Early Mountebank Stages," *Publication of the Modern Language Association*, March 1946.

McGill, Kathleen. "Women and Performance: The Development of Improvisation by the Sixteenth-Century Commedia dell'Arte," *Theatre Journal*, Vol. 43, No. 1, March 1991.

McKee, Mary J. "*Aria da Capo*: Form and Meaning," *Modern Drama*, September 1966.

McLellan, Joseph. "The Spirit of Spoleto: Conquering Charleston With the Lively Arts," *The Washington Post*, May 1984.

McMahan, Jane. "The Polish Puppet Theatre: A Report from the Unima Conference," *Soviet and East European Performance*, Summer 1990, Vol. 10, No. 2.

Meeker, Marilyn. "Picasso, Massine, and Stravinsky: Putting Punch in Pulcinella," *Dance Magazine*, April 1981.

Mellamphy, Ninian. "Pantaloons and Zanies: Shakespeare's *Apprenticeship* to Italian Professional Comedy Troupes," *New York Literary Forum*, 1984, Vol. 5-6.

"Molière Comedy Acted," *The New York Times*, January 26, 1922.

"Molière's *L'Avare* at the Colombier," *The New York Times*, March 20, 1918.

Monnier, Philippe. "The Venetian Theatre and Italian Comedy in the Eighteenth Century," *The Mask*, January 1911, Vol. III, Nos. 7-9.

"More of Barrie and Three Barry-Mores," *The New York Times*, December 26, 1905.

Moody, C. "Vsevolod Meyerhold and the *Commedia dell'arte*," *Modern Language Review*, Vol. 73, October 1978, pp. 859-869.

Moody, Richard. "Negro Minstrelsy," *Quarterly Journal of Speech*, October 1944, Vol. 30, No. 3.

N.J.A. "Theatre: Arte Troupe," *The New York Times*, July 5, 1957.

Nathan, George Jean. "Pantaloons A-Posture," *The Mask*, 1923, Vol. IX.

Nicholson, David. "Gozzi's *Turandot*: A Tragicomic Fairy Tale," *Theatre Journal*, December 1979, Vol. 31, No. 4.

Nicoll, Allardyce. "A Company of Masks," *Opera News*, January 16, 1965.

Nietzsche, Friedrich. "A Word on Masks," translated by Helen Zimmern. *The Mask*, April 1910, Vol. II, Nos. 10-12.

Oliver, Roger W. "Performance, Italian Style," *American Theatre*, January 1988, Vol. 4, No. 10.

Orani, Aviv. "Realism in Vakhtangov's Theatre of Fantasy," *Theatre Journal*, December 1984, Vol. 36, No. 4.

P. "Foreign Notes," *The Mask*, July 1912, Vol. V, No. 1.

Paolucci, Anne. "Comedy and Paradox in Pirandello's Plays (An Hegelian Perspective)," *Modern Drama*, Vol. 20, 1977.

Pearson, Tony. "Evreinov and Pirandello: Twin Apostles of Theatricality," *Theatre Research International*, Vol. 12, No. 2.

Perrucci, Andrea. "The Commedia dell'arte or Professional Comedy. Directions as to the Preparation of a Performance from a Scenario, Translated from the *Arte Rappresentativa ed all'improviso* of Andrea Perrucci, 1699," *The Mask*, October 1911, Vol. IV, No. 2.

Peterson, D.L. "Two Productions by Copeau: *The Tricks of Scapin* and *Twelfth Night*," *The Drama Review*, Spring 1984, Vol. 28, No. 1, T101.

Phialas, P.G. "Massinger and the Commedia dell'arte," *Modern Language Notes*, February 1950.

Phillips, James E. "A Commedia dell'arte," *Quarterly of Film, Radio, TV*, Fall 1954.

Pilikian, H.I. "Max Reinhardt and Total Theatre," *Drama*, Winter 1968, Vol. 91.

Pirrotta, Nino. "Commedia dell'arte and Opera," *Musical Quarterly*, July 1955, Vol. XLI.

Place, E.B. "Does Lope de Vega's *Gracioso* Stem in Part from Harlequin?" *Hispana*, 1934, Vol. XVII.

Poli, Giovanni. "Commedia dell'Arte: A Renewal of the Theatre," *Players Magazine*, January 1963, Vol. 39.

"Quaint Play Opens the Punch and Judy," *The New York Times*, November 11, 1914.

Quinn, Michael L. "The Comedy of Reference: The Semiotics of Commedia Figures in Eighteenth-Century Venice," *Theatre Journal*, Vol 43, No. 1, March 1991.

Rea, Kenneth. "Reconstructing the Commedia dell'arte," *Drama*, 1986, 1st Quarter, No. 159.

_____ . "Review," *The Guardian*, January 20, 1989.

Rehin, George F. "Harlequin Jim Crow: Continuity and Convergence in Blackface Clowning," *Journal of Popular Culture*, Winter 1975.

Reinhardt, Max. "New Life for the Theatre," *Bookman*, April 1934, Vol. 86.

_____ . "Of Actors," *The Yale Review*, 1928, Vol. 18, No. 1.

Riccoboni, Luigi. "A Note on the Meaning of the Word *Lazzi*," *The Mask*, October 1911, Vol. IV, No. 2.

_____ . "Riccoboni's Advice to Actors; Translated and Epitomized, with a Biographical Note on the Author by Pierre Rames [pseudonym of Dorothy Nevile Lees]," *The Mask*, April 1911, Vol. III, Nos. 10-12.

Rich, Daniel. "Jacques Callot: Three Hundred Years After," *Theatre Arts Monthly*, December 1935.

Roeder, Ralph. "Copeau, 1921," *Theater Arts Monthly*, October 1921, Vol. 5.

Rolfe, Bari. "The Mime of Jacques LeCoq," *Drama Review*, 1972.

Royce, Anya Peterson. "The Venetian Commedia: Actors and Masques in the Development of Commedia dell'arte," *Theatre Survey*, Vol. XXVII, Nos. 1 and 2, May and November 1986.

_____ . "Who Was Argentina? Player and Role in Late Seventeenth Century Commedia dell'arte," *Theatre Survey*, Vol. XXX, Nos. 1-2, May and November 1990.

Ruljancic, Dagmar. "Otomar Krejča's Gearing Up for Postrevolutionary Theatre," *Euromaske*, No. 1, Fall 1990.

Saint-Denis, Michel. "The Modern Theatre's Debt to Copeau," *The Listener*, February 16, 1950.

Sarton, May. "Copeau in Florence. Modern Theatre in a Corral," *Theatre Arts Monthly*, September 1935.

Sawyer, Paul. "The Popularity of Pantomime on the London Stage, 1720-1760," *Restoration and 18th Century Theatre Research*, 2nd Series, Vol. 5, No. 2, Winter 1990.

Scherillo, Michelle. "Capitan Fracassa," *The Mask*, April 1911, Vol. III, Nos. 10-12.

_____ . "The Commedia dell'arte," *The Mask*, January 1911, Vol. III, Nos. 7-9.

_____ . "The Genealogy of Pulcinella," *The Mask*, July 1910, Vol. III, Nos. 1-3.

Schiller, Leon de Schildenfeld. "Two Theatres, Introduction to *An Essay on the Grotesque Theatre*," *The Mask*, January 1909, Vol. I, No. 11.

_____ . "Two Theatres (concluded)," *The Mask*, February 1909, Vol. I, No. 12.

Schrickx, Willem. "Commedia dell'arte Players in Antwerp in 1576: Drusiano and Tristano Martinelli," *Theatre Research International*, February 1976.

Scott, Virginia P. "The Infancy of English Pantomime: 1716-1723," *Educational Theatre Journal*, May 1972, Vol. 24, No. 2.

_____ . "The Jeu and the Role: Analysis of the Appeals of the Italian Comedy in France in the Time of Arlequin-Dominique," *Western Popular Theatre*. Edited by David Mayer and Kenneth Richards. London: Methuen and Co., 1977.

Scott, Walter B. "Commedia dell'arte and Molière," *Charleston Drama Bulletin*, 1931.

Semar, John [pseudonym for Gordon Craig]. "The Commedia dell'arte or Professional Comedy," *The Mask*, October 1910, Vol. III, Nos. 4-6.

_____ . "The Commedia dell'arte or Professional Comedy," *The Mask*, April 1911, Vol. III, Nos. 10-12.

_____ . "Editorial Notes," *The Mask*, July 1910, Vol. III, Nos. 1-3.

_____ . "The Pre-Shakespearean Stage: Some Facts About It. The Men Before Shakespeare," *The Mask*, October 1913, Vol. VI, No. 2.

Senelick, Laurence. "Nikolay Evreinov's *Inspector General*," *Performing Arts Journal*, 1984, 22, Vol. VIII, No. 1.

Shergold, N.D. "Ganassa and the *Commedia dell'arte* in Sixteenth Century Spain," *Modern Langauge Review*, July 1956, Vol. LI.

Signorelli, Maria. "Puppets and Marionettes in Italy Today," *World Theatre*, 1962, Vol. XI, No. 2.

Smith, Winifred. "The Academies of the Popular Italian Stage in the XVIth Century," *Modern Philology*, April 1911, Vol. viii.

_____ . "A Comic Version of Romeo and Juliette," *Modern Philology*, October 1909, Vol. 7.

_____ . "The Earl of Essex on the Stage," *Publication of Modern Language Association of America*, 1926, Vol. xli.

_____ . "G.B. Andreini as a Theatrical Innovator," *Modern Language Review*, 1922, Vol. xvii.

_____ . "Italian and Elizabethan Comedy," *Modern Philology*, April 1908, Vol. 5.

_____ . "Two Commedia dell'arte on the *Measure for Measure* Story," *Romanic Review*, 1922, Vol. xiii.

Sologub, Fyodor. "The Theatre of One Will," translated by Daniel Gerould. *The Drama Review*, December 1977, Vol. 21, No. 4 (T76).

Spiers, A.G.H. "Modern Stage-Setting," *The Nation*, December 27, 1917, Vol. 105, No. 2739.

Steele, Eugene. "Shakespeare, Goldoni, and the Clowns," *Comparative Drama*, Fall 1977.

Steele, Eugene, and David Welsh, "The Commedia dell'arte in Eighteenth-Century Poland and Russia," *Forum Italicum*, 1975, Vol. 9, No. 4.

Stone, Rochelle. "Aleksandr Blok and Bolesław Lesmian as Proponents and Playwrights of the New, Symbolist Drama: A Comparison," *Theatre Journal*, December 1984, Vol. 36, No. 4.

Storey, Robert F. "The Pantomime of Jean-Gaspard Deburau at the Théâtre des Funambules (1819-1846)," *Theatre Survey*, May 1982, Vol. XXIII, No. 1.

_____ . "Verlaine's Pierrots," *Romance Notes*, 1979, Vol. XX.

Strehler, Giorgio. "The Giants of the Mountain," *World Theatre*, May/June 1967, Vol. 16, No. 3.

Svehla, Jarolslav. "Jean Gaspard Deburau: The Immortal Pierrot," translated by Paul Wilson. *Mime Journal*, 1977, No. 5.

Tessari, Roberto. "Actor Training in Italy," *New Theatre Quarterly*, May 1988, Vol. IV, No. 14.

Tonelli, Franco. "Molière's *Don Juan* and The Space of the Commedia dell'Arte," *Theatre Journal*, December 1985, Vol. 37, No. 4.

Torda, Thomas Joseph. "Tairov's *Princess Brambilla*: A Fantastic,

Phantasmagoric *Capriccio* at the Moscow Kamerny Theatre," *Theatre Journal*, December 1980, Vol. 32, No. 4.

Toscan, Richard, and Kathryn Ripley, "The San Francisco Mime Troupe: Commedia to Collective Creation, *Theatre Quarterly*, June 1975.

Trimpi, Helen P. "Harlequin-Confidence-Man: The Satirical Tradition of Commedia dell'arte and Pantomime in Melville's *The Confidence Man*," *Texas Studies in Literature and Language*, Spring 1974.

Uraneff, Vadim. "Commedia dell'arte and American Vaudeville," *Theatre Arts Monthly*, October 1923.

Vautel, Clement. "M. Jacques Copeau at the Comédie-Française, As It Might Have Been," *Theatre Arts Monthly*, October 1929, Vol. 13.

Volbach, Walther R. "Memoirs of Max Reinhardt's Theatres, 1920-1922," *Theatre Survey*, Vol. XIII, No. 1A, Fall 1972.

Wells, Mitchell P. "Some Notes on the Early Eighteenth Century Pantomime," *Studies in Philology*, October 1935, Vol. XXXII.

Williams, David. "*A Place Marked by Life*: Brook at the Bouffes du Nord," *New Theatre Quarterly*, February 1985, Vol. 1, No. 1.

Wilmeth, M.W. and J.R. "Theatrical Elements in Voodoo: The Case of Diffusion," *Journal for the Scientific Study in Religion*, March 1977, Vol. 16.

Wolff, M. "Shakespeare und die Commedia dell'arte," *Shakespeare-Jahrbuch*, 1910, Vol. xlvi.

Woollcott, Alexander. "The Play," *The New York Times*, December 24, 1920.

Worrall, Nick. "Meyerhold Directs Gogol's *Government Inspector*," *Theatre Quarterly*, July-September 1972, Vol. 11, No. 7.

_____ . "Meyerhold's Production of *The Magnificent Cuckold*," *The Drama Review*, March 1973.

Wright, Louis B. "Will Kemp and the Commedia dell'arte," *Modern Language Notes*, December 1926, Vol. XLI, No. 8.

330

Yorick [pseudonym for Gordon Craig]. "A History of Puppets, Puppets in England," *The Mask*, January 1914, Vol. VI, No. 3.

_____ . "A History of Puppets, Puppets in France," *The Mask*, July 1914, Vol. VII, No. 1.

_____ . "A History of Puppets, Puppets in Italy," *The Mask*, January 1913, Vol. V, No. 3.

_____ . "A History of Puppets, Puppets in Italy," *The Mask*, April 1913, Vol. V, No. 4.

_____ . "A History of Puppets, Puppets in Italy," *The Mask*, July 1913, Vol. VI, No. 1.

_____ . "A History of Puppets, Puppets in Spain," *The Mask*, October 1913, Vol. VI, No. 2.

Zacha, Richard B. "Iago and the *Commedia dell'arte*," *Arlington Quarterly*, 1969, Vol. 2, No. 2.

Zaiser, Rainer. "*En Attendant Godot*: Reflections on Some Parallels Between Beckett and Pirandello," *Journal of European Studies*, 1988, Vol. xviii.

Dissertations:

Barker, Walter Lawton. *Three English Pantalones: A Study in Relations Between the Commedia dell'arte and Elizabethan Drama*. Ph.D 1966, University of Connecticut. Dissertation Abstracts International, Order No. AAD67-04524, Page 3419 in Volume 27/10-A, 222 pages.

Cappelletti, Salvatore. *Dalla Commedia dell'arte agli inizi della* Commedia Borghese: *Luigi Riccoboni e la sua riforma del teatro*. Ph.D 1978, Brown University. Dissertation Abstracts International, Order No. AAD79-06527, Pt. A US ISSN 0419-4209, Pt. B US ISSN 0419-4217, Ann Arbor, Michigan, 1979, 39: 6155A-56A, 187 pages.

Cautero, Salvatore Gerard. *Studies in the Influence of the Commedia dell'arte on English Drama: 1605-1800*. Ph.D 1962, University of Southern California. Dissertation Abstracts International, Order No. AAD62-06045, Page 2516 in Volume 23/07, 262 pages.

Cheron, George. *The Dramas of Mixail Kuzmin*. Ph.D 1982, University of California, Los Angeles. Dissertation Abstracts International, Order No. AAD82-29660.

Groves, William McDonald. *The Commedia dell'arte and the Shakespearean Theatre: A Study of the Relevance of Applying Commedia dell'arte Techniques to Shakespearean Production*. Ph.D 1983, University of Colorado at Boulder. 44/09A, p. 2626, PUV84-00896, 310 pages.

Helder, Jack. *The Commedia dell'arte Tradition and Three Later Novels of Henry James*. Ph.D 1974, Bowling Green State University. Dissertation Abstracts International, Order No. AAD74-17177, Page 1047 in Volume 35/02-A, 235 pages.

King, William Lupo. *The Treatment of Commedia dell'arte Characters in the Dramatic Works of Regnard, Dufresny, and Marivaux*. Ph.D 1968, The University of North Carolina at Chapel Hill. Dissertation Abstracts International, Order No. AAD69-10177, Page 328 in Volume 30/01-A, 216 pages.

Lubé, Jane R. *Commedia dell'arte Elements in Some German Twentieth-Century Dramas*. Ph.D 1973, University of Pennsylvania. Dissertation Abstracts International, Order No. AAD73-24178, Page 1920 in Volume 34/04-A, 224 pages.

Mathews, Darrell Eugene. *The Commedia dell'arte on the High School Stage: A Production Analysis of Jerry Blunt's "A Gap in Generations"*. M.A. 1976, California State University, Fullerton. Masters Abstracts, Order No. AAD13-09233, Page 61 in Volume 15/01, 181 pages.

McDowell, John H. *An Iconographic Study of the Early Commedia dell'arte (1560-1650)*. Ph.D 1937, Yale University. University Microfilms International, Page 83 in Volume W1937.

Mead, Mary. *Through the Zani's Mask: Examining Blok's* Balaganchik *and Evreinov's* Veselaja Smert. Ph.D 1975, Harvard University.

Rotta, John Bernard. *The Commedia dell'arte in the Theatre of Cervantes*. Ph.D 1976, State University of New York at Stony Brook. Dissertation Abstracts International, Order No. AAD76-19719, Page 1598 in Volume 37/03-A, 203 pages.

Salerno, Henry Frank. *The Elizabethan Drama and the Commedia dell'arte*. Ph.D 1956, University of Illinois at Urbana-Champaign. Dissertation Abstracts International, Order No. AAD00-18195, Page 1901 in Volume 16/10, 209 pages.

Schwartz, Isadore Adolphe. *The Commedia dell'arte and Its Influence on French Comedy in the Seventeenth Century*. Ph.D 1931, New York University. Dissertation Abstracts International, AAD73-20840, Volume S0146, 203 pages.

Smith, Winifred. *The Commedia dell'arte, A Study in Italian Popular Comedy*. Ph.D 1912, Columbia University. University Microfilms International, Page 39 in Volume L1912, 291 pages.

Sostek, Edward Leon. *The Commedia dell'arte: A Study in Dramatic Form*. Ph.D 1976, The University of Iowa. Dissertation Abstracts International, Order No. AAD77-03775, Page 4715 in Volume 37/08-A, 180 pages.

Steele, Eugene Joseph. *The Improvisational Art in Shakespeare and the Commedia dell'arte*. Ph.D 1975 The University of Michigan. Dissertation Abstracts International, Order No. AAD75-20457, Page 1488 in Volume 36/03-A, 142 pages.

Thompson, Juli Ann. *Ariane Mnouchkine and the Théâtre du Soleil*. Ph.D 1986, University of Washington, Seattle. Dissertation Abstracts, Order No. AAD87-06684.

Trapido, Joel. *An Encyclopaedic Glossary of the Classical and Mediaeval Theatre and of the Commedia dell'arte*. Ph.D 1943, Cornell University. University Microfilms International, Page 88 in Volume W1943.

NOTES

Introduction

1. Dion Clayton Calthrop and Granville Barker. *The Harlequinade. An Excursion.* Boston: Little, Brown, and Company, 1918, pp. 86-87.

2. One twelfth century French medieval myth (retold in modern times most memorably by Anatole France (Jacques-Anatole-François Thibault; 1844-1924) under the title "Our Lady's Juggler") told the commedic story of a poor *jongleur* who has nothing material to offer the Virgin Mary on her feast day. As the story ends, a couple of churchmen come upon him juggling at the altar of the Holy Mother. As the churchmen are about to protest this blasphemy, the statue of the Virgin comes to life, descends from her altar, and wipes the sweat from the brow of the little juggler. Clowns and fools appear regularly in other religious rituals, stories, and documents, including the Talmud and the Koran.

3. The name commediadell'arte was not given to improvising actors until the eighteenth century, when it was deemed necessary to create a descriptive title that belied the declining fortunes of improvised comedy.

4. The first known contract bringing together a small troupe of actors to play improvised comedy is dated 1545 and identifies Matio de Rei (d. 1553) as organizer. He performed under the stage name Zanini.

5. Their names varied and included Isabella, Lucia, and Florinda for the women. Octavio and Lelio are the names which recur most often for the men.

6. Some of the names taken by actors playing Pantalone include Zanobio da Piombino, Facanappa, Il Bernardone, Cassandre, and Il Biscegliese.

7. Joseph Spencer Kennard. *Masks and Marionettes* Port Washington, N.Y.: Kennikat Press, 1967, p. 52.

8. Among the most frequent names used by actors portraying Dottore were Gratiano, Forbizon, and Partesana.

9. Some of the recorded names used by various actors playing Capitano and similar characters include Spavento della Valle Inferna, Fracassa, Terremoto, Scaramuccia, Rinoceronte, Crispin, Pasquino, Rodomont, Giangurgolo Calabrese, Coccodrillo, Rogantino, Spezzafero, Grillo, Il Vappo, Il Smargiasso, and Matamoros. Francesco Andreini was among the first actors to play this role. It was later popularized by Tiberio Fiorilli (c.1605-1694) in France as Scaramouche.

10. Pierre L. Duchartre. *The Italian Comedy.* Authorized translation from the French by Randolph T. Weaver. N.Y.: Dover Publications, Inc., 1966, p. 132.

11. Other names of *zanni* similar to Arlecchino include Trivellino, Truffa or Truffaldino, Guazzeto, Zaccagnino, and Bagatino.

12. Brighella was originally a thief and a bully, but he later became a servant who retained an affinity for lying and trickery.

13. Scapino was a crafty and amoral character who avoided danger at all costs. The first actor associated with this role was Francesco Gabrielli (? -1654).

14. Pulcinella was nearly identical to Maccus, an absurdly stupid servant found in Atellan farce. He is a hump-backed and slow-witted grotesque, dressed in an oversized, baggy white costume and a cap similar to a fez.

15. Characters similar to Columbina also played under such names as Ricciolina and Franceschina.

16. In English, see the works by Pierre L. Duchartre, Allardyce Nicoll, Winifred Smith, Joseph Spencer Kennard, and Giacomo Oreglia, listed in the bibliography, for more detailed information on the diverse characters of commedia.

17. In *The Triumph of Pierrot* by Martin Green and John Swan (Macmillan, 1986), a study of the influence of commedia's Pierrot on modern art and literature, the authors coin the word "commedic," thus avoiding overuse of the infelicitous "commedia-inspired" or "commedia-style." I shall borrow their adjective throughout this book.

18. The *commedia erudita* plays of Lodovico Ariosto (1474-1533), Bernardo Dovizi da Bibbiena (1470-1520), Pietro Aretino (1492-1556) share many common qualities, especially stereotypical characters, with *commedia dell'arte*. Even writers of tragedies dabbled in *commedia erudita*. Giambattista Della Porta (1535-1615), the last major writer of *commedia erudita*, developed *commedia grave* (serious comedy), which paved the way for later tragi-comedies. His plays, including *The Moor* (1607), were a rich source of plots, characters, and comic business for the scenarists of *commedia dell'arte*. Ludovico Dolce (1508-1568?), best remembered for his tragedy, *Marianna* (1565), wrote five comedies: *The Boy* (1541), *The Captain* (1545), *The Husband* (1545), *The Pimp* (1551), and, the finest and most original, *The Play of Fabrizio* (1549). Aside from the obvious Plautine inspiration, Dolce's comedies include elements from Machiavelli and *commedia dell'arte*, especially a similar set of stereotypical characters.

19. Niccolo Machiavelli. *The Mandrake*. Introduction by Christian Gauss. The Oxford University Press "World's Classics" translation from Luigi Ricci, revised by E.R.P. Vincent. New York and Scarborough, Ontario: New American Library, 1980, p. 90.

20. Niccolo Machiavelli. *Clizia*. Introduction and translation by Oliver Evans. Great Neck, N.Y.: Barron's Educational Series, Inc., 1962, pp. 25-26.

21. Angelo Beolco, "Ruzzante Returns from the Wars," English version by Angela Ingold and Theodore Hoffman, *The Classic Theatre*, edited by Eric Bentley. Garden City, N.Y.: Doubleday and Company, Inc., 1958, p. 77.

22. French commedia character derived from Italy's Pedrolino, a *zanni* role first played by Giovanni Pellesini (c.1526-1612). The character incorporated elements of Pulcinella, but is best known in the variation made famous by Deburau in which the character became a gentle mime pining away for a lost or unrequited love.

23. Martin Green and John Swan. *The Triumph of Pierrot*. New York: Macmillan, 1986, p. xiii.

24. Gordon Craig, "The Commedia dell'arte Ascending," *The Mask*, Vol. V, No. 2, October 1912, p. 104.

Chapter 1. The Finger in the Eye: Commedia in Italy

1. "Dario Fo: Andiamo a Ridere," *A.R.T. News*, 7, 4 (May 1987), p. 6.

2. Carlo Goldoni. *The Comic Theatre*. Translated from the Italian by John W. Miller. Lincoln, Nebraska: University of Nebraska Press, 1969, p. 31.

3. Goldoni and Gozzi influenced many nineteenth century Italian dramatists, especially Francesco Augusto Bon (1788-1858), whose trilogy of Ludro plays, *Ludro's Big Day* (1832), *Ludro's Marriage* (1837), and *Ludro's Old Age* (1837), were written partially in Venetian dialect. Bon's plays also demonstrate the commedic influence of Molière and Beaumarchais. In the middle of the nineteenth century, Paolo Ferrari (1822-1889) turned to Goldoni for the very subject matter of his play, *Goldoni and His Sixteen New Comedies* (1852). Drawing on Goldoni's memoirs, Ferrari depicts Gozzi as the villainous Carlo Zigo in a psychological treatment of the intrigues of Goldoni's personal and professional life.

4. Antonietta Portulano, Pirandello's wife and the mother of his children Stefano, Lietta, and Fausto.

5. cited in Jana O'Keefe Bazzoni, "The Carnival Motif in Pirandello's Drama," *Modern Drama*, Vol. XXX, No. 3, September 1987, p. 421.

6. cited in A. Richard Sogliuzzo. *Luigi Pirandello: The Playwright in the Theatre*. Metuchen, N.J. and London: The Scarecrow Press, 1982, p. 77.

7. Ibid.

8. cited in Eric Bentley, ed. "Pirandello and Performance," *Theatre Three*, No. 3, Fall 1987, p. 70.

9. Oscar Büdel. *Pirandello*. New York: Hillary House Publishers Ltd., 1966, p. 97.

10. cited in Bazzoni, "The Carnival Motif in Pirandello's Drama," *Modern Drama*, p. 414.

11. cited in Bentley, ed. "Pirandello and Performance," *Theatre Three*, p. 69.

12. Ibid.

13. cited in Sogliuzzo, *Luigi Pirandello: The Playwright in the Theatre*, p. 77.

14. Ibid., p. 244.

15. Luigi Pirandello. *On Humor*. Introduced, Translated, and Annotated by Antonio Illiano and Daniel P. Testa. Chapel Hill, North Carolina: The University of North Carolina Press, 1960, p. 5.

16. Ibid., p. 93.

17. Ibid.

18. Ibid., p. 103.

19. Ibid.

20. Ibid.

21. Ibid., p. 113.

22. Luigi Pirandello, "Introduction to The Italian Theater," translated by Anne Paolucci. *The Genius of the Italian Theater*. Edited by Eric Bentley. New York: Mentor Books, 1964, p. 23.

23. Ibid., p. 24.

24. Ibid., p. 24.

25. Ibid., pp. 24-25.

26. Ibid., p. 25.

27. Ibid.

28. Ibid.

29. Ibid., p. 21.

30. Ibid., p. 26.

31. Ibid., pp. 26-27.

32. E. Gordon Craig, "Introduction," *The Liar. A Comedy in Three Acts*. By Carlo Goldoni. Translated by Grace Lovat Fraser. With decorations by C. Lovat Fraser. London: Selwyn and Blount, Ltd., 1922, p. 7.

33. Pirandello, "Introduction to The Italian Theater," *The Genius of the Italian Theater*, p. 27.

34. Ibid.

35. Ibid., p. 28.

36. Ibid.

37. Ibid.

38. Ibid.

39. Ibid., p. 29.

40. Luigi Pirandello. *Sicilian Comedies. Cap and Bells. Man, Beast and Virtue*. Translated by Norman A. Bailey and Roger W. Oliver. New York: Performing Arts Journal Publications, 1983, pp. 27-28.

41. Eric Bentley. *The Pirandello Commentaries*. Evanston, Illinois: Northwestern University Press, 1984, p. 29.

42 Luigi Pirandello. *Right You Are*. A Stage Version with an Introduction and Notes by Eric Bentley. New York: Columbia University Press, 1954, p. 115.

43. Ibid., p. 130.

44. Ibid.

45. Ibid.

46. Stark Young. *Immortal Shadows*. New York: Charles Scribner's Sons, 1948, p. 86.

47. Bentley. *The Pirandello Commentaries*, p. 7.

48. Luigi Pirandello. *Three Plays. The Rules of the Game. Six Characters in Search of an Author. Henry IV*. Translated by Robert Rietty and Noel Cregeen, John Linstrum, Julian Mitchell. London: Methuen, 1985, p. 74.

49. Ibid., p. 96.

50. Ibid., p. 115.

51. Ibid., p. 133.

52. Ibid.

53. Ibid.

54. Luigi Pirandello, "Preface to *Six Characters in Search of an Author*," *Naked Masks*. Edited by Eric Bentley. New York: E.P. Dutton & Co., Inc., 1952, p. 366.

55. Pirandello, *Three Plays. The Rules of the Game, Henry IV, Six Characters in Search of an Author*, p. 197.

56. Ibid., p. 200.

57. Ibid.

58. cited in Sogliuzzo, *Luigi Pirandello, Director: The Playwright in the Theatre*, p. 43.

59. In a characteristic gesture of his admiration for *Six Characters in Search of an Author*, Reinhardt practically took it apart structurally and made many changes.

60. Luigi Pirandello. *To-Night We Immprovise*. Translated from the Italian, and with an Introduction by Samuel Putnam. New York: E.P. Dutton & Co., Inc., 1932, p. 18.

61. Pirandello, *To-Night We Improvise*, p. 25.

62. Ibid., p. 26.

63. cited in Sogliuzzo, *Luigi Pirandello, Director: The Playwright in the Theatre*, p. 41.

64. Ibid.

65. cited in F.L. Lucas. *The Drama of Chekhov, Synge, Yeats, and Pirandello*. London: Cassell and Co., 1963, p. 364.

66. Pirandello, *Naked Masks*, p. 209.

67. cited in Lucas, *The Drama of Chekhov, Synge, Yeats, and Pirandello*, p. 357.

68. Kenneth Macgowan. *The Theatre of Tomorrow*. New York: Boni and Liveright, 1921, p. 252.

69. Giovanni Calendoli, "The Theatre of the Grotesque," *The Drama Review*, Volume 22, No. 1 (T77), March 1978, p. 14.

70. Other playwrights of the era were indebted to commedia. Ugo Betti (1892-1953) wrote realistic plays which are somewhat narrower in scope, but he also clearly owes much to Pirandello. His plays show characters as victims of contradictory impulses and in need of the judgment of others, while in search of a viable religion. His early plays, including *The Wonderful Island* (1930) and *The Women of the Shield* (1927), are strikingly similar to the *fiabe* of Gozzi. At approximately the same time, Raffaele Viviani's (1888-1950) Neapolitan dialect theatre continued the modern tradition which earlier in the twentieth century had found expression in the plays of Salvatore Di Giacomo (1860-1934), and would later influence the plays of Eduardo De Filippo. The roots of these plays are, of course, commedia, especially in that the form and content of them depends on the personality and experience of the actor. As an actor himself, Viviani played the *scugnizzo* (Neapolitan street urchin) and his earliest plays were rough and loosely connected sketches (*macchiette*) involving stereotypical personalities on the Neopolitan street scene. His play *The Alley* (1917) is typical of his work in that Naples in not just the background, but the *subject* of the play as well.

71. As it had in earlier times, commedia found its way onto puppet stages. The Ferrari family of Parma, under the direction of Giordano Ferrari (son of Italo Ferrari), and the Manteo family of Sicily, under the direction of Miguel Manteo (1909-1989), attempted to preserve aspects of commedia in their marionette theatres. Italo Ferrari had declared that modern puppeteers were "the successors to the Commedia dell'Arte, our works sometimes merely follow a theme that we embroider. But this is only possible because we know all the characters who take part. We have studied each one for years so that before parading them before the footlights we already know exactly how they will react to any situation, familiar or unexpected. . ."(Maria Signorelli, "Puppets and Marionettes in Italy Today," *World Theatre*, Vol. XI, No. 2, 1962, pp. 182-183).

72. Paolo Grassi, "The Milan Piccolo Teatro," *World Theatre*, Vol. XI, No. 2, 1962, p. 168.

73. Strehler led the Piccolo Teatro continually except for a brief period between 1968 and 1973, when he returned and Grassi moved on to the directorship of La Scala.

74. Since 1962, Ferruccio Soleri has distinguished himself with well over two thousand performances as Arlecchino at the Piccolo Teatro.

75. Ibid., p. 174.

76. Ibid.

77. Paolo Grassi and Giorgio Strehler, "Sixteen Years of the Piccolo Teatro," *Tulane Drama Review*, Vol. 8, Spring 1984, p. 30.

78. Ibid.

79. Jan Kott. *Theatre Notebook. 1947-1967*. Translated from the Polish by Boleslaw Taborski. Garden City, N.Y.: Doubleday & Company, Inc., 1968, p. 28.

80. Ibid.

81. Ibid., p. 173.

82. Giorgio Strehler, "The Giants of the Mountain," *World Theatre*, Vol. 16, No. 3, May/June 1967, pp. 263-264. Strehler puts considerable energy to staging operas, although his love of commedia surfaces in many of his selections, including *Ariadne auf Naxos, The Marriage of Figaro*, and *Love for Three Oranges*.

83. Ronald Spiers. *Bertolt Brecht*. New York: St. Martin's Press, 1987, p. 155.

84. Strehler, "The Giants of the Mountain," *World Theatre*, p. 265.

85. Ibid.

86. Jan Kott. *The Bottom Translation*. Evanston, Illinois: Northwestern University Press, 1984, p. 134.

87. Rosette Lamont, "Reviews of *La Tempesta* and *Minna von Barnhelm*," *Performing Arts Journal* (23), Vol. VIII, No. 2, 1984, p. 56.

88. Kott, *The Bottom Translation*, p. 138.

89 Lamont, "Reviews of *La Tempesta* and *Minna von Barnhelm*," *Performing Arts Journal*, p. 58.

90. Kott, *The Bottom Translation*, p. 141.

91. Lamont, "Reviews of *La Tempesta* and *Minna von Barnhelm*," *Performing Arts Journal*, pp. 58-59.

92. Ibid., p. 60.

93. Venetian-born Giovanni Poli led two *teatro stabile* troupes, Teatro Ca'Foscari and Teatro L'Avogaria, both of which produced commedic productions, including *La commedia degli zanni* (1960), which won the grand prize at the Festival of Nations in Paris. Poli admitted that his approach to commedia was inspired by Strehler's work, especially in "the staging; the interpretation; the characterizations." (cited in John D. Mitchell. *Theatre: The Search for Style*. Midland, Michigan: Northwood Institute Press, 1982, pp. 139-140) Noting that commedia was "the most important thing that Italy gave to world theatre,"(Ibid., p. 140) Poli stressed that it "is related to the anti-naturalistic, in which the interpretation of the actor is not an expression of reality nor an imitation of daily reality, but is an abstraction of daily reality." Especially

conscious of the rhythmic qualities of commedia, Poli's productions of commedic plays by Goldoni and Gozzi emphasized the significance of movement and music. His commedia was "halfway in the direction of dance. The two elements, music and mime, dominate the style of commedia."(Ibid.) Other *teatro stabile*, including the Teatro d'Arte of Genoa, founded in 1951, and the Teatro Stabile of Turin, founded in 1955, followed the lead of the Piccolo Teatro.

94. Grassi left in 1967, after which a variety of directors led the school, including critic Luigi Ferrante, actor Checco Rissone, Roberto Leydi, and Renato Palazzi, who has recently taken over.

95. cited in Roberto Tessari, "Actor Training in Italy," *New Theatre Quarterly*, Vol. IV, No. 14, May 1988, p. 187.

96. Ibid., pp. 187-188. A number of other training schools for the actor sprang up in Italy during the 1970's, when a major upswing in interest in theatre performance occured among the young. The Florence Initiation Centre, The Rome Performance Laboratory, The Florence Theatre Workshop, among others, attempt to bring commedia, and other Italian stage traditions into contemporary theatre, not as museum theatre, but as an energizing force for both actor and audience.

97. The Teatro di Roma recently presented Roberto Rossellini's (1906-1977) previously unproduced *Pulcinella*, in an adaption by Manil Santanelli, under the direction of Maurizio Scaparro. The production, a "delicate paean to the theatre and the actor,"(Roger W. Oliver, "Performance, Italian Style," *American Theatre*, Vol. 4, No. 10, January 1988, p. 50) was set against a plain cyclorama and emphasized "the magical, transformational quality of the theatre."(Ibid.) It was viewed by some critics as a homage to Strehler in its celebration of commedia, and connected as well to the plays of Pirandello. *Pulcinella* was performed at New York's Italy on Stage Festival in 1987, where director Luca Ronconi's (b. 1933) commedic production of Goldoni's *The Loving Servant*, a "complex embodiment of Italian performance traditions,"(Ibid., p. 51) also appeared. Ronconi's first production as a director was Goldoni's *The Good Wife*, in 1963, and his subsequent staging of Ariosto's *Orlando Furioso*, in 1969, mingled the traditions of Italian folk spectacle with state-of-the-art staging practices. Like most directors of his generation, Ronconi has proudly allied himself with commedia and the other greatest traditions of Italian theatre. Gianfranco De Bosio (b. 1924) put together a student company in 1949 which he christened Il Ruzzante. He produced the commedia plays of his company's namesake in open air productions, but also produced a variety of classical and modern plays. Vito Pandolfi (b. 1917), a graduate a D'Amico's Accademia d'Arte Drammatica, wrote many books on his theories of theatre art, especially commedia, and staged a highly successful revival of original commedia scenarios in 1947, which he called *The Masks' Fair*.

98. Kenneth Rea, "Reconstructing Commedia dell'arte," *Drama*. 1st quarter 1986, No.159, p. 18.

99. Ibid.

100. Ibid.

101. Ibid.

102. Ibid., p. 19.

103. Kenneth Rea, "Review." *The Guardian*, January 20, 1989.

104. Ibid. Contemporary commedia can also be found in the work of a smaller troupe, a pair of clowns, Carlo Colombaioni and Alberto Vitali, brothers-in-law and inheritors of a family commedia tradition that dates back to the seventeenth century. Their production, *I Saltimbanchi*, has toured extensively, and it was a featured attraction at the 1986 Chicago International Theatre Festival. Their particular brand of commedia derives from those commedic traditions that had been absorbed by circus clowns. Carlo spent his early years in the circus, but the simplicity of their performances (no scenery and their props include a few ordinary objects such as a broom, a colander, a blanket, and a couple of chairs) and the mixture of silent mime, verbal interplay, slapstick, and topical satire is pure commedia. Their performances are typically divided into three parts: a classic commedia routine, contemporary treatments of commedia style, and a sketch that moves beyond the bounds of traditional commedia. They lampoon high art, such as Shakespeare or grand opera, as well as myths (their William Tell spoof hilariously presents Carlo devouring the apple on his head before Alberto can fire a single arrow). At the Chicago Festival, they performed a sketch as two hobos which was based on a four-hundred year old scenario that stunningly resembled the existential clowning in Beckett's *Waiting for Godot*. In 1983, the Colombaioni brothers performed Dario Fo's *Patapumfete*, a clown show.

105. Marvin Carlson. *The Italian Stage. From Goldoni to D'Annunzio*. Jefferson City, N.C. and London: McFarland and Company, Inc., 1981, pp. 172-173.

106. Silvio D'Amico, "Petrolini," *Theatre Arts*, November 1935, p. 842.

107. Ibid.

108. Ibid., p. 850.

109. cited in Stanley Vincent Longman, "The Modern *Maschere* of Ettore Petrolini," *Educational Theatre Journal*. October 1975, p. 386.

110. Ibid., p. 377.

111. Peppino (1903-1980) went on to become a well-known film actor and specialized on the stage in light Italian comedies and farces, as well as the plays of Molière. Titina (1898-1963) worked mostly with Eduardo, appearing in leading roles in many of his plays.

112. Eduardo De Filippo, "The Intimacy of Actor and Character," *Actors on Acting*. Edited by Toby Cole and Helen Krich Chinoy. New York: Crown Publishers, Inc., 1970, p. 471.

113. Ibid.

114. Eric Bentley, *What is Theatre? Incorporating The Dramatic Event and Other Reviews 1944-1967*. New York: Atheneum, 1968, p. 338.

115. De Filippo, "The Intimacy of Actor and Character," *Actors on Acting*, p. 472.

116. Mario Prosperi, "Marina Confalone: A Neapolitan Actress," *The Drama Review*, Vol. 29, No. 4 (T108) Winter 1985, p. 14.

117. cited in Mimi D'Aponte, "From Italian Roots to American Relevance: The Remarkable Theatre of Dario Fo," *Modern Drama*, Vol. XXXII, No. 4, December 1989, p. 537.

118. Dario Fo, "Dialogue with an Audience," *Theatre Quarterly*, Vol. IX, No. 35, Autumn 1979, p. 15.

119. Dario Fo, "Some Aspects of Popular Theatre," translated by Tony Mitchell. *New Theatre Quarterly*. Vol. 1, No. 2, May 1985, p. 136.

120. "Dario Fo: Andiamo a Ridere," p. 6.

121. cited in Luigi Ballerini and Giuseppe Risso, "Dario Fo Explains. An Interview," *The Drama Review*, Vol. 22, No. 1 (T77), March 1978, p. 36.

122. Ibid.

123. Ibid.

124. Ibid.

125. Ibid.

126. Ibid., p. 38.

127. Ibid.

128. cited Tony Mitchell. *Dario Fo. The People's Court Jester*. London: Methuen, 1984, pp. 15-16.

129. Fo, "Some Aspects of Popular Theatre," *New Theatre Quarterly*, pp. 135-136.

130. Ibid., p. 136.

131. cited in Mitchell, *Dario Fo. The People's Court Jester*, p. 44.

132. *Dario Fo and Franca Rame Theatre Workshops at Riverside Studios, London. April 28th, May 5th, 12th, 13th & 19th 1983*. London: Red Notes, 1983, p. 8.

133. Ibid.

134. Ibid.

135. Ibid.

136. Ibid.

137. cited in Marvin Carlson. *Theories of the Theatre*. Ithaca and London: Cornell University Press, 1984, p. 477.

138. Fo, "Some Aspects of Popular Theatre," *New Theatre Quarterly*, p. 133.

139. *Dario Fo and Franca Rame Theatre Workshops at Riverside Studios, London. April 28th, May 5th, 12th, 13th & 19th 1983*, p. 26.

140. cited in Mitchell, *Dario Fo. The People's Court Jester*, p. 72.

141. Ibid., p. 73.

142. Fo, "Some Aspects of Popular Theatre," *New Theatre Quarterly*, p. 135.

143. Ibid., p. 131.

144. Commedia has also had some impact on cabaret entertainments in Italy. For example, Aldo Trionfo's *La Borsa di Arlecchino*, founded in 1957, staged avant-garde international plays, many with commedic elements. Trionfo has directed the National Academy of Theatre Arts in Rome since 1980.

145. Dario Fo, "Author's Note," *Accidental Death of an Anarchist*. Adapted by Gavin Richards from a translation by Gillian Hanna. Introduced by Stuart Hood. London: A Methuen Paperback, 1987, p. xviii.

Chapter 2. The Bonds of Interest: Commedia in Spain

1. cited in Reed Anderson. *Federico Garcia Lorca*. New York: Grove Press, 1984, p. 28.

2. Some evidence suggests that commedia players appeared in Seville as early as 1538. During the 1580's Ganassa appeared several times before the royal family and in 1584 he appeared in one of Madrid's two new permanent theatres.

3. The greatest playwright of the Spanish Golden Age, Lope de Vega (1562-1635), was also influenced by commedia. In 1599 he is known to have appeared himself in a entertainment at carnival time dressed in the red costume of Pantalone. His more than two thousand plays demonstrate his interest in the form.

4. The Portugese theatre, which was fundamentally an outgrowth of the neighboring Spanish stage, was the scene of much experimentation with modern theatrical theories. In the twentieth century, playwrights such as Jose de Almada Negreiros (b. 1893) rejected the highly intellectual approach to drama and worked toward a theatre which was disassociated from the self-conscious intellectualism typical of Spanish dramatists in the early twentieth century. For him, the theatre should be considered a figurative art for the creation of amusing spectacles. His light-hearted *Pierrot and Arlequin* (1924) ties him to commedia in its spirit and use of the traditional characters. Commedia even spread to South America. Guatemalan dramatist Adolfo Drago Bracco (1894-1937), atypically for early twentieth century South American drama, ignored any sort of nationalistic flavor in his works, preferring instead the appeal of fantasy and the theatrical. His commedic work included *Colombina Wanted Flowers* (1928), a comedy set in the era of Madame Pompadour. Argentine playwright and director Osvaldo Dragún (b. 1929) committed himself to denouncing social injustices in his plays, particularly the materialism and hypocrisy of contemporary times. His play *Stories to Be Told* (1957) was performed in the style of commedia by Dragún's Teatro Popular Fray Mocho.

5. cited in David George, "The *commedia dell'arte* and the Circus in the Work of Jacinto Benavente," *Theatre Research International*, Spring 1981, p. 102.

6. Walter Starkie. *Jacinto Benavente*. Oxford: Humphrey Milford Oxford University Press, 1924,

p. 36.

7. cited in Marcelino C. Penuelas. *Jacinto Benavente*. Translated by Kay Engler. New York: Twayne Publishers, Inc., 1968, p. 110.

8. cited in Starkie, *Jacinto Benavente*, p. 161.

9. Ibid., p. 151.

10. Wilma Newberry. *The Pirandellian Mode in Spanish Literature from Cervantes to Sastre*. Albany, N.Y.: State University of New York Press, 1973, pp. 100-101.

11. Robert Lima, "The *Commedia dell'Arte* and *La Marquesa Rosalinda*," *Ramón del Valle-Inclán*. Edited by Anthony N. Zahareas. New York: Las Americas Publishing Co., 1968, p. 386.

12. Another popular form in turn-of-the-century Spain owing to commedia were the *costumbrismo* plays. These were usually one-act works depending on atmospheric local color and traditional folk types.

13. John Lyon. *The Theatre of Valle-Inclán*. Cambridge: Cambridge University Press, 1983, p. 70.

14. Lima, "The *Commedia dell'Arte* and *La Marquesa Rosalinda*," *Ramon del Valle-Inclán*, p. 395.

15. Ibid., p. 415.

16. cited in Anderson, *Federico Garcia Lorca*, p. 48.

17. Ibid., p. 51.

18. J.L. Styan. *Modern Drama in Theory and Practice, II, Symbolism, Surrealism and the Absurd*. Cambridge: Cambridge University Press, 1981, p. 86.

19. Pamela E.C. Robertson. *The Commedia dell'arte*. Natal: The University Press, 1960, p. 65.

20. Lorca was taken from his house and shot by the Fascists.

21. Marion P. Holt. *The Contemporary Spanish Theater (1949-1972)*. Boston: Twayne Publishers, 1975, p. 101.

Chapter 3. "Here We Are Again!": Commedia in England

1. Gordon Craig, "Critics Criticised," *The Mask*, Vol. V., No. 2, October 1912, p. 182.

2. Among Scala's scenarios, a comic version of *Romeo and Juliet* (c.1595-1596) can be found, and commedic traces in characters and passing references can also be discovered in Shakespeare's *Henry IV, Parts I and II* (1590-1592), *The Taming of the Shrew* (c.1592-1593), *Two Gentlemen of Verona* (c.1592-1593), *The Merchant of Venice* (c.1596), *Much Ado About Nothing*

(c.1598-1599), *Hamlet* (c.1600-1601), *All's Well That Ends Well* (c.1602-1603), *Othello* (1604), *Cymbeline* (1609-1610), and *The Winter's Tale* (1611). In *Love's Labor's Lost* (c.1593), several of the characters, Don Adriano de Armado, Moth, and Holofrenes mirror Capitano, a zanni, and Dottore, respectively.

3. The most useful and thorough source on the influence of commedia on English drama in this period is Kathleen M. Lea's *Italian Popular Comedy*, published in 1934.

4. Molière's plays arrived in England in the early 1670's, bringing many French commedic traditions to the English stage. Thomas Otway (1652-1685) adapted Molière's *The Tricks of Scapin*, which appeared successfully in 1676 as *The Cheats of Scapin*. Edward Ravenscroft's (1643-1707) *Scaramouch a Philosopher, Harlequin a Schoolboy, Bravo, Merchant and Magician. A Comedy After the Italian Manner* (1677), produced at the Drury Lane with comedian Joseph Haines (d. 1701) in the lead, offered an Anglicized version of commedia, and Ravenscroft's *The Anatomist* (1697), was also indebted to commedic influences. In the eighteenth century, John Vanbrugh (1664-1726), in collaboration with William Congreve (1670-1729) and William Walsh, presented *Squire Trelooby* (1704), based on Moliere's *Monsieur de Pourceaugnac*. In 1707, Vanbrugh wrote *The Cuckold in Conceit*, taken from Molière's *Sganarelle*. Plays inspired by Molière, as well as plays in the "Italian manner," like William Mountfort's (1664-1692) *The Life and Death of Doctor Faustus. . .With the Humours and Harlequin and Scaramouche* (1685), kept the commedic flame burning in England before the arrival of pantomime in the early eighteenth century.

5. George Speaight's *The History of the English Puppet Theatre* (London, 1955) and *Punch and Judy* (Boston: Plays, Inc., 1970) offer thorough accounts of the history of Punch and Judy, and the influences on their creation.

6. Behn's model for her play was a French farce, *Harlequin, Emperor of the Moon* (1684), which Giuseppe-Domenico Biancolelli (c.1636-1688) had produced in Paris.

7. Throughout the eighteenth century, pantomimes were only performed as afterpieces, although they ultimately became more popular than the works they accompanied. Rich trained actor Harry Woodward (1717-1777) in the skills of pantomime, and Woodward began producing them at the Drury Lane Theatre in 1738, solidifying a tradition that was to become a permanent part of the fabric of English theatrical life. Even tragedians like David Garrick (1717-1779), who wrote and produced *Harlequin's Invasion* (1759), and Edmund Kean (1787-1833), occasionally delighted audiences as Harlequin in pantomimes.

8. The popularity of pantomime, particularly in England and France, lasted well into the twentieth century. Many playwrights wrote pantomimes along with their "serious" works, and some, like the great French melodramatist René-Charles Guilbert de Pixérécourt (1773-1844), were particularly influenced by pantomime (in Pixérécourt's case, the serious, sentimental pantomimes of Jean François [Arnould-] Mussot; 1734-1795). Others, like James Robinson Planché (1795-1880), remembered now for his scene designs for Charles Kemble's (1775-1854) antiquarian Shakespearean productions, wrote prolifically for the pantomime stage. Pantomime led to enormous popularity for Pierrot troupes all over England during the later part of the nineteenth century. The success of these troupes reached a pinnacle in *The Co-Optimists* (1921) by Davy Burnaby (1881-1949), a musical revue based on the traditions of Pierrot troupes. Pierrot and pantomime fundamentally faded with the death of the memorable clown Andre Séverin (1863-1930), by then, Pierrot and other manifestations of commedia had profoundly influenced many contemporary artists.

9. cited in Gerald Frow. *"Oh, Yes It Is!" A History of Pantomime*. London: British Broadcasting Corporation, 1985, p. 172.

10. *The Page* (1898-1901), *The Mask* (1908-1929), and *The Marionnette* (1918-1919), and his book *The Art of the Theatre* (1905).

11. Gordon Craig, "European Theatre from 1500 to 1900," *Unpublished Manuscript*, Bibliothèque Nationale, Paris, n.p.

12. Gordon Craig, "To the Editor of Theatre Arts Monthly," *Theatre Arts Monthly*, Vol. VIII, No. 10, October 1924, pp. 714-715.

13. Letter: Edward Gordon Craig to David Allen, May 4, 1955, 3 pp.

14. Edward Gordon Craig. *Index to the Story of My Days*. New York: The Viking Press, 1957, p. 127.

15. The tradition of Pierrot shows, particularly as seaside entertainment, began in the 1890's and usurped the popularity of nineteenth century blackfaced minstrel productions.

16. Martin Shaw. *Up to Now*. London: Oxford University Humphrey Milford Press, 1929, p. 25.

17. *The Masque of Love* was adapted from Henry Purcell's (1659-1695) music for Francis Beaumont's (1584-1616) and John Fletcher's (1579-1625) drama *The Prophetess; or, The History of Dioclesian*.

18. Max Beerbohm, "Mr. Craig's Experiment," *Around Theatres*. London: Rupert Hart-Davis, 1953, pp. 201-202.

19. Allan Wade, ed. *The Letters of W. B. Yeats*. New York: The Macmillan Company, 1955, p. 366.

20. Ibid.

21. Craig. *Index to the Story of My Days*, p. 235.

22. *Acis and Galatea* featured music by George Frideric Handel (1685-1759) and text by John Gay (1685-1732).

23. Yeats was excited by attempts to move away from the naturalistic stage. He admired Oriental forms and, most particularly, argued for the use of masks.

24. These contributions included essays by Girolamo Tiraboschi (1731-1794), Michelle Scherillo (1860-1930), Umberto Fracchia (1889-1930), Cesare Levi (1874-1926), Philippe Monnier (1865-1911), along with contributions from the assistant editor of *The Mask*, Dorothy Nevile Lees (c.1872-1966).

25. Gordon Craig, "The Characters of the Commedia dell'Arte. A List Compiled by Gordon Craig," *The Mask*, January 1912, Vol. IV, No. 3, p. 200.

26. John Semar [pseudonym for Gordon Craig], "Editorial Notes," *The Mask*, Vol. III, No. 1-3,

July 1910, p. 50.

27. Craig looked to many original commedia sources in his research on the form, and is known to have purchased a copy of Adolfo Bartoli's *Scenari inediti* in 1909. Many of Craig is unpublished works are in the Bibliotheque Nationale.

28. Ibid., p. 51.

29. Craig was only one of many modern theatre artists inspired by Oriental and Indian art forms, and to see in them parallels with commedia. The ritual dramas of China and Japan utilized masks and mime, in highly detailed and stylized ways. Traditional forms of Oriental theatre are analogous to commedia, most obviously in their use of masks, emphasis on movement, and de-emphasis of literary scripts. In *The Chinese Conception of Theatre* (Seattle and London: University of Washington Press, 1985), Tao-Ching Hsü wrote that commedia was "a type of theatre which, like the modern Chinese theatre, rose out of the popular theatre and bore prominent marks of popular taste. In both types of theatre the form had hardened before aristocratic patronage and literary interests could change it. The *commedia dell'arte*, like the Chinese theatre of to-day, had no literary value and could not be judged properly by literary standards."(p. 423) Carrying the parallel further, Hsü points out that the Chinese theatre was and is, like commedia, an actor's theatre where "the subjects of drama are such that the actors' physical skill have ample opportunity to be shown."(p. 428) Early Turkish farces were absorbed into *orta oyunu* (middle play), which involved live actors instead of puppets which were, until that time, extremely popular in Turkey. It resembled commedia in that its characters represented various ethnic groups and actors imitated their dialects while depicting their occupations and professions in daily life. It involved improvisation, broad comedy, and was played on a simple stage platform. Some scholarship has suggested that *orta oyunu* evolved from either the ancient Greek mimes via Byzantium or commedia. Others see it as a relatively new form (post-1790) that evolved from *Karagöz*. Greek *omilias*, much like commedia, involved performers reciting and improvising political verse couplets often set to music and presented in public places. Equally interesting similarities with commedia can be found in a multitude of emerging cultures, suggesting that commedia was an especially adaptable and pleasing theatrical manifestation of a basic set of human impulses common to most peoples.

30. Craig, *Index to the Story of My Days*, p. 125.

31. J.S.[pseudonym for Gordon Craig], "Madame Bernhardt and Variety," *The Mask*, Vol. III, No. 7-9, January 1911, p. 145.

32. Edward Gordon Craig, *Daybook II*, January 7, 1911, p. 165.

33. J.S. [pseudonym for Gordon Craig], "The Commedia dell'Arte or Professional Comedy," *The Mask*, Vol. III, No. 10-12, April 1911, p. 148.

34. Craig, "Critics Criticised," *The Mask*, p. 183.

35. Gordon Craig, "Shakespeare's Plays," *The Mask*, Vol. VI, No. 2, October 1913, pp. 166-167.

36. J.S.[pseudonym for Gordon Craig], "The Commedia dell'Arte or Professional Comedy," *The Mask*, Vol. III, No. 7-9, January 1911, p. 100.

37. Edward Gordon Craig, *Daybook II*, October 22, 1910, n.p.

38. Craig, *Daybook II*, February 3, 1909, p. 77.

39. Ibid.

40. Ibid.

41. Ibid.

42. Craig, *Daybook II*, May 24, 1909, p. 127.

43. Gordon Craig, "Conversations With My Real Friends," *The Mask*, Vol. V, No. 3, January 1913, p. 232.

44. Gordon Craig, "Letters to the Editor. The Music Hall and the Church," *The Mask*, Vol. VI, No. 3, January 1914, p. 258.

45. John Semar [pseudonym for Gordon Craig], "The Pre-Shakespearean Stage, Some Facts About It. The Men Before Shakespeare," *The Mask*, Vol. VI, No. 2, October 1913, p. 152.

46. Ibid.

47. Edward Gordon Craig. *The Theatre Advancing*. Boston: Little, Brown, and Company, 1919, p. 118.

48. Friedrich Nietzsche, translated by Helen Zimmern, "A Word on Masks," *The Mask*, Vol. II, No. 10-12, April 1910, p. 164.

49. Craig, *The Theatre Advancing*, p. 121.

50. Craig, *Daybook II*, January 22, 1909, p. 71.

51. Edward Gordon Craig, "The Actor and the Über-marionette," *The Mask*, Vol. I, No. 2, April 1908, p. 5.

52. Edward Gordon Craig, "A Plea for Two Theatres," *The Mask*, Vol. VIII, No. 6, September 1918, p. 22.

53. Gordon Craig, "A Note on Italian and English Theatres," *Anglo-Italian Review*, April 1919, p. 298.

54. Craig, *The Theatre Advancing*, p. 113.

55. Sheldon Cheney. *The Theatre. Three Thousand Years of Drama, Acting and Stagecraft*. New York: David McKay Company, Inc., 1967, p. 222.

56. Letter: Edward Gordon Craig to David Allen, May 4, 1955, 3pp.

57. Bernard Shaw, "Preface," *Three Plays for Puritans*. New York: Brentano's, 1929, p. xxxvi.

58. George Bernard Shaw. *Our Theatres in the Nineties*. London: Constable, 1932, Vol. II, p. 121.

59. J.M. Barrie. *What Every Woman Knows and Other Plays*. New York: Charles Scribner's Sons, 1930, p. 262.

60. Ibid.

61. Harley Granville Barker. *On Dramatic Method*. London: Sidgwick & Jackson, 1931, p. 9.

62. These include *The Marrying of Ann Leete* (1899), *The Voysey Inheritance* (1903-1905), *Waste* (1906-07), and *The Madras House* (1908-1910).

63. Laurence Housman and Granville Barker. *Prunella; or Love in a Dutch Garden*. Boston: Little, Brown, and Company, 1937, p. 23.

64. Ibid., p. 53.

65. Ibid., p. 88.

66. Laurence Housman. *The Unexpected Years*. New York and Indianapolis: The Bobbs-Merrill Company, 1936, p. 193.

67. Ibid., p. 192.

68. C.B. Purdom. *Harley Granville Barker*. London: Salisbury Square, 1955, pp. 32-33.

69. *The New York Times*, October 27, 1919, p. 9. The play was produced by the senior class of New York's Theatre Guild school in June, 1926, again under the direction of Winthrop Ames (1871-1937), with Sylvia Sidney (b. 1910), later a well-known stage and film actress, as Prunella. The production was received cordially by critics, one stating that in every respect "it came very near perfection."(*The New York Times*, June 16, 1926, p. 23).

70. Eric Salmon, ed., *Granville Barker and His Correspondents*. Detroit, Michigan: Wayne State University Press, 1986, p. 506.

71. Ibid., p 480.

72. Housman, *The Unexpected Years*, p. 205.

73. Dion Clayton Calthrop and Granville Barker. *The Harlequinade. An Excursion*. Boston: Little, Brown, and Company, 1918, pp. v-vii.

74. Ibid., pp. 6-7.

75. Ibid., p. 20.

76. Ibid., pp. 20-21.

77. Ibid., p. 23.

78. Ibid., pp. 24-25.

79. Ibid., p. 36.

80. Ibid., pp. 70-71.

81. Ibid.

82. Ibid., p. 75.

83. Ibid., p. 78.

84. Ibid., p. 79.

85. Ibid., pp. 86-87.

86. Purdom, *Harley Granville Barker*, p. 146.

87. *The New York Times*, May 11, 1921, p. 20.

88. Sacha Guitry. *Deburau*. English version by Harley Granville Barker. New York and London: G.P. Putnam's Sons, 1921, p. 221.

89. Some of these include John Hastings Turner's (b. 1892) *Punchinello*, a fictional drama about the legend of Punch; Harold Chapin's (1886-1915) *The Marriage of Columbine* (1921), which places Scaramouche and Columbine in nineteenth century Dunchester; Oliphant Down's *The Maker of Dreams* (1911), which is a Pierrot play similar to Barker's and Housman's superior *The Harlequinade*; Reginald Arkell's (1882-1959) *Columbine*; Ferdinand Bessier's *A Pierrot's Christmas*; and Thomas Dibdin's many pantomimes.

90. cited in Howard Goorney and Ewan MacColl, eds. *Agit-Prop to Theatre Workshop, Political Playscripts 1930-1950*. Manchester: Manchester University Press, 1986, p. 36.

91. Peter Brook. *The Empty Space*. New York: Avon, 1968, p. 63.

92. Ibid.

93. David Williams, "'A Place Marked by Life': Brook at the Bouffes du Nord," *New Theatre Quarterly*, Vol. 1, No. 1, Feb. 1985, p. 59.

94. David Selbourne, *The Making of "A Midsummer Night's Dream"*. London: Methuen, 1982, p. 211.

95. Clive Barnes, "Theater: Historic Staging of *Dream*," *The New York Times*, August 28, 1970, p. 15.

96. Harley Granville Barker, "The Heritage of the Actor," *Actors on Acting*. Edited by Toby Cole and Helen Krich Chinoy. New York: Crown Publishers, Inc., 1970, p. 391.

97. Ibid.

Chapter 4. Dr. Dapertutto and Company: Commedia in Russia

1. Edward Braun, trans. *Meyerhold on Theatre*. London: Eyre Methuen, 1969, p. 130.

2. Antonio Sacchi's troupe appeared in Russia as early as 1742.

3. Edward Gordon Craig. *Daybook 1909*, p. 139.

4. Vladimir Nemirovich-Danchenko (1859-1943) was Meyerhold's mentor and co-founder of the Moscow Art Theatre with Constantin Stanislavsky (1863-1938). Although he maintained a closer allegiance to Stanislavsky, he was also drawn to many of Meyerhold's concepts. Both a playwright and a director, Nemirovich-Danchenko was the Russian theatre's most skillfully diplomatic figure, managing to work effectively under both the Imperial and Soviet regimes. His philosophy of the theatre, which was somewhat more theatrical than Stanislavsky's, is well-chronicled in his autobiography, *My Life in the Russian Theatre* (1937). Although he had seen an Italian troupe perform in commedia style in Naples in 1910, Stanislavsky with a few exceptions, kept to the contemporary and fundamentally realistic drama. Danchenko, however, shared with Meyerhold an admiration for the traditions of past theatre forms, like commedia, that might enliven the modern stage.

5. cited in Paul Schmidt, ed. *Meyerhold at Work*. Austin, Texas: University of Texas Press, 1980, p. 11.

6. Vera Komissarzhevskaya (1864-1910), Russian actress and theatre manager, strenuously encouraged Symbolist productions in her theatre. In 1907 following her brief, but fruitful collaboration with Meyerhold, she replaced him with her brother, Theodore, and Nikolai Evreinov. She disbanded her company in 1908. Theodore Komissarzhevskaya (1882-1954) - emigrated to England in 1919, where he married actress Peggy Ashcroft (1907-1991) and worked with the Shakespeare Memorial Theatre as a designer and director. While there he staged productions of *The Comedy of Errors* (1938) and *The Taming of the Shrew* (1939) that included touches of commedia, obvious remnants of his early years in Russia. He viewed commedia as a form which poked fun at "militarism, profiteering, hypocrisy, false morals, ignorance, learned pomposity," and it offered "oppressed people joy and hope of a better existence."(Theodore Komisarjevsky. *The Theatre and a Changing Civilisation*. London: John Lane The Bodley Head Limited, 1935, p. 8).

7. Meyerhold directed productions of Richard Wagner's *Tristan and Isolde* (1909), Richard Strauss' *Elektra* (1913), and Igor Stravinsky's *Nightingale* (1918).

8. While working on *Columbine's Scarf*, Mikhail Kuzman suggested that Meyerhold adopt the pseudonym "Doctor Dapertutto," a character from Hoffmann's *Adventure on New Year's Eve*, so that he could work in the experimental theatres of St. Petersburg while also employed in Imperial theatres. Meyerhold also used this pseudonym for many of his published theories, especially between 1914 and 1916 in his journal, *Love for Three Oranges*, a title inspired by Gozzi's commedic fantasy which combined elements of both literary and improvisational styles.

9. German poet, novelist, composer, and stage director, Ernst Theodor Amadeus Hoffmann (1776-1822), whose short stories and novels were often dark fairytales populated with various grotesque characters, was a seminal influence on modern theatre artists attracted to the grotesque.

10. Marjorie L. Hoover. *Meyerhold. The Art of Conscious Theater*. Amherst: University of Massachusetts Press, 1974, p. 57.

11. C. Moody, "Vsevolod Meyerhold and the *Commedia dell'arte*," *Modern Language Review*,

Vol. 73, October 1978, p. 862.

12. Braun, trans. "The Fairground Booth," *Meyerhold on Theatre*, p. 129.

13. Ibid., p. 122.

14. Ibid., p. 123.

15. Ibid., p. 129.

16. Ibid., p. 127.

17. Ibid., p. 134.

18. Ibid., p. 136.

19. Ibid., p. 135.

20. cited in Schmidt, ed. *Meyerhold at Work*, p. 155.

21. Hoover, *Meyerhold. The Art of Conscious Theater*, p. 84.

22. Braun, ed., *Meyerhold on Theatre*, p. 38.

23. Ibid., pp. 131-132.

24. Ibid., p. 131.

25. cited in Schmidt, ed., *Meyerhold at Work*, p. 154.

26. Braun, ed., *Meyerhold on Theatre*, p. 81.

27. Ibid., p. 124.

28. Ibid., p. 147.

29. Meyerhold learned much about the grotesque from the writings of Ernst von Wolzogen (1855-1934), who opened the first literary cabaret in Berlin in 1901.

30. Braun, ed., *Meyerhold on Theatre*, p. 138.

31. Braun, ed., *Meyerhold on Theatre*, p. 139.

32. Hoover, *Meyerhold. The Art of Conscious Theater*, p. 47.

33. Most of Alexander Blok's (1880-1921) few other plays are similar to *The Fairground Booth* in their lyrical expression of his concern about the survival of the sublime and beautiful in a commonplace and drab world. Among his later plays, *The Rose and the Cross (1912),* which depicts the struggle between the forces of good and evil, is not as overtly commedic as *The Fairground Booth*, but it is an effective modern evocation of the spirit of commedia.

34. *The Fairground Booth* was subsequently revived in 1908 and 1914 on a double bill with Maeterlinck's *The Miracle of St. Anthony*, also directed by Meyerhold.

35. Poet Mikhail Kuzmin (1875-1936) was also a novelist, critic, translator, and cafe performer. He composed music for Meyerhold's production of *The Fairground Booth*. His interest in commedia was given its most obvious play in his poems, wherein he wrote about the "intoxicating lips of Pierrot."(Martin Green and John Swan. *The Triumph of Pierrot*. New York: Macmillan, 1985, p. 36) Kuzmin was impressed by Meyerhold's productions of the plays of Maeterlinck and Blok, and in his own *The Venetian Zanies* (1912), set in the Venice of Goldoni, Gozzi, and Longhi, he creates a tragicomic version of Otway's *Venice Preserved* in which a male friendship is destroyed over the love of a woman. It also owes a debt to Mikhail Lermontov's (1814-1841) commedic play *Masquerade*, for which he had also composed the music under Meyerhold's direction.

36. cited in Avril Pyman, *The Life of Aleksandr Blok. Volume I. The Distant Thunder 1880-1908*. Oxford: Oxford University Press, 1979, p. 268.

37. Virginia Bennett, "Russian *pagliacci*: symbols of profaned love in *The Puppet Show*," *Themes in Drama*. Edited by James Redmond. Cambridge: Cambridge University Press, 1982, p. 174.

38. Ibid., p. 173.

39. cited in Edward Braun. *The Theatre of Meyerhold* New York: Drama Book Specialists, 1979, p. 70.

40. cited in Ibid., pp. 70-71.

41. Braun, ed., *Meyerhold on Theatre*, p. 113.

42. Ibid., pp. 113-114.

43. cited in Hoover, *Meyerhold. The Art of Conscious Theater*, p. 258.

44. Braun, ed., *Meyerhold on Theatre*, p. 132.

45. Ibid., p. 133.

46. Ibid., p. 146.

47. Ibid., p. 148.

48. Meyerhold's students included film director Sergei Eisenstein (1898-1948).

49. Norris Houghton. *Moscow Rehearsals, The Golden Age of the Soviet Theatre*. New York: Grove Press, Inc., 1962, pp. 95-96.

50. Fernand Crommelynck (1885-1970), Belgian actor and dramatist, found theatrical power in the use of the mask, the grotesque, and the notion of self-inflicted torture and pain. His three-act play, *The Sculptor of Masks* (1911), labelled "theatre of the unexpressed," shows feelings and emotions through gesture, protracted silences, and sound effects. The environment is realistic, but emotions are hidden in this play about Pascal, the theatrical mask-maker, whose personal

struggle is his attempt to mingle sensual passion with beauty. The play is an important contribution to modern commedia in its use of the carnival spirit and masks as a means of expelling mass anger, hysteria, and frenzy. Crommelynck is best remembered today for *The Magnanimous Cuckold* (1920), a twentieth century re-enactment of the Greek *comus* which, in the landmark 1924 production, served as a memorable vehicle for Meyerhold's biomechanics. Crommelynck's *A Woman Whose Heart is Too Small* (1934), depicting a prudish woman's resistance to her husband's advances until she is advised by a "big-hearted" woman to share her husband's bed, presents its simple story through the use of pantomime, ballet, and music, and owes much to Molière and commedia.

51. Nikolai A. Gorchakov. *The Theater in Soviet Russia*. Translated by Edgar Lehrman. New York: Columbia University Press, 1957, p. 205.

52. Houghton, *Moscow Rehearsals. The Golden Age of the Soviet Theatre*, p. 95.

53. Braun, ed., *Meyerhold on Theatre*, p. 286.

54. Fyodor Sologub, "The Theatre of One Will," translated by Daniel Gerould. *The Drama Review*. Vol. 21, No. 4 (T76), December 1977, p. 99.

55. Ibid., p. 147.

56. Other playwrights of the period were also touched by commedia. Aleksey Nikolayevich Tolstoy (1883-1945), remembered more for his novels and science fiction than for his plays, wrote works for the theatre ranging from drama to comedy. Partly inspired by commedia, he wrote what he called "fantastic scenes" and "pamphlet bouffe," and among his more fantastic works is a one-act harlequinade, *The Young Writer* (1913). Eugene Ivanovich Zamyatin (1884-1937), a novelist, literary critic, and playwright, was invited by the Moscow Art Theatre's Second Studio to dramatize Nikolai Leskov's short story, "The Tale of the Cross-Eyed Lefty from Tula and the Steel Flea." The extremely popular result, *The Flea*, attempted in its depiction of Tsarist Russia and Victorian England to revitalize Russian folk theatre by using commedic techniques.

57. Leonid Andreyev, "The Failure of the Symbolist Theatre," *The Russian Symbolist Theatre*. An Anthology of Play and Critical Texts edited and translated by Michael Green. Ann Arbor, Michigan: Ardis, 1986, p. 365.

58. Leonid Andreev, "Letters on the Theater," *Russian Dramatic Theory from Pushkin to the Symbolists*. Translated and edited by Laurence Senelick. Austin, Texas: University of Texas Press, 1981, p. 244.

59. Andreyev, "The Failure of the Symbolist Theatre," *The Russian Symbolist Theatre*, pp. 361-362.

60. Valery Briusov, "Against Naturalism in the Theatre," *The Russian Symbolist Theatre*. An Anthology of Play and Critical Texts edited and translated by Michael Green. Ann Arbor, Michigan: Ardis, 1986, p. 25.

61. Spencer Golub. *Evreinov. The Theatre of Paradox and Transformation*. Ann Arbor, Michigan: UMI Research Press, 1984, pp. xvii-xviii.

62. Ibid., p. 35.

63. Nikolay Evreinov, "Introduction to Monodrama," *Russian Dramatic Theory from Pushkin to the Symbolists*. Translated and edited by Laurence Senelick. Austin, Texas: University of Texas Press, 1981, p. 194.

64. Nicolas Evreinoff. *The Theatre in Life*. Edited and Translated by Alexander I. Nazaroff. New York: Brentano's, 1927, p. 145.

65. Ibid., p. 23.

66. Ibid., p. 128.

67. J. Michael Walton, ed. *Craig on Theatre*. London: Methuen, 1983, p. 21.

68. Evreinoff, *The Theatre in Life*, p. 55.

69. Ibid., p. 145.

70. Tony Pearson, "Evreinov and Pirandello: Twin Apostles of Theatricality," *Theatre Research International*, Vol. 12, No. 2, Summer 1987, p. 157.

71. Theodore Komissarzhevskaya asserted that Meyerhold's interest in commedia had been inspired by announcements of a commedia season at The Ancient Theatre, but clearly Meyerhold's interest in commedia pre-dates that season by several years.

72. Nicholas Evreinoff. *The Chief Thing*. Translated by Herman Bernstein. Garden City, N.Y.: Doubleday, Page & Co., 1926, p. xii.

73. Alexander Tairov. *Notes of a Director*. Translated, and with an introduction by William Kuhlke. Coral Gables, Fla.: University of Miami Press, 1969, p. 42.

74. Ibid., p. 40.

75. Ibid., p. 100.

76. Ibid., p. 78.

77. Ibid., p. 40.

78. Ibid., p. 98.

79. Ibid., p. 95.

80. Konstantin Mardzhanov (1872-1933) influenced Tairov's ideas, especially his interest in and emphasis on pantomime. He often quoted Arthur Symons' (1865-1945) 1898 essay on the subject, which noted that pantomime was not merely a replacement of words or an equivalent of words, but that it was thinking overheard.

81. Tairov, *Notes of a Director*, p. 43.

82. Ibid., p. 44.

83. Ibid., p. 52.

84. Ibid.

85. Ibid.

86. Ibid.

87. Ibid., p. 53.

88. Ibid.

89. Ibid.

90. Ibid., p. 124.

91. Thomas Joseph Torda, "Tairov's *Princess Brambilla*: Fantastic, Phantasmagoric *Capriccio* at the Moscow Kamerny Theatre," *Theatre Journal*, Vol. 32, No. 4, December 1980, p. 491.

92. Tairov, *Notes of a Director*, p. 104.

93. Gorchakov, *The Theater in Soviet Russia*, p. 228.

94. Tairov, *Notes of a Director*, p. 126.

95. Ibid., p. 139.

96. Ibid., p. 140.

97. cited in Aviv Orani, "Realism in Vakhtangov's Theatre of Fantasy," *Theatre Journal*, Vol. 36, No. 4, December 1984, p. 463.

98. cited in Ibid., p. 469.

99. Eugene V. Vakhtangov, "The School of Intimate Experience," *Actors on Acting*. Edited by Toby Cole and Helen Krich Chinoy. New York: Crown Publishers, Inc., 1970, p. 508.

100. cited in Orani, "Realism in Vakhtangov's Theatre of Fantasy," *Theatre Journal*, pp. 466-467.

101. cited in Ibid., p. 467.

102. Ibid.

103. cited in Ibid., p. 469.

104. One of Vakhtangov's assistants, Boris Zakhava (1898-1976), played Timur in the production. After Vakhtangov's death, he joined Meyerhold's company and later became head of the Shchukin School of Acting in Moscow, holding true to many of Vakhtangov's principles.

357

105. cited in Gorchakov, *The Theater in Soviet Russia*, p. 253.

106. cited in Orani, "Realism in Vakhtangov's Theatre of Fantasy," *Theatre Journal*, p. 476.

107. Ibid.

108. Vakhtangov, "Fantastic Realism," *Directors on Directing*, p.190.

109. Brooks Atkinson, "Dutch to Russian," The New York Times, October 23, 1927, Section VIII, p. 1.

110. Oliver M. Sayler. *The Russian Theatre*. New York: Brentano's, 1922, p. 205.

111. Valentin Nikolayevich Pluchek (b. 1909), a director who also studied with Meyerhold during the 1920's, demonstrated the influence of commedia in his productions of Beaumarchais's *The Marriage of Figaro* and Gogol's *The Inspector General*. He became director of Moscow's Theatre of Satire in 1957, where he revived the recently liberated plays of Mayakovsky, as well as a popular production of Molière's *The Tricks of Scapin*.

112. Norris Houghton. *Return Engagement. A Postscript to "Moscow Rehearsals"*. New York: Holt, Rinehart and Winston, 1962, p. 102.

113. cited in Gorchakov, *The Theater in Soviet Russia*, p. 275.

Chapter 5. A Fist in the Eye: Commedia in Eastern Europe and Scandinavia

1. Jindřich Honzl, "Dynamics of the Sign in the Theater," *Semiotics of Art*. Edited by Ladislav Matejka and Irwin R. Titunik. Cambridge: The MIT Press, 1977, p. 74.

2. P., "Foreign Notes," *The Mask*, Vol. 5, No. l, July 1912, p. 84.

3. Ibid., p. 85.

4. Ibid.

5. Alexander Hevesi, "Introduction," Edward Gordon Craig. *On the Art of the Theatre*. London: Mercury Books, 1962, p. xvii.

6. Ibid.

7. Stanisław Wyspianski (1869-1907) anticipated the scenic innovations of Edward Gordon Craig and Adolphe Appia, creating a complete *mise-en-scène* for his productions.

8. After World War I, Schiller worked for a time for the Polski Teatr in Warsaw and the Reduta Theatre in Osterwa before starting the Bogusławski Theatre in 1924. There he directed a number of European classics and contemporary plays, which, along with his well-known left-wing political interests, led to the closing of the theatre in 1930. He moved his base of operations to Lwów and staged works in a number of Polish cities until he was interned at Auschwitz, where he remained until 1941. The Nazis had closed all Polish theatres, so Schiller secretly produced early Polish liturgical dramas in a Warsaw convent. At the conclusion of the

war he became director of a theatre in Łódź.

9. Rochelle Stone, "Aleksandr Blok and Bolesław Lesmian as Proponents and Playwrights of the New, Symbolist Drama: A Comparison," *Theatre Journal*, Vol. 36, No. 4, December 1984, p. 456.

10. Ibid., p. 456.

11. This troupe named itself for an earlier Russian team, Bim-Bom, which began in 1891 with I. Radunsky and F. Kortezi. Radunsky and Kortezi were later replaced by other comics, but Bim-Bom continued in Russia until well into the middle of the twentieth century.

12. cited in Daniel Gerould, "Bim-Bom and the Afanasjew Family Circus," *The Drama Review*, Vol. 18, No. 1 (T-61), March 1974, p. 103.

13. Ibid., p. 102.

14. Honzl, "Dynamics of the Sign in the Theater," *Semiotics of Art*, p. 74.

15. Ibid., p. 75.

16. Ibid., p. 74.

17. Ibid., p. 86.

18. Ibid.

19. Ibid., p. 89.

20. cited in Barbara Day, "Czech Theatre from the National Revival to the Present Day," *New Theatre Quarterly*, Vol. II, No. 7, August 1986, p. 256.

21. Ibid., p. 257.

22. Ibid.

23. Jarka Burian, "Otomar Krejča's Use of the Mask," *The Drama Review*, September 1972, p. 48.

24. Ibid., p. 49.

25. Ibid., p. 48.

26. Jarka M. Burian, "Czech Theatre, 1988: Neo-Glasnost and Perestroika," *Theatre Journal*, Vol. 41, No. 3, October 1989, p. 392.

27. Vaclav Havel's (b. 1936) plays, which focus on the failure of language to communicate, have been the principal examples of Absurdism seen in Czech theatres. He, too, owes something to commedic traditions.

28. August Strindberg, "Preface to Miss Julie," translated by E.M. Sprinchorn. *Dramatic Theory*

and Criticism, edited by Bernard F. Dukore. New York: Holt, Rinehart, and Winston, 1974, p. 572.

29. Eugenio Barba. *Beyond The Floating Islands*. With a postscript by Ferdinando Tavianai. Translations by Judy Barba, Richard Fowler, Jerrold C. Rodesch, Saul Shapiro. New York: PAJ Publications, 1986, p. 199.

30. Ibid., p. 200

Chapter 6. From Hanswurst to Handke: Commedia in Germany and Austria

1. Max Reinhardt, "On the Importance of the Actor," *Max Reinhardt and His Theatre*. Edited by Oliver M. Sayler. New York: Brentano's Publishers, 1924, pp. 61-62.

2. Kasperl was first seen in the Viennese folk comedy and was created by Johann Laroche (1745-1806), an actor at the Leopoldstadt Theatre.

3. Hanswurst has proven to be a powerful influence on several generations of theatre artists, writers, and composers, including Richard Wagner. Peter Schumann, founder of The Bread and Puppet Theatre, among other contemporary artists, has found Hanswurst's image an inspiring clown of the people.

4. Neuber and Gottsched attacked the Hanswurst tradition in their *Play of Hanswurst's Banishment* (1737).

5. Johann Wolfgang von Goethe. *Italian Journey 1786-1788*. trans. by W.H. Auden and Elizabeth Mayer. New York: Schocken, 1968, p. 87.

6. The first important German cabaret was the *Bunte Bühne* (motley stage) which was started by Baron Ernst von Wolzogen (1855-1934) and Otto Julius Bierbaum (1865-1910) in 1901 with the expressed goal of satirizing contemporary society and empowering the popular stage with the techniques of the music hall. Nearly fifty cabarets opened between 1900 and 1905 -- and many others followed. The Dada and Symbolist movements were a significant factor -- and cabaret thrived until the rise of the Nazis. In 1901, Reinhardt started the *Schall and Rauch* (noise and smoke) cabaret in Berlin, and, in Munich, the *Elf Scharfrichter* (eleven executioners) featured Frank Wedekind performing grotesque commedic songs of his own composition. Wedekind (1864-1918), an important German playwright of the era, was influenced by commedia. He had started his career working in a circus. Although his early works were most influenced by Naturalism, his greatest plays, *Spring's Awakening* (1891) and *Pandora's Box* (1904), foreshadowed the Expressionist movement. His *Lulu* plays, of which *Pandora's Box* is one, feature an amoral heroine who is clearly inspired, in part, by commedia's Columbine. These works are commedic in Wedekind's characters, who are often grotesque one-dimensional caricatures, and in his brisk episodic style which contributes an air of improvisation and spontaneity.

7. cited in Michael Patterson. *The Revolution in German Theatre 1900-1933*. Boston, London and Henley: Routledge and Kegan Paul, 1981, p. 31.

8. Gottfried Reinhardt. *The Genius. A Memoir of Max Reinhardt*. New York: Alfred A. Knopf, 1979, p. 16.

9. G.N. [pseudonym for Gordon Craig], "Foreign Notes," *The Mask*, Vol. III, No. 7-9, January 1911, p. 144.

10. Sheldon Cheney. *The New Movement in the Theatre*. New York: Mitchell Kennerley, 1914, pp. 58-59.

11. Ibid.

12. Margaret Dietrich, "Music and Dance in the Productions of Max Reinhardt," *Total Theatre*. Edited by E.T. Kirby. New York: E.P. Dutton & Co., 1969, p. 163.

13. Max Reinhardt, "The Enchanted Sense of Play," *Actors on Acting*. Edited by Toby Cole and Helen Krich Chinoy. New York: Crown Publishers, Inc, 1970, pp. 298-299.

14. Max Reinhardt, "Of Actors," *The Yale Review*, 18 (1928) 1, pp. 36-37.

15. Reinhardt, "The Enchanted Sense of Play," *Actors on Acting*, pp. 296-297.

16. Max Reinhardt, "On Actors," *Max Reinhardt. 1873-1973*. Edited by George E. Wellwarth and Alfred G. Brooks. Binghamton, New York: Max Reinhardt Archive, 1973, p. 4.

17. Ibid., p. 5

18. Max Reinhardt. *The Part of the Director*. Binghamton, New York: Max Reinhardt Archive, State University of New York at Binghamton, n.p.

19. Hugo von Hofmannsthal, "Reinhardt the Actor," *Max Reinhardt and His Theatre*. Edited by Oliver M. Sayler. New York: Brentano's, 1926, p. 72.

20. Kenneth MacGowan, "Reinhardt and the Formal Stage," *Max Reinhardt and His Theatre*. Edited by Oliver M. Sayler. New York: Brentano's, 1926, p. 160.

21. Max Reinhardt, "The Salzburg Project I. In Search of a Living Theatre," *Max Reinhardt and His Theatre*. Edited by Oliver M. Sayler. New York: Brentano's, 1926, p. 187.

22. Ibid., pp. 187-188.

23. Ibid.

24. *A Midsummer Night's Dream* was staged by Reinhardt at the following cities: Neues Theater, Berlin, January 31, 1905; Kunstler Theater, Munich, June-July, 1909; Vienna, May, 1910; Munich, June-August, 1910; Stockholm and Christiania, 1915; Zurich, Berne, Basle, St. Gallen, Davos, Lucerne, January, 1917; Grosses Schauspielhaus, Berlin, March 12, 1921; Theater in der Josefstadt, Vienna, 1925; Salzburg Festival, August 6, 1927; Century Theatre, N.Y., November 17, 1927; Deutsches Theater, Berlin, September, 1930; Boboli Gardens in Florence (with Italian players), May 13, 1933; Oxford, England, Summer, 1933; Hollywood Bowl, September-October, 1934; War Memorial Opera House (San Francisco), Greek Theatre (L.A.), and the Chicago Auditorium, October-November, 1934. The film version premiered at the Hollywood Theatre, N.Y. on October 9, 1935.

25. Gottfried Reinhardt, *The Genius. A Memoir of Max Reinhardt*, p. 280.

26. Ibid.

27. Huntley Carter. *The Theatre of Max Reinhardt*. New York: Mitchell Kennerley, 1914, p. 156.

28. J. Brooks Atkinson, "According to Reinhardt," *The New York Times*, November 18, 1927, p. 21.

29. Walther R. Volbach, "Memoirs of Max Reinhardt's Theatres 1920-1922," *Theatre Survey* Vol. XIII, No. 1a, Fall 1972, p. 25.

30. *Twelfth Night* was staged by Reinhardt at the following cities: Budapest, May, 1909; Munich, June-July, 1909; Frankfort-on-Main, July, 1909; Vienna, May, 1910; Munich, June-August, 1910; Stockholm and Christiania, 1915; Rotterdam, The Hague, Amsterdam, April-May, 1916; Zurich, Berne, Basle, St. Gallen, Davos, Lucerne, January, 1917; Bucharest, June, 1917; July 26, 1931 at Leopoldskron, Salzburg; November 11, 1931 at the Theater in der Josefstadt, Vienna.

31. Julius Bab, "Reinhardt's Management of the Chorus," *Max Reinhardt and His Theatre*. Edited by Oliver M. Sayler. New York: Brentano's, 1926, p. 114.

32. Ernst Stern. *My Life, My Stage*. London: Victor Gallancz Ltd., 1951, pp. 102-103.

33. Ibid.

34. George Brandes, "(Denmark)," *Max Reinhardt and His Theatre*. Edited by Oliver M. Sayler. New York: Brentano's, 1926, p. 330. *The Merchant of Venice* was staged by Reinhardt at the following cities: Vienna, May, 1910; Munich, June-August, 1910; Bucharest, June, 1917; Copenhagen, Goteborg, Stockholm, Aarhus, November-December 1920; Grosses Schauspielhaus, Berlin, March 12, 1921; 1924, Theater in der Josefstadt, Vienna; and Venice with Italian players in 1935.

35. George R. Marek, "The Lord of Leopoldskron," *Max Reinhardt. 1873-1973*. Edited by George E. Wellwarth and Alfred G. Brooks. Binghamton, New York: Max Reinhardt Archive, 1973, p. 87.

36. Gottfried Reinhardt, *The Genius. A Memoir of Max Reinhardt*, p. 54.

37. Siegfried Jacobsohn, "Vignettes from Reinhardt's Productions," *Max Reinhardt and His Theatre*. Edited by Oliver M. Sayler. New York: Brentano's, 1926, p. 323.

38. *Much Ado About Nothing* was staged by Reinhardt at the following cities: Deutsches Theater, February 23, 1912; Deutsches Theater, November 21, 1913; and Volksbuehne, January 25, 1916.

39. Jacobsohn, "Vignettes from Reinhardt's Productions," *Max Reinhardt and His Theatre*, p. 325.

40. *The Servant of Two Masters* was staged by Reinhardt at the following cities: Kammerspiele Theater, Berlin, October 26, 1907, Kammerspiele Theater, Berlin; Theater in der Josefstadt, Vienna, April 1, 1924; Komodie Theater, Berlin, November 1, 1924; Kammerspiele, Vienna, June 3, 1925; Salzburg Festival, Summer, 1926; Cosmopolitan Theatre, N.Y., January 9, 1928; Salzburg Festival, August, 1930; Deutsches Theater, Berlin, September, 1930; Kammerspiele,

Vienna, December 3, 1930; Salzburg Festival, Summer, 1931; Riga, 1931; Italian and Swiss cities, 1932; under the title *At Your Service* at the Assistance League Playhouse, Hollywood (Max Reinhardt Workshop), May 31, 1939; San Francisco, 1939/40.

41. Augusta Adler, "Max Reinhardt in Salzburg," *Max Reinhardt. 1873-1973*. Edited by George E. Wellwarth and Alfred G. Brooks. Binghamton, New York: Max Reinhardt Archive, 1973, p. 18.

42. Otto Preminger, "An Interview," *Max Reinhardt. 1873-1973*. Edited by George E. Wellwarth and Alfred G. Brooks. Binghamton, New York: Max Reinhardt Archive, 1973, p. 111.

43. Helene Thimig (1889-1973), who had begun her acting career in 1907, moved to Reinhardt's company in 1917. They were married later that same year, and she continued acting in his productions and helped him manage his School of Acting in Hollywood. After Reinhardt's death, and the conclusion of World War II, she returned to Vienna to act at the Theater in der Josefstadt. The other Thimigs, Hermann (1890-1976), Hugo (1854-1944), and Hans (b. 1900), had distinguished careers on German and Austrian stages.

44. Donald Freeman, "News of Reinhardt," *The New York Times* November 30, 1924, VIII, p. 7.

45. As an actor, Kurz (1717-1783) played a variation on Hanswurst with his character Bernardon, before turning to playwriting. He is credited with over three hundred dramatic works, including a version of *Faust*.

46. Preminger, "An Interview," *Max Reinhardt. 1873-1973*, p. 110.

47. The 1926 Salzburg production of the play was designed by Clemens Holtzmeister, but it depended heavily on the inspiration provided by Laske's design.

48. Robert Ryan, "Essay," *Max Reinhardt. 1873-1973*. Edited by George E. Wellwarth and Alfred G. Brooks. Binghamton, New York: Max Reinhardt Archive, 1973, p. 129.

49. Ibid.

50. Some years before, in 1917, Busoni composed a short opera, *Arlecchino*, which placed the commedia clown in a light anti-war satire, as well as his own treatment of Gozzi's *Turandot* (1917).

51. Carter, *The Theater of Max Reinhardt*, p. 258.

52. Edda Leisler and Gisela Prossnitz. *Max Reinhardt und Die Welt der Commedia dell'Arte*. Salzburg: Otto Muller Verlag, 1970, p. 24-25. Translated by Judith Greene.

53. Gottfried Reinhardt, *The Genius. A Memoir of Max Reinhardt*, p. 345.

54. George Marek, "The Lord of Leopoldskron," *Max Reinhardt. 1873-1973*. Edited by George E. Wellwarth and Alfred G. Brooks. Binghamton, New York: Max Reinhardt Archive, 1973, p. 18.

55. Stern, *My Life, My Stage*, p. 125.

56. Ibid., pp. 125-126.

57. Michael Hamburger, ed. *Selected Plays and Libretti of Hugo von Hofmannsthal*. London: Routledge & Kegan Paul, 1964, p. xxxi.

58. Volbach, "Memoirs of Max Reinhardt's Theatres 1920-1922," *Theatre Survey*, p. 6.

59. Ibid.

60. Reinhardt's other productions of Molière included *Tartuffe*, produced at the Deutsches Theater in April, 1906; *The Forced Marriage*, staged at the Kammerspiele on a double bill with Shakespeare's *Comedy of Errors* in October, 1910; *George Dandin*, presented on a fixed stage anticipating that of Jacques Copeau's Vieux Colombier at the Deutsches Theater in April, 1912; and, *The Miser* produced at the Deutsches Theater in April, 1917, in a highly controversial production which incorporated suggestive expressionist pantomimes.

61. *The Imaginary Invalid* was staged by Reinhardt at the following cities: Kammerspiele, Berlin, March 10, 1916; August 20, 1923 at Leopoldskron, Salzburg; August 21, 1923 at Municipal Theater, Salzburg; November 26, 1924 at Komodie Theater, Berlin.

62. Oliver M. Sayler, "Reinhardt's Salzburg," *Max Reinhardt and His Theatre*. Edited by Oliver M. Sayler. New York: Brentano's, 1926, p. 184.

63. Adler, "Max Reinhardt in Salzburg," *Max Reinhardt. 1873-1973*, p. 15.

64. Willi Handl, "The Artists of the Deutsches Theater," *Max Reinhardt and His Theatre*. Edited by Oliver M. Sayler. New York: Brentano's, 1926, p. 108.

65. Ibid.

66. *A Venetian Night* also played at the Kammerspiele in August, 1913. Karl Vollmoeller (1878-1948) also wrote the scenario for *The Miracle*, which was Reinhardt's best-known and most acclaimed production.

67. Carter, *The Theatre of Max Reinhardt*, p. 241.

68. Hamburger, ed., *Selected Plays and Libretti of Hugo von Hofmannsthal*, p. xvii.

69. Hiram K. Moderwell. *The Theatre of To-Day*. New York: John Lane Company, 1914, p. 234.

70. Green and Swan, *The Triumph of Pierrot*, p. 97.

71. Among other commedic writers of this era was Austrian poet and novelist Stefan Zweig (1881-1942). He was not widely known for his plays, but he adapted Ben Jonson's commedic play *Volpone* into an acid farce, emphasizing its commedic aspects. In a tragic parallel with his fellow commedist Viktor Arnold (1873-1914), he committed suicide while exiled in Brazil, during the Nazi reign in Germany.

72. Brecht's many plays include *The Rise and Fall of the City of Mahagonny* (1927), *The Three-Penny Opera* (1928), *Happy End* (1928), *Mother Courage and Her Children* (1941), *The Rise and Fall of Arturo Ui* (1941), *The Life of Galileo* (1943), *The Good Woman of Setzuan* (1943), and *The Caucasian Chalk Circle* (1944-45).

73. John Willett, ed. *Brecht on Theatre. The Development of an Aesthetic*. New York: Hill and Wang, 1964, pp. 155-156.

74. Ronald Spiers. *Bertolt Brecht*. New York: St. Martin's Press, 1987, p. 63.

75. Willett, ed., *Brecht on Theatre. The Development of an Aesthetic*, p. 153.

76. Ibid., p. 154.

77. Ibid.

78. Ibid., p. 110.

79. cited in Patterson, *The Revolution in German Theatre 1900-1933*, p. 168.

80. Ibid.

81. Martin Esslin. *The Theatre of the Absurd*. Harmonsworth: Penguin, 1980, p. 375.

82. cited in Patterson, *The Revolution in German Theatre 1900-1933*, p. 169.

83. Katherine Bliss Eaton. *The Theater of Meyerhold and Brecht*. Westport, Conn.: Greenwood Press, 1985, p. 103.

84. In Antwerp, International Nieuwe Scene (New International Stage), a bilingual political theatre group begun in 1973, borrowed influences from commedia, Brecht, Dario Fo, and Arturo Corso. Their first production was a reworking of Fo's commedic play, *Mistero Buffo*, and the performance techniques of commedia proved to be essential in their attempt to mirror aspects of Brecht's epic style.

85. Friedrich Dürrenmatt. *Plays and Essays*. Edited by Volkmar Sander. New York: Continuum, 1982, p. 255.

86. Some of Ciulli's productions showing the evidence of commedic influence are *Electra* (1983), *Kasimir and Karoline* (1984), *Tartuffe* (1984), *Danton's Death* (1986), *Lulu* (1986), *Waiting for Godot* (1986), *The Croatian* (1987), and *Cathy from Heilbron* (1989).

Chapter 7. The Tricks of Scapin: Commedia in France

1. cited in Marie-Hélène Dasté, "Foreword. Jacques Copeau's School for Actors," *Mime Journal*, Nos. Nine and Ten, 1979, p. 4.

2. New playwrights were influenced by Molière's plays and the surviving traditions of commedia. Jean-François Regnard (1655-1709), was particularly inspired by the works of Molière (and

those of Plautus, which he adapted), and his most commedic play, *Harlequin the Lady Killer* (1690), was produced with great success by the Italian players. Charles-Rivière Dufresny (1648-1724) also wrote a number of comedies for the Italian actors before their abrupt departure in 1697. Other playwrights of this era affected by commedia include Alain René Lesage (1668-1747), who is best remembered for his play *Tucaret* (1709), although he also wrote numerous vaudevilles, comic operas, and farces, including the particularly commedic *Crispin, Rival of His Master* (1707). French poet Alexis Piron (1689-1773) wrote many parodies, farces, and comic-opera texts (as well as some unsuccessful tragedies), and his first play, *Arlequin Deucalion* (1722), a three-act work in the form of a series of monologues, featured Arlequin as the sole survivor of a flood, who amuses himself by recreating characters according to their social useful-ness, foreshadowing the socially-conscious commedic productions of the early twentieth century. The influence of commedia on the golden age of French drama is superbly documented in Virginia Scott's *The Commedia dell'arte in Paris. 1644-1697* (Charlottesville and London: University Press of Virginia, 1990).

3. The last Italian Arlecchino in France was Carlo Antonio Bertinazzi (1713-1783), known as Carlin. Legendary English actor David Garrick, who himself played the role occasionally, considered Carlin one of the most expressive actors in Paris. By the middle of the eighteenth century, however, the dominance of the Italian actors in Paris had ended.

4. Grand Guignol performances spread from Paris to the rest of Europe, first appearing in London in 1908 and in America in 1923.

5. Pierrot had derived from a transformation of commedia's Pedrolino attributed to an Italian actor named Giuseppe Giaratone (or Giratoni) sometime around 1665 at the Comédie-Italienne. Giaratone exaggerated the character's fundamental simplicity and awkwardness, and dressed in a crude version of the now familiar white Pierrot costume.

6. The influence of Pierrot on nineteenth century French literature is fully chronicled in Robert Storey's studies, *Pierrot. A Critical History of a Mask* (Princeton, N.J.: Princeton University Press, 1978) and *Pierrots on the Stage of Desire* (Princeton, N.J.: Princeton University Press, 1985).

7. Jean-Pierre Claris de Florian (1755-1794), novelist and translator, wrote plays and harlequinades. Florian's Arlequin seems, in part, to have inspired Jarry's Ubu plays.

8. cited in Gay Manifold. *George Sand's Theatre Career*. Ann Arbor, Michigan: UMI Research Press, 1985, p. 56.

9. Ibid., p. 119.

10. cited in Pierre L. Duchartre. *The Italian Comedy*. Authorized translation from the French by Randolph T. Weaver. New York: Dover Publications, Inc., 1966, p. 132.

11. cited in John Rudlin. *Jacques Copeau*. Cambridge: Cambridge University Press, 1986, p. 3.

12. Antoine, the greatest French exponent of Naturalism, experimented with commedia techniques and theatrical Symbolism, including productions of *La Nuit Bergamasque* (1887) and *Pierrot Assassin of His Wife* (1888), but he fared better with more literal plays.

13. Marie-Hélène Dasté, "Foreword," *Mime Journal*, p. 4.

14. Ibid.

15. Jacques Copeau, "An Essay of Dramatic Renovation: The Theatre du Vieux-Colombier," *Educational Theatre Journal*. Translation by Richard Hiatt. Vol. XIX, No. 4, December 1967, p. 450.

16. Michel Saint-Denis, "The Modern Theatre's Debt to Copeau," *The Listener*, February 16, 1950, p. 284.

17. Copeau, "Remembrances of the Vieux Colombier," *Educational Theatre Journal*, p. 4.

18. cited in Rudlin, *Jacques Copeau*, p. 39.

19. Léon Chancerel (1886-1965), playwright and director, had been Copeau's secretary during the final Vieux-Colombier season, and he greatly admired Copeau's ideas. Although he was never an official member of *les Copiaus*, he became one of the most vocal disciples of Copeau's concepts. In 1935, he founded Le Théâtre de L'Oncle Sebastien, a company of young actors who played in commedia style with particular emphasis on improvisation, for children. Many of the productions were adaptations of the plays of Molière and medieval tales.

20. Jacques Copeau, "Notes on the Actor," *Actors on Acting*. Edited by Toby Cole and Helen Krich Chinoy. New York: Crown Publishers, 1970, p. 219.

21. cited in David Whitton. *Stage Directors in Modern France*. Manchester: Manchester University Press, 1987, p. 41.

22. Jacques Copeau, "To Bring the Actors Back to Fervor," *Boston Transcript*, December 19, 1917, p. 11.

23. Copeau, "Notes on the Actor," *Actors on Acting*, p. 219.

24. Jacques Copeau, "On Diderot's Paradox," *Actors on Acting*. Edited by Toby Cole and Helen Krich Chinoy. New York: Crown Publishers, 1970, p. 225.

25. cited in Rudlin, *Jacques Copeau*, p. 95-96.

26. Kenneth Macgowan and Robert Edmond Jones. *Continental Stagecraft*. London: Benn Brothers, 1923, p. 171.

27. Saint-Denis, "The Modern Theatre's Debt to Copeau," *The Listener*, p. 284.

28. cited in J. Chiari, "Jacques Copeau," *World Review*, January-June 1952, p. 38.

29. Copeau, "Notes on the Actor," *Actors on Acting*, p. 219.

30. Copeau, "Remembrances of the Vieux Colombier," *Educational Theatre Journal*, p. 7.

31. Michel Saint-Denis. *Training for the Theatre*. New York: Theatre Arts Books, 1982, p. 30.

32. cited in Rudlin, *Jacques Copeau*, p. 48.

33. cited in Albert M. Katz, "The Genesis of the Vieux-Colombier," *Theatre Journal*, Vol. XIX, No. 4, December 1967, p. 446.

34. The Fratellinis were born of an Italian circus family (their father was acrobat Gustavo Fratellini (1842-1905)), and developed a superb clown act that toured in America and throughout Europe. The brothers, Paolo (1877-1940), the subtle comedian, Francesco (1879-1951), an elegant white-faced clown, and Alberto (1886-1961), the grotesque butt of the comedy, began to perform in 1905, and later settled in Paris at the Cirque Médrano, before moving to the Cirque d'Hiver. In an extraordinary testament to their high quality clowning, the Comédie-Française invited them to join as affiliates in 1922.

35. Jacques Copeau. *Copeau. Texts on Theatre*. Edited and translated by John Rudlin and Norman H. Paul. London: Routledge, 1990, p. 148.

36. cited in Barbara Kusler Leigh, "Foundations: 1879-1914. Jacques Copeau's School for Actors," *Mime Journal*, Nos. Nine and Ten, 1979, p. 16.

37. Copeau, "Remembrances of the Vieux Colombier," *Educational Theatre Journal*, p. 8.

38. Ibid., p. 16.

39. cited in Rudlin, *Jacques Copeau*, p. 72.

40. Ibid., p. 95.

41. These productions were Paul Claudel's *The Exchange*, which opened January 15, 1914, at the Vieux-Colombier; Marivaux's *Love's Surprise*, first presented January 31, 1918, during the American seasons, and subsequently revived at the Vieux-Colombier on October 27, 1920; Beaumarchais's *The Marriage of Figaro*, which debuted in New York on October 21, 1918, with Copeau as Figaro, and was revived twice at the Vieux-Colombier, on October 25, 1921, and October 14, 1922; Evreinov's *The Merry Death*, which opened March 7, 1922, at the Vieux-Colombier; and, Gozzi's *Turandot*, which opened at the Vieux-Colombier on February 2, 1923.

42. Norman Marshall. *The Producer and the Play*. London: Davis-Poynter, 1975, pp. 61-62.

43. *Twelfth Night* was subsequently staged by Copeau on December 25, 1917, at the Garrick Theatre, New York; December 22, 1920, December 5, 1921, and December 14, 1922, at the Vieux-Colombier; December 23, 1940, at the Comédie-Française.

44. cited in Rudlin, *Jacques Copeau*, p. 15.

45. Copeau, "Remembrances of the Vieux Colombier," *Educational Theatre Journal*, p. 4.

46. Saint-Denis, *Training for the Theatre*, p. 34.

47. Waldo Frank, "The Art of the Vieux Colombier," *Salvos. An Informal Book About Books and Plays*. New York: Boni & Liveright, 1924, pp. 159-160.

48. cited in Ralph Roeder, "Copeau, 1921," *Theatre Arts Monthly*, October 1921, Vol. 5, p. 289.

49. Geraldine Bonner, "M. Copeau's Players," *The New York Times*, March 17, 1918, IV, p. 5.

50. Ibid.

51. John Corbin, "Shakespeare's *Twelfth Night*," *The New York Times*, February 25, 1919, p. 9.

52. *Love's the Best Medicine* was revived March 5, 1918, at the Garrick Theatre, New York and May 27, 1921, at the Vieux-Colombier.

53. "Double Bill at the Vieux Colombier," *The New York Times*, March 6, 1918, p. 10.

54. *The Miser* was revived on March 19, 1914, at the Vieux-Colombier; March 19, 1918, at the Garrick Theatre, New York; January 6, 1919, at the Garrick Theatre, New York; and March 11, 1922, at the Vieux-Colombier.

55. "Molière's *L'Avare* at the Colombier," *The New York Times*, March 20, 1918, p. 11.

56. Ibid.

57. *The Jealousy of Barbouillé* was revived December 5, 1917, at the Garrick Theatre, New York; October 27, 1920 and February 26, 1922, at the Vieux-Colombier.

58. A.G.H. Spiers, "Modern Stage-Setting," *The Nation*, Vol. 105, No. 2739, December 27, 1917, pp. 727.

59. Similar movement-oriented productions were given to *The Imaginary Invalid*, which opened during the New York seasons, on November 25, 1918 (it was revived October 15, 1920, January 6, 1922, and March 8, 1923, at the Vieux-Colombier; and August 15, 1925, at the Repertoire of the Copiaus); *The Misanthrope* was also first produced in New York on March 17, 1919 (it was revived January 25, 1922, December 6, 1922, March 22, 1923, and January 3, 1924, at the Vieux-Colombier; December 7, 1936 and September 8, 1940, at the Comedie-Française); and *The School for Wives*, produced in Burgundy on October 25, 1925.

60. *The Tricks of Scapin* was revived at the Vieux-Colombier on April 27, 1920.

61. cited in Rudlin, *Jacques Copeau*, p. 75.

62. Ibid., p. 51.

63. Frank, "The Art of the Vieux Colombier," *Salvos. An Informal Book About Books and Plays*, p. 160-161.

64. John Corbin, "Molière Reborn," *The New York Times*, IX, December 2, 1917, p. 1.

65. Ibid. Among other things, *The Tricks of Scapin* was an important step in the introduction of the "new stagecraft" onto the American stage. The most obvious aspect of this was exemplified by Copeau's notion of the *mise-en-scène*, which he defined broadly as "the arrangement of movements, gestures and poses, the blending of faces, voices and silences, the totality of the scenic spectacle springing from a single mind which conceives it, regulates it and harmonises it."(cited in Whitton, *Stage Directors in Modern France*, p. 62). The *treteau*, and Copeau's use of it, was a striking challenge to the Belasco-style Realism that pervaded New York's stage during that period.

66. Spiers, "Modern Stage-Setting," *The Nation*, p. 728.

67. "French Company in Molière Farce," *The New York Times*, November 28, 1917, Section 2, p. 1.

68. Ibid.

69. Copeau, "Remembrances of the Vieux Colombier," *Educational Theatre Journal*, p. 5.

70. Ibid. p. 16.

71. Edmond Rostand (1868-1918) wrote the perennial *Cyrano de Bergerac* (1897), a tragi-comedy featuring a commedic lover trapped behind the grotesque "mask" of a hideously deformed nose. He also wrote *The Two Pierrots, or The White Supper* (1891), one of the many nineteenth century French plays offering a variation on the character of Pierrot. In his last play, *The Last Night of Don Juan*, published after his death in 1921, Rostand includes a symbolic puppet show staged for Don Juan, featuring Punchinello. The puppeteer reveals himself ultimately as Satan come to claim the soul of Don Juan in a transformation that mirrors the demonic elements of Blok's *The Fairground Booth*. Georges Courteline (1858-1929) and Georges Feydeau (1862-1921) were just two of many French playwrights who churned out rambunctious commedic farces in modern settings. "Boulevardier" Sacha Guitry (1885-1957) was touched by the spirit of commedia, especially in his play, *Deburau*, first produced in Paris in February, 1918, as a vehicle for his father, the great French actor Lucien Guitry (1860-1925). The bittersweet story of the great Pierrot, Deburau, was unfolded in a play that captured the "fragrance, the glamour and the wistfulness"(Alexander Woolcott, "The Play," *New York Times*, December 24, 1920, p. 14) of the clown's troubled life. Even the dramas of playwright and poet Paul Claudel (1868-1955), also a sometime diplomat and essayist, broke not only with Realism, but with the formal verse tradition represented by the works of Rostand. Among his many works, *The Rape of Scapin* (1949), his final play, was a farcical comedy based on Molière. Impressionist Jean Giraudoux (1882-1944) turned to playwriting late in his career, but, like Claudel, he became a leader in a steadily developing movement away from the strictly realistic stage to a more imaginative and creative one. For Giraudoux, "theatre ceased to be restrictively psychological, social, moral, of manner, or character, and became a synthetic creation, the distilled essence of all genres, a fusion of reality, idealism, and poetry in a kind of modern *commedia dell'arte sui generis*"(Barrett H. Clark and George Freedley, editors. *A History of Modern Drama*. New York and London: D. Appleton-Century Company, Inc., 1947, pp. 306-307). His lyrical and fantastic plays, including *Amphitryon 38* (1929), *Electre* (1937), *The Paris Impromptu* (1937), *Ondine* (1939), and especially *The Madwoman of Chaillot* (1945), were clearly influenced by the Symbolist movement in France, but it is Giraudoux's own extravagant sense of theatre that connects him to commedia. In *The Paris Impromptu*, a play inspired by Molière's *The Rehearsal at Versailles*, he revealed his ideas for a more theatrical theatre in his depiction of Jouvet's company in rehearsal, debating the relative merits of critics, theatre and literature, and reality. He incisively articulates both the need for style in the theatre, and for what many modern writers found in commedic theatre, its ability to be real within the unreal. Jean Cocteau (1889-1963), poet, artist, novelist, film director, and one of the leading French intellectuals between the two world wars, also wrote many dramas, but his most significant involvement in modern commedia was his ballet *Parade*, produced in 1917 with the participation of an extraordinary group of artists. It featured designs by Pablo Picasso, choreography by Serge Diaghilev, and music by Erik Satie. The ballet was created out of a whirlwind of influences, from Craig and Reinhardt through Meyerhold and Chaplin. Picasso had painted, sketched, and sculpted Pierrots, Harlequins, and Columbines for many years, and his vision of commedia

masks as eloquent human symbols was particularly effective in *Parade*. Yvan Goll (1891-1950) was influenced by the Symbolists, especially in his play, *Die Chaplinade* (1920), written under the spell of silent film comedy. It combined poetry with filmic images, using Chaplin's "Little Tramp" as the central character. He later wrote several plays which were more influenced by Greek tragedy and Shakespeare, than by film comedy or commedic forms. His interest in commedia, and for that matter, ancient drama, had to do with his fascination with the possibilities of masks.

72. cited in Frantisek Deak, "Antonin Artaud and Charles Dullin: Artaud's Apprenticeship in Theatre," *Educational Theatre Journal*, October 1977, p. 349.

73. Antonin Artaud. *The Theater and Its Double*. Translated from the French by Mary Caroline Richards. New York: Grove Press, Inc., 1958, pp. 39-40.

74. Ibid., p. 142.

75. Ibid., p. 43.

76. Ibid., p. 42.

77. Ibid., p. 91.

78. Ibid., p. 109.

79. Martin Esslin. *The Theatre of the Absurd*. Harmondsworth: Penguin, 1980, p. 337.

80. Ibid., p. 334.

81. Ibid., pp. 328-329.

82. ibid., p. 330.

83. Roger Blin (1907-1984), the French director who produced the original *Waiting for Godot*, was a major influence on the creation of Beckett's "tramps" in the play, as well as its many commedic resonances.

84. Samuel Beckett. *Waiting for Godot*. London: Faber and Faber, 1959, p. 34.

85. Jacques Lecoq, "In Search of Your Own Clown," *Commedia dell'arte and the Comic Spirit. Classics in Context Festival*. Michael Bigelow Dixon and Michelle Togami, eds. Louisville, Kentucky: Actors Theatre of Louisville, 1990, p. 43.

86. Esslin, *The Theatre of the Absurd*, p. 169.

87. Another Absurdist, Jean Genet (1910-1987) viewed theatre as a vehicle for revolt, and his powerful, often realistic plays, including *The Maids* (1947), emphasized masquerade. The highly structured plots and polished language of his plays made his work seem less commedic than those of the other major Absurdist dramatists.

88. cited in Copeau, *Copeau. Texts on Theatre*, p. 237.

89. Two other directors influenced by Copeau were sometime students of the master, although they were not completely won over to the techniques of commedia. Gaston Baty (1885-1952), also fell under the spell of the theories and productions of the modern Russians and Germans, and he created a theatre form in which the actor and the playwright were subordinated to the control of the director. In 1936, he became director of the Comédie-Française where he was credited with reanimating the classical repertory. Russian-born Georges Pitoëff (1887-1939) directed his own amateur company in St. Petersburg, where he admired the work of both Stanislavsky and Meyerhold. From 1915-1921, he lived in Geneva where he was significantly influenced by Jacques-Dalcroze's eurythmics. After 1921, he settled in Paris where he worked with Copeau and shared with him the concern that the French theatre was bankrupt, both in ideas and vision. Under severe financial constraints, he attempted to produce the best work of foreign dramatists including Shakespeare, Shaw, Chekhov, and Pirandello, as well as French works by Claudel, Cocteau, and Anouilh.

90. cited in Whitton. *Stage Directors in Modern France*, p. 71.

91. Ibid.

92. Charles Dullin, "The Birth of Life and Characters," *Actors on Acting*. Edited by Toby Cole and Helen Krich Chinoy. New York: Crown Publishers, Inc., 1970, p. 230.

93. cited in Mira Felner. *Apostles of Silence. The Modern French Mimes*. Rutherford, N.J.: Fairleigh Dickinson University Press, 1985, p. 34.

94. "Molière's *L'Avare* at the Colombier," *New York Times*, p. 11.

95. "M. Dullin Acts *The Miser*," *New York Times*, January 7, 1919, p. 11.

96. Marshall, *The Producer and the Play*, pp. 80-81.

97. Jean-Louis Barrault. *The Theatre of Jean-Louis Barrault*. Translated by Joseph Chiari. New York: Hill and Wang, 1959, pp. 100-101.

98. One significant member of Dullin's company, Jean Vilar (1912-1971), achieved success as both an actor and a director with the particular goal of recreating theatre as a communal celebration or ceremony. He acknowledged his debt to German, Russian, and Oriental theatre, and added, "Let's not forget the *Commedia dell'Arte*, either."(Jean Vilar, "Theater Without Pretensions," *Directors on Directing*. Edited by Toby Cole and Helen Krich Chinoy. New York: The Bobbs-Merrill Company, Inc., 1953, p. 267) Despite the obvious success that Copeau, Dullin, and others had with commedia techniques, Vilar doubted "whether we have the means to convey to contemporary audiences the explosive Italian comedy, for instance, with its lazzi and scenarios. It was a specialized actors' art, and died with them."(Ibid., p. 269) Director André Barsacq (1909-1973) had also started his career with Dullin as a scene designer creating settings for *Volpone*. In 1936, he founded the Compagnie des Quatre Saisons where he directed and designed Gozzi's *The King Stag*, Molière's *The Tricks of Scapin*, and other commedic plays.

99. Bettina L. Knapp. *Louis Jouvet. Man of the Theatre*. New York: Columbia University Press, 1957, p. 45.

100. Louis Jouvet, "Comedian and Actor," *Actors on Acting*. Edited by Toby Cole and Helen Krich Chinoy. New York: Crown Publishers, Inc., 1970, p. 241.

101. Ibid.

102. Ibid., p. 243.

103. Ibid.

104. Ibid., p. 242.

105. Ibid., p.245.

106. Knapp, *Louis Jouvet. Man of the Theatre*, p. 243.

107. Ibid., p. 245.

108. Ibid., p. 251.

109. Jean-Louis Barrault, "Four Directors. 1. Jean-Louis Barrault," *Theatre Quarterly*, Vol. III, No. 10, April-June 1973, p. 4.

110. cited in Felner, *Apostles of Silence. The Modern French Mimes*, p. 105.

111. Ibid., p. 77.

112. Barrault, *The Theatre of Jean-Louis Barrault*, pp. 101-102.

113. Ibid., p. 102.

114. Ibid., p. 101.

115. Ibid., p. 104.

116. Ibid.

117. Barrault, "Four Directors. 1. Jean-Louis Barrault," *Theatre Quarterly*, p. 5.

118. Barrault, *The Theatre of Jean-Louis Barrault*, p. 103.

119. Ibid., pp. 103-104.

120. cited in Felner, *Apostles of Silence. The Modern French Mimes*, p. 82.

121. Jean-Louis Barrault, "Pantomime," *Actors on Acting*. Edited by Toby Cole and Helen Krich Chinoy. New York: Crown Publishers, Inc., 1970, p. 247.

122. Barrault, *The Theatre of Jean-Louis Barrault*, pp. 76-77.

123. Jean-Louis Barrault, "Dramatic Art and the Mime," *Mimes on Miming*. Edited by Bari Rolfe. London: Millington, 1981, p. 109.

124. Ibid. p. 110.

125. Barrault, *The Theatre of Jean-Louis Barrault*, p. 29.

126. cited in Felner, *Apostles of Silence. The Modern French Mimes*, p. 102.

127. Barrault, *The Theatre of Jean-Louis Barrault*, p. 30.

128. Ibid., p. 92.

129. Ibid., p. 206.

130. Etienne Decroux. *Words on Mime*. Translated by Mark Piper. Claremont, California: Mime Journal, 1977, p. 3.

131. Ibid., p. 8.

132. Ibid.

133. Etienne Decroux, "Each Art Has Its Own Territory," *Mimes on Miming*. Edited by Bari Rolfe. London: Millington, 1981, p. 107.

134. Thomas Leabhart, "An Interview with Etienne Decroux," *Mime Journal*, 1 (1974), p. 28.

135. Decroux, "Each Art Has Its Own Territory," *Mimes on Miming*, p. 106.

136. Thomas Leabhart, "Etienne Decroux on Masks," *Mime Journal*, 2, (1975), pp. 57-58.

137. Decroux, *Words on Mime*, p. 36.

138. Ibid., p. 35.

139. Ibid.

140. cited in Felner, *Apostles of Silence. The Modern French Mimes*, pp. 128-129.

141. Rebecca Cox, "Marcel Marceau Speaks," *Prompt*, No. 11 (1968), p. 10.

142. cited in Felner, *Apostles of Silence. The Modern French Mimes*, p. 139.

143. Brooks Atkinson, "Theatre -- Marcel Marceau," *New York Times*, September 22, 1955.

144. cited in Felner, *Apostles of Silence. The Modern French Mimes*, p. 20.

145. Jacques LeCoq, "Mime, Movement, Theatre," *Mimes on Miming*. Edited by Bari Rolfe. London: Millington Books, 1981, p. 151.

146. Ibid.

147. Ibid.

148. Ibid., p. 153.

149. Ibid.

150. cited in Felner, *Apostles of Silence. The Modern French Mimes*, p. 148.

151. Ibid.

152. Ibid., p. 156.

153. cited in Bari Rolfe, "The Mime of Jacques LeCoq," *The Drama Review*, 1972, p. 36.

154. cited in Felner, *Apostles of Silence. The Modern French Mimes*, p. 157.

155. Ibid., p. 164.

156. French actors less oriented toward mime also excelled in commedic productions. Daniel Sorano (1920-1962) was widely acclaimed as Scapin in Maurice Sarrazin's Le Grenier de Toulouse production of *The Tricks of Scapin* (1950), and later as Sganarelle in *Don Juan* and Figaro in *The Marriage of Figaro*, before his untimely death. Robert Hirsch (b. 1926), like several centuries of predecessors in the Comédie-Française company, excelled in Harlequin roles in many of Molière's plays, continuing a tradition that has made the Comédie-Française the "House of Molière."

157. Among 1950's French theatre artists interested in commedia, Jacques Fabbri (b. 1925) was acclaimed for his productions, including C. Santelli's *The Family of Harlequin*, staged at the Théâtre du Vieux-Colombier in 1955, that overtly employed commedic techniques and *lazzi*.

158. cited in Whitton, *Stage Directors in Modern France*, p. 255.

159. Françoise Kourilsky and Leonora Champagne, "Political Theatre in France Since 1968," *The Drama Review*, Vol. 19, No. 2 (T-66, June 1975), p. 52.

160. cited in David Brady and David Williams. *Director's Theatre*. New York: St. Martin's Press, 1988, p. 96.

Chapter 8. The Show Booth: Commedia in the United States

1. Joan Holden, "Comedy and Revolution," *Arts in Society*, Vol. 6, No. 3, 1969, p. 418.

2. The cast also included Emily Rigl as Columbine and Fox's brother, Charles Kemble Fox, as Pantaloon.

3. Produced by Fox's brother-in-law, George C. Howard, at Purdy's National Theatre in 1853.

4. Laurence Senelick. *The Age and Stage of George L. Fox. 1825-1877*. Hanover and London: University Press of New England, 1988, p. 219.

5. Richard Moody, "Negro Minstrelsy," *Quarterly Journal of Speech*, Vol. 30, No. 3, October 1944, p. 327.

6. Edward Harrigan, "American Playwrights on the American Drama," *Harper's Weekly*, Vol. 33, February 2, 1889, p. 98.

7. W.D. Howells, "Editor's Study," *Harper's New Monthly Magazine*, Vol. 73, June-November 1886, p. 316.

8. Ibid.

9. Ibid.

10. At the turn of the century, modern European commedia began to assert itself on America's stages. The first of these was Michel Carne's French pantomime *The Prodigal Son,* produced by Augustin Daly in March, 1891, with the beloved Ada Rehan as Pierrot. Although it was tremendously successful in France and England, Daly's production achieved only modest commercial and critical success here, and most of that was due to Rehan's enormous popularity. *The Prodigal Son* was revived by Winthrop Ames on September 16, 1916, at the Booth Theatre. Praised by virtually every New York critic, this time it was an unqualified hit, running one-hundred sixty-five performances. Much of the credit went to Marjorie Patterson's performance as the wayward Pierrot. It was revived again, on March 6, 1925, under the title *Pierrot the Prodigal*, in a production of The Actors' Theatre, starring perhaps the finest American actress of her generation, Laurette Taylor. Incredibly, the production was a thudding failure, and closed after a mere fourteen performances. *The Prodigal Son* has never been revived on the New York stage.

11. *Pantaloon* was produced by Charles Frohman in New York in December, 1905, on a double bill with Barrie's *Alice-Sit-by-the-Fire*, as a rare opportunity for the three young Barrymores, Ethel, Lionel, and John, to appear together. Ethel did not act in *Pantaloon*, although she had one of her first triumphs in *Alice-Sit-by-the-Fire*. She had seen both plays produced in England the previous year and recalled in her memoirs that *Pantaloon*, acted by Gerald du Maurier, "had so devastated me and made me cry so hard that I could not go that night to see *Alice-Sit-by-the-Fire*." (Ethel Barrymore. Memories. New York: Harper and Brothers, 1955, p. 150) She encouraged production of the plays in New York where the bill ran for eighty-one performances at the Criterion Theatre. One critic declared *Pantaloon* to be a "delicate and whimsical bit, thoroughly charming."("More of Barrie and Three Barry-Mores," *The New York Times*, December 26, 1905, p. 7) Lionel Barrymore later appeared in *Laugh, Clown, Laugh* by David Belasco (1853-1931) and Tom Cushing (1879-1941), based on Fausto Martini's *Ridi Pagliaccio*, which was produced and directed by Belasco and opened on November 28, 1923, for a run of one hundred thirty-three performances. The play's circus background and combined use of both theatrical artifice and near-tragic drama owes something to Meyerhold's grotesque commedia.

12. *Prunella* opened in October, 1913, under the management of Winthrop Ames. A short-lived failure in London in 1904, it found a somewhat more appreciative audience in New York, where it ran for over one hundred performances, starring Marguerite Clark as Prunella and Ernest Glendinning as Pierrot. Critics found Ames's production to be "fantastic as a dream, the dainty and elusive mood of the play is perfectly attained in the acting and setting. . ."("Exquisite Fantasy of Rhapsodic Love," *The New York Times*, October 27, 1913, p. 9) *Prunella* was revived in June, 1926, for six performances at the Garrick Theatre by the seniors of the Theatre Guild school, again under the direction of Ames. The cast included Sylvia Sidney, later a respected film and stage actress, as Prunella.

13. *The Harlequinade*, opened May 10, 1921, at the Neighborhood Playhouse, for twenty-five performances before it moved and reopened on June 14, 1921, for fifteen performances at the Punch and Judy Theatre. *The Harlequinade* was revived for forty performances at the Garrick Theatre beginning on October 1, 1928, but did little to promote any major revival of commedia.

14. *Deburau*, in a translation by Harley Granville Barker, who also directed, was produced in New York by David Belasco in December, 1920, beginning a highly successful run of nearly two-hundred performances. Alexander Woollcott gushed that the "fragrance, the glamour and the wistfulness of a quaint and singularly beautiful Parisian play have been caught and held there for American audiences." (Alexander Woollcott, "The Play," *The New York Times*, December 24, 1920, p. 14) The cast included Lionel Atwill as Deburau. The second act of *Deburau* was revived in December, 1926, on a double bill with Guitry's *Mozart*, with Guitry himself appearing as Deburau. Critics found it to be "amiable and without distinction,"(J. Brooks Atkinson, "Guitry et Femme," *The New York Times*, December 28, 1926, p. 16) and it lasted for only thirty-two performances.

15. In November, 1914, the new Punch & Judy Theatre opened with *The Marriage of Columbine*, a new play "touched with the spirit of fantasy," written by Harold Chapin (1886-1915). Produced by Charles Hopkins, who also played Scaramouche opposite his wife as Columbine, the play only managed thirty-one performances. It concerned the awkwardnesses that occur when Columbine realizes, as the result of becoming a member of small town English society, that although she has been living for many years with Scaramouche, she has never been properly married to him. According to one critic, the play's improvisatory spirit left the impression "of an unfinished sketch, as though its manuscript were still waiting for a more skillful and a more determined hand to sharpen its outlines and to distribute its values."("Quaint Play Opens the Punch & Judy, *The New York Times*, November 11, 1914, p. 13) Similarly, Oliphant Down's *The Maker of Dreams*, was produced with modest success at the Neighborhood Playhouse in March, 1915, and is strongly reminiscent of Barker and Calthrop's *The Harlequinade*.

16. Pirandello's commedia influence was far-reaching, even finding its way into the works of Russian dramatists who had already fallen under the spell of Meyerholdian commedia. Having failed with both Spanish and Italian modern commedia, the tenacious Theatre Guild tried the Russian brand, producing Evreinov's *The Chief Thing* in March, 1926, in a translation by Herman Bernstein and Lee Bandole, with a cast including Estelle Winwood, Edward G. Robinson, Helen Westley, and Lee Strasberg. It was unenthusiastically received in its "colorful but seldom crisp" performance (J. Brooks Atkinson, "Intellectual Comedy at the Guild," *The New York Times*, March 23, 1926, p. 24). The production failed to find an audience and disappeared from the Guild repertory after a mere forty performances. *The Chief Thing* was revived at the Greenwich Mews Theatre in April, 1963. Acknowledging that Evreinov's techniques must certainly have seemed novel forty years before, critic Paul Gardner noted that "once his statement is made -- and it is announced almost immediately -- the playwright never moves from the truth-illusion question, which he repeats as steadily as a child who wonders when Christmas will come."(Paul Gardner, "Theater: *Chief Thing*," *The New York Times*, April 30, 1963, p. 27) It was condemned as "historically interesting without being theatrically moving,"(Ibid.) and it closed after twenty-four performances.

17. Along with Rollo Peters, the cast of *The Bonds of Interest* also included Dudley Digges as Polichinelle, Edna St. Vincent Millay as Columbine, and Helen Westley as Dona Strena.

18. One of the last great actor-managers of the American theatre, Walter Hampden, revived *The Bonds of Interest* in New York on October 14, 1929, using the same Underhill translation produced by the Theatre Guild. Brooks Atkinson wrote that it was "commedia dell'arte in spirit"("Hampden Harlequinade," *The New York Times*, October 15, 1929, p. 34) and applauded the performances of Hampden and his company, including Etienne Giradot as Pantaloon. It managed only twenty-four performances. Critics pointed to the fundamental inability of American actors to master commedic acting skills, and this criticism dominated reaction in 1951, when *The Bonds of Interest* was revived, this time by the Loft Players at the Circle in the Square Theatre. Featuring a cast of unknowns, Atkinson noted that the players "are not yet ready for stylized acting."("Benavente in the Round," *The New York Times*, December 1, 1951, p. 7) It was again revived in 1958, in a new translation by Philip Minor, who also directed, at the Sheridan Square Playhouse. The cast of unknowns included several actors who would later thrive in television and film careers, including Peter Falk as Crispin and David Doyle as the Prosecutor. Critics again noted the inability of the actors to understand commedic style, and the production folded after only twenty-four performances. Despite its failure with Benavente's *The Bonds of Interest* in 1919, the Theatre Guild mounted other commedic productions, including Luigi Chiarelli's *teatro grottesco* play *The Mask and the Face* in 1933, translated by W. Somerset Maugham, under the direction of Phillip Moeller, with sets by Lee Simonson. *Teatro grottesco* was dominating the Italian stage, due largely to the works of Chiarelli and the early plays of Pirandello. Most, however, failed to prove much more than curiosities. *The Mask and the Face* had been previously presented on Broadway for a mere thirteen performances in 1924 by producer Brock Pemberton. The Guild production also failed to find an audience, achieving just forty performances despite a bright young cast featuring Shirley Booth, Judith Anderson, Leo G. Carroll, and Humphrey Bogart.

19. *The Merry Death* was revived November 9, 1959, at St. Mark's Theatre for one performance.

20. A producing organization that boasted a board of directors including Arthur Hopkins, Robert Edmond Jones, Nicholas Roerich, Padraic Colum, Ruth Draper, Serge Prokofiev, and Uraneff, who also served as General Director, "American Commedia dell'arte, Inc." set out to introduce Russian modernist commedia to the New York stage.

21. Program, *The Show Booth* and *The Song of Songs*, April, 1923, 4 pp. New York Public Library.

22. Gordon Craig, "The Commedia dell'Arte Ascending," *The Mask*. Vol. V, No. 2, p. 104.

23. Vadim Uraneff, "Commedia dell'Arte and American Vaudeville," *Theatre Arts*, October 1923, p. 328.

24. Ibid., p. 325.

25. Ibid.

26. Ibid., pp. 326-327.

27. The cast included musical comedy performer James Watts as The Clown, Burford Hampden as The Author, E.J. Ballantine as Pierrot, Edna James as Columbine, William Kirkland as Harlequin, Mary Corday and Romney Brent as The Pink and Blue Lovers, Edna St. Vincent Millay and Denis Auburn as The Medieval Lovers, and Marshall Vincent, James Carroll, Jacques Cartier, and Brent as the Mystics (here called Occultists).

28. Ralph Pendleton, ed. *The Theatre of Robert Edmond Jones*. Middletown, Conn.: Wesleyan University Press, 1958, p. 162.

29. Robert Edmond Jones. *The Dramatic Imagination*. New York: Theatre Arts Books, 1941, p. 143.

30. Ibid., pp. 143-144.

31. B.F., "*Song of Songs* and *The Show Booth* at Matinees," *The New York Tribune*, April 4, 1923.

32. John Corbin, "Barrieized Pinero," *The New York Times*, April 8, 1923, Section VIII, p. 1.

33. Ibid.

34. Late nineteenth and early twentieth century commedic plays included *The Pierrot of the Minute* by Ernest Dowson (1867-1900), *An Old Story* by actress Ruth Draper (1884-1956), *Mr. and Mrs. P. Roe* by Martyn Johnson, *Pierrot and Pierrette* by T. MacDonald, *A Thousand Years Ago* and *Caliban of the Yellow Sands* by Percy MacKaye (1875-1956), and *Pierrot in the Clear of the Moon* by Gretchen Riggs.

35. "The Artist of the Theater: A Colloquy Between Eugene O'Neill and Oliver M. Sayler," *Shadowland*, 7.2 (1922), p. 77.

36. Despite his disdain for the idea of modern commedia, O'Neill nevertheless experimented with theatrical elements that were a traditional and central part of commedia. He suggested his allegiance to a commedic style of theatre by pointing out that "we agree in the main point: the theater of the present must be destroyed."("The Artist of the Theater: A Colloquy Between Eugene O'Neill and Oliver M. Sayler," *Shadowland*, Vol. VI, No. 2, April 1922, p. 77.) O'Neill was especially drawn to masks, although his interest in them grew out of his admiration for ancient Greek drama, with O'Neill wondering why "not give all future Classical revivals entirely in masks?"(Eugene O'Neill, "Memoranda on Masks," *The Unknown O'Neill*. Edited with commentaries by Travis Bogard. New Haven and London: Yale University Press, 1988, p. 407). He even advocated the use of masks "for stage crowds, mobs -- wherever a sense of impersonal, collective mob psychology is wanted."(Ibid., p. 409) Anticipating that actors would object to masks because they would "extinguish their personalities and deprive them of their greatest asset in conveying emotion by facial expression,"(Ibid., pp. 410-411) O'Neill felt that masks would "give them the opportunity for a totally new kind of acting, that they would learn many undeveloped possibilities of their art if they appeared, even if only for a season or two, in masked roles."(Ibid.) O'Neill himself used them in his more experimental works of the 1920's, such as *The Great God Brown* (1923).

37. Goodman wrote two other one-act commedic plays, *Dancing Dolls* (1914) and *A Man Can Only Do His Best* (1914), both of which were produced successfully in little theatres in America and England.

38. Kenneth Sawyer Goodman and Ben Hecht. *The Wonder Hat and Other One-Act Plays*. New York: Appleton, 1925, p. 39.

39. Brooks Atkinson. *Broadway*. New York: Macmillan Publishing Company, Inc., 1974, p. 110.

40. *Aria da Capo* was performed December 5-8, 1919, April 23-May 6, 1920 and June 8-July 1, 1921, with Millay's sister, Norma, as Columbine, and Charles Ellis, designer of sets and costumes as one of the shepherds. James Light played another shepherd, Harrison Dowd played Pierrot, and Hugh Ferris was Cothurnus. Millay directed the production in Ellis's set made up of a small set of screens.

41. Mary J. McKee, "Millay's *Aria da Capo*: Form and Meaning," *Modern Drama*, September 1966, p. 166-167.

42. Edna St. Vincent Millay, "Aria da Capo," *Thirty Famous One-Act Plays*. Edited by Bennett Cerf and Van H. Cartmell. New York: The Modern Library, 1943, p. 470.

43. Allan Ross Macdougall, ed. *Letters of Edna St. Vincent Millay*. New York: Harper & Brothers, Publishers, 1952, p. 90.

44. *Aria da Capo* was performed by Gats of Manhattan at the 1923 Little Theatre tournament. It was revived by the students of the Abbe Workshop in 1950, and again in 1958, on a double bill with *Guest of a Nation*, both directed by Neil McKenzie and designed by Mordecai Gorelick at the Theatre Marquee. The revival ran for one-hundred two performances.

45. Although American actors had virtually no training in its unique techniques, European artists noticed elements of commedia in the work of some American actors. When the celebrated acting duo of Alfred Lunt and Lynn Fontanne were performing in the successful American adaption of Jean Giraudoux's *Amphytrion 38*, Giraudoux, in an interview in the The *New York Herald Tribune*, noted that the Lunts "have some of the freedom of improvisation and the accuracy of gesture that exists in commedia del arte[sic]. That to me is the best kind of theatre. I think a playwright should write for publication and permit the actors to do as they please in the way of interpretation."(*The New York Herald Tribune*, November 7, 1937)

46.Eva Le Gallienne. *At 33*. New York and Toronto: Longmans, Green and Co., 1934, p. 78.

47. Antiquarian interest in commedia continued with The Theatre Guild's production of Molière's *The School for Husbands*, which was adapted by Laurence Langner and Arthur Guiterman. It was staged in commedic settings by Lee Simonson, had music by Edmond W. Rickett and lyrics by Guiterman, and featured Osgood Perkins as Sganarelle. To underline director Langner's commedia concept, the actors were permitted modest opportunities for ad-libbing in an attempt to create the illusion of improvisation. Although Brooks Atkinson found the production to be "a charming bit of make-believe,"(Brooks Atkinson, "The Play," *The New York Times*, October 17, 1933, p. 26) he lamented the ad-libs interpolated to create an illusion of improvisation, and found the direction to be "patronizing and sometimes it is a frank travesty. Some of the interpolations have a bucolic motive. If you are a stickler for style in professional theatre, you will object to the sort of amateur stage quips that please holiday audiences in the Summer theatres."(Ibid.) Despite the quibbles, *The School for Wives* was very well received and had a healthy run at New York's Empire Theatre. Molière's commedic plays were rarely seen in performances by American actors or companies until the explosion of repertory theatres around the country after 1960. There were some exceptions. In 1917, Charles Coburn, one of the last of the actor-manager breed, and later, a character actor in Hollywood films, produced *The Imaginary Invalid*, in a translation by himself and his wife, Ivah Wills, who also played Toinette. Its brief engagement was well-received, necessitating a change in theatres to continue its run. It was revived in 1922 at Columbia University's gymnasium, with the cooperation of the Department of English and Comparative Literature and Romance Languages and the

Institute of Arts and Sciences, and was well-received by one critic who stated that it was performed with "gusto and evident affection."("Molière Comedy Acted," *The New York Times*, January 26, 1922, p. 26) In recent years, many of Molière's plays have been produced on the New York stage, and Richard Wilbur's verse translations of *Tartuffe*, *The Misanthrope*, *The School for Wives*, and *The Learned Ladies* inspired several excellent productions beginning in the late 1960's.

48. Hallie Flanagan. *Arena. The History of the Federal Theatre*. New York: Benjamin Blom, 1965, p. 70.

49. Ibid., p. 176.

50. Three one-act plays opened the Greenwich Village Theatre in November, 1917, under the direction of Frank Conroy, who had fashioned a resident company in the style of the Washington Square Players. The bill, which featured Arthur Schnitzler's *The Festival of Bacchus*, also included *Behind a Watteau Picture* by Robert L. Rogers, a two-scene drama which featured Pierrot, Harlequin, and Columbine. One rare popular success among American productions of commedia was a bill of two ballets and a commedia playlet, titled simply *Commedia dell'Arte*. It was based on an original Martinelli scenario, translated by Amelia Defries and adapted into an acting version by Ann MacDonald. It was produced by the Neighborhood Playhouse in April, 1927. In 1951, an original commedia play was produced by the Equity Library Theatre at the Lenox Hill Playhouse. *The Great Magician* by Lawrence Carra (b. 1909), "proved a gallant try by a group of earnest players, but a general disappointment"(L.C., "A Go at Commedia Dell'Arte," *The New York Times*, November 22, 1951, p. 45) due mostly to the fact that Carra's "conception of what constitutes a commedia dell'arte performance is a bit too broad,"(Ibid.) in its use of "Shouting, groaning, hiccoughing and some ill-advised imitations. . ."(Ibid.) In 1957, an evening entitled *Commedia dell'Arte*, a series of three sketches, "Isabella's Weekend," "Pierrot's Rose," and "Small Planet Girls", was presented at the Bleecker Street Theatre. According to the program, the actors improvised from scenarios. One critic cynically acknowledged: "We are informed at the onset that the dialogue is unrehearsed in the the tradition of the ancient company. This, unfortunately, is not difficult to believe. . . There should be a law against an off-Broadway troupe such as the current Bleecker Street Players borrowing the respected name of 'Commedia dell'Arte."(N.J.A., "Theatre: Arte Troupe," *The New York Times*, July 5, 1957, p. 13)

51.Michael Kirby, "Nonmatrixed Performances: Happenings," *Actors on Acting*. Edited by Toby Cole and Helen Krich Chinoy. New York: Crown, 1970, p. 651.

52. cited in Eugene Van Erven. *Radical People's Theatre*. Bloomington and Indianapolis: Indiana University Press, 1988, f.p.

53. cited in Carlson, *Theories of the Theatre*, p. 477.

54. Carlo Mazzone-Clementi, "Commedia and the Actor," *Mimes on Miming*. Edited by Bari Rolfe. London: Millington, 1981, p. 198.

55. Ibid.

56. Carlo Mazzone-Clementi, "Commedia and the Actor," *Drama Review*, Vol. 18 (T61), March 1974, p. 60.

57. Mazzone-Clementi, "Commedia and the Actor," *Mimes on Miming*, p. 199.

58. Ibid., p. 199.

59. Mazzone-Clementi, "Commedia and the Actor," *Drama Review*, p. 64.

60. Misha Berson, "The Dell'Arte Players of Blue Lake, California," *Drama Review*, Vol. 27 (T98), No. 2, June 1983, p. 69.

61. Mazzone-Clementi, "Commedia and the Actor," *Drama Review*, p. 60.

62. Ibid., p.63.

63. Ibid.

64. R.G. Davis. *The San Francisco Mime Troupe: The First Ten Years*. Palo Alto, California: Ramparts Press, 1975, p. 31.

65. "Guerrilla Theatre," *Time*, October 18, 1968, p. 72.

66. Joan Holden, "Comedy and Revolution," *Arts in Society*, Vol. 6, No. 3, 1969, p. 418.

67. Ibid., p. 416.

68. Davis, *The San Francisco Mime Troupe: The First Ten Years*, p. 32.

69. Ibid.

70. Ibid.

71. Lee Gallup Feldman, "A Brief History of Improvisational Theatre in the United States," "Tonight We Improvise," *Yale/Theatre*, Vol. 5, No. 2, 1974, p. 150.

72. The troupe appeared at the 1986 International Theatre Festival in Nicaragua. They encountered a number of theatre groups, including the *Justo Rufino*, which originated as a childrens' television company, but now perform in Managua using dance and commedia training to create a popular theatre.

73. "Guerrilla Theatre," *Time*, p. 72.

74. Ibid.

75. Jeffrey Sweet. *Something Wonderful Right Away*. New York: Avon, 1978, p. xvi.

76. Interview with Paul Sills by Charles Mee, "The Celebrating Occasion," *Tulane Drama Review*, Vol. 9, No. 2, Winter 1964, p. 174.

77. Throughout the 1960's, other commedic productions appeared. In June, 1966, a group called The Theater in the Street, presented Goldoni's *The Servant of Two Masters* actually on the street, in the poverty-ridden, troubled streets of Bedford-Stuyvesant. The company, which included Raul Julia, contended with thrown bottles and mattresses, to give their simply staged

free performance to audiences who would not normally see live theatre. The South Coast Repertory in Costa Mesa, California, presented *The Three Cuckolds*, based on a commedia scenario by Leon Katz in the fall of 1968. It was a ribald, actor-oriented performance, directed by Martin Benson, and it made *The Three Cuckolds* one of the most popular modern commedias in theatres around the country.

78. Early in the 1970's, Rumanian-born director Andrei Serban staged controversial revisionist productions of a number of operas and modern and ancient classics before turning to Gozzi's *The King Stag*, for the American Repertory Theatre, and Beaumarchais' *The Marriage of Figaro*, for the Guthrie Theatre in 1982. Referring to its contribution in shaping the French Revolution, Serban called *The Marriage of Figaro* "the most political play in history!"(Arthur Bartow. *The Director's Voice. Twenty-One Interviews*. New York: Theatre Communications Group, Inc., 1988, p. 298) To Serban, however, "the political aspects of the play are no longer ardent. But to see the vaudeville aspects of the plot, to see how this play came out of the roots of commedia dell'arte following the plays of Gozzi and Goldoni, to see how the clown and the aristocrat, the master and the slave relate to each other in a kind of universal, archetypal way, are of great interest. I tried to present it in modern costume for the first act and in eighteenth century costume in the second act just to create modern equivalents. The critics wanted to see the serious political statement. That didn't interest me. And they didn't see that what I did was to try to find a commedia dell'arte equivalent for today."(Ibid., pp. 298-299) Other directors followed Serban in seeking a modern commedia "in service of the truth of theatre, not in imitation of life. That's why Meyerhold loved Gozzi. Gozzi has been completely neglected in this country, and Europe, too. He actually reinvented the theatre."(Ibid., p. 299) In 1981, a play called *Pierrette* by Mamako and Company was presented at the American Conservatory Theatre in San Francisco. Combining elements of commedia with Japanese performance techniques, particularly in the areas of movement, (surprisingly similar to Meyerhold's interest in both commedia and Oriental theatre forms) it satirized the American musical theatre. A few years earlier, the American Conservatory Theatre had produced a memorable production of Shakespeare's *The Taming of the Shrew*, directed by William Ball, with the characters and traditions of commedia super-imposed over Shakespeare's original. It was extremely popular, subsequently broadcast on public television stations, and enthusiastically received by critics, confirming the increasingly familiar practice of giving plays by Shakespeare, Molière, and others, productions conceived along commedia lines. Productions of virtually unknown classics also abounded, including Gianlorenzo Bernini's *The Impresario*, a work that "is written in the free-wheeling style of the commedia dell'arte, and is peppered with pratfalls, knockings of heads, sexual oglings and scatological banter."(Dan Hulbert, "A Rare Old Play Comes to Light," *The New York Times*, April 25, 1982, Section II, p. 4)

79. Dan Issac, "Ronald Tavel: Ridiculous Playwright," *The Drama Review*, Vol. 13, No. 1 (T41), Fall 1963, p. 108.

80. Stefan Brecht, "Family of the f.p. Notes on the Theatre of the Ridiculous," *The Drama Review*, Vol. 13, No. 1 (T41), Fall 1968, p.119.

81. Ibid.

82. Isaac, "Ronald Tavel: Ridiculous Playwright," p. 108.

83. "Interview: Charles Ludlam," *Performing Arts Journal*, Vol. III, No. 1, Spring/Summer 1978, p. 79.

84. Bartow, *The Director's Voice. Twenty-One Interviews*, p. 55.

85. Ron Jenkins. *Acrobats of the Soul. Comedy & Virtuosity in Contemporary American Theatre*. New York: Theatre Communications Group, Inc., p. xi.

86. cited in Ibid., p. 143.

87. Ibid., p. xii.

88. Ibid., p. 164.

89. During the 1920's and 30's, American scholars began to take note of commedia, perhaps inspired by the few American productions of it, or by the publications of Craig and many other Europeans on the subject. Books and articles by Brander Matthews (1852-1929), Winifred Smith (1879-1939), and Rosamund Gilder (1891-1987), among others, appeared with regularity. Although the most useful general resources on the history of commedia came from France's Pierre L. Duchartre and England's Allardyce Nicoll, American scholars have continued to examine commedia. In recent years, Bari Rolfe's adaptations of commedias and work on masks, and Mel Gordon's collection of *lazzi*, have been useful to those wishing to perform commedia. Henry F. Salerno's collection of translations of Scala's scenarios, and Thomas F. Heck's recent bibliography, are indispensable resources.

90. Martin Green and John Swan. *The Triumph of Pierrot*. New York: Macmillan, 1986, p. xiii.

Appendix

1. Charles Chaplin, "Pantomime and Comedy," *The New York Times*, January 25, 1931, Section VIII, p. 6.

2. Ibid.

3. Ibid.

4. Ron Jenkins, "Reagan's Last Laugh: Supply Side Comedy and the Americanization of Arlecchino," *Commedia dell'arte and the Comic Spirit. Classics in Context Festival 1990*. Louisville, Kentucky: Actors Theatre of Louisville, 1990, p. 48.

INDEX